CON EL PERRO

The Story of the Walk and the Dog
that Brought Me Back to Life

COLBY MILLSAPS

Cover Design by BespokeBookCovers.com
Cover photo from author.

Printed in the United States of America.
First Printing, 2022.
Paperback ISBN: 978-1-7336996-2-4
Hardcover ISBN: 978-1-7336996-3-1

For my parents
The best people in my life
I don't know what I would do without you
This journey, this book, would have never been possible if not for
you and your undying support and belief in me.

Contents

Disclaimer

This is a work of creative nonfiction.

I have been lucky enough to remember my time along the Camino in the most vivid of memories, almost as if I was walking the very path again while writing. I also have count-less pictures and the journal entries I wrote each day while walking to supplement me in this writing endeavor.

With that being said, the conversations portrayed throughout this memoir come from my recollections and are not word-for-word transcripts. I have done my best to capture the tone, mood, and meaning of what was discussed in all instances so that the essence of the dialogue remains accurate.

Please note that distances at the start of each chapter were recorded from my Fitbit each day. Often, these distances are quite different than what guidebooks have for each stage. Walking with Maverick meant adding kilometers that took us to every swimming hole he found, along after-noon walks despite already hiking over 20 kilometers during the day, or wandering through towns in search of places that sold dog food.

Also note that some names and descriptions may have been changed or omitted to maintain anonymity for those I did not gain express permission from. Others have remained as vibrant and pure as I remember them and I hope they are happy to see the wonderful impact they had on our Camino experience come to life on the page.

Author's Note

This is more than just the story of my Camino, a five-hundred-mile trek across Spain. It's more than just the story of Maverick's Camino. It's also my story with depression. That's what ultimately led me to El Camino de Santiago: Depression. You see, when I had to drop out of Ohio State in the spring of my sophomore year because I was too suicidal to continue with college, I thought I was a failure. When I came back home, and started working as a waitress, I was lost and alone. Getting Maverick as a Support Animal that September should have helped with my mental state, but I still ended up in a ward in October. The ward didn't fix me. Leaving college hadn't fixed me. A Support Animal hadn't fixed me. But I was determined to find something that would. Maybe if I just added it all together…

So paired with Maverick, I thought the Camino de Santiago was the answer I was looking for. A purpose. A goal. Hope. They say miracles happen on the Camino.

You see, people walk El Camino de Santiago for all sorts of reasons. The pilgrimage dates back to the Middle Ages and even nor it draws thousands of pilgrims every year from all corners of the world. Some still walk for religious reasons. Some walk for deeply personal reasons. Some walk to lose weight. Some walk to travel and meet new people. If you asked me why I was walking, I would have told you it was my way to finally kick depression. Except, the thing is, you don't have any control over what you get out of the Camino. It has its own power - its own magic. It might sound silly to you now, but it's true.

I'd like to tell you that walking El Camino was a beautiful experience of finally living again. I'd like to tell you I was magically healed of depression and never have to feel sad again. But that's not the truth.

The truth is, the Camino was hard. I cried probably as much as I laughed. I was stressed and confused probably more than I was content. I was alone more than I made beautiful connections with amazing people.

The truth is, you can't just beat depression. It's always there. Did you know that even if you think you're better, they only say that you're "in remission"? Just like cancer. It means it never truly goes away. You can't just take a long walk and wind up better. You can't just determine you're cured. If we're being brutally honest, there is no cure.

But that doesn't mean there isn't a reason to try. To try to live. To keep going. To put one foot in front of the other and keep walking. My Camino wasn't constant laughter among the endless miles, but that doesn't make it any less beautiful. It doesn't make it any less profound. My Camino brought me back to life.

Camino Vocab

Con el perro – with the dog, or with my/your dog. Spaniards don't use personal pronouns when it comes to pets, so when I was continually asked about doing things with my dog, it would always be "¿con el perro?"

Buen Camino – the typical pilgrim greeting

Peregrino/a – pilgrim (-o for masculine and -a for feminine) also note *bicigrino* (pilgrims on bikes) or our favorite *perro-grino* (a dog pilgrim)

Albergue – pilgrim hostel. Only pilgrims walking El Camino de Santiago are permitted to stay by proof of their pilgrim's passports, which get stamped at each lodging along the way. Typically, these hostels are very cheap and often have options to eat a communal breakfast or dinner in house with fellow pilgrims

Hospitalero/a – the caretakers of albergues. Sometimes these are families, sometimes they are volunteers from all over the world, sometimes they are religious persons depending on the lodging

Credencial/credenciales – Pilgrim's Passport. These are paper documents, long and folded like an accordion, with little grids for places to stamp at different stops along the route. Your *credencial* much show at least one stamp every day along your journey, typically at the place you stay for the night and two stamps per day during the final 100km of your walk in order to receive a *compostela* in Santiago

Compostela – the document that certifies that a pilgrim has completed the Camino de Santiago. This is awarded at the pilgrim's office in Santiago de Compostela upon verifying a pilgrim's *credencial.* These documents date back to the 9th century when the tomb of Saint James was given official status

Sello – stamp. These go in a Pilgrim's Passport. You need one a day to certify that you have walked the Camino. Typically, pilgrims get these at the places they stay for the night. Once you reach Sarria, the last 100km of the trek, pilgrims are required to get two per day

Concha – a symbol of the Camino connected with Saint James. It is a seashell. Often, pilgrims carry one on their packs to denote that they are a pilgrim. Signage along The Way utilizes the *concha* in various forms, often accompanied by a yellow arrow

Tortilla Española – a typical Spanish breakfast. It is a bit like an omelet, though denser, made with egg and potatoes and served in slices of a large, round pie

Sanfirmines – the festival that takes place in Pamplona that includes the legendary running of the bulls

Pensión – not quite a hostel, not quite an albegue, but not a hotel. They're normally very affordable lodgings (and as such, are not the most luxurious places to stay) often with single rooms and shared bathrooms, though some have private bathrooms

Farmacía – pharmacy

Fuente – fountain

Casa rural – a guest house of sorts. Typically where a family resides who have rooms for rent. One of the more expensive lodging options along the Camino, slightly less than a full hotel would be

Plaza – a square in town, often surrounded by bars and restaurants as well as shops where locals will sit and relax with one another. *Plaza mayor* often signifies the main square in towns that have more than one

Siesta – nap, a time in the early afternoon (anywhere between 1 p.m. and 6 p.m. depending on the town) where all businesses close for a few hours during the heat of the day

Bocadillo – sandwich

Paella – a traditional Spanish rice dish. It comes in many varieties, including the classic Valencian, or seafood, mixed, vegetarian, or even a black option made with squid ink

Río – river

Empanada Gallego – Spanish pie from Galicia. These are different from the empanadas found in central America or even southern parts of Spain. The Galician empanadas are often flat, thin pies often filled with tuna or pork

Palloza – these buildings date to pre-Roman times and are still used in Galicia. They are circular or oval structures with short stone walls and conical roofs that are covered in thick thatch or rye. The structures were meant to house families and their livestock.

Pulperia – restaurant specializing in octopus, or *pulpo*, a key dish in Galicia

Horreos – long, thin structures found in Galicia that hold grain, produce, or feed. They are raised off the ground in an effort to keep out rodents

Botafumeiro – literally meaning "smoke expeller," the massive incense burner found in the Cathedral de Santiago measures five feet tall and weighs in at 120 pounds when empty. It takes a team of eight men pulling on a rope to get the *botafumeiro* swinging. Like its much smaller counterparts, the *botafumeiro* is used as a priest would use a censor at the altar. It symbolizes the attitude of the true believer with smoke rising to the ceiling just as prayers rise to God.

Tiraboleiros – the team of eight men who transport, carry, and pull the rope to both swing the *botafumeiro* and slow it down after the ceremony. The *botafumeiro* swings at speeds up to forty-three miles per hour and reaches a maximum height of sixty-five feet as it swings across the length of the nave

Prologue

"No," I shook my head, eying the concrete with the little piles of sun-dried dog poop. "No, gracias. Mi perro nunca está sin mí. Nunca duerme solo."

The young Spanish girl swiveled her head between me and the tiny concrete patio where a couple little yappy-dogs gave me a sad look. I had been in Spain long enough now that I knew the girl wouldn't understand me at all. Oh, my Spanish was fine. Not perfect, but it got me around and I could communicate well enough. However, the concept of Maverick as never being separated from me? Well, that…that concept wasn't easily translated.

I made my way back around the side of this albergue and came to stand in front of my two friends, Amy and Beth. We had just met this morning. Ah, the magic of Camino friendships – quickly formed and everlasting. They could have been asleep in a nice bunk by now. Or at the very least they could have been taking a shower. Yet for some reason, they were kind enough to be sticking with me. Maverick hopped up from beside Amy and tugged at the leash, yanking her arm forward as he saw me come around the corner, as excited as if we hadn't just spent the last twelve days together 24/7. And I mean *twenty-four-seven*. As in, I knew the face-he-made-when-he-was-about-to-poop kind of twenty-four-seven. As in, I-was-jealous-that-he-could-take-a-dump-in-any-old-place-but-I-had-to-find-a-bathroom kind of twenty-four-seven.

"No?" Amy asked now as I flopped down on the sidewalk beside her and Beth. I unhooked Maverick's leash from his collar and he bounded into the deserted little street in front of us, eyes to the ground as he chased the shadows of birds in circles until they disappeared and he waited for a new shadow to swoop past.

"No. I mean, they allow dogs in the sense that dogs can stay the night out on their patio. But Maverick always sleeps with me. I would never just leave him outside without me. He'd freak."

Although, he didn't look too torn up about it at the moment. He ran back and forth in the empty street before turning his head to look at us with his tongue lolling out as if he was saying, *See, Mum? This is fun!* He was not at all fazed by the fact that we had trudged close to thirty-six kilometers today, most of that in the beating sun. He was definitely unbothered about the prediction of thunderstorms coming in tonight that we would need to tent out in if we couldn't find somewhere that would let us in.

I sat back up and folded my legs under me before leaning my palms back on the hot concrete. My brain was tired. Heck, my body was tired. Even though we had walked the last eleven kilometers with Amy and Beth, making the time pass by easier, it had still been a long day of walking. *Seriously, John Brierley?* I internally cursed the author of the guidebook we were using once again. It wasn't the first time I questioned his judgment on this journey. *Who voluntarily walks this much in one stage? Logroño to Nájera?* That hadn't been my plan at all. The only reason we had done it was because the albergue at the halfway point in Ventosa that was supposed to allow dogs had turned us down and the threat of bad thunderstorms tonight made me leery to tent out in that hilltop village.

"You guys don't need to stay with us." I told Amy and Beth. "You can go grab a bed somewhere else. Or here. I'll figure something out for me and Maverick."

And I would. I always did.

Pre Departure

June 18th

Today I was boarding a plane bound for a final destination of Saint Jean Pied de Port, France. Just a tiny little town nestled in the foothills of the Great Pyrenees Mountains. My friends and family were all so excited for me to be off on some big, new adventure. And I had smiled and played the part of bubbly, enthusiastic traveler well. I didn't let them see that simmering anxiety under the surface as it grew larger and larger.

What I hadn't told anyone else was that I was scared. I was full of doubts. I had been so busy prepping and planning and researching for this trip that I hadn't stopped to think... all those other people who had told me I was nuts for trying this? They were right.

This was nuts. Absolutely crazy.

"Will you just pee already? Actually, poop would be good. Go poop. You know you want to." I crossed my arms over my chest and tapped a foot impatiently.

Maverick looked up at me with those big, soulful German Shepherd eyes, then went back to intently sniffing the extra hard, plastic, neon-green grass that the Boston-Logan International Airport thought might actually entice a dog into peeing on it. *Right*, I thought. *I'm sure.*

I sighed and finally slipped his vest back on. He gave me a side-eye but didn't put up a fight before walking back out to the terminal with me. We were officially alone. Just me and my dog.

I had first heard of El Camino de Santiago when I was fourteen years old. Like many pilgrims who walk it now, I had originally fallen in love with the epic pilgrimage through the movie, *The Way*. While I won't promote going off on a trek simply because you watch a movie (though many pilgrims do) I *do* promote watching the movie. It's definitely worth it.

Since first seeing the film in theaters that summer, I've probably watched it close to a dozen times. Twice being in a Spanish class. That's because it's more than just a movie; it's a look into one of the most historic walks in the world that cuts its way across Spain and gives you a firsthand look into Spanish life. The more I learned about it, the more I wanted to do it. Five years ago, I jokingly said, "One day, I'm going to walk the Camino."

I distinctly remember one of the final phone calls I had with my mom before leaving Ohio State last spring. It was cold and grey and I was walking from my dorm to the RPAC to work out, crying to her over the phone like I did most days. At that time, I think I cried every single day. Walking to class, studying, in my dorm room, walking home from a night out. I wasn't even sure why I was crying half the time. I just knew I was immeasurably *sad*. That was before I would even admit that I could possibly have…*depression*. Gasp. I could never.

I remember saying to my mom that day, "If I'm going to come home, I want to do something worthwhile. I want to walk the Camino." At the time, I was in no mental capacity to do that. I struggled to focus on wanting to be alive, let alone wanting to walk five hundred miles. Yet here I was now, sitting in the international terminal in Boston, waiting for my flight to Paris.

You're probably wondering then why this was such a crazy thing. Lots of people walk El Camino. Thousands every year. What's so interesting about that?

I watched as Maverick laid his head down on my foot and drifted off, unfazed by the commotion of a last-minute terminal change for a flight. Yep. Him. That sleeping nugget was why this whole thing was so utterly insane. From what I gathered before setting out on this endeavor, it quickly became apparent that nobody in their right mind would walk El Camino de Santiago with a dog.

Good thing I wasn't in my right mind.

I had scoured the internet for any tips on walking El Camino with a dog, reached out to Camino forums for any advice, asked any person I could on Camino Facebook pages if they had seen it done, yet I got nothing but criticism in return. Reactions ranged from snide comments of "leave Fido at home" to chastising me for animal abuse. "No dog wants to walk 500 miles," they said. "Just because you want your dog to come with you doesn't mean you can just force him to walk every day."

Regardless, I refused to be deterred. I knew what we were getting into. Maverick wasn't some itty-bitty dog who couldn't handle miles on miles. He was a young German Shepherd in perfect health. He was bred for stuff like this. We hiked up 4,000-foot mountains in New Hampshire regularly, so hiking was already his thing. He had booties for the hot tar that so many people warned me of. I had researched what brands of dog food were available in Spain and had already carefully switched him over before we left so he was acclimated to it. He had been training in public situations since he was eight weeks old so he could handle trains and planes as an Emotional Support Animal. Despite the false claims of ESAs running rampant in the U.S. currently, Maverick is actually prescribed by my therapist who we saw weekly. We didn't abuse the power of Emotional Support Animals, which were allowed access to transportation and housing only. I had my letter documenting his status from my prescriber.

So armed with international health certificates, letters of training and documentation, and lists of albergues along the way that I had painstakingly researched to see if they would allow a dog, we were ready. Or so we thought…

Put One Foot in Front of the Other

Day One: Saint Jean Pied de Port to Roncesvalles

Approx. 33 km ~ 47,000 steps

June 19ᵗʰ

The air in the room was still, like everything was teetering on some sort of ledge, just waiting for a push to set it in motion. Or maybe that was just my anxiety talking. I tapped my phone until the screen lit up and the numbers *4:59* glowed back at me. There was no need for an alarm to go off. I hadn't been able to sleep last night, anyway.

The sheets rustled quietly as I slipped out of the four-poster bed and my feet landed on the creaky, wooden floors. Everything in this albergue, or pilgrim hostel, was old. It had probably been serving pilgrims for decades. I wondered how many others had felt the same trepidation of crossing the Pyrenees on their very first day as I was feeling right now.

Tens of thousands to be sure. Hundreds of thousands. Perhaps even millions.

My eyes scanned the gloom of the room, briefly meeting with Maverick's amber ones where he laid on the bed. For a second, a sense of calm washed over me just knowing he was here with me. I wasn't completely alone. He stood up on the bed, stretched out the sleep from his limbs, and plopped down onto the floor beside me. His paws barely made a sound as they connected with the wood, but his tail thumping against the bedpost did.

"Shh," I hissed. The hospitaleros here had been adamant that all guests should be as quiet as possible until eight a.m. No one wanted to be woken up by the rudeness of other pilgrims, regardless of if that pilgrim was a dog or a human. I caught Maverick's tail just before it made contact with the bedpost again and nudged him forward before dishing him out a bowl of food. I left him eating and tiptoed to the adjoining bathroom to brush my teeth and gather up my toiletries. As I tucked away the few belongings I had, I caught a glimpse of myself in the mirror over the sink.

There was still that numbness to my eyes that no one else seemed to notice. A hollowness. I hadn't really felt much of anything in quite some time. But as I stared back at my reflection, I could see a bit of something there. Just a tiny bit of fear. Maybe that wasn't the most desirable emotion to have, but to me, it was better than feeling nothing at all. I scooped up my toothpaste and all-in-one soap and headed back to the bedroom.

I had already laid out all of my gear and then repacked it into my backpack last night, so there was nothing I could do to put off the inevitable. It was time to go. I tucked the bag of toiletries into the pack, pulled the drawstring shut, and clipped the flap down. Each action echoed in the quiet room, counting down until our journey really started. Maverick's pack was next. Even in the dim light from the wide-open shutters, it appeared to glow. I tucked his food dish and bag of kibble back into the open saddlebag, then slipped the bright red harness over his head. He steadied himself under the new weight and lifted his front paw for me to slip through the straps.

"Ready?" I whispered. He shook in response, the seashell that marked him as a pilgrim clinking against the metal tag it was attached to on his pack. Through my nerves, I gave him a soft smile. We could do this.

The heavy, wooden door creaked as we slipped into the hall of the albergue and an automatic light switched on that momentarily blinded me. Maverick teetered out of the room behind me, his pack bumping against my legs and knocking against the doorframe, and I winced at the sound of it. I probably should have waited until we were outside to put his pack on. I hustled down the short flight of stairs to meet him at the side door and pushed it open. The cool, morning air bit at my face and caused me to suck in a deep breath before I could sling my pack over my shoulders.

Everything around us was shrouded in mist and dew clung to the plants in the lush garden we stepped out into. As quietly as I could, I eased the door closed behind us and heard the lock automatically snap into place. My fingers closed over the thick, antique key the hospitalero had given me when I checked in yesterday. Along with his lengthy list of rules, he had told me I would need to deposit the key in the mailbox by the gate to the garden if we chose to leave before eight a.m. For now, I still had the option to unlock the door and crawl back into bed.

My feet shuffled forward over the paving stones in the garden, inching further from the door and closer to that mailbox, but when I got there, I hesitated. My hand paused just above the box, the rusted key dangling precariously.

Once I dropped it in, there was no turning back. We were really on our way. As if the two planes, one train, one taxi, and one bus we had taken to arrive here in the tiny town of Saint Jean Pied de Port hadn't been enough to solidify that fact.

With one last deep breath, my fingers released the heavy metal. It fell with a *clang* to the bottom of the mailbox, and just like that, we tipped over the ledge. The world, or at least our world on this Camino, was set in motion.

There were no pilgrims crowding the narrow, French street this morning like there had been yesterday evening. No shops were open and, unfortunately for me, there was no chance of getting any euros out of an ATM this early. *Well*, I thought sullenly as I followed Maverick's beacon of a red pack down the cobblestones. *Good thing I brought a couple granola bars.*

The Pilgrims' Office hadn't even woken yet. I paused for a moment to stare through the dark windows, thinking of how crowded it had been when we got our first stamps in our *credenciales* yesterday. The Frenchman filling out our information had just about glared a hole through Maverick's head when we sat down in front of him.

"There is no way," he had said in that lilting French accent, thick with disbelief. "You will not be allowed to stay. Nowhere will allow the dog."

"I have a tent," I replied calmly while Maverick bumped his way over to a girl and her mom who had been on the same bus from Bayonne as us. His pack bounced against pilgrim legs in the crowded little shop and I had been on the brink of making apologies when the young girl started gushing over him.

"To do the whole way with a dog. It is just not smart."

I only shrugged my shoulders and offered a forced smile. "We'll manage." I pushed my second credential across the desk towards him, the one with "Maverick K. Millsaps" printed on the inside of the very first page.

"I have already stamped you," the Frenchman said brusquely, clearly ready for the next pilgrim to take a seat.

"Right, but this is Maverick's credential."

His eyes had met mine in a mix of disbelief and exasperation then, but he slid the paper passport closer and punched the stamp down onto the first open space. "Buen Camino," he had muttered. "And good luck."

I grinned at the recent memory, my own reflection smiling back at me in the darkened windows of the office. *Right then*, I thought. *No one ever said this journey would be easy.* It didn't take long for us to make our way through the rest of Saint Jean and then begin the winding climb up into the Pyrenees. The fog we hiked through was soon left behind as we climbed higher and higher in elevation and the sun finally started to peek over the rolling hills. Below us, the valleys of France were laid out as beautifully as if Monet himself had painted the scene. Hills of emerald green were poking up through the low clouds and mist like little islands on a sea of white foam. The rays of the sun cut through the water droplets as it rose, giving the whole world a golden hue. It was one of the most perfect things I had ever seen.

It was also a hard-ass hike.

I gasped in air as Mav and I took a break off to the side of the paved road that curved up the mountain range. I knew everyone said this stage was brutal, but I hadn't really believed it until now. Maverick and I were experienced hikers. We regularly hiked in the White Mountains of New Hampshire. But shit, this was no joke. It was just one steady incline for the entire day. There weren't any boulders to scramble over, or super steep sections of trail. Instead, the route from Saint Jean to the top of Roncevaux Pass followed a tar road, guaranteeing a solid, albeit exhausting calf workout.

Soon enough, our quiet pilgrimage became crowded. As the sun warmed the air and all the clouds burned off for the day, more and more pilgrims passed by us. We recognized a group of men that we had befriended on our bus ride in from Bayonne yesterday afternoon and walked with them for a bit until they outpaced us. We even ran into a man who was also from New Hampshire of all places, and enjoyed walking the last few kilometers to the albergue in Orisson with him.

Many pilgrims chose to stay a night in Orisson so they didn't have to do the entire stretch from Saint Jean to Roncesvalles in one day. Since we started so early and it was only eight kilometers from Saint Jean, Maverick, our new friend Tyler from New Hampshire, and I were only stopping for a quick rest at the picturesque albergue. Tyler stopped just long enough to buy some breakfast from the albergue and then was on his way with a wave goodbye, but Maverick and I took a seat at one of the wooden picnic tables outside.

Since this little mountain hut had no way to accept a credit card, I was stuck eating my last granola bar I had packed. It wasn't exactly the breakfast of champions. Maybe my mom had a point when she had told me I should have stayed an extra day in Saint Jean Pied de Port before beginning our walk. It would have given me time to take euros out of an ATM. We could have had more time to rest after a full day of travel. But I was never one who wanted to rest, and I was itching to get into Spain.

So many pilgrims were out on the trail now, we were never alone after leaving Orisson. They laughed as Maverick darted back and forth, chasing the shadows of butterflies. Many asked if they could take his picture since they were enamored with his pack and his very own pilgrim shell, *la concha*. We all exchanged the expected "Buen Camino" and told each other where we were from and shared small talk, but Maverick was the star of the show. Despite the grueling walk and almost four-thousand-foot elevation gain, there was nothing but smiles on this day and Mav was a huge reason for that.

We made it another hour past Orisson before flopping down on a grassy knoll off the side of the road. The Napoleon Route was notorious for its nasty weather, so the fact that we were getting a cloudless sky and a light breeze was incredible. I slipped Maverick's heavy pack over his head so he could have some time free from the weight and pulled out my journal from my own pack, then leaned back to write.

Mav bounced back and forth through the grass and little white wildflowers. Every so often I would hear his jaws snap shut on thin air, clearly missing yet another butterfly, and I would smile to myself. It wasn't until I heard someone laughing out loud that I looked up and realized what a crowd he had drawn with his antics. There were at least eight other pilgrims on this knoll now and half of them had their phones out, clearly videoing Maverick.

I turned my attention back to him as he pounced forward and then stood stock still, his eyes and ears on high alert as his tongue lolled out from the side of his mouth. For a brief second, his eyes flashed to where I was laying in the grass, making sure I was still safe, but then he caught sight of another butterfly and he took off again. I could feel my own smile tugging at my cheeks while our fellow pilgrims continued to laugh and I was suddenly struck by the thought…did he even know what we were doing? Did he realize he was in a new country? Did he understand that when he boarded that plane in Boston and slept for that entire flight, he woke up a whole ocean away from where he had started? I wondered if he could smell a difference. Did the air in France smell different than the air in New England to him? I knew everyone wished their dogs could talk to them, but I had never wished for that as much as I did now. With a sigh, I tucked my journal back into my pack, then called Maverick off from his wild-butterfly-chase and hooked him back into his own pack. He didn't even flinch in putting it back on, just trotted back towards the asphalt road and started up the mountain pass once more.

Our break time had been so nice, I almost forgot that we were completely out of water. Apparently there were no water fountains between Orisson and here. So not only had I emptied my own water bladder, I had even polished off some of Maverick's water as well. I gave him a side-eye as he paused beside the road to drink from a trickle of water coming down a rock face.

"Must be nice," I muttered. There was a tiny voice in the back of my head that wondered if it would be frowned upon if I tried drinking from here as well.

Mav's ears twitched in my direction just before he laid down completely, mud squelching out from beneath his stomach and up around the sides of the pack. His tongue poked out to lap up some of the muddy water around his paws. "Ew, gross. Can't you stick to just drinking it from the rocks? At least I know that's semi-clean for you."

He paused his drinking and cocked his head, then flopped sideways as much as his pack would allow, getting himself nice and comfy in the cool mud. I scrunched my nose in response. Some pilgrims passed behind us and laughed at our exchange, so I smiled at them before turning back to Maverick with my eyes narrowed. I was officially jealous of a muddy dog. At least he wasn't also a *thirsty* dog.

However, one of the most common sayings on this journey is "the Camino provides." It turns out that adage is quite true. A roadside café soon appeared by the trail. It was tiny, and it honestly reminded me of an ice cream truck more than anything, which was fitting because I had about the same amount of excitement upon seeing it as little kids have for ice cream trucks. Only...my excitement didn't last very long because, well, I still had no cash. Maverick, oblivious to my issues, tugged to keep going, but I sat down dejectedly on a carved wooden bench.

"What would you like?" a thickly French-accented voice asked from behind me. I swiveled around.

"Me?" I asked. Of course it was directed at me, though. I was the only other person sitting here besides the cute old couple now talking to me. The man nodded. "Oh, no. I'm okay. Thank you, though," I tried to decline. I'm not exactly sure why. I guess it was a prideful American thing to decline help even when you really did want it. Luckily for me, the man would not take no for an answer. Without my asking, he bought me a banana, a granola bar, and a bottle of water from the little food truck. He still thought this was barely adequate, but I couldn't thank him enough. I'm pretty sure I thanked him in English, French, and Spanish just to make sure I got my point across. His wife only laughed at my appreciation, and then they were off without another word. Just like that. My first Camino Angel experience.

We weren't alone at the café for long. Dario soon appeared cresting the last hill towards the food truck and broke into a large grin. I smiled back at Maverick's biggest fan, an Italian man from the bus we took to Saint Jean yesterday. "Ciao! Che bello!" he called out as he came up to us, immediately dropping to his knees to smother Maverick in attention. After catching up on how our respective mornings had gone, I left Maverick with his admirer so I could take a closer look at the map on the side of the food truck.

According to this, we should only have to keep going "up" for another five kilometers and then it would be all downhill from there. My face broke into an involuntary grin. No news could have sounded any better at the moment. Even me, who adored hiking, was ready for some downhill. With that happy news, we bid farewell for now to Dario and set off with a fresh pep in our step.

Except, I don't know who measured out those five kilometers, but I am here to tell them they are *wrong*. You hear that, French Food Truck Man? *Wrong!* It was more like five *hundred* kilometers.

That may be a slight exaggeration, but I'm telling you now…if you ever see that truck with the map on it, do not believe it.

Mav and I continued to trudge onward and upward, still with just a tiny bottle of water between the two of us. The Camino had turned off the asphalt road and now cut through grass and along dirt cart paths before finally, *finally*, reaching the height of the pass just before the Fountain of Roland. I was exhausted. Too exhausted to even bother trying to get Maverick out of yet another mud puddle. I just sighed while I watched him.

"You do realize we're supposed to be sharing a tent tonight, right?" His tongue rolled out of his mouth as he panted in response. "And now you're gonna be all disgusting and it's an itty-bitty backpacking tent and we're going to have to be pressed together and…ugh," I sighed.

As much as he was gross, if that's what he needed to do to be happy, so be it. The past hour of our hike I had spent wondering if this really had been the right choice after all. What if he didn't want to walk eight-hundred kilometers across Spain? What if his pack was too heavy? What if he was tired? What if all the things those people said on the internet before we came were true? What if that man who stamped our *credenciales* yesterday was right? Doing this with a dog was just not smart.

I couldn't seem to break from my doubts until we reached the Fountain of Roland. There was a crowd of pilgrims there, everyone filling up on water for the first time in several kilometers. While I stood and waited for my turn, Mav took the opportunity to splash through the puddles on the paving stones from the runoff of the fountain. He had found yet another butterfly and was chasing its shadow across the stones, shoving his nose into puddles in his attempt to "catch" it. All around me, the other pilgrims were laughing and videoing him yet again. I swear, he was in more pictures and videos in one day along the Camino than any of the other pilgrims combined.

I finally looked around me and really took in what was happening here. Maybe I hadn't been the only pilgrim feeling defeated after that long, grueling climb. Maybe some of these pilgrims surrounding me were absolutely exhausted, too. Maybe they didn't know what they had been thinking, setting out on a journey like this. Yet here was Maverick, bringing each and every one of them a smile. Their laughter was ringing through the birch forest behind us. Their joy was palpable. More than anything else, Maverick gave all of us something to smile about. He had been doing that for me since the moment I met him when he was just two days old. But this? Seeing how he could do it for others? This was something special.

The descent into Roncesvalles felt never-ending. I'm sure if I hadn't been so exhausted I would have appreciated the forest we walked through and the same woodland path that had been trodden by pilgrims for centuries. As it was, each tree blurred into another in my weary mind. Ten hours after setting out from Saint Jean Pied de Port, we reached the outskirts of Roncesvalles where a river crossed the trail.

Pilgrims were gathered by the stream, their boots kicked off, soaking their aching feet in the frigid mountain water. Maverick gained a burst of energy at the sight of running water and happily plunged in, wading around while I rummaged in his pack before producing a tennis ball. It may have added some extra weight to bring a toy with us on this trek, but he was absolutely obsessed with balls. It wouldn't have been right to travel without at least one.

I tossed the ball upriver, away from relaxing pilgrims, and Mav took off after it. Within a second, he was bounding back to me, water splashing around him as other pilgrims smiled. However, his fatigue from the day caught up to him quick and after a few throws, he was ready to lay down in the cool water. Except, that meant he wasn't paying attention to his ball. It went floating downstream, right under the little bridge I was sitting on, and down through the brush that grew into the river beyond.

"Maverick!" I gasped. He only tilted his head from where he was laying in the water. "Hurry up! Go get it!" I waved my arm urgently as the tennis ball floated away. Despite my pleas, it took Mav another five minutes before he realized that his ball had gone missing. At which point the ball was long gone, but I let him wade through the plants downstream in search of it while I gathered up our things.

Eventually, I had to call him off his search so we could hobble the last few steps into the town of Roncesvalles. Although calling this a "town" was pretty generous. In truth, it wasn't much more than the massive monastery and two bars that serve hungry pilgrims. Sitting at a little table outside the first bar were a pair of Irish girls we had made friends with on the bus from Bayonne to Saint Jean and a boy I had yet to meet. They eagerly leapt up to greet us and offered me the last free chair at their table. After catching up quickly and asking if they would mind watching over Maverick for a minute, I ducked into the bar to finally buy myself some food.

I scanned the dark interior of the old building for an ATM but came up empty. *Of course there wasn't an ATM here,* I thought. *Just my luck.* I stepped further inside and towards the counter that had a huge sign displaying food options hanging overhead. In tiny print in the corner, the sign claimed they accepted credit cards. Only…with a twenty-five euro minimum. I mean, I was hungry but not *that* hungry. I bit my lip and turned to see another woman scanning the menu above the counter.

"I'll buy whatever you're getting," I told her eagerly. She startled at my voice and whipped around.

"Oh, no," she smiled once she realized I was just a fellow pilgrim. "No, that's alright, I can get it."

"Yeah, but I need to buy a certain amount to use a card anyway." I waved the plastic card in question in the air as proof. "So I might as well buy whatever you were planning on getting."

"Are you sure?" she hesitated, and I was struck once more by how hard it was for us Americans to simply accept help from others. The Camino provides, right? I had already witnessed that today. It was the least I could do to pay it forward.

"Yeah, whatever you want." I smiled and waved her to the counter.

In the end, she ordered food for herself and her husband, and I was able to order the first of what would be many *tortilla Españolas* along my journey and a glass of Spanish wine before rejoining my friends outside. The wine, I found, was bitter and strong and I quickly pawned it off to one of my Irish friends. It didn't take much convincing for her to accept it and down it. The *tortilla* was delicious, though it wasn't at all what an American would think of as a tortilla. Instead, it was almost like a breakfast food. I'm pretty sure there were chunks of potato in there. And it was definitely made from eggs as the primary ingredient. It reminded me of an omelette more than anything.

"You're staying in the albergue, right?" the boy asked as we stood from the table once I had finished eating. He was a fellow American who had befriended the girls about halfway through the walk today.

"Oh, no," I smiled as I slung my pack back over my shoulders and picked up Maverick's red one from beside my chair. "No, we'll just tent tonight I think. I should check in with the hospitaleros to see where it would be okay to pitch a tent, but I know they don't allow dogs inside."

I had done plenty of research before setting out and everywhere I looked had warned that nowhere in Ronces-valles would allow dogs. However, it was also known that the monastery had no problem with pilgrims pitching a tent outside, so long as you asked first. Talking with the hospi-taleros who ran the place would also allow me to get our credentials stamped and maybe, just maybe, I could convince them to let me use their showers. I think I had sweat out about half my body weight today.

"You're going to tent? After this long day?" one of the Irish girls gasped. I laughed and nodded as I fell into step with them. We made our way towards the monastery complex that connected the massive albergue with the church, *Real Colegiata de Santa María*, as well as cloisters and crypts, a library, and a museum. In the middle of this inter-connected complex was a massive courtyard where various pilgrims were scattered about lounging, chatting, and resting after the long day.

Mav and I and our three new friends continued on to the

entrance of the albergue where a team of hospitaleros were buzzing around. Some were checking new arrivals in by taking their passports and stamping *credenciales*. Others were directing pilgrims on where to put their shoes and which beds to take. Still more at the counter looked to be outlining when pilgrim mass and dinner services would take place. This was the largest albergue along the entire route and it was clear these hospitaleros were used to the mayhem.

I joined a queue with my friends and finally reached a hospitalera who was happy to direct me to a grassy area outside the walls of the monastery that would be a fine place to pitch my tent for the night. She informed me that using the bathroom and showers would cost three euros, which my friends were quick to pool together for me since I still had no cash, and then both Maverick and my *credenciales* were stamped without a second thought and the hospitalera was already moving on to help the next pilgrim.

I blinked in surprise at the speed of that process, then backed out of the glass doors of the office and into a shady corner of the courtyard that had a bench. I dropped my pack off my shoulders and plopped Maverick's bag beside it. "Thank you guys again for the euros," I said emphatically. "Seriously, you didn't have to do that."

One of the girls waved off my appreciation. "Ah, it was just one euro from each of us. You'll feel better after a shower. They're actually quite nice."

"Well thank you again," I said once more as I bent and looped Maverick's leash around the leg of the bench before reattaching it to his collar. I went about dishing him out some dinner, since it was already past time for his meal, and squirted out water into his other collapsible dish.

"Would you like us to sit with him? While you go in and shower?" The other girl nodded her head towards the albergue.

"You would do that?"

"Of course!"

"Wow, yeah, that would be great. If you need to be somewhere else, I'm sure he'll be fine for just a minute tied here. He's got his food and water. I won't be long." I dug in my bag for my travel towel, fresh clothes, and soap.

"Take your time, really."

Even with their assurances, I took the fastest shower I had ever taken. The idea of leaving Maverick without me, for even a minute, wasn't one I enjoyed. I rushed back down through the albergue and the endless bunks, which had clearly seen a renovation since *The Way* had been filmed here, and popped back out into the courtyard with my hair still dripping. In the time I had been gone, the Irish girls had disappeared and Maverick was now accompanied by the young man we ate with earlier and two new arrivals I hadn't met yet.

After thanking them for keeping an eye on Maverick for me, they headed off to dinner and Mav and I stayed to people watch in the courtyard. Some hospitaleros came out to talk, all curious about how I planned to do this whole journey with a dog. They thought it was insane that someone as young as me, all alone, was planning to walk five hundred miles across Spain with a dog. The Camino wasn't known to be dog friendly. It would be a long grueling journey, even without a dog. Yet again, I wondered if all of our doubters were right. Maybe this was a horrible idea. But we had already set out. I had no intention of turning back now.

Once I finally had built up enough strength to think about pitching our tent for the night, I gathered up our gear and shuffled off through the vaulted walkway to the lush grass outside of the complex. We picked a spot just beneath the towering walls of the monastery and I got to work unraveling my tent and snapping the poles together. Maverick, of course, was no help in this endeavor. He chose to "supervise" rather than pitch in, although his supervision looked a lot like sleeping.

Regardless, it was a pretty simple tent to set up and soon enough I had everything inside - a tiny green blip beneath the towering walls of the monastery. The sun was still out even though it was after nine at night so while I felt like I should still be awake, I was beat and chose to crawl into my sleeping bag right away. Maverick plodded over from his spot in the grass to inspect our new sleeping arrangements but had no desire to stay inside when I attempted to zip the flap shut. Reluctantly, I tied him up and let him stay outside. That lasted all of twenty minutes before I decided that wasn't okay. For one, he was getting dewy. And two, I missed him. It just wasn't right with him outside. With a tug on his leash, I forced him into the tent and zipped us in together.

Too bad, so sad Nugget. It's me and you for the next fifty days.

Follow the Yellow Brick Road

Day Two: Roncesvalles to Zubiri

27.7 km ~ 39,136 steps

June 20th

I know I was the one who insisted that Maverick sleep inside the tent with me, but that was before I realized he would take up the *entire* sleeping pad. And the sack of clothes I was using as a pillow. And that he would demand to be the little spoon no matter how many times I tried to roll over throughout the night. I groaned when the sky finally started to lighten outside and pushed myself up to sit. Maverick hopped up beside me, already pawing to be let out of the confines of the tent.

I crawled out after him and stretched, hearing my bones creak and pop after a night of restlessness. Dew adorned the blades of grass and coated our tent while mist hung in the cool, mountain air. After a trip into the albergue to use the bathroom and brush my teeth, I filled our waters from the fountain outside, then made quick work of packing up our tent site.

"Oh, God," I groaned as soon as I slung my pack over my shoulders. "I swear this was not as heavy yesterday." Maverick looked over at me from where he was lifting his leg against the towering stone walls of the monastery. "Do you think because the tent is still damp it gained ten pounds?" I asked while I attempted to hike my pack up further on my back and buckled the hip belt. Maverick trotted over to my side and sniffed at his own pack still in the grass.

"Yep," I told him. "You too." With a grin, I slipped his saddlebags over his head and buckled him in across his stomach. He shook, settling the bags over his back, then looked up at me as if saying he was ready to go. Clearly, he took the weight better than I did.

We set off around the monastery walls and made our way back onto the road that led from the little hamlet. Already, pilgrims were hitting the road or grabbing breakfast at the bar we had eaten at yesterday afternoon. Before leaving Roncesvalles, almost all of them stopped for a picture beside the famous road sign at the edge of town.

SANTIAGO DE COMPOSTELA – 790.

I tilted my head to look at it. "Seven hundred and ninety kilometers to go. No big deal," I said under my breath to Maverick.

As much as I wanted to take a picture with the sign, there were too many pilgrims out and about for me to take out my mini tripod and remote control. It would look too strange to do that. I would have to suck up my anxiety and actually *ask* someone to take our picture. You would think that something as small as asking a fellow pilgrim to take a picture for me wouldn't be a big deal. In reality, it filled me with more trepidation than knowing we had over seven hundred kilometers to walk.

I waited until there were just two pilgrims around the sign, then finally stepped forward with Maverick in tow. "Excuse me?" I asked the older woman with the dark hair who had just taken a picture for her friend. "Would you mind taking a photo for me?"

"Of course! Oh, and a dog!"

See? My mind tried to tell me. *That wasn't hard at all.* The anxiety still churning in my gut disagreed.

Mavy and I climbed up the little embankment on the side of the road and posed beside the sign. Pilgrims walking by called out and waved. "Hi, Maverick! Buen Camino, Maverick's mom!" It made the smile on my face for that first picture genuine.

"Okay, now act shocked! You've gotta have a picture with this sign looking in total dismay!" the woman called to me as she made to snap more pictures. I had already been about to climb back down to the road to reclaim my phone, but I couldn't help but smile at her enthusiasm and do as she said. By the time she had finished taking pictures, both of us were laughing. It was only natural to fall into step beside her as we headed down the path beside the road leading out of Roncesvalles.

"I'm Tricia, but you can call me Trish. I'm walking with my friend up there, Margie." She indicated another woman ahead of us on the trail who I recognized as the one she was taking a picture of earlier. "Who are you with?"

"I'm Colby, but I'm quickly learning that most people on this journey just know me as Maverick's mom. I guess there are worse things to be known for." I smiled. "It's just me and him."

"No one else? Just you and your dog?" she asked in astonishment. I nodded. "Well, I hope you brought enough poop bags for him."

With a rueful grin, I unzipped a pocket on my hip and

pulled a full roll of bags free. He was carrying five more rolls in his own pack. Trish's laughter rang out. From then on, we fell into easy conversation. Everyone I had come across so far was excessively open and chatty, diving into deep or difficult topics that would typically be avoided almost immediately. *That was the magic of the Camino*, I thought as Trish told me more about her life back home and what had brought her here while I listened attentively. *It took all of five minutes walking with someone to get into their life story.* There was a sort of beauty in that. That out here, no one felt judged.

Trish and I finally caught up to Margie at the next town when we all stopped for breakfast. She made a quick intro-duction between us as I hooked Maverick to a nearby table. Margie was already eating a croissant for breakfast so Tricia and I ducked inside the café, me to see if they would possibly accept a credit card and her to attempt a breakfast order in Spanish. I hung back while she tried to communicate what she wanted, but it wasn't going well. I shifted my weight from one foot to the other until finally, I couldn't take it anymore. Her order poured out of my mouth in Spanish. The barista flashed me a relieved, if somewhat surprised look then quickly got to work on the coffee in question.

Trish turned to me with her mouth slightly open. "You speak Spanish?" she asked.

I smiled sheepishly and gave her a little shrug. "Un poco," I joked. *A little.*

Even in my home life, I found it hard to keep the Spanish at bay when someone wasn't a native English speaker. It seemed wrong of me to let them struggle to find the words they wanted to say if I could just as easily say them in Spanish. But it also felt rude for me, a little white girl, to simply start speaking to them in Spanish just because they were Hispanic. It was a fine line of being culturally conscious that I balanced back home, but here? It was silly not to use

my Spanish. I would have to get over holding back. Maybe
this would be fun.

Trish insisted that she pay for my breakfast as a thanks
for being her interpreter. The barista had told me they didn't
accept card here, but there was an ATM not too far down the
road. Once again, my first instinct was to wave off Trish's
offer with the typical, "oh no, you don't have to." But I really
was hungry. I was also starting to accept that these sorts of
things just happened here. So I let her buy my breakfast and
just said thank you. Sometimes, all you needed to do was say
thanks.

I made sure to say thanks once more as I left the pair of
friends behind at the café before heading off in search of the
elusive ATM that was supposed to be in this village. It was a
cute town, with sidewalks of slate stones and little drainage
canals that ran between sidewalk and street. Even though the
sun hadn't gotten too hot yet, Maverick took it upon himself
to walk through the water instead of staying on the sidewalk.
He became a hit with pilgrims as they passed us, laughing at
the way Maverick with his big, red pack was plodding
through the canals, splashing water onto the slate stones each
time he had to jump around a grate. Unfortunately for him,
the yellow arrows guiding us along The Way turned right
onto a dusty road at the edge of town. To the left, just before
open farmland, was the coveted ATM.

I practically skipped over to the little kiosk in excitement.
No more relying on others for food or drinks! No more
feeling awkward for having no cash! No more having to ask
bars and cafés if they accept cards! Huzzah!

Only…the older man currently at the ATM looked to be
plucking at the keys of the machine fruitlessly. When he
looked back to see me and Maverick, he gave a little start and
inched away from the dog. I suppose Mavy could be considered intimidating to some. Though the lopsided pack and

wet paws from his recent puppy-like behavior kind of ruined the scare factor if you asked me.

When the man shifted away from the machine, I was able to clearly see the message displayed on the screen. It was out of order. For a moment I just stared at the screen in disbelief. Then a laugh burst out of me unbidden. I had to laugh. That was all you could do at this point. The older man looked at me in confusion from where he stood a safe ten feet away from Maverick. I swallowed down my laughter and turned to him, but a smile of disbelief was still on my face.

"It's broken," I told him with a chuckle. *Of course it was broken*, I thought sardonically. He continued to gaze at me in confusion. I read him back the message on the screen. "Fuera de servicio." Again, he looked at me blankly. *Hm. No English. No Spanish. This is fun.* I attempted to convey the message with a few more gestures, but when it was clear we weren't getting anywhere I just sighed and muttered a "Buen Camino" before continuing down the dirt farm road ahead.

Today's trail was certainly less of a climb than yesterday, yet it was still hard. We dipped in and out of some scattered villages, though none that had an ATM, and ran into pilgrims we had already made friends with along with many new faces. We walked with the same boy from last night for quite a while this morning, then waved goodbye to him when we joined up with the Irish girls that we all knew as they took a break on the crest of a ridge. We skirted the edge of a field bursting with tall, lush grasses and passed over a farmer's fence with a pair of older Spanish gentlemen who delighted in the fact that I could speak Spanish with them. I rested on the edge of a river that crossed the trail while Maverick chased after some pebbles I threw for him and

Trish and Margie soaked their feet in the cool waters. And on and on and on the day went.

I kept thinking we had to be in Zubiri soon. We had to be almost done. Yet the trail just kept going. The last town we passed through before our destination was supposed to have a water fountain in it, though. Thank God, because both Maverick and I were out of water yet again. Maybe I wasn't good at this whole pilgrim thing. What pilgrim runs out of water two days in a row? That had to be rule number one of long-distance walking – never run out of water – and I had broken it twice already.

As we came into town, we passed by the empty shell of some old building that may have been a factory at some point and a trio of stray dogs emerged from it. Maverick lifted his head and the dogs growled low in their throats. "Leave it," I commanded. I tried to scan the area for wherever this water fountain may be hiding, but I was a bit preoccupied now. The dogs circled closer, heads lowered, sniffing the ground Maverick had just passed over. He trotted beside me, oblivious to our tagalongs. Luckily, he never paid attention to other dogs. I just wished these street dogs could do the same.

The closer they came, the faster we walked. "Okay, Mav. Come on," I ushered, completely giving up on my search for water. I would stay thirsty if it meant we avoided a dog fight. The trio hadn't outright attacked and didn't look like they were about to, but I wasn't going to push their boundaries anymore than we already had. Their low growls and raised hackles made it quite clear that they didn't want Maverick on their turf. Only once we had passed through the village and started to climb the road that led out of town did they finally stop trailing us. The brown one was wandering off to the left now, lifting his leg against a broken-down wall. One that looked like it should have been white but was mostly grey had already given up and was making his way back to the shell of a building they called home.

I let out a breath I didn't realize I had been holding and my shoulders drooped. "Right then," I sighed to Maverick. He paused from his climb up the asphalt ahead of me and looked back down. "So much for fresh water," I grumbled.

The sun was beating down on us by that point in the afternoon and even though the hill out of town wasn't a mountain, it sure felt like one. I dragged myself up it after Maverick as best I could until we finally made it into the blessed shade of a forest. I threw myself down on a rock that had dislodged from an old stone wall and slid my pack off my shoulders. It would have been a great spot to stop and have a drink, if we had had anything to drink. That was where Tyler found us, the man we had met yesterday who was also from New Hampshire.

"Rough day?" he chuckled as he paused beside our rest area. He dropped his pack to the forest floor and scratched Maverick's head when he bent over to rummage through his bag.

"Long day," I laughed back. "We ran out of water again. I'm afraid I'm not a very good pilgrim."

Immediately, he pulled the bottle from his lips where he had been taking a drink and held it out to me as an offering. I shook my head. "Oh, no. That's yours. We'll be okay, just taking a little rest before continuing on."

"You sure? Let me at least give some to Maverick."

I couldn't deny him that. I unhooked Mav's collapsible water dish and popped it open so he could pour some water in. Maverick greedily lapped it up, then snuffled around the dirt in search of a stick to bring Tyler as thanks. I stood and pulled my pack over my shoulders once more, buckling back into the hip belt and tightening the shoulder straps again as Tyler tucked his water away. Without a word of agreement needed, we fell into step on the wooded path along what seemed to be a ridgeline of sorts.

"It's weird, isn't it?" he asked after we had walked in companionable silence for a while. Maverick was jogging ahead of us, a stick protruding from between his jaws.

"What is?"

"The idea of walking so much. Literally all we do is walk. Your whole life goes from all these different things constantly going on to…nothing. Just walking. It feels like we've been out here a lot longer than just two days."

I paused before answering him, taking in his words. He was right, of course. Our whole world had been reduced to the ground beneath our boots and how many miles we covered each day. "Yeah, you make a point. And every time we pass a new place, it seems like we've gone so far. Like so much has happened already and we've seen so much. But it's only been two days now, like you said. It seems like we've covered so much ground, but we really haven't at all."

Tyler laughed. "I'd like to keep thinking I've covered a lot of ground, thank you very much." I tossed a smile back at him and we lulled into silence again. There were a lot of miles to go, almost five hundred to be exact, but it was nice to share it with others.

Our trek down the notoriously hard descent into Zubiri really wasn't all that hard. The guidebook had overestimated that (for once). Tyler and I even took a break at the cutest little food truck/café that was parked about halfway down the trail. Little tables with shady umbrellas were spread out before it like a mirage in the desert, only this was a mirage for weary pilgrims on the trail. Before I could so much as shake my head, Tyler had already bought two water bottles from the truck for me and Maverick.

"Thank you," I said gratefully as we sat at one of the picnic tables together.

"You can buy me a beer when we get to town to pay me back," he smiled.

"I will! I'm not joking, I so will!" He only laughed and shook his head at me before loosening the laces of his hiking boots and kicking his feet free.

While Tyler got comfortable to rest for a while, Mav and I decided to finish the slog down to Zubiri. The rest of the descent was a bit of a daze, much like the final descent into Roncesvalles yesterday. I was shocked to feel almost as tired today as I had been yesterday. By the time we came to the river that formed the boundary of town, I could have cried tears of joy. We didn't even cross the bridge into town; Mav and I headed straight for the water. I slipped his pack over his head and he plunged in, immediately laying down in the shallows so his stomach was submerged. I followed suit, toeing off my boots and peeling back my socks to join him.

Maverick was acting completely unfazed by the tempera-ture of the water so when I splashed in, I was not at all expecting the icy needles that dug into my skin. I hopped onto a rock sticking up from the river and cautiously dipped my toe back in.

"Aren't you cold?" I gasped, before gritting my teeth to submerge one foot.

Mavy responded with a piercing whine before shoving his muzzle under the water and digging with his paws. He came up a moment later with a waterlogged stick dripping from his mouth. I laughed as I hopped from one rock to the next, dunking my other foot. The stick was wet and slimy between my fingers, but I took it from him nonetheless and chucked it upstream. He took off in a wave of water droplets, causing me to screech as the freezing spray hit me, and I toppled off the rock I was balancing on with a splash. As quickly as I could, I scrambled back onto another rock just as Maverick returned with the same damn stick in his mouth. Somehow he had managed to find it again, even though I was sure it sank to the bottom immediately.

He dropped the log with a plop by my rock and proceeded to bounce from one paw to the other in a little dance in front of me. Even in my exhausted state, I couldn't help but laugh. Here we were, an ocean away from home, but it felt completely normal. Just me and him playing by a river. Once again, I wondered if he knew just how much had changed for us over the past three days. His bark broke my train of thought and he stomped his front paws dramatically until I dipped my hand under the water and fished around for the sodden log. This time I threw it down river, towards the two massive arches that made up the bridge into town, *Puente de la Rabia*. According to legend, if an animal passed under the arches of the bridge or around the central pillar, it would be cured of rabies. Interesting theory, though I'm glad we have a bit more advanced ways of avoiding rabies nowadays.

Although Maverick would have been happy to spend hours down by the river, eventually we had to make our way into town and find the place I had written down, Zaldiko, that was supposed to allow dogs to stay. Just a few steps from the bridge, we came across the albergue in question, complete with a haggard-looking man sitting outside with a dog of his own. With a sheepish smile, we slipped by the pair and into the entry room of the albergue.

The hospitalera here was so kind, reassuring me that it would be no problem at all to have a place to stay with Maverick. Due to the older man outside having already checked in with his own dog, she asked if we would be okay with a private room in another property they owned down the street for the same price as a spot in the albergue, that way there wouldn't be any unexpected hostility between dogs. I quickly told her we were more than okay with that arrangement. Just having a hospitalero treat us normally and not as an oddity was enough for me. I already had a feeling this wouldn't be a typical response to a pilgrim with a dog, so I would take any and all kindness I could get.

It was interesting to interact with Spanish hospitality workers, actually. There was no need to put on a fake smile or add in any extra pleasantries. The hospitalera was kind, that much was apparent, and yet she had no use for small talk, no need to smile warmly at me just to put me at ease. She simply did her job, leading us down the road and to the left, showing me the keys to the other building where she led me up and into a four-bedroom apartment of sorts. She pointed out the kitchen, washer should I need to wash my clothes, two separate bathrooms, and a room for me and Maverick before giving me the keys she had just used. According to her, there was an ATM just down the street and I could just bring the money back to her at the main albergue whenever I was ready. And then she was gone, just as quickly as she had led me here.

I stood in the room with Maverick with a bemused smile on my face. No extra frills with that girl, that's for sure. And she was unconcerned about me paying her right away. She didn't care if I ate and took a shower or even took a nap before I paid, though I wouldn't do that. I planned to get euros out of the ATM and pay her right away, but still. It was kind of nice to meet a person who still has that sort of faith in humanity – that trust that a person will do the right thing. It's not something you see often.

As soon as we settled into our room, I grabbed Maverick's leash and we headed out in search of the ATM. At the corner of the two main streets in town, we came across the group of men who shared the bus with us from Bayonne to Saint Jean. They were occupying most of the patio of the restaurant, enjoying beers and some food. Upon seeing us, a raucous call went up as they urged us to join them.

"Okay, okay," I laughed. "I just need to pay the albergue. One minute," I promised. A cheer went up in response, courtesy of the overly friendly English bloke, Chris. My smile was so wide on the short walk back to the main Zaldiko albergue that my cheeks were starting to hurt.

The hospitalero behind the desk now was happy to take my payment and stamp my pilgrims' passport, but he was definitely thrown off when I asked if he could stamp Maverick's credential as well. Just like the man from the Pilgrim's Office in Saint Jean, he did a double take at the second *credencial.*

I read his confusion. "Es para el perro," I clarified. I nodded at the name printed on the inside of the paper passport. *Maverick K. Millsaps.*

The hospitalero's eyes flicked between the *credencial* and Maverick, who was laying on the cool tile beside my feet. He shook his head in disbelief, but I caught the grin he tried to hide as he pressed the Zaldiko stamp down against the thick paper. "Buen Camino," he said.

We made our way back to the patio and snuck into an empty seat at the table next to the guys. Immediately, Dario came over to crouch down next to Maverick, cooing "ciao, bello," over and over again. Maverick soaked up the attention with a wolfy grin. Except, when the loving Italian man went to stand again, he stumbled back with a groan. In the next second, he toppled backwards onto his ass. Despite already having four Caminos under his belt, the grueling terrain of the first two days had taken its toll, and his legs had cramped so bad he couldn't move from his spot on the stone patio.

"Are you okay?" I gasped, making to help him. Chris and Graham hooted in laughter, not bothering to offer their new friend a hand. He waved off my attempt to help and shot back insults to the guys, all with a smile. Once it was clear he was okay, I allowed myself to laugh as well.

While Dario sat on the stone next to Maverick, Chris struck up a conversation with me. "So you're out here all alone? Just you and the dog?"

"Yep," I replied, the 'p' popping off my lips as I nodded a thanks to the waiter who had just delivered my drink.

"How old are you? Have I asked that yet? You look so young."

"Twenty." I answered just as I took a sip, but I saw the shock that came over the faces of the men around me; saw Graham choke on the beer he had just drank.

"You're twenty?" he asked incredulously once he had gotten the drink down. I nodded sheepishly.

"Damn, girl. You've got balls of steel," Chris drawled in his British accent. Immediately, the table erupted in laughter again. My lips quirked in a self-deprecating smile, but I didn't respond.

Maybe he was right. Maybe I did have some courage. Or maybe I was just crazy. Once again, I wondered if all the trolls on the internet before we set out had been right. If the grump from the Pilgrim's Office in Saint Jean knew more than I did. I guess there was just one way to find out…keep going.

Either way, in that moment, I was struck by how strange it was to feel so comfortable in a foreign place surrounded by people who were essentially strangers. In the midst of it all, I realized how completely and utterly at ease I was here. I may not have responded to their praise or participated in their continued jabs and stories that much, but I couldn't keep the smile off my face.

Over the afternoon beers and *pintxos*, I learned that the man from France was named "Gaillaume" and Chris, who had also befriended him on the bus from Bayonne to Saint

Jean, had yet to be able to pronounce his name properly. Apparently, his solution to this predicament had been to call his newfound friend "Gollum" ... as in the creepy little hairless thing from *Lord of the Rings*. Let it be noted that this poor Frenchman looked nothing like Gollum, but regardless, that's what his comrade had been calling him for the past three days.

While this story came to light for those of us who had yet to hear it, Gailluame, exasperated with his friend's antics, attempted to explain to the rest of us what his name *really* was. Emphatically, he told us that it wasn't a hard name at all.

"You know, like Gaillaume the Conqueror," he explained slowly in his thick accent.

I, for one, had no idea what he was talking about and the accent made it no easier to understand. But at this new explanation, Chris slapped his hands on the table and cried out, "*William*? William the Conqueror? Your name is William?! You mean to tell me I could have been calling you Bill this whole time?!"

The table erupted in laughter and Maverick, startled from his slumber at the sudden commotion, jumped up and added his bark to the mix.

The past two days may have exhausted us but *this*? This was what the Camino was all about.

Calling All Angels

Day Three: Zubiri to Pamplona
24.4 km ~ 34,376 steps

June 21ˢᵗ

Most pilgrims spent the rest of the evening talking of Pamplona and how excited they were to get there. Though we had only been on trail for three days, it felt like so much longer. When life shrank down to just the miles you walked and the faces you passed, time seemed to warp. Safe to say, the excitement to reach the legendary city was high. Pamplona was the first major town along the trail, almost like a small city, and it held plenty of allure no matter who you were. While Hemingway aficionados may have recognized it from the author's classic *The Sun Also Rises*, the city was most famous for its *Las Fiestas de San Fermín*. A week-long celebration originally meant to honor the saint Fermín, the festivities are nothing without the Running of the Bulls, which occurs each day of the festival at eight a.m. The insane ritual is recognizable worldwide for the men who dress in bright white clothing, red belts, and vibrant red scarves in order to sprint ahead of bulls as they charge down the narrow city streets. The bulls who run each day later participate in the afternoon's bullfights in the center of the city. Each year, Pamplona floods with Spaniards and international tourists alike who come to witness the spectacle, take in the many parades and bullfights, and drink Sangria among friends.

Luckily for us, *Sanfermines* occurs each year between noon on July sixth and midnight on July fourteenth. Though many pilgrims may want to witness the activities of the festival, it is notoriously hard to find a place to stay during that week and walking through town could take a full day in itself. As interesting as the tradition is, I was totally okay with passing through Pamplona before the crowds descended. Like my fellow pilgrims, I would be happy to see the city, but I wasn't even planning on making it there today.

From my endless internet searching, I had discovered that the albergue of Trinidad de Arre supposedly allowed dogs to stay the night. It was only three and a half kilometers shy of the city, but I was happy to put off our arrival at the first major town if it meant a warm welcome for both Maverick and myself. Plus, knowing we weren't making the full walk from Zubiri to Pamplona today gave me the impression that I could take a late start this morning.

Clouds hung thick over Zubiri as we made our way down from our little apartment and through the empty streets that had been so abuzz with pilgrim chatter late last night. Apparently, the excitement of reaching Pamplona meant that most pilgrims had set out early from town despite the dreary weather. I shuffled through the puddled sidewalk to the same café we had eaten at last night and tied Maverick to a lamp post just outside the door.

"I'll be right back." My voice was still rusty from sleep.

With no other humans around, I had no reason to talk until now. I slipped into the café and ordered a slice of *tortilla* and a tea before hurrying back out to Maverick. I still wasn't comfortable leaving him outside alone, even if it was just for a minute. By the time I reemerged from the café, a man in a bread truck was pulling up to make the morning delivery. He hopped out of the back with a foot-long baguette in his hand and made his way directly to us.

"¿Por el perro?" he asked, extending the bread towards Maverick. I laughed and nodded that yes, it was okay to give him the bread.

Of course, Maverick being the little snob that he is, doesn't actually like human food. Particularly carbs. Apparently, he's put himself on the dog version of the Keto Diet. He merely licked the loaf, tentatively took it from the Spaniard, and promptly dropped it onto the sidewalk. The man shot me a befuddled look.

"Está bien," I reassured him. "No tiene hambre ahora. Pero llevamos por la tarde." With a shrug of confusion, because really…what dog didn't eat human food?? the man wished us a "Buen Camino" and hopped back into the truck as it rumbled down the sleepy street. If Maverick wouldn't eat it, I definitely would. I scooped up the loaf and brushed off any gravel before shoving it into the mesh pocket on the side of my pack. *More for me*, I thought happily.

We ambled out of town, back over Puente la Rabia, and bore right up the hill in pursuit of the next village. The road out of Zubiri wasn't exactly pleasant. It skirted around some sort of quarry or factory, then looped into a forgotten village that had little more than a water fountain and some stray cats who took an interest in Maverick. They quickly scrambled over the broken down walls and disappeared once he released an excited bark. And still, no other pilgrims.

"I need a sign," I sang out since no other soul was in

sight. No one but Maverick could tell me I had a horrible singing voice. "To let me know you're here." Mavy trotted a stick back to me and plopped it by my feet. I grinned and tossed it ahead and watched him launch into the brush beside the narrow road out of town. "All of these lines are being crossed over the atmosphere."

Even with the singing and fetch, I still had the crushing feeling of being completely alone. Sure, I had Maverick, but it wasn't like he could answer when I spoke to him or sing off-key with me. I pulled my phone from my hip pocket and shot a text to my dad about how alone I was. More than anyone else, I missed him when on a trail through forest. He would have some fun historical fact to share about the area. He would know what species of tree was what; what animals lived here.

A moment later, my phone vibrated. I tossed the stick for Maverick once more and slid open the text.

Isn't the point to be alone?

I read the text once. Then again. Then, with a huff, I shoved it back into my pocket.

No, I thought sullenly. I thought of all the pilgrims I had met so far, already grouping up. The band of men from the bus who had already formed a coalition. The two Irish girls and the young boy they met on the walk to Roncesvalles. I thought of the countless stories about finding a "Famino" – your Camino Family. I remembered the whole premise of *The Way* and the reluctant group from such diverse backgrounds that came to be one.

So no, I didn't think the point of the Camino was to be alone. I didn't need to be alone to find myself. Maybe God's plan for me along this journey was to confront my social anxiety; to teach me to be a bit more social. It certainly had felt like that up until today. But maybe the whole lesson here was to be more confident in myself, whether I was alone or among others. I could fully admit that I was a walking contradiction. When I was alone, like now, I craved the company of others. Yet when I was in a large group, I battled constant social anxiety and wished I could slip away to hang out with Maverick on my own.

I had never even considered the idea that I had anxiety before I started seeing a therapist after returning home from Ohio State. The first few weeks of this therapy had been spent going over my state of mind – what had happened, how I felt, taking personality tests and depression scales. It was just a matter of multiple choice and rating feelings for me, but apparently these things could give a lot of insight for people who know how to read them. Also, you had to actually fill them out honestly. That's the hardest part about getting treatment for depression, I think. You finally have to put all those walls away and be honest about it for the first time. That was a new one for me.

So after all those surveys, when my therapist mentioned anxiety to me, I laughed. *Listen*, I thought. *You've managed to diagnose me with one issue. Let's just stick to that, shall we? I'm a sad, hollow, shell of a human. Isn't that enough?*

Apparently not.

Just as I tried to pretend I didn't have depression, I didn't believe I had anxiety, either. To me, anxiety was shaking in the corner because you had to give a presentation in class. Anxiety was overreacting over little things that shouldn't have been an issue. Anxiety was hiding in your room because the world was too scary. I didn't have any of these problems. I didn't have anxiety.

I was wrong.

"Have you ever had trouble asking for help?" my therapist asked me after she had brought up anxiety.

Hah! Girl, if you only knew, I thought. "Yes," I answered.

"You'll say yes to things even when you really want to say no and it causes you stress?"

"Yes."

"So you struggle over saying no?"

"Yes."

"You don't like people touching you, getting too close to you?"

"Right..."

"And you don't do well in groups; you prefer to be one-on-one?"

"Yeah."

"Have you ever thought these all might be aspects of social anxiety?"

I hadn't. Not until then. I hadn't considered that any of those things weren't normal behaviors. I had just assumed that everyone worried about what others thought of them when they stood up to use the restroom while out to dinner with a group of friends. I assumed all people had that fear of others getting too close to them, seeing them clearly and picking apart everything that they saw. Apparently that wasn't the case. Apparently, when I was put in a social setting, my brain ran like a hamster on a wheel with all these worst-case scenarios and self-deprecating thoughts that other people don't ever think of.

Maybe, just maybe, this time alone on the Camino would teach me how to quiet those thoughts. Maybe if I was lucky, somewhere along this trail, I would find a balance. I would gain some confidence and maybe even a little bit of self-love.

"I need to know, that things are gonna look up," I sang softly as Mavy boinged along beside me. "'Cause I feel us drowning in a sea spilled from a cup."

The day grew hotter, but the trail remained lonely. We bumped into a few pilgrims at various villages along the way, but when it came to walking, we continued alone. At a fork in the trail, we opted for the "scenic route" and climbed the scrubby land towards Zabaldika and the old stone church that crouched amongst overgrown grasses at the top of a steep hill. Though I had never been to California, never walked the Pacific Crest Trail, I imagined it was somewhat like the ridgeline this trail ran along. Dry dirt cracked beneath my boots, the sun burnt the grass beside the trail, and I could hear the slight rattle of what might have been a rattlesnake in the brush ahead. *Wait…rattlesnake?!*

"Maverick!" I shouted, launching into a sprint to catch up to where he was poking into the scrubby bushes to the left of the trail. "No! *Hier!*" His German command for *come* poured from my mouth and he immediately snapped to attention, backing out of the bushes and coming to my side. The rattling sound faded as I unfurled his leash and clutched the end of it tightly, as if the feel of the leather biting into my palm made it real that he was still okay.

I could be overreacting. It could have just been the sound of some odd bug. *Were there even rattlesnakes in Spain? In this region?* I wondered. How could I not know? Here I was, thinking I had done my research on walking this trail with a dog, and I didn't even know if there were snakes on it. I didn't know what plants were toxic or what bugs or animals could hurt him. What if Maverick got bitten by something? What if he ate something he shouldn't? How could I have been so careless that I hadn't researched any of this?

Mav tugged at the leash, not at all used to being restrained while we were hiking. He was so obedient off-leash that I rarely held him back when we went out on walks. "Listen, kid," I scolded. "You will stay on this leash. You're not getting bitten by a snake on my watch. You got that?"

Maverick cast me a baleful look and shook out his pack across his shoulder blades before trotting on. Within an hour, the scenic route we were walking on linked back up to the main trail where a man had set up a makeshift table to sell pilgrims fresh fruit and bottled water. Our friend Tyler from New Hampshire was leaning against the half-crumbling cement wall here, his pack resting by his feet. At the sight of a familiar face, I sighed out the tension I hadn't realized I was still holding onto since the snake encounter. I pulled out some euros from my pack (since I finally possessed my own money now) and bought a banana from the vendor before leaning into the wall of an abandoned stone building opposite the vendor and Tyler.

"Are there poisonous snakes here?" I asked without preamble.

"Snakes?" the vendor asked.

"¿Los seprientes?" I clarified, making sure he understood what I was asking about.

"Ah, sí, serpientes. Why?" he asked.

"I think Maverick was almost bitten by a rattlesnake."

"Rattlesnake…hm," he muttered, a look of confusion crossing his features.

"Are there rattlesnakes around here?" Tyler asked.

"Beats me," I shrugged and took a bite of my banana, feeling way more nonchalant about the encounter than I had been a half hour ago.

"No. Only five poisonous snakes in Spain," the man piped up. "Not near here."

"Really?" I rushed out. "Oh, thank goodness." Not that it excused me not doing my research before coming, but hearing we weren't in immediate danger of venomous snakes was a relief nonetheless. At least now I knew that if Maverick happened to get bitten by a snake in these parts, it likely wouldn't be deadly. Although, the thought of Maverick getting bitten didn't make my next bite of banana go down all that smoothly.

"So," I said once I had managed to swallow. "No rattlesnakes then?"

"What is…rattlesnake?" the vendor asked.

"You know…snake that shakes its tail? Makes the rattle noise?" I was met with another blank stare. I wiggled my finger in an impersonation of a rattling tail, but still nothing. "You know…" After a moment of hesitation, I attempted my best rattle sound. Tyler let out a snort of laughter, then straightened up when I glared at him.

"Sorry, sorry," he muttered as he slung his bag onto his shoulders, but he couldn't wipe the grin from his face.

I narrowed my eyes at him, but then huffed out defeat. "Never mind," I groaned.

"Well, good luck with that," Tyler laughed. "Adiós." He waved to the vendor and then headed up the trail.

Mav and I didn't dally much longer and soon we were following Tyler's tracks, on our way to Trinidad de Arre and the monastery that supposedly allowed dogs. It was only one o'clock as we crossed over the stately, medieval bridge into Arre and I was in desperate need of a bathroom. I was starting to grow jealous of Maverick's ability to relieve himself at any point along the trail. We bypassed the monastery in search of somewhere I could use the bathroom. Except, every bar or café or store we passed all said the same thing. *Cerrado.* Closed. Even the pharmacies had put up signs claiming they would be back later.

"Is this a joke?" I grumbled under my breath. If there had been any doubt at all that *siesta* was a real thing in the Spanish culture, this was my resounding answer. We were in the heart of midafternoon naptime. Just after the center of town, we came across a library or museum of some sort that looked like it was open to the public. Surely it would have a bathroom.

"Wait here," I told Maverick and I looped his leash around a tree out front and dropped my pack down next to him. "Eat some bread." I broke off an end of the baguette the man had given us that morning then rushed into the imposing building. *Servicios* was printed just inside the doors on the left and I sent up a quick prayer of thanks for my good fortune before ducking inside.

When I pushed through the pristine glass doors back out into the heat of the Spanish afternoon, Maverick was surrounded by a gaggle of children. From the looks of it, they were part of a summer camp program and were taking a break of their own on the lawn. After so much solitary time on trail this morning, I welcomed the bustle and excitement of the kids. I tried to answer their many questions about Maverick as best I could in Spanish and munched on the hard loaf of bread that had been tucked into the outside pocket of my pack all morning while we lounged in the shade of the tree. It was so pleasant I had the urge to keep walking straight into Pamplona. The afternoon wasn't *that* hot, and really, what was four kilometers? We would be able to catch up with our fellow pilgrims, the same ones we had been with since the bus from Saint Jean. What could possibly go wrong?

So after an hour or more of relaxation under that tree, I shrugged my heavy blue pack back onto my shoulders and took hold of Maverick's leash. "Onward, good sir," I giggled to him as we clomped our way along sidewalks, following the *conchas* inlaid beneath our feet until we reached the towering city walls of Pamplona.

The ancient city of Pamplona was nothing short of impressive. Massive stone walls surround part of the city where pilgrims have entered for centuries over the drawbridge at the medieval *Portal de Francia* and into the tight, winding alleyways that serve as streets here with countless balconies overlooking them. The entire area had its own energy, as if a bull could come charging down the street at any moment and it wouldn't be a surprise at all, even if it wasn't *Sanfermines*. Both Spaniards and pilgrims alike crowded the narrow streets, spilling out of bars and cafés at every curve of the road. It was impossible to even take three steps without hearing Maverick's name called from a bar stool or being intercepted by a fellow pilgrim we had bumped into along the trail so far. Most didn't know my name. I was still only referred to as "Maverick's Mom" or "the girl with the dog" by the majority of our comrades. Except for Chris and Dario – they knew who I was.

"The girl with the balls of steel," Chris greeted me as I spied them leaving a café near the center of town. I grinned and rushed to hug them both. It wasn't that I felt scared out here or like I didn't know what I was doing. I had yet to meet anyone else as young as me on the trail, but that hadn't made me feel like what I was doing was treacherous. Regardless, seeing Chris and Dario bathed me in a sense of security, as if I had some father figures looking out for me.

With their coaxing, I agreed to check out the municipal albergue where the majority of pilgrims were staying for the night. I hadn't read anything about this particular albergue being accepting of dogs, but I allowed their positivity to buoy me. In the end, it was a moot point. The hospitaleros at the nice, modern municipal albergue would not budge in their "no dogs allowed" stance even with Dario and Chris's pleading.

"It's okay," I laughed at Chris and his pouting. It seemed odd for a grown man to pout, but it was cute they cared so much about me. "I'll keep looking."

"But you'll be all alone," he said.

I shrugged. I better get used to that feeling of being all alone. As my dad pointed out this morning, being alone was a very big part of this journey. "I have Maverick. Who says that's all alone?" I scratched between Mavy's shoulder blades and he glanced up at me in appreciation. With a wave goodbye and a "maybe" to their offer of getting dinner later, I continued on in search of a place to stay.

However, my optimism was quickly fading after getting turned down by the fifth albergue I tried. Instead of prolonging my fruitless search on foot, I found a bench to sit on while I propped open my guidebook and began dialing numbers of places to stay here in Pamplona. Being the first real "city" along the Camino meant the list of accommodations was seemingly endless. Surely one of them would allow a dog. Finally, a number I dialed agreed to allow both Maverick and I to stay the night. I matched up the name of the hostel with its dot on Brierley's map and we set off in that direction. The peaceful feeling that had carried us on from Trinidad de Arre was long gone, as was the excitement of finding Dario and Chris. Now, all I wanted was a shower and to take off these boots.

The *pensión* was seedy at best and located past the center of town where the tourists were few and far between and the buildings that crowded tight on either side of the streets were coated in a thick layer of grime. I pressed my finger to the call box where the *pensión* was supposedly located and a moment later a dull buzz told me the door had been unlocked. I exchanged a tentative look with Maverick before stepping into the dank entryway. A wooden staircase looped upward in a rectangular pattern and I followed it with my eyes until it disappeared into the gloom in the stories above us. I had a feeling this could have been a light, airy chamber but instead it was shrouded in shadows with a faint smell of rot.

"Well," I muttered to Maverick as we began the climb, his pack bumping against the banisters with every step. "Beggars can't be choosers, right?"

We didn't spend much time in our room. Just long enough to drop our packs and for me to take a shower in the adjoining bathroom. I suppose I should be thankful our accommodations had a private bathroom and one of Pamplona's iconic balconies looking out over the street three stories below. I glanced back up at said balcony as we made our way back towards the main part of town, noting my clothes that were now hanging from the banister to dry. No fancy washer here like Zubiri had. It was back to the pilgrim way of washing clothes in the sink.

The crowds were even thicker in the main part of the city than they had been when we first came through a couple hours ago. Apparently, it was a Friday night and many were eager to kick off the weekend. It was funny how quickly I had lost track of the days out here. Tuesday, Wednesday, Friday, it made no difference to us. We would wake up and we would walk and eventually we would find a place to sleep and do it again the next day. There were far more important things to worry about than what day of the week it was. Things such as, *where was the next water fountain?* Or, *do we have a place to stay for the night?*

The sudden influx of people felt wrong after a day of such solitude, so I found myself ducking away from the main roads and wider streets in favor of the twisty side alleys of the city. Finally, we found a whole street that was blessedly empty; not a soul in sight. I looked up and down the street once more, then grinned down at Maverick. A second later, I had unclipped his leash from his collar and he bounded forward in freedom, then came right back to pant up at me.

"Race ya?" I asked him. Before I knew what I was doing, I had taken off at a sprint down the deserted alleyway. In an instant, Maverick was at my heels. I skidded to a stop and turned to face him, playfully tapping him on the cheek so he turned and tried to catch my hand in his mouth. I bopped his other cheek before he could catch me, then took off again in the other direction. He darted after me, yapping happily, the sound echoing in between the buildings that pressed in on either side of us. I spun when he caught me again, dropping into a crouch to meet him on eye level and tapping him on a shoulder this time. He lunged in an effort to catch me and I dodged away, this time zigging and zagging down the street again. I was having so much fun, laughing over my shoulder as I watched Maverick chase after me, that I almost crashed right into a woman who had just rounded the corner into our deserted alley.

Maverick collided with the back of my legs at my sudden stop and I lurched forward before righting myself again. "Lo siento," I gasped, out of breath from all my laughter and running. I couldn't wipe the grin from my face.

The woman blinked rapidly, taking in my haggard appearance and breathless state, and then noticed Maverick panting beside me. She smiled ruefully. "Está bien."

I bit my lip to hold in my laughter and reached down to clip Maverick's leash back on him, straightening up to the picture of civility. She tossed us one more backwards glance, and then strode past us. I looked down at Maverick out of the corner of my eye and grinned.

"Whoops," I whispered to him, ruffling the fur between his ears one more time. "Come on, then. Let's go pretend to be adults."

We wandered the streets some more, took in the cathedral from afar but didn't go in because I didn't feel right leaving Maverick tied outside, and found our way back to the busy thoroughfare through town.

"Colby!" I turned, shocked to hear my own name and not just "Maverick's owner."

Trish and Margie were seated at a high table just outside of a bar and they waved me over, demanding I take a seat and eat some *pinxtos* with them. I settled in beside them with a smile, Maverick at our feet, and thought I may just be finding that Camino family after all. Chris and Dario. Trish and Margie. They all felt like a little slice of home even though they were from all different corners of the world. I may have felt lonely on the trail this morning, but arriving in Pamplona had changed all of that. Maybe we were getting the hang of this whole Camino thing: the quiet, solo times *and* the times spent with friends. Maybe the key was to find the balance.

Foreplay / Long Time

Day Four: Pamplona to Uterga

21.1 km ~ 29,723 steps

June 22nd

It's so nice to sit in the comfort of your own home and watch a movie about someone walking a trail, or read a book on it, or maybe scroll through your Instagram feed and see the pretty pictures people post about traveling. It's easy to say, "I want to do that" or "I want to go there." It's another thing entirely to actually go there and do those things. It turns out those books and movies? Those pretty pictures? That's just the highlight reel. Actually living the experience? Well that? That's really fucking hard.

Maverick got sick last night. I'm talking *really* sick. I'm pretty sure the entire contents of his stomach was spewed across the floor of our *pensión* at one a.m. The smell was atrocious. It's a miracle I didn't puke just from the smell and sight of it. Trying to clean it up was a nightmare. But trying to clean it up when I had nothing but what I carried in my pack? That was even worse. I'm sorry to say the owner of this *pensión* would not be pleased when he saw the state of his towels. But what was I supposed to do?

This was all my fault. How could I have let this happen? How had I not realized Maverick wasn't feeling good? Did he drink bad water yesterday when I wasn't paying attention? Was he dehydrated? Was this a result of walking in the heat yesterday afternoon? Had we walked too far? I must have pushed him too hard. Everyone we had talked to before leaving was right. What had I been thinking, taking a dog on a Camino? This was no place for a dog. Why had I foolishly thought we could beat the odds? Why hadn't I listened to the hundred people who had told me this was a stupid idea before setting out? They had been right. We couldn't do this.

So I did the only thing I *could* do at one in the morning, in a crisis, sad and completely alone. I called my mom. What was it Rory Gilmore said? *I need my mommy and I don't care who knows it.*

She answered on the fourth ring; it was only seven p.m. back home. But what could she possibly do for me from an ocean away? "Colby?"

The very thin measure of control I had been holding onto snapped at the sound of her voice. I started sobbing then. Through my tears, she talked me down. She reminded me that this was okay. Dogs got sick. It happened. It didn't mean he was dying, no matter how much I wailed about the amount of vomit there was. This was all new to him. He wasn't used to walking every day and staying in a new place every night. Even if he didn't outwardly show it, this was probably stressful to him, too.

Once again, I berated myself. Why hadn't I thought of that before? As humans, we could understand the concept of a long-distance walk. You walk a certain distance, then stop for the night. Every day is somewhere new. I was aware of this; I had wrapped my head around it. But Maverick didn't understand this concept at all. Even if we did hike often, or go camping, we weren't in a new place every night. We always came home to our house after a hiking trip or a camping trip. We had our car that he knew well. There was familiarity there.

There was absolutely nothing familiar here.

"Maybe he just needs an extra night to get his bearings," my mom offered over the phone. "Why don't you stay in Pamplona for an extra day? Spend the day together and relax before walking again tomorrow. You both could use the time to reset. Get some sleep now, it's late, and in the morning you can make a new plan. You can do this," she assured me. I wasn't so sure.

Out loud, I agreed with her. But in my head, I had already made up my mind. There was no way we were staying in this sketchy *pensión* for an extra day. I suppose I could have found some other place to stay, but something was pulling me forward despite every part of me screaming that I had messed up; that I couldn't do this. I may not know exactly what the morning would bring, but I knew we needed to move on from here.

At five-thirty, Maverick and I trudged down the block of stairs and spilled out into the streetlight of the sketchy alley. Once again, we were completely alone as we trekked out of Pamplona. Only this time, it was because *we* were the early birds. It wasn't until we had left the city limits and started our climb that the sun began to peek over the horizon.

As I followed Maverick's fluffy tail up the sidewalk from Cizur Maior and into the endless fields that led up to

Zariquiegui, I tried to plan out our day. I was carrying Mavy's pack today so he wouldn't have the burden of that weight. We would take plenty of breaks. I would make sure he drank a little bit of water at each stop. Maybe I could even get him to lay down and rest when we stopped. We would take our sweet time today. This was no race. This was a pilgrimage and damnit, we were going to make it all the way to Santiago. With the rising sun came my determination. In the light of day, things no longer seemed so dire. My mom was right. We could do this.

Thanks to the snail's pace I insisted on today, many of our fellow pilgrims had caught up to us by the time we reached Zariquiegui for breakfast. Maverick ate up the attention from Chris, Guillaume, and Dario while we shared a table and chatted over our *tortilla españolas* and croissants.

"He looks fine today," Chris commented as he scratched between Maverick's ears. I had just finished telling them of our horrible night. I swallowed my bite of egg and potato mixture that had quickly become my standard breakfast here and squinted my eyes at Maverick. I had been watching him like a hawk all morning and I had yet to see any abnormal behavior in him. By all accounts, Chris was right. He did look fine. In fact, he looked extremely happy to be amongst friends spending another day hiking. Maybe getting sick last night was just a fluke, but I wasn't about to risk it.

"Yeah, so far he's seemed perfectly normal today. I'm planning to just do a short day regardless. I don't want to push him."

"That is smart. Where will you stop?" Dario asked as he sipped a *café con leche*.

"I'm thinking Uterga."

Dario smiled. "A nice town," he said. He would know, this was his fifth pilgrimage after all.

"Just seventeen kilometers from Pamplona. That

shouldn't be too bad for him. I'm guessing you guys are on to Puente la Reina?" According to Brierley's guidebook, that was the next main stop along the route. The trio nodded their agreement and before long they were off again, laughing and jesting with one another like teenage boys, not middle-aged men.

When Maverick and I set off a few minutes later, we took a considerably slower pace up the steep incline to the top of Alto de Perdón, one of the more famous spots along the Camino Francés. If I thought the wind had been strong on our climb up, it was nothing compared to the way it was whipping across the summit when we arrived. The massive pilgrim monument drew my attention immediately, but the view was just as impressive from this spot. No one talks about the view from Alto de Perdón, but it deserves to be mentioned. Before I could even take a closer look at the metal monument, I took the time to look out over all the land we had covered.

Spread out below us was a patchwork of rolling fields, the same ones we had just walked through on the outskirts of Pamplona, which then melted into the city limits before the landscape rose once again towards the foothills of the Pyrenees we had descended over the past few days. To think, we had just walked all that way and it had taken days to do it. And now, looking from above, it seemed so short. Like if you had a strong enough arm, you could throw a stone and it would reach Pamplona at the very least, maybe even the green hills on the edge of the great Pyrenees mountains. I had seen many mountaintop views, but for some reason this was more humbling than all of them combined. I deftly reached down, brushing back Maverick's fur where the wind was blowing it up in tufts. He let me, leaning his weight into my side, and for a moment I forgot all about the uncertainty and fear I had been feeling this morning. For a moment, all I could feel was the wind against my face and his Maverick's fur pressing against my leg and half a world away, I felt like I was home.

With a deep breath, I turned my view from the horizon to the monument that stretched across most of the summit of Alto de Perdón. The statue, made from iron, depicts twelve pilgrims and bears the famous saying at its center, "Where the path of the wind crosses with that of the stars." While all pilgrims who have walked the Camino Francés surely know this monument well, what isn't common knowledge is that the procession of the twelve pilgrims actually represents the change from the very first pilgrims, through the Middle Ages, to modern times. The true name of the monument is *Pilgrims Through the Ages.* Quite fitting.

The first pilgrim is shown alone, curiously forging a path on this ancient way. He's quickly followed by two others, indicating the increased popularity of this pilgrimage. The center of the statue, and the most recognizable part since it holds the inscription, depicts the height of the route's popularity during Medieval Times where many people from all different classes walked The Way on horseback, with their dogs (hey Mavy look, it's you!), or with mules to carry their belongings. The next two figures are shown spread apart, alone, to denote the decline in the popularity of the trek due to various reasons such as political, religious, and social unrest up until the twentieth century. The last two figures, when looked at more closely, can clearly be seen as more modern pilgrims. They walk together, wearing what appear to be backpacks and modern clothing, and show the recent popularity of the Camino in modern times.

I ran my hand over the metal one last time, feeling the raised inscription beneath my fingers, before turning with Maverick and starting our descent which, might I add, is far steeper than the so-called wretched descent into Zubiri. This path was all loose gravel and rocks that would roll beneath my boots as I skittered down the trail, doing my best not to lose my footing with every step. When we finally made it back to level ground after what felt like hours, we were greeted with rolling wheatfields that were dotted with bright red poppies on either side of the farm trail the Camino followed. It felt like something out of a painting, the vibrant crimson against the dull gold wheat waving lazily in the breeze. I smiled as Maverick romped ahead, chasing after a butterfly yet again, and let my hand brush over the soft tops of the wheat while I walked. It was hard to imagine there was anything more peaceful in the world than this moment right here.

With one final climb, we reached our destination: the tiny village of Uterga. It wasn't hard to find the place I hoped to stay tonight. There were only two albergues in this tiny town, directly across from each other on the main road. Mav and I turned right into the huge, open door of Casa Baztan and immediately, a young man appeared behind the front desk with a welcoming smile.

"¡Buen Camino!" he called, not at all deterred by Maverick's presence. In fact, he did not appear surprised at all that Maverick was here. Instead, he went about bringing me water, a plate of fresh olives, and various sodas despite my laughing protests before giving both Maverick and my *credenciales* a stamp. We were the first pilgrims to arrive, so I had my choice of bunk bed in the large dormitory. I would have been happy with any bunk. It was our very first true albergue experience and I had a sinking feeling it would be one of our only true albergue experiences. The room was long and dim, but sunlight was still shining through some of the windows that lined the road, little flower boxes bursting with color on each sill. I found a bunk in the corner and dumped our bags on it to claim it, gratefully rubbing my forearms which were now numb from carrying the weight of Maverick's pack all day. Then Mav and I trailed after the hospitalero as he showed us the bathrooms and large sinks to wash clothes in, the *jardín* (which was really just a backyard, not a garden) equipped with endless clotheslines and welcoming hammocks, and then instructed me when and where I could find dinner.

I looped Maverick's leash around a leg of our bunk and promised I would be right back before scurrying off to the bathroom to shower and wash my sweaty, dusty clothes in one of the industrial sinks. We spent the rest of our afternoon in the *jardín* while my clothes were drying on the line. Maverick spun in circles in the lush grass, darting after the shadows of butterflies and snapping his jaws on empty air each time one came close to his head. I pushed off the dirt with a foot, my bright blue hammock swinging back and forth lazily while I smiled at him.

Everything about this place was full of color. The flowers in every window, the multicolored hammocks, the bright yellow butterflies. My fingers swirled the handful of shockingly red cherries I had in my palm. They rolled from one hand to the next and then back again as I absentmindedly played with them. A man who had been selling fruits and vegetables from his farm truck had stopped us on our way into the village and insisted I take them.

As I watched the bright red cherries roll back and forth, felt their smooth surfaces against my rough skin, I thought back to a very different time. When I was coming into a different town. When everything was black and white; not at all vibrant.

Leaving college the previous spring hadn't been much of a choice. I wasn't considered "safe" anymore. My mental health had deteriorated so rapidly that year that the idea of taking my own life had become more and more appealing.

My dad had flown out to get me and the next day, we were on our way home. As he drove me into the town I had spent my entire life in, with all my stuff from college packed into the back of the rental car, I watched the snowy fields and trees roll by while tears streaked down my cheeks. He didn't ask why I was crying. I'm not sure I would have been able to give him an answer if he had. He only rubbed my shoulder with one hand and told me everything would be okay.

Except, he couldn't know that. No one could know that. They weren't inside my head. They didn't cry themselves to sleep every night and feel the same pain every day. They only saw the smile I pasted on in public. I had been doing it for so long I didn't even notice it anymore. I couldn't even remember what it was like to feel things.

What so many people don't ever know is that some depressions are silent.

I wasn't a person who shut herself in her room and wouldn't come out. I wasn't the one who could never leave her bed or cried all the time. I didn't eat way too much or go days without eating. I didn't lose contact with all of my friends. I wasn't someone who never responded to invites or showed up late for class or work. My grades didn't slip. I kept going to the gym. These were all things we've been trained to recognize in someone who's suicidal.

Maybe that's why I refused to get help for so long. I couldn't believe I really did have depression because I wasn't that person. I wasn't the stereotype of depression. Even when I finally admitted something was wrong and I came home that bleak spring day, I still functioned. I went on hikes. I got a job. Heck, I got two jobs. I finished my first book. I was doing fine.

Now, less than a week into the Camino, I could see how very wrong that had been. I hadn't been doing fine. Sure, I was still living, but once that crushing sadness I felt at school had faded, I was left feeling...nothing. I was living in a world of black and white. My brain couldn't comprehend color. There were no peaks of excitement, no valleys of sadness. I think that was even worse than being excessively sad all the time. At least then I would have a definite thing to be fighting.

But when you felt nothing at all? Well, there really was no reason to fight then. There was no light at the end of the tunnel. No hope in the future. There was no future at all. It's not that I had an immediate plan of suicide anymore, there was simply no way to picture myself older.

I couldn't picture a life in the future. I couldn't picture a version of me in my thirties. I couldn't picture finding a husband or having children. I couldn't picture working a steady job or owning my own house. I couldn't picture any of it. Depression had stripped me of a future and it stripped me of a life right now.

I couldn't feel anything at all.

Maverick bumped into my knees, sending my hammock rocking again, and a cherry jostled from my palm, bouncing into the emerald grass. Within a second, he was skittering off again, his teeth snapping behind an orange butterfly this time. I blinked a few times, shaking myself from my reverie, and took in this place. This beautiful, vibrant place that had welcomed us with open arms and was bursting with color. Color I could fully see.

Castle on the Hill

Day Five: Uterga to Villatuerta

31 km ~ 44,884 steps

June 23rd

The tiny village of Uterga, in all its welcoming beauty, did not attract many pilgrims to stay the night. The town of Puente la Reina was just a little over six kilometers away and that was where most pilgrims chose to spend the night. So while we got the pilgrim experience of sleeping in a dormitory… I think there were a total of six other pilgrims sleeping there with us. It made no matter. Last night, we had gone across the street to the only other albergue in town for dinner and had run into Trish and Margie who were staying there. Maverick and I were able to lounge with them on the patio for most of the evening, where Trish appointed herself as my "Camino Mom."

I was in need of a mom right about now, Camino or real.

Since yesterday had gone so well for Maverick, I thought it would be best if we started out super early again to beat the afternoon heat. So at four-thirty this morning, we had struggled our way out of the massive wooden door of Casa Baztan and started down the main road. It had been a straight shot out of the village and then we were into more fields. Of course, I could only see what fell within the light of my flashlight. Half the time I couldn't even see Maverick until the beam would swing over him and reflect his ghostly eyes back at me.

It was so quiet. Only the crunch of gravel beneath my own boots echoed back at me. And the sky was so clear. I could see thousands of stars, more than I had ever been able to see back home. There was no light pollution for miles and the sun hadn't even begun to tint the horizon yet. And... we were lost. My feet stuttered to a stop. That couldn't be right. The trail we were on led straight into a new field of wheat. Or barley. Or whatever it was they grew here. I certainly couldn't make it out in just the light of my flashlight. I dropped down a little rise to the field, checking to make sure the trail didn't bend off to the right, but no. It just stopped. It came to the field and stopped. I was officially lost. I spun in a circle. Still lost. Looked up at the sky, then back the way we came. Yep. Still lost.

"How the heck did we go the wrong way?" I asked aloud to Maverick. The sound of my voice shattered the silence, completely out of place in the predawn air. Of course, Maverick didn't respond. Not that I needed him to. We had stayed on the trail. I hadn't seen any other turns. Where had we gone wrong?

Okay, I thought to myself. *This could be worse.* All I had to do was retrace my steps. Go back the way we came. Surely, I would come across some arrow I had missed. Some sign that had been hidden in the almost suffocating darkness. I could fix this. No need to panic.

I called out for Maverick, once more breaking the almost sacred silence. I heard him running towards me in the dark and then he was there, his head tilted to look at me curiously in the beam of my flashlight. "Let's go," I muttered to him, turning to trudge back up the little hill we had just come down. Only…we made it all the way back to the outskirts of Uterga and nothing popped out at me. No sign to turn. No yellow arrows. Nothing.

I vaguely debated walking straight back to Casa Baztan and crawling back into bed, but then remembered that the door would be locked. There was no going back. I was frustrated and lost and sad and disappointed in myself. More than anything, I was alone. Maverick was too busy chasing bugs to realize I was in desperate need of a friend.

Which brought me to the point: I was in desperate need of a mom right about now.

"Honey, we can't help you." My mom's voice was still scratchy with sleep as it came through the line. This made two days in a row that I called my mom in tears. I could hear her talking to my dad in the background, trying to explain where I was while I sniffled from my spot in the dirt under the never-ending night sky. My mom and I always shared our locations with one another on our phones, so I knew she must be looking at my little blue dot on the screen while my dad tried to match it up with the maps of the guidebook they had back home.

"It doesn't say anything about turns," I heard my dad say.

"I know that," I grumbled. I had read the guidebook, too. I had read it multiple times. I even had it open in my lap now. I knew it wasn't fair for me to be upset with them. I *had* been the one to call them at midnight their time and woke them up to…what? Help me? They couldn't very well help me from New Hampshire.

"You're just going to have to keep going. There has to be something you missed. Can you see what it looks like, Jon?" my mom asked my dad.

"Her dot is just in the middle of fields. Just fields for miles," he replied, referencing my lovely locator.

I groaned. Maverick caught a moth that was hovering in the light of my flashlight and I rolled my eyes, frustrated at anything and everything. "I'll just keep walking," I snapped.

"I wish we could do something," my mom tried.

I sighed, feeling even shittier for treating them so poorly. "I know," I mumbled. "I love you. I'll let you know if I find anything."

I stood and brushed the dirt from my pants, slinging on my pack again and hoisting Maverick's bag onto one forearm. He paused in his pursuit of some other flying thing and looked at me expectantly.

"Yeah," I muttered. "We're still going."

Not five minutes down the trail, the beam of my flashlight swung over a stone marker with the famous yellow *concha*. An arrow below it directed us to turn right. "No way," I groaned. I had missed this twice now, and for good reason. The stone was set far enough back that the crops almost swallowed it up. If I hadn't been scouring both sides of the trail like a madwoman, I would have missed it yet again. I pulled my phone out to shoot a quick text to my parents so they wouldn't keep worrying that their daughter was wasting away in a field somewhere. Then, with a sigh, Maverick and I turned to the right and finally continued on our way.

If only my mood was so easily fixed. Blame it on lack of sleep, or lack of food as the day wore on because the first four towns we passed through would prove to have nothing open, or simply my own depressed brain, but I was *not* having a good day today. I spent almost as much time crying as I did walking. I cried while I drank water. I cried while I walked up and down dusty hills and through villages. I cried while I sat down right in the dirt because I no longer cared if there was a bench or a comfortable patch of grass to sit on. I cried while we passed over the stunning bridge, *Puente la Reina*. I hadn't cried this much since I was at Ohio State.

In the months just before I came home, I used to walk across campus with tears pouring down my face. I didn't even care if other people saw me crying. It didn't matter to me. Just as I didn't care now. Only today, instead of fellow students passing by, I was being passed by fellow pilgrims. Same depression, different location. Just like then, I couldn't even pinpoint what I was crying about. I was just *sad*. Defeated. Hopeless. I didn't even realize I was crying half the time. It wasn't a conscious decision. It just happened.

I used to believe that depression was a choice. When I was in high school, back before my depression had fully taken hold of me, I had to write a response to a reading of *Tuesdays with Morrie*. I distinctly remember writing that every person had the power to decide to be happy or to be miserable. Bold statement? Not really. We heard it all the time. "It's all in your mindset," they tell you. "It's all how you look at things." You have the power to change your own thoughts. I truly believed that back then. I thought that if you looked around at the world with rose-colored glasses, with the mentality that the glass is half full, then you would be happy.

What a bunch of bullshit.

I couldn't will myself out of depression no matter how hard I tried. Not through therapy. Not through pills. I thought I had made some progress, but clearly not enough.

Because here I was, half a world away, still sobbing. I couldn't even will myself into happiness as Maverick and I passed through Puente la Reina.

The town, which took its name from the formidable Romanesque bridge that spanned the river Arga, was the meeting point of the route I had been traveling and that of the Camino Aragones. As a melting point of two Camino routes, the medieval town became popular and grew up around the massive bridge it was named for. It is said to have been built by a twelfth century queen, hence the name *Queen's Bridge*, to allow pilgrims safe passage across the river.

Maverick and I shuffled through town wearily and without much fanfare. No shops were open yet, no bars to serve breakfast. The sun had barely begun to lighten the sky at that point. We paused to take in the sprawling bridge, over three-hundred feet long, peaked in the center, with six massive arches supporting it, and then we shuffled across that as well. The scenery throughout the day was beautiful…when I could make it out through my tears. A part of me vaguely wondered if this was what Tuscany looked like with all its hilltop villages. Each town we passed through sat at the crest of a hill, meaning Maverick and I trudged up and down countless dusty farm roads and even parts of road that were laid by the Romans themselves, the slabs of stone ancient and worn smooth by thousands of feet.

I'd like to say I reveled in the good things. That they seemed so much sweeter in the midst of all my sadness today and taught me profound lessons, but I know that isn't true. I still smiled through my tears, though. Just before leaving Cirauqui, we ran into a family of four who were biking the Camino. The two sons looked to be no older than eight and five. They didn't speak a lick of English, but that was fine. I gave them a watery smile and welcomed them to play with Maverick in the shade of the archway that led out of town.

The younger of the two boys insisted on being the one to use the self-serve stamp station here to give both Maverick and my *credenciales* a stamp to mark our progress. I thanked him profusely but denied his attempt to give Maverick his sandwich.

His mother tried to apologize, but I quickly waved her off. They were the first people I had actually interacted with all day and for a little while talking with the boys and smiling as they danced around Maverick, I didn't feel so defeated. Kids had that same purity that dogs did. Maybe because they didn't understand the heavy emotions or maybe just because they're full of energy and excitement for anything and everything. It was nice to be reminded of the wholesome things in life like a child's laughter and a dog's wagging tail or the selfless help of strangers.

Later in the day, when the sun had begun to bake us and even Maverick was showing signs of slowing down, we came across a little oasis of sorts. In a grove of olive trees, countless hammocks had been strung up and benches strewn about in the shade. A little wooden hutch full of water bottles and power bars welcomed pilgrims to take whatever they may need. Since Maverick and I had already been making terrible time today thanks to all my crying and the slow, painful pace I had kept all day, I saw no reason why we shouldn't lay down among the trees. We certainly weren't going to be making it to Estella anytime soon.

By the time we reached the river that formed the boundary of the village of Villatuerta, I was completely spent. Somewhere between the olive grove and the river, I had ditched my hiking boots in favor of my Chacos so it was easy to slip from them and dunk my feet into the river while Maverick laid down. The water was no longer the frigid mountain streams of the Pyrenees. Here, it still felt refreshing on my tired feet, but it was warm from the late afternoon sun beating down.

While Maverick plodded amongst the reeds of the river, I looked up at the town we had reached. Villatuerta. From what I could see, it wasn't much of a town. Just a small cluster of dusty buildings situated close to the river. I couldn't fathom the thought of walking further today. Just the thought alone made me want to puke, but I had no knowledge of this village. In all my prior research, nothing had come up about this town having dog friendly accommodations.

"Come on, Maverick," I croaked. My voice was raw from all the crying I had done today and coated with dust from the road. "Let's see what we can find."

Fortunately, there was an albergue just beyond the tiny bridge into town. With no idea if they allowed dogs or not, we pushed our way out of the hot sun and into the cool, tiled entryway of what appeared to be a very nice albergue. I took a seat in one of the woven chairs across from the front desk and waited for a *hospitalero* to arrive so I could plead my case. A man came down the stairs a moment later with a huge grin on his face which faltered for just a moment at the sight of Maverick.

I hopped up with as much enthusiasm as I could muster. "¡Hola! ¿Tiene un cuarto libre esta noche?" I was pretty positive from what I had seen so far that we were the only pilgrims in the albergue. There was no way he had no empty rooms for the night.

The man stayed quiet, his eyes flicking to Maverick who was laying on the floor quietly. "Por favor, señor," I pleaded when I saw his hesitation. "Estamos muy cansados. Él es un perro muy amable." I wasn't sure what else I could say. I would just have to wait and pray this stranger would let us stay for one measly night.

He hesitated again, but this time he focused on me. He must have seen something in my face. It could have been the residue of all my tears from the day, or maybe just the defeated slump of my shoulders, but he took pity on me. While I was never one to be pitied, in this situation, I would take it. "No permitimos perros aquí. Pero, haré una excepción para ti. Ven."

I felt my shoulders collapse as a sigh of relief escaped me. All the tension I had been carrying seemed to flow out of me at his kind words. An exception. He would make an exception for me. I didn't think anything had ever sounded so sweet.

"Pasaporte." I scrambled over to the front desk and handed my passport to him so he could transcribe my information into his logbook. When he was finished, he gave me a wan smile. "¿Credencial?" I slid mine across the wooden desk and he punched a stamp onto the thick sheet.

"Gracias, señor." I tucked my credential into the waterproof pouch I kept them in and pulled out Maverick's. "Pues...¿señor? ¿Es posible tener una silla en esta credencial también? Es la credencial del perro."

The man looked up at my request and a true smile broke out on his face now. He let out a chuckle, no doubt amused that Maverick had his own credential that needed a stamp as well. "Claro," he said as he pushed down onto the credential with a flourish. We shared a smile then, my first genuine smile of the day. Somehow, Maverick had made everything okay while simultaneously making everything so much more difficult than it was for any other pilgrim.

The man led me out to the gardens, then up the stairs and to the room we were to have for the night. There were five beds in the room, and just as I had suspected when we first arrived, there were no other pilgrims here. I shared a secret smile with Maverick, who was still firmly connected to his leash and displaying the best behavior. After ensuring that there would be no dogs on the beds, pointing out the bathrooms, and informing me when and where to find dinner tonight, the hospitalero ducked back into the hall and disappeared down the stairs.

We hadn't even gotten settled into our room fully when I heard the door to the albergue push open again and a female voice call out. Being the curious person I am, I peaked my head out over the balcony of the second floor to see into the lobby and found none other than Trish and Margie with their massive packs.

"Hey!" Trish waved upon seeing me. I smiled and waved back. I really thought I was going to have this whole albergue to myself for the night, which would have been mildly creepy, so this was a welcome surprise.

The three of us ate dinner in the cramped kitchen/dining room combo of the albergue with the hospitalero and his wife, then lounged together in hammocks that were hung on a balcony overlooking the garden. We lamented over the heat of the day and all the hills we had to climb up and down. Trish laughed about how much stuff she had packed in her bag and how she had already shipped so much ahead to Santiago where she would pick it up at the end of the journey.

I thought I could do this trek alone, with just Maverick by my side. I wanted to prove that I could beat depression; that I was strong enough to do anything on my own. But today had shown me that I wasn't beating depression like I hoped. And it turns out, I really did need the support of other humans. Both the support of my family back home with their ever-comforting voices through the phone, and my very own Camino family. My Famino. So when Trish told me about her relationship with her daughter back home and how grateful she was to have found me as a Camino daughter, I felt a warmth I didn't know I needed. After a grueling day of endless tears, I fell asleep with my head on a pillow, Maverick on the floor by my side, and a smile on my face.

All My Friends

Day Six: Villatuerta to Villamayor de Monjardín

20.7 km ~ 29,210 steps

June 24th

For the first time, we were waking up amongst other pilgrims. I packed my bags beside friends, and clomped down the stairs with them, and the three of us echoed a chorus of "adiós" and "gracias" to the hospitalero together. I didn't realize then that it would be one of the only times I felt such pilgrim camaraderie but even still, I knew it was special. Margie popped her headphones in and continued at a quicker pace while Trish and I trailed behind Maverick. When I started to outpace Trish, we exchanged no words of parting, just continued on our way with unspoken understanding that we would meet up again. I wondered if this was how most pilgrims walked. With a group around them but not always tethered to them. It allowed for both a feeling of community but also individual growth and experience along the trail.

Maverick and I reconnected with Margie just outside of Estella where she was waiting for us, perched on some ruins overlooking a river down below. To the left of the trail, across from where she was standing, a small church seemed to rise out of nowhere. There were no other buildings to be seen, just this stone structure that had an abandoned, desolate feel in spite of its intricately carved façade.

Along the top of the building, the twelve apostles stood meticulously carved in naves. The entrance was set back into the façade with delicate arches that drew the eye to the carved scene just above the massive wooden doors. Christ on the cross sat surrounded by soldiers in the peak of the arch. Beneath that scene were even more carved figures. One depicted the three Marys visiting the tomb of Jesus as an angel oversaw them, another showed Jesus's descent into Hell marked by the mouth of a dragon, and one more had Jesus appearing to Mary Magdalene. The final scene just above the door was a rendition of the last supper, so perfectly carved as to show the folds in the tablecloth and even the plates laid in front of each man. A statue of St. James himself stood to the left of the door, easily towering over me in his pilgrim garb. An archbishop stood guard to the right, just as massive as James. Even with all these impressive features, it was clear that this church had never been completed and looked to be rarely visited. There would be no stamp to obtain from this place. Instead, Margie, Trish, and I could only take in the façade in silent wonder.

We walked the short distance into Estella together, the town where most pilgrims were sure to have spent the night, and found a café for breakfast. I knew from our morning outside of Roncesvalles that my companions took a more leisurely time eating breakfast than I normally did, so before long I gave up my chair at their table to a mother and daughter duo who had just arrived. I needed to find food for Maverick. This was one of the bigger towns along the Camino, one I had planned to resupply dog food at, which meant I would need to step off the trail and go in search of the pet store I knew was in town. Hopefully by the time I located it, I wouldn't be too far behind my friends and Mavy and I could catch up to them again.

Within just a few minutes, we came across the little pet store. After walking the length of the store three times, scouring the shelves of dog food and the various displays around the store, I still hadn't found the food I was looking for. I had researched what dog food brands were available in both Spain and the U.S. and switched Maverick over to Eukanuba months before we came. It shouldn't have been a problem to find this brand, yet here I was, having a problem.

"¿Perdón?" A young store attendant hurried over at the sound of my voice. "¿No tiene comida de perro grande?"

He looked down at the display I was standing next to. Eukanuba covered the table, but they were all for small breeds. There was no bag of dog food for large breeds in sight. He looked back up with a sad smile and shook his head. "¿De ese? No, solamente tenemos esto. Lo siento."

I paused and looked back at the Eukanuba for small breeds. It looked similar enough. "Pues… ¿qué es la diferencia?" I asked. I mean, really. What *was* the difference between food for a large breed and small breed? Minus the size of the kibbles, could it really be that different?

"Ah…" The young man paused, tilting his head from side to side. "Las croquetas son más pequeñas, obviamente. Hay más energía en comidas para perros pequeños." He launched into a further discussion on why food for small dogs was packed with more energy followed by how similar the ingredients were in each. "Pero…pienso que es todo."

I pondered his response. Smaller kibbles and more energy. That could work. "Bueno," I said once I was sure he was finished explaining. "Es perfecto." He gave me a curious look, but I heaved a bag into my arms and led the way to the checkout with a smile.

Back outside, armed with new food and a new fancy pink ball to replace the one we had lost on Day One, I unzipped Maverick's pack and pulled out the two dry sacks I used to hold his kibble, which were both very light now, and got to work transferring the new food into them. Mav shoved his face in, trying to catch a few of the raining kibbles until I pushed him away with a laugh. When all was set, we made our way a couple blocks down to a *farmacía* where I tied his leash to a lamppost so I could pop in for my own feminine needs. Just like that, we had resupplied and were ready to head back to the trail and out of this little city.

We left the suburbs of Estella behind and began a steady climb up yet another dirt road, but this time sprawling vineyards took over the landscape. A makeshift welding shop appeared to the right of the trail where a grizzled man was working iron, but he welcomed Maverick and I to come take a look around his open-air setup. Tables held various trinkets he had made, from necklace charms and bracelets to door knockers and horseshoes. The shop was adorned with even more of his work. Lampposts, candleholders, and chandeliers sprouted from the walls and dangled from the rafters. I signed my name into a log of pilgrims who stopped to visit and listened in as the man told another woman about the history of the shop. How his grandfather had passed it to his father before him and how his own son would take over when he grew too old to man the fires. I purchased a metal *concha* strung on a strip of black leather for my mother and had just finished tucking it safely back into my pack when we came upon our next gem of the day: *Bodegas Irache*, the famed wine fountain of the Camino.

Estella has been known for its good wine and bread for centuries, and *Bodegas Irache* was happy to supply all pilgrims with a sample of that wine. Each day, one hundred liters of red wine could be dispensed from the famous wine fountain for free. Of course, there was also a spigot for water as well. Margie was here when Maverick and I arrived and I quickly snapped a picture for her as she sipped from the iconic fountain. Even though I had already found I didn't enjoy the taste of Spanish wine, I couldn't pass up the opportunity to try some here. It was a pilgrim rite of passage along the Camino Francés.

While Maverick scampered around the gated courtyard where the fountain was, his new pink ball clutched between his jaws, I untied his pilgrim's *concha* from his pack and brought it to the fountain. If I was going to drink this wine, I would drink it like the pilgrims of past centuries. Straight from a shell. According to one of the signs beside the spigot, if I wanted to arrive in Santiago with strength and vitality, I better drink.

Margie had just finished gathering up her gear. She nodded her head uphill, to a shady corner by the Benedictine *Monasterio de Irache* across from the wine museum that fed this fountain. "I'm going to wait in the shade for Trish. You're welcome to join."

Tricia arrived not long after with the mother-daughter duo they had met at breakfast. I had just finished filling both my water bladder as well as Maverick's from the spigot beside the one for free wine when they walked up. After those first couple of days on trail, I had learned my lesson. Fill up on water at every fountain. There was no telling when the next one would come. I capped the bladders and moved aside as the women practically skipped to the wine fountain in excitement.

Even as the day grew steadily hotter, and I worried if Maverick was too hot or if he was developing a slight limp, everything was slightly better in the company of friends. Maverick and I would walk ahead of the others, through short stretches of forest or along the edge of fields on dusty farm tracks, then find a cool place to sit and wait in the shade for our companions to catch up. It was the perfect mix of solitude and community. At each fountain, I drenched Mav's cooling collar in fresh water and slipped it over his head. I wasn't sure if it was actually accomplishing anything, but it made me feel like I was helping him somewhat, even though his mostly-black coat was sure to be scorching in the sun.

I had just re-wet his cooling collar again after a long lunch break in Azqueta and slipped it over his head, not pulling it all the way down this time so that it might keep the top of his head cool. I stepped back from my handiwork and promptly doubled over in giggles from the sight of him. His ears were pinned back beneath the blue of the cloth, his tongue lolling out to the side with his wolfy grin, and I swear he looked just like the wolf from *Little Red Riding Hood* dressed in Grandma's clothing. Mav cocked his head at me, his tongue flopping out even further, as if wondering what was wrong with *me*.

"My," I gasped in laughter. "What big teeth you have!"

At that, Maverick shook his entire body, the cooling collar slipping to its proper place on his neck, and his ears sprung back to their normal position. He looked at me out of the corner of his eyes as if he was not at all amused by my

antics, then trotted on up the dusty lane towards the imposing, conical peak of Monjardín. A massive garage rose up out
of the landscape to our left, but it looked completely abandoned. There was no glass in the windows and the enormous
bay doors were left gaping open. It was odd to see such a
large structure in the middle of nowhere, with no other businesses surrounding it, no people passing by aside from
pilgrims. I incorrectly assumed it was empty.

An angry, thundering bark echoed to us from the bowels
of the garage and both Maverick and I whipped around to
face the previously innocuous structure. What could only be
described as a small horse was making its way towards us
through an open bay. "Oh no," I gulped. "Not good. Not
good, not good, not good."

The massive dog's barks doubled, deep and rumbling, as
he caught sight of us on the road beside his home. I vaguely
remembered many threads on Camino Facebook pages and
forums about "vicious street dogs" and "packs of wild dogs"
and needing to carry a walking stick to beat them back, but I
hadn't paid them much mind. I was regretting that now.

"Go, go, go, go, go," I urged Maverick, who didn't seem
to realize that giant mass of fur was most-decidedly *not*
friendly. I picked up my pace, hoping against hope that the
dog would somehow, for whatever reason, not follow us up
the trail. Pilgrims walk by here every day, right? He wouldn't
follow a helpless pilgrim, would he?

I finally dared to look back and immediately let out a
groan. "Not good." The dog had burst from the shelter of the
garage and was just rounding the corner, charging after us up
the lane. Out of nowhere, there was the resounding *snap* of
metal being yanked tight and the beast was jerked back, his
front paws in midair as he fought to break free. For the first
time, I noticed a heavy metal chain attached to a thick
leather collar on his neck.

Clang! Clang! Clang! The iron beat angrily against the concrete with each attempt the dog made to reach us. There was froth pouring from his mouth and his jaws snapped shut on the air a few times before he settled into a steady, menacing bark.

My feet stuttered to a stop in the dust and I breathed out a massive sigh. Maverick pressed himself against my thigh and gave a wary look back to the barking beast. I let my fingers drop down and bury into the thick fur on his shoulders. "It's okay," I breathed. "We're safe."

Despite saying it out loud, I couldn't shake the feeling of terror as we continued our uphill slog to Villamayor. I was in a fog, lost in my thoughts. I hadn't given any actual thought to a dog attack happening on this trek. Clearly that was another careless oversight on my part. If that dog hadn't been chained...I don't know what I would have done. Beat it back with my bare hands? Hoped for the best? I didn't know the protocol for being attacked by a vicious, Spanish guard dog. Do you try to make yourself big and imposing while slowly backing away like you do with black bears? Maybe avoid eye contact and play dead like you do with Grizzlies? I felt like there should be a checklist for these things.

I was so consumed with various ways to survive a mauling by Spanish mutt that the triangular structure of *Fuente de Los Moros* caught me off guard when it appeared on the right side of the trail just before Villamayor. I don't know what I had been expecting when the guidebook said we would come across this fountain, but it hadn't been this. The brick building was shaped like one of those houses that every elementary school kid knows how to draw, with a triangle roof and short, square sides. But instead of a small, rectangular door in the middle, this structure's face was open. Two delicate arches welcomed you into...stairs. Once inside, the staircase spanned the entire length of the building and dropped down to a rectangular pool at the bottom of the structure. The floor was simply one giant, rectangular well that the stairs dropped straight into. It was the strangest, most beautiful thing. This was no fountain of running water. It was something completely different.

Maverick galloped headlong down the stairs and into the water below without pause. His front legs disappeared beneath the surface on a lower step while he dipped his muzzle to drink. A part of me thought I should call him back; this was a pilgrims' fountain after all. But this certainly wasn't a fountain to drink from, there were even coins tossed into the bottom of it, so really, what harm was it if he stepped in and cooled himself down?

The mother and daughter duo from Denmark laughed from their perch on some of the top stairs and I looked over at them as I made my way into the cool shade of the building. "Do you think it's fine?" I asked them. "That he's in the water?"

"Oh, yes," the mother said. "We put our feet in! And wet our bandanas."

I lifted a brow and nodded as I considered their response. *That's fair*, I thought. If humans could wade in it, dogs should be able to as well. I followed their lead and slipped off my shoes and socks, then made my way down to Maverick, who was now attempting to balance on one skinny step so he could lay down in the water. I joined him on the first submerged stair and immediately gasped. It was much colder than I had anticipated. Actually, the entire structure was cold, which was shocking given how hot it had grown this afternoon. I gratefully took a seat on one of the higher steps and leaned my back against the cool brick to face the Danes. We chatted for a while as they slipped on their boots once more and gathered their gear. The next moment, they were gone, off to the nearby village of Villamayor for something to eat while Maverick and I continued to enjoy the blessed shade of the fountain.

I had just closed my eyes, completely at ease, when I heard a scratching sound coming from just outside the arches. I cracked one eye open and squinted against the sun streaming into the little haven. Maverick was pawing at his red pack with both paws, taking a break every so often to nudge it with his nose. "What are you doing?" I muttered. He didn't acknowledge me, just redoubled his efforts to break into the pack. "Hey, stop," I scolded. He stopped for all of one second, cocked his head to one side to look at me, then let out a shrill bark and resumed pawing. I scrambled up the last few stairs to where I had left our packs.

"Stop that," I chastised. "What do you want?" I stooped to unzip the saddlebag he had been pawing at and his nose immediately dove inside, shoving my hands out of the way. "You're hungry? It's not even suppertime yet. What are you-"

He pulled his head back out, his entire body lighting up in that way only dogs had. "Ohhh," I breathed. "That makes sense."

The new pink ball I had gotten him in Estella was in his mouth, his tail waving proudly from side to side. He eagerly plopped it down just in front of my toes and then backed up half an inch, his head still bowed over the ball, eyes looking up at me eagerly. I sighed and reached forward. His front feet bounced up and down as I plucked the pink rubber out of the dust.

"Now you listen to me," I said sternly as I tested the weight of it in my hand. It was surprisingly heavy for such a small thing. Maverick's eyes stayed glued to the ball, not even bothering to look at my face. "Do *not* drop this down the stairs. If you drop this, I am not going to get it. You got that? You drop it, it's your problem."

He whined, but I knew it had nothing to do with what I

was saying and everything to do with the fact that I had yet to throw the ball down the dirt road. I sighed and launched the ball down the path we had just come up. A cloud of dust immediately assaulted me as Maverick took off at breakneck speed. *So much for the slight limp*, I thought sardonically.

I was just about to sit back down on the cool brick of the stairs when he was back, his tongue still managing to peek out from the side of his mouth even while he held the ball. "Okay, *aus*," I said, his German command for *leave it*.

He didn't move, just kept staring at me with the ball clutched firmly in his jaws. A little whine escaped him.

"You have to give it to me if you want me to throw it. *Aus*," I repeated. He inched a bit closer and dipped his head, then chomped the ball a few more times before finally releasing it into the dirt. "Gross," I grumbled, picking it up and chucking it towards the fields ahead of us. This time when he came charging back, he headed straight for the stairs. And dropped his ball. His ball that was made of rubber. Which bounced...and bounced...and bounced. Until it *splashed* right into the bottom of the well and...sank.

"You did *not*," I groaned. He charged down the stairs after it until he was at the surface of the water and then whined, the high-pitched noise echoing in the chamber. He reached one paw forward and poked the water in an attempt to find the next stair but couldn't seem to get his footing on it. He backed up and tried with his other paw, whining the whole time. The water was clear, easy to see the pink ball in the depths, but impossible to get to. Maverick fruitlessly pawed at the water as if that would somehow help. His whines picked up in intensity as I made my way down the stairs until I was next to him

"You've got to be kidding me."

He danced from one foot to the other, still not anywhere close enough to reach the ball. Even if he jumped in, he would have to dive down to retrieve it and I had never known him to do that. I stepped onto the first step beneath the water and hissed at the frigid temperature. The stair was slimy beneath my feet and I had to be careful not to lose my footing. Then the next step, this one even more slippery, and the next. Maverick watched me and tentatively tried to follow my steps to little success. The water was up to my knees now. I reached my hand down to grab the ball, but it was still too far.

"This is ridiculous," I told him, but he didn't seem to mind. I looked back up the stairs, checking to see if anyone else was coming. I dropped down another step and gasped. It truly was freezing and it was now up to the hem of my shorts. "The things I do for you." I stuck out one leg, trying to see if I could reach towards the pink ball and possibly swish it over my way. There was no way I was going down one more step to the very bottom of the well.

After another minute of failed attempts and sloshing water, I closed my eyes and pinched the bridge of my nose. "Seriously, Maverick. You're lucky you have me as a mother." And then I stepped off the last stair. "Oh, God," I groaned. "This is way deeper than it looks."

The water was up past my belly button as I held my arms up away from the cold. I tried to grab the ball with my toes, but it was no use. There really was no other option. I leaned down and shoved my whole arm under the water, practically pressing the side of my head against the surface as I blindly grasped until my fingers touched rubber. I yanked it free and scampered back up the steps as quickly as I could.

"Cold, cold, cold, cold," I gasped as I burst from the *fuente* and back into the hot sun. The burning stones felt wonderful beneath my freezing toes. Maverick bounced happily by my side, trying to weasel his mouth around the ball in my hand.

"Oh, no you don't." I shoved the ball deep into his pack and zipped it shut. "You have lost that privilege." He drooped his head and made a haphazard attempt to paw at the pack again.

"Get over it," I grumbled, digging in my own pack for my sack of clean clothes. I pulled it out and then realized I was in the middle of a very open area. Where exactly did I think I could change? And what if a pilgrim came walking up right at the moment I pulled my shorts off? Granted, no one else had passed during this whole debacle, but knowing my luck someone would come along just as I stripped off my sopping wet bra. *Oh, hello. Nothing to see here, folks.*

I sighed at the thought but still grabbed my new clothes and scurried to the back corner of the building. At least here, if I saw someone coming up the trail I could duck to one side, and if I saw someone coming from the village...well, I would kind of be hidden. Sort of. Not really.

Maverick followed me into the underbrush and stared at me curiously. "This is your fault," I grumbled as I stripped off my t-shirt and attempted to wrestle out of my bra. Which, if you've ever tried to change a sports bra when you're wet, you know did not go well at all. I finally fought my way free and stood up straight, whipping my head to check the trail from both directions. Maverick sniffed at a bush and lifted his leg, completely unconcerned by my struggles. I grumbled incoherently as I switched shorts in record time and gathered my dripping clothing. *There better not be any ticks or bugs on these now*, I thought.

A pair of pilgrims were approaching just as I rounded the corner of the structure and I breathed a sigh of relief that they hadn't come even one minute earlier. They responded kindly to my overly friendly "Buen Camino" and continued on their way with barely a glance at *Fuente de Los Moros*.

Not long after, we trailed behind them to the village of

Villamayor de Monjardín, which was just a stone's throw away from the fountain. It was a small village with just a couple of bars in town and only one or two albergues. I quickly found all four of our walking friends from the day gathered at the bar in the center of the village. After settling their bill, they joined me and Maverick by a concrete wall of the *plaza* where a tree cast shade over us. While they took up seats on the wall itself or on a nearby bench, I settled down right on the concrete ground beside Maverick, relishing in the coolness seeping up through my shorts thanks to the shaded corner of the *plaza*. Our four companions were debating on when they should walk on to Los Arcos. According to the guidebooks, that was the best place to stay for the end of this stage.

"It's really hot now," one of the women was saying. I positioned my pack as a pillow and lay back. *Oh, that was nice.*

"What if we take a *siesta* and then walk on tonight?" someone offered. I let my eyes flutter closed. Maverick was tipped over on the cool concrete next to me, his leash looped around my wrist, so if he tried to take off after a pigeon I would know.

"Would the albergues let us in later?" another of the ladies asked.

"We could call in advance, right? Make a reservation?" That must have been the mother from Denmark. The accent was easy enough to pick up.

"Colby? What are you two planning?"

I peeked one eye open. "I think I'll stay here."

"Here? In Villamayor?"

"Yeah." I shrugged from my reclined position. "Mav had a bit of a limp today. And to be honest, I'm tired. I don't really want to walk on to Los Arcos. It's way too hot now."

They pondered my words for a while. "It's only..." I

heard the pages flipping as one of them thumbed through a guidebook. "Twelve or so kilometers to Los Arcos."

"*Only?*" I scoffed. "Yeah, hard pass. I think I'm good here." Maverick groaned into a more comfortable position beside me. The daughter, Freya, took up a spot on the concrete next to us.

"Well, we should at least wait until it's cooler to walk any further. We could just take a nap here," she offered as she settled in.

"What do you think, Margie?" Trish asked her friend.

"You could all stay here," I offered before Margie even had a chance to answer. "There's an albergue right there. We could all stay the night and walk together tomorrow."

My idea was met with silence. *Or not*, I thought.

After what had to have been at least an hour of debating (during which I stayed mostly silent from my prone position on the ground) the ladies agreed it would be best to stay the night in Villamayor de Monjardín. Tactfully, I held in my thoughts of *I told you that two hours ago* and simply smiled at their decision. I kind of liked this whole Camino Family thing. I was happy they would be in the same town as me tonight.

My companions had no problem securing bunks in the albergue just off the *plaza*. Unfortunately, the hospitaleros there were adamantly against allowing Maverick in for the night. They were super kind about it, insisting we *had* to come back and have dinner there with them, but Maverick was not welcome inside. After agreeing to come back for dinner and telling my friends not to be worried about us, Mav and I continued on to check with the other albergue in town and even a *casa rural* we were able to find. Neither would allow us in. Defeated, I ended up wandering into the one store in the village for a snack, where the woman at the cash register offered the idea of pitching my tent in the churchyard.

"¿Está seguro de que yo puedo?" I tried to affirm. I didn't want to be doing anything illegal. When we camped outside of the monastery in Roncesvalles, I knew that was allowed. The woman just shrugged her shoulders and claimed it would be fine. So with that absolutely stellar reassurance, Maverick and I went in search of the tiny, old church. It wasn't hard to find, since the village was extremely small, and we picked out a spot of flat ground to pitch our tent on behind the stone chapel overlooking the valley below.

It was a surprisingly lively night at the albergue for dinner. There were far more pilgrims staying in this midway town than I would have anticipated, including quite a few Germans who kept us all in hysterics and a group of lively young pilgrims who were planning to hike up to the ruins of *Castillo de San Esteban* on the peak of Monjardín tonight. I'm pretty sure I agreed to accompany them, but by the time I had passed the last dish of dinner to the pilgrim next to me, I was too full and far too exhausted to think of hiking up any mountain. I could barely make the hike back to our tent.

Still grimy from the hot day, but slightly cleaner thanks to my dip in *Fuente de Los Moros*, I crawled into our tent and quickly passed out with Maverick pressed against my side.

Take Your Time

Day Seven: Monjardín to Logroño

14.5 km ~ 20,491 steps

June 25th

To say I tossed and turned all night would be an understatement. Actually, it would be a flat-out lie. Last night was *miserable*. The ground here? Hard. I mean *really* hard. I'm sure it had something to do with the sunburnt earth of this region, but I wasn't feeling very understanding at the moment. Aside from that, the wind last night was an absolute nightmare. It was whipping our tent around so much that I had to crawl out in the middle of the night and move the entire thing closer to the church walls in hopes that they would offer some sort of protection. Even then, with the wind only able to pummel us from three sides instead of four, it was still impossible to sleep. Maverick was whining most of the night, clearly not pleased by our situation, and at some point the wind tore the fly off the tent so there was just thin mesh between us and the frigid air. I didn't even bother crawling out to try to reattach it.

The wind didn't die down until the sky was starting to lighten. I knew I was supposed to be meeting the other girls at seven to walk with them to Los Arcos, but I had yet to get a wink of sleep. The idea of packing up in less than two hours to walk miles on end wasn't something I wanted to entertain. So with just a stiff breeze blowing, I rolled over in my sleeping bag and buried my nose in Maverick's fur, planning to sleep as much as I could. They could walk on without me. We would catch up eventually. Maybe.

Maverick woke me up by nine, pawing to get out of the tent. As much as I would have liked to sleep in longer, the sun was blinding through the exposed mesh of our tent so I reluctantly followed him out, stretching my stiff limbs as I stood. I didn't feel at all rested, it was still cold, and I had absolutely zero desire to walk today. Which was rather unfortunate seeing as this entire journey was about walking. What did people do when they woke up and just did *not* want to walk? I wondered. There had to have been thru-hikers or pilgrims who woke on the trail and thought, "wow, this is really stupid. I don't feel like strapping a pack to my back today and trudging fifteen miles." Certainly I wasn't the first person to have felt this way. Did they just stay in one spot all day? Or did they pack up their gear, like I was doing now, shrug it onto their stiff shoulders from their horrible night's sleep, and walk on?

The day's endless, dusty farm trails didn't improve my mood at all. After dipping off the rise that was Monjardín, the wind we had battled all night was gone and a small part of me (a very small part after the torment of last night) wished it hadn't left. Instead, the sun beat down relentlessly. On top of being brutally hot and dry, the path we trekked on today was clearly taking its toll on Maverick's paws. Brierley touted such lovely "natural paths" in his guidebook for much of the Camino, so I hadn't anticipated any issues for Maverick. I only brought a pair of booties for use in emergency situations if it was extremely hot and we were walking on tar. However, I found myself pulling the red boots free from his saddlebags and slipping them over each of his paws.

See, these perfect, "natural paths" Brierley loved so much were actually hard-packed, dry dirt scattered with thousands of tiny rocks no bigger than an acorn in size. Sometimes, entire stretches were made up solely from teenie-tiny rock fragments. If you've ever walked on a dirt road and stepped on a pebble with your bare feet, you know how painful that can feel as the rock bites into the soft flesh. Now imagine that, times four, as a dog walks across these paths with his paws day after day, mile after mile. For the first time, I realized that's what Maverick had been going through for most of our journey.

He didn't fight the booties. For a quarter mile, he walked like an awkward duck unsure of how to place his feet, but after that he was chasing butterflies without a care in the world. The slight limp I had been worrying over yesterday had disappeared entirely.

Unfortunately, aside from the amusement that came from watching Maverick's failed attempts to catch butterflies, today was monotonous. Sure, the endless rolling fields were beautiful at first. Majestic even. I remembered how enamored I had been by them just a few days earlier on our way into Uterga. Now? Not so much. If I never saw another mile of hay, it would be too soon. The only positive of that long slog from Villamayor de Monjardín to Los Arcos were the signs that kept steadily counting down to a rest stop. As the kilometers ticked on, that rest area was sounding more and more like paradise. Only, as it turned out, "paradise" was closed. In June.

I paused at the turn-off to what looked like a dilapidated shack. *It was June*, I whined in my head. *What pilgrim stop was closed in June, high traffic time on the Camino?* I must have let out an involuntary whimper because Maverick came back to sniff my knee in concern.

I huffed out a sigh and tangled my fingers in his fur briefly before shuffling onward. "It's fine," I moaned. "It's not like my throat is coated in dust or anything." Another beleaguered sigh. "It's not like I would have wanted a *tortilla* or anything."

And so went our trek into Los Arcos. The trail was busy today, oddly enough. I suppose that's what happens when you don't start walking before the sun even rises. In a way, it was nice to walk with other pilgrims. It helped to take my mind off the monotony of the grain fields. But I was quickly coming to anticipate every question they asked. How old Maverick was. Did he like walking every day. Were we planning to do the entire Camino Francés. When did we start. If it was hard to find places to stay. The questions were becoming as familiar to me as the side eyes we garnered once we finally reached the outskirts of Los Arcos. Nothing malicious of course, just simple curiosity. What was some blonde girl doing walking eight-hundred kilometers with a big dog in tow? Farmers would do a double-take, watch us curiously, then offer a hearty "Buen Camino" once we were within earshot.

Once into the old part of Los Arcos, I found a table in the *plaza* that was bustling with fellow pilgrims who had stopped for lunch, ordered some food of my own, and tried to plan my next move. It was already noon, the heat of the day, and my desire to walk hadn't increased at all since this morning. I was tired, mentally and physically, and the idea of walking all the way to Logroño today was laughable. I had planned a side trip up to the northern coast, Bakio to be exact, to see San Juan de Gaztelugatxe. Our train was set to leave from Logroño tomorrow afternoon which meant one way or another, I had to make it the twenty-eight kilometers from here to there by then. If I wanted to walk there, I needed to get a move on. Now.

Maverick lunged at an offending pigeon, which took off with a *squawk!* and my chair jerked from where his leash was attached to it, promptly pulling me out of my thoughts. Pilgrims at the surrounding tables laughed while Maverick shook out his coat, letting his fur fall flat again after that show of toughness. I simply rolled my eyes at him and found that my *bocadillo* had been delivered without me even realizing it. I took a bite and spoke around it to Maverick, who was now prowling around our table in an effort to thwart any wayward pigeons.

"So here's the deal," I mumbled around the bread. "We can walk to Torres del Río. That's only eight kilometers from here. That's not that bad." I paused to take a swig of the iced tea I had ordered. "Then tomorrow morning we can do the twenty kilometers to Logroño in time to catch the train."

Maverick let out an angry growl at an approaching bird, who quickly sidestepped and headed towards a more friendly table. Seeing our zone was clear, he flopped himself down in the shade with a huff. "Mmm," I agreed. "Not ideal. Of course, we could take a cab from Torres del Río? Though, do you think that means we're cheating? We can't exactly skip part of the trail. Think that would mean we're not true pilgrims?"

At the moment, I wasn't all that sure if I cared what made a "true" pilgrim or not. No part of me was looking forward to walking on. So in an effort to stall even further (the exact opposite of what I should have been doing) I finished up my lunch and decided to check out the church that opened onto the main *plaza*. I found Maverick a shady corner on the porch, made sure it was pigeon free, and looped his leash around a banister before heading inside the stone building.

My jaw dropped. Truly, the inside of this cathedral was stunning. *Could this even be considered a cathedral?* I wondered. It wasn't all that big. *Is that a prerequisite to be considered a cathedral? Size?* Whatever it was, it certainly was incredible. There was gold *everywhere*. The entire apse looked to be gleaming. And the cloisters in the back, surrounding a rather wild-looking garden, were the perfect place to enjoy a moment of peace. Everything about this church was stunning. The stonework, the attention to detail, the gold that seemed to shine from every corner, the delicately painted ceilings. It was unbelievable to think about how much work went into these places of worship. We didn't have anything like it in my part of the world. There wasn't a single tiny town in New Hampshire that would have anything close to this magnificence.

Whether it was the sheer beauty of the church, or the damp, cool air inside, or just getting to pop a new *sello* in my *credencial*, I felt revitalized as I made my way back outside to Maverick. I could do this. We would make it to Torres del Río tonight. Easy peasy.

Maverick perked up as soon as I stepped out of the church and tugged to be at my side. I unhooked him from the banister he was tied to only for him to bark at some more pigeons and send them into a fit. No matter. All was well. "Let's go, Bud," I singsonged, hefting his pack into my arms as we headed out of the *plaza* and through the massive stone gate to leave Old Town behind.

We hopped and skipped our way over the bridge just outside the gates and…Maverick plopped himself down in some grass under the shade of a tree. "Really, dude?" I asked exasperatedly. "We barely went thirty steps."

He panted up at me in reply.

Just then, a bus rolled up to the stop by the river crossing. It was only a few feet from where we stood. I quickly glanced between Maverick and the bus. Bus back to Maverick. It had to be a sign. A bus coming at that exact time? What were the odds? Maybe this made us bad pilgrims, but oh, well.

My hopes were quickly dashed when the bus driver shook his head adamantly. No dogs allowed on the bus unless they were guide dogs for the blind. Maverick and I slunk back to the shady spot in the grass and I flopped myself down next to him as the bus squealed away. My short-lived optimism after leaving the church was now completely gone. But so was my idea that it was imperative that we walk every single step of this Camino. There was no law against skipping one tiny section. Twenty-eight kilometers. That wasn't that bad…right?

With that thought, I pulled out my phone to Google up a taxi company nearby. All I'm saying is that if pilgrims in the Middle Ages had access to such technology, they definitely wouldn't have stuck their noses up at the idea of using it. That's my story and I'm sticking to it.

After calling three separate listings, I finally was able to connect to one that would allow Maverick in the car. Within fifteen minutes, we were piling into a minivan-looking thing with all of our meager belongings. It wasn't a long ride at all, and the woman who drove was very pleasant, asking about our trek so far and what our plans were and where we were from. She wished us luck as she dropped us outside the train station.

Logroño was a far bigger city than I had been expecting, which is to say I had been pretty much ignorant before arriving. I have since learned it is the capital of La Rioja region of Spain and as such is a bustling metropolis. Much of what we walked through from the train station was like any modern city, with plenty of high-end shopping and modern amenities. It was a bit strange to find myself in the midst of a city like this after a week in rural villages and small cities like Pamplona. After seeing this, I wasn't sure I could even consider Pamplona a true city. Eventually, we ended up in Old Town, which was bustling with tourists and pilgrims alike, just as Pamplona had been. The streets were narrow here, with cafés and bars spilling out into them, and a large *plaza* by the ancient church.

I worked my way through Brierley's listing of places to stay and finally came across one that would allow Maverick that also happened to be right on the main street of Old Town. It was a *pensión*, which meant it was more like a hostel than an albergue (which allowed only pilgrims) and we would have our own room. Honestly, after the hard ground and whipping wind of last night, I was A-okay with that. If I wasn't going to be a "true" pilgrim, what with taking a taxi and all, I might as well go all out today. *Watch out, world*, I thought. *We have a bedroom with our own bathroom.*

Whenever God Shines His Light

Days Eight to Ten: Bakio

June 26th-29th

   The train situation the following morning was a debacle to say the least. Luckily, after snagging a croissant on our walk back to the train station, we arrived early enough to smooth out any snafus. And boy, was there a snafus. See, the thing with Spain is that they don't exactly recognize support animals. Quite frankly, they don't recognize service animals much at all unless it's a seeing eye dog for the blind. The idea that Maverick would be allowed on the train despite being a large dog was preposterous to the man and woman behind the ticket counter. I have heard that in recent years Spain has become more accepting of dogs, especially on trains, but this was certainly not the case in 2018.

   After approximately twenty minutes of discussion in a mixture of both Spanish and English, and an alarmingly close inspection of both my letter from my therapist as well as the email I had from Renfe themselves (a major train carrier in Spain) which stated that I did indeed have permission to travel on their trains with Maverick, the clerks finally granted me a ticket to Bilbao. Once on the train, we luckily had no problems. One attendant questioned why my letter from the therapist was not written in Spanish, but other than that we were free and clear. At least we were until we reached Bilbao where we hit another snag. Bakio, the place where we were set to stay at an Airbnb on the coast, was still a half hour from this northern city. While I had thought ahead enough to contact Renfe to ensure that a support animal would be allowed on trains in Spain, I hadn't really anticipated the idea of taxis or buses.

None of the buses that ran from Bilbao to Bakio allowed any dogs unless they were seeing eye dogs. I called ten cab companies before I found one that said he would accept a dog, and even then it seemed debatable that Maverick would fit in such a tiny car. But fit we did and off we went to an apartment I would be sharing with a man I had never met before. Ah, the joys of Airbnb. The taxi deposited us in the "heart" of Bakio…which was the definition of a sleepy beach town in the off-season. Despite it being late June, there was a chill to the air this close to the coast and mist hung low and shrouded the streets.

The people of Bakio were inviting and helpful, but none more so than Cesc, our host and roommate for the next two nights at his apartment overlooking the sea. We climbed the steep hill that crowded up against the tiny town to reach an apartment complex that was undergoing renovations. At the top floor of the building, Cesc greeted us on the balcony and ushered us inside his little apartment, immediately showering Maverick in affection. One massive window took up most of the far wall of his place, the town and beach spread out perfectly below us. Even with the gloomy weather, it was breathtaking.

"Does he like cats?" Cesc asked after helping to deposit our bags in his guest room and welcoming us into his space.

"Hm?" I mumbled, tearing my eyes from the view beyond his living room window. "Oh, yeah, we have cats at home. He doesn't mind. Do you have one?"

"Yes," he replied with an easy smile, his accent thick even in one word. "But only one. I have lost the others."

"Lost?" I questioned sadly. "I'm so sorry."

In just a few minutes, I could already tell the smile on his face would be a permanent fixture. "It is okay. I would take them in all the time in the city. They never would last long."

I let out a huff of laughter. *O-kay then.* "Did you live in Bilbao?"

"No, in Barcelona. There are many street cats. I would take in strays. But they would still run away. Get hit by cars. Not always the smartest, are they?" he laughed. "I used to have three. But now only him."

My eyes followed where he had nodded to a wide armchair set in front of the enormous window. There, almost completely blending in with the cream color of the chair, was the rattiest cat I had ever laid eyes on. "Oh," I managed to squeak out upon spying him. "Is he...is part of his ear missing?"

Cesc grinned. "Yes. He was not the nicest kitty."

In response to Maverick shuffling closer to sniff his head, the cat in question let out a low growl. Apparently, it took too much effort for him to work up to a full-on hiss. Maverick stumbled back a couple steps, then picked his pink ball up and trotted back to look out the window, unfazed.

Cesc continued to point out anything we may need in his apartment, invited me to play any music on his impressive sound system, and offered up his washer and dryer for my smelly clothes. It wouldn't hurt to wash them for real rather than scrubbing them with one measly drop of my all-in-one soap in a sink. He offered recommendations for where to eat in town, which resulted in an interesting paella dinner that turned my teeth black, and we talked of my plans to walk to San Juan de Gaztelugatxe at first light tomorrow to beat any crowds. For my first time sharing an Airbnb with a host living there as well, it couldn't have been any better.

———

Of course, my bright plans to wake up at the crack of dawn and walk the five or so kilometers to the hermitage were quickly dashed. The bed in Cesc's guest room was incredibly comfortable and the weather really wasn't all that nice and it wasn't like I had anything else I needed to do later in the day…really, I could have come up with a million excuses for why I should sleep in. We did leave before Cesc had woken, but it was certainly not at five a.m. as I had intended.

Once again, the clouds hung low over the ocean, which was a steely grey. Humidity clung to my skin as we made our way down the steep cliff from the apartment, through town, and began to climb up into the coastal cliffs again. Spain's northern coastline is striking to say the least. Lush and green with rolling hills that cut off in jagged cliffs that drop to the sea. The region of Basque Country is like a world of its own and walking just a little bit through it was a joy.

It makes sense that the vibe here felt so different from the rest of Spain. The Basque Country, or País Vasco, has been battling for independence for centuries. Technically, the region spans the border between Spain and France and has its own distinct cultural characteristics, origins, and language. The people here speak Euskera, or Basque, perhaps the oldest living language in Europe. It has no known ties to any other languages and has stumped linguists for generations, but it is a point of great pride for the Basques. While most people in the region also speak Castilian Spanish, the signs, menus, and newspapers are all commonly printed in Euskera. There is even an initiative to increase the number of Basque-speakers in the region in coming years with the projection that Euskera will be the first language for over half of the upcoming generation.

Our destination of the morning, San Juan de Gaztelugatxe, clearly shows ties to the Euskera language. *Gaztelu* actually means castle in Euskera, while the *aitz* sound derives from the Euskera for rock or crag. It only made sense that this tiny island, nothing more than a large rock that was remarkably connected to the mainland by a stone bridge and a steep, winding staircase, would take this name. The church on this rock, dedicated to Saint John the Baptist, has been sacked, burned down, and rebuilt countless times. The first hermitage was said to be built here in the 9th century and some even claim John the Baptist himself once set foot on the tiny island. It seemed like quite a lot of trouble to go through to build such a tiny church on a rock out at sea and connect it with a stone bridge that would withstand the tides, but so be it. It certainly made for a stunning place to visit.

As I huffed and puffed up the steep climbs and dips on our way to the island, I thought of how much attention this place had garnered lately. You wouldn't be able to tell from the sleepy hamlet of Bakio, but San Juan de Gaztelugatxe was definitely becoming quite the tourist attraction in recent years. Thanks, *Game of Thrones*. Remember that impressive walkway up to Dragonstone? Yeah. That's real. And it's here. Except instead of an imposing, towering fortress that was constructed from CGI, the end of that winding stone walkway was none other than the tiny rock that was home to the even tinier church with the bright, terracotta roof.

Despite today's gloom, the roof of the church shone like a beacon from the rock out at sea. It was low tide as Mav and I cut through the trees and began to descend down to the start of the stone walkway. Instead of a sandy bottom beneath the towering stone walls of the bridge, the bare ocean floor was rough rock that looked almost volcanic, cut in layers that resembled rings of a tree, one on top of the other. With no water hammering against the stone, it made the drop from the top of the walls of the walkway to the sea floor a good forty feet or more.

It was still early enough that tour buses hadn't arrived yet with their hoards of tourists, although individual day trippers were already streaming down to the bridge. I couldn't imagine what these narrow stairs would look like midday. You probably wouldn't be able to move. As it was, I just made sure to have Maverick on his short leash amongst the fellow tourists.

At the very start of the bridge, I motioned for Maverick to put his paws up on the wall so that I could get a nice photo of him with the stairs and church in the background. Before I could even comprehend what was happening, he had full-on leaped up to the barely five-inch-wide crest of the wall rather than simply putting his front paws up. For one torturous second, he tottered unsteadily on the surprisingly narrow ledge. I was suddenly immeasurably thankful that I had Mav on a leash for once. In a blinding panic, I yanked hard on my end and he toppled off the ledge, back onto the walkway. I stumbled backwards until the backs of my legs bumped into the cool stone on the opposite wall of the bridge.

That saying, the one about your heart being in your throat? I had never understood it before. Not until now. Not until I saw Maverick on that ledge with an almost fifty foot drop down to jagged rock below him. I gulped in a breath of air, then another. I could hear the blood rushing in my ears, knew my legs were shaking, but I couldn't do anything to stop it. Maverick looked up at me in concern as I dropped to my knees, wrapping my hands around his neck.

"Holy shit," I mumbled into his fur. "Oh my God. You could have died. You could have *died*. Holy shit."

He clearly did not share my panic and after humoring me for a moment, he shook free of my hold and tugged closer to the wall again. I yanked back on his leash. "Let's just stay right in the middle, shall we?" I said shakily. Once more, I rose to my feet and shuffled slightly closer to the wall, peering over. The height I had barely made note of before now appeared dizzying to me and images of Maverick plunging over the edge flashed through my mind unbidden. I backed away again. It hadn't happened. It could have. But it didn't. He was fine.

"Don't ever scare me like that again," I muttered to him. He panted back in reply.

There were two hundred and forty-one stone steps that zigzagged their way up the rock to the hermitage at the very top of San Juan de Gaztelugatxe. Different crosses marked our way once we had crossed the bridge. We paused for pictures, took breaks at various hairpin turns, and I marveled at the idea that Kit Harrington, Emilia Clarke, and Peter Dinklage had walked these very same steps. The only thing it was missing were some dragons swooping overhead. There was no need for a massive castle at the top of the island like the one from *Game of Thrones*; the tiny hermitage was more than enough. With each new arrival, its bell tolled three times. A long rope dropped down the front façade of the church for guests to pull. According to legend, after making the long climb, if you ring the bell three times and make a wish, it will come true. I'm not sure if that is the case or not, but I rang the bell all the same.

The steps were growing more and more crowded as we made our way back down and onto the mainland. Despite the sun remaining hidden behind clouds for the rest of the morning, the humidity here by the coast made walking back to Bakio feel like we were wading through soup.

"I take back what I was thinking earlier," I panted out to Maverick. "Screw the Camino del Norte. I think I would die trying to walk this route."

Not that the del Norte, a separate Camino route to Santiago de Compostela, passed through Bakio. It remained south of here, passing through the major city of Bilbao. But still. My point remained. "One, it's constant hills. Up and down and up and down. Do people not get that's what this coastline is?" I huffed as I followed Maverick's tail up yet another rise that was about to drop down once more. "Two, even if you do have a 'sea breeze,'" I scoffed, "you're still going to be battling humidity. Overall temperature might not be as bad as the Meseta, but I think I'd take dry heat over suffocating humidity any day."

Judging from the intensity of Maverick's panting, I assumed he agreed. Camino del Norte would not be on our short list of upcoming hikes.

We spent the remainder of our day lounging, sleeping, exploring what little parts of Bakio we had yet to explore, and hanging out with Cesc. Aside from Maverick dropping his ball off the top floor of the apartment building straight down into an open bucket of white paint, the rest of the day was uneventful. Cesc had rushed down the four flights of stairs, retrieved the little pink ball, and made sure to thoroughly clean it. He then went on to book us a taxi back to Bilbao in the morning that was sure to allow dogs. I'm not sure how most Airbnb hosts acted, but he was really setting the bar high.

Unfortunately, we just had one more night of comfort and relaxation before it was an early morning departure to get back onto the trail. I was already nervous. What if this *wasn't* a good idea? What if, instead of rejuvenating us, this side trip just made me all the more reluctant to start walking again? What if Maverick started limping again on our first day back walking?

Even with Cesc's comfortable guest bed, I barely got any sleep that night. I was up before the sun and decided I might as well go sit out on the deck and watch the waves below. Except, when Maverick came trotting out of the guest room after me, he must have scared the ancient cat from its perch on the arm of the oversized chair. Rather than jumping off to hide as a normal cat would have done it just kind of…tipped over. My feet stuttered to a halt.

All four paws of the cat were still dug firmly into the covering of the armchair, and yet the cat was now dangling from the side of the chair a few inches above the floor, completely horizontal. It was as if it had made to jump from the chair but then completely froze, its claws and limbs all locked in place. I had called Maverick away from terrifying the poor thing any more than it already was and began to step forward to help it when it suddenly began to retch.

"Oh, no," I whispered, now stepping back in the opposite direction. My nose wrinkled. "I'm sorry," I pleaded with the cat, who clearly couldn't understand anything I said. For one, it was a cat. Two, it was a Spanish cat. Maybe I should have been talking to it in Spanish? "I just can't. I'm a sympathetic puker. If I see puke…or smell it… I'll puke too." I turned away. "Just…come down off the couch, kitty. I'm sure

your dad will be up soon and can clean up your mess. Maverick," I hissed while slowly backing away. I coaxed him back
towards the guest room before he could decide that cat vomit
was appetizing.

"We're just gonna…wait in here. 'Til Cesc wakes up. It's
fine. It'll be *fine*." I didn't have to wonder who I was trying to
convince more. It was definitely myself. But there was no
way in hell I would be going near that cat puke. With no
better ideas, I laid back down on the bed and stared at the
ceiling some more, waiting until I could hear Cesc stirring so
I could explain what had happened.

It didn't take long. Within an hour, I heard his bedroom
door crack open from down the hall and I quickly made to
intercept him. Only, before I could make it past the door of
my room, I heard his voice call out.

"Oi! The cat!"

I rushed down the hall to see what that decrepit cat was
doing now, only to realize it hadn't moved. Not even an inch.
It was still suspended, its claws all locked into the covering of
the armchair, legs out stiff as a board, with a puddle of throw
up under it. My eyes widened, immediately feeling even
worse. I thought by now it would have surely climbed down
and gone on its way, just leaving the vomit behind. But no.
However, despite Cesc's initial outburst, he didn't seem at all
fazed by this.

I crept up behind him as he leaned over and began gently
unlatching the cat's claws from the cotton covering. "Does
this…" I started, then paused. "Does this happen often?"

"Oh, yes," Cesc answered genially, his permanent smile
in place even though he was detangling a cat from a chair
where it was hovering over a pool of vomit. As if this was a
morning ritual for them. "He is very old. Sometimes, he gets
stuck."

"I see." Once all claws had been successfully removed

from the chair, Cesc popped the cat back on its feet upright and made to stand up. In the next moment, the cat had toppled over, flopping to the floor with its legs still locked in place just as they had been when it was holding onto the chair.

"Oi!" Cesc bent and quickly righted it again. Only this time, he didn't take his hands off it.

"This…is normal?" I questioned.

Cesc moved his hands away from the cat's body slightly, but it swayed, still not able to stay upright on its own. He righted it again, lifted it slightly, and set it back on its feet as if it was a child's toy that you had to place *just right* in order to prevent it from toppling over.

"Sí," he muttered, once again trying to release the cat to no success. "Oi, Dios mío."

With one final lift and plop, the cat's legs seemed to understand what was being asked of them and for the first time, it stood of its own volition. "There." Cesc finally straightened, facing me with his smile. "All better."

I looked around his shoulder to where the cat was wobbling its way towards the massive window on very unsteady legs. I would bet five dollars it would tip over in the next ten minutes, but I let Cesc have his win. "He just locks up like that?"

"Yes. Old legs. Very sad. But not to worry." He brushed off his hands and started towards the kitchen, but I cleared my throat.

"Oh, uhm, I think…I think it might have gotten sick." I tipped my head in the direction of the chair again. Because I *totally* didn't know it had gotten sick an hour ago. Definitely not. I gave him a small smile and lifted my shoulders in commiseration. *Pets, what can you do, am I right?*

Of all the things I had spent the previous night overthinking about returning to the Camino, I hadn't anticipated what was the most upsetting of all: simply saying goodbye to Cesc. We had barely interacted in the past couple days. A few words in passing. Laughing over my attempts to figure out the washer and dryer. This hardly constituted a new friendship. And yet, saying goodbye to him as he helped load Maverick and I into the taxi with our gear almost brought me to tears. He had been my safety blanket when I hadn't even known that's what I needed. He was a reprieve when I was sure I was failing. I was so used to closing off from everyone and handling everything on my own, that I hadn't even known I needed someone to get me out of my own head. Cesc had broken open my tough exterior to show me that it was okay to just relax. That I could be happy and goofy and not hold up the weight of the world all on my own shoulders. He gave me a new perspective that I so desperately needed at just the right time.

Leaving behind his genuine kindness and easy, open manner was hard. Far harder than I expected. I was going to miss him. But the Camino was calling, and we were due back.

Don't Stop Believin'

Day Eleven: Logroño to Nájera

35.9 km ~ 50,386 steps

June 30th

Despite all my nerves about returning to the trail, I was excited when I woke up in the *pensión* this morning. By the time 5:45 rolled around, Maverick and I were already packed up and out on the deserted streets of Logroño. The guide-books claimed that finding your way out of Logroño as a pilgrim was difficult, and if it was later in the morning, I could definitely see that being the case. Most markers in this city are circular plaques inlaid into the sidewalks or streets that direct you where to turn. With the light of the street-lamps and no one else in our way, it was easy enough to pick them out, but if there had been morning traffic or the streets of Old Town were as congested as they had been when we were here the other day, I couldn't imagine how hard it would be to try to follow the Camino out of the city and into the park on the outskirts of town.

Maverick seemed just as excited to be back on the trail as I was. He kept bounding ahead on the park's walkways, then darting back to show me whatever stick he had found, or pausing to sniff at one of the many snails that were littering the sidewalk. I had never seen anything like it before. If I wasn't paying careful attention to where I set my feet, I would hear the tell-tale crunch of a shell getting smushed beneath my boot. Weren't snails found on beaches and near the ocean? Not just sluffing along sidewalks? What was this?

After an hour or so of walking mostly on our own, the Camino was coming to life around us while the sun slowly climbed the sky. We began to play a game of leapfrog with an older Spanish gentleman without even meaning to. It seemed every time we would pause for water or breakfast, he would pass us, and when he paused for whatever reason, we would pass him until finally, we fell into stride with one another as we came to the reservoir outside of Logroño. He immediately warmed to Maverick, who was thrilled to have someone else that would admire his sticks now.

As we walked, I came to find out that he was from the north of Spain and was walking the Camino in sections whenever he got the chance. It reminded me of how some thru-hikers in the US hiked the Appalachian Trail or the Pacific Crest Trail in sections as well. It definitely made the trek easier to accomplish since you wouldn't have to take months off from your job, but personally, I didn't think I would find it as meaningful if I walked in that manner. In my mind, long walks like this, especially a pilgrimage, just begged to be completed as one. I didn't think there was anything wrong with section hiking, and it made perfect sense logistically, but for me, I would want to do it all in one go. Although, who am I to have an opinion on the matter at all? Maverick and I were just getting back from our own trail hiatus.

"Ah, Maverick, no," I called out, pulling myself from my reflections to focus on my derpy dog, who was currently balancing on the concrete wall of the reservoir, looking very much like he was about to dive in. "No you don't." I unclipped his leash where it always hung looped around his neck and took the end of it so that I could wrap it around my wrist. I couldn't be too safe, not after he had almost toppled over the wall at San Juan. Only once we were back into the shade of the trees by the reservoir did I loop the leash back in a circle and clip it, thinking it was fine for him to run free again. Of course, I was wrong. Within a minute, he had spotted a few ducks who were pecking along the grass and lazily floating in an inlet.

"Maverick..." I barely had time to warn.

He was already off with a thunderous bark I wasn't even aware he had yet. *When had my baby grown into a man?!* But there was no time to worry about that. "Maverick, no!" I yelled as he came dangerously close to one duck's tail feathers. "No!"

His paws skidded to a halt as the ducks took off with shrill quacks, some taking flight, others charging deep into the water as fast as their webbed feet would carry them. Maverick looked back at me with wide eyes, then back to the ducks that were gathering together out in the middle of the reservoir shaking off their traumatic experience, then back to me.

"Bad dog," I hissed, glancing around the little grove we found ourselves in. No one else was in sight, luckily. We had outpaced our old Spanish friend before the climb up to the water, so no one else was witness to Maverick almost mutilating the wildlife.

He drooped his head, knowing from my tone that he had

done something wrong. I sighed at his sad expression as he trudged back up the bank towards the trail. "I mean...you *did* almost get it," I told him. His ears perked back up and I could tell he wasn't sure if I was still mad at him or not. "It was kind of impressive."

His mouth popped open again and he smiled at me in that wolfy way. "But don't do it again!" I admonished.

Although we had officially been walking through the region of La Rioja since we arrived in Logroño, it hadn't been apparent until today. Our taxi ride from Los Arcos to Logroño meant that we had missed whatever sign there was that welcomed us to a new autonomous region. La Rioja, a tiny region sandwiched between Navarra to the east, Basque Country to the north, and the massive Castilla y León to the south and west, is known above all for its wines. We were treated to our first real experience of walking through vineyards today with rich, red clay beneath our feet. Since it was still early in the summer, the grapes were mostly just small buds, pure green before they grew into a deep purple. Pilgrims who walk later in the year would be sure to see the vineyards in all their glory, heavy with grapes.

We weren't in the vineyards for long, as the trail climbed steeply uphill with a chain-link fence on our right to keep us from slipping down the slope and into the bustling highway below. It certainly wasn't the nicest atmosphere we had come across so far, but it could have been worse. Past pilgrims had taken to decorating the fence with wooden crosses of various sizes, weaving wood in between the chain-link. Some were from large sticks, others were made of strips of bark, and still more were tiny twigs. It wasn't exactly moving, but it made what could have been an eyesore a bit more...spiritual I suppose? Maverick, however, had no idea what all those sticks were doing stuck in the fence. He let out a shrill whine from just ahead of me and I quickly realized he was trying to pry one of the crosses from its spot in the fence.

"Mavy, no!" I couldn't quite get enough conviction behind the scolding, though. It was too funny to be truly mad at him. He grunted as he tried to fit his nose in between the links to grab onto one of the sticks. "Mave*rick*," I groaned. "Leave it."

His answer was a series of whine-grunts until he finally managed to yank a strip loose. He snatched it up in his teeth in triumph and bounced over to me to show me his prize. I looked to the fence where a cross was now missing its vertical post and cringed. "Yes," I sighed. "I see your stick." He whined happily and loped away from me, tossing his head back and forth as he scampered down the trail.

I took one last look at the now half-complete cross, then hurried after Maverick as the trail turned away from the highway to cross over a smaller roadway and began to descend towards Navarrette through more vineyards. Navarrette was a welcome sight to be sure because my stomach was beginning to growl. We were just about to enter the medieval town when we caught up to a mother with her young son. I could tell as soon as we got near them that something was off. The way she kept the boy close to her and how she was holding herself was a tip-off.

"Can you put him on a leash?" the mother barked as soon as I was in hearing distance.

"Oh, yeah, of course," I responded, a little caught off guard by her tone. Her eyes were glued on Maverick as I called him back to me and unfurled his leash. "All good," I called out.

She nodded but the stiff set of her shoulders didn't relax at all. "You know some people don't like dogs."

I bristled a bit. Obviously, I knew that. Not everyone had to like everything, of course. Her tone was pretty rude, though, and I had to fight down my first nasty retort. "I know."

We were closer together now and she kept her son on the far side of her so that her body was between him and Maverick. She was acting as if he may lunge at any given moment. I fought the urge to roll my eyes. I'm sure she wouldn't take kindly to that. "And you thought it was a good idea to bring your dog? That's not very considerate to people who are afraid of dogs."

I sucked in a breath. I was cool, calm, and collected. "He's a very good dog and mostly ignores the people we pass. He's also an Emotional Support Animal for me and very well trained," I said calmly.

She sniffed at that. "I was attacked by one of those when I was younger."

"I'm sorry to hear that," I said genuinely. It wasn't fair she had been attacked by a dog. I couldn't fault her fear. But she was instilling that fear in her young son now. I bet he had no experiences of his own with dogs to go off of and had to rely on what his mother told him. Which was horrible. I felt bad for him. "Well," I said, as we were now almost past them. "Buen Camino."

She didn't return the sentiment and Maverick and I hurried on to put some distance between us before we got to town. We climbed up to the main street and found ourselves a spot at the first bar we came across. I dropped our packs on a chair and then hooked his leash to the leg of it before going inside to use the restroom and order a *tortilla*. By the time I came back out with my food, the mother and son were taking a spot at the furthest possible table from us on the patio.

"You really can't just leave him out all alone. What if he were to go after someone?" she called to me.

Okay, I thought. *I had played nice. Now I was just annoyed.* There was another café just down the road! If she had seen Maverick tied out at this one, why the heck had she chosen to stop here? Keep walking, woman! I gritted my teeth and bit back my first response. "He's not going to attack anyone."

"You don't know that," she said snidely, sending daggers at Maverick through her eyes. For his part, he couldn't be bothered to even acknowledge their presence. He had already lapped up some water and had flopped himself down on the cool pavement. I realized some battles weren't worth fighting and I ignored her, choosing instead to focus on my *tortilla* and flip through the guidebook to see how much further we had to walk today, but I could still feel her glaring at us.

My plan was to take the alternate route to Ventosa today. In my research, I had come across an albergue that claimed to accept dogs in that town. Plus, the route through Ventosa seemed much more enjoyable than staying right next to the highway for a solid chunk of time like the main trail seemed to do. If I scoffed down my breakfast quickly, we could hit the road with enough time to have a solid buffer between ourselves and the mother and son pair. I slung my pack back over my shoulders and picked up Maverick's. He immediately jumped up, more than ready to keep going, and I was careful to lead him in a wide berth around the woman's table.

The next section of trail alternated between more vineyards, past what I believed to be a winery, and then back into fields of wheat before turning up the road to Ventosa. It was still relatively early in the day, not even noon despite the fact that we had already walked over eighteen kilometers. I wasn't sure if the albergue would be open yet, so Maverick and I settled in at an outdoor patio of one of the cafés on the main street of town and relaxed. After a while, we decided to explore the tiny town and wandered up to the church. It was situated at the top of a hill that over-looked the entire village with a beautiful expanse of lush, green grass surrounding it. *If only the church we had tented next to in Monjardín had been so nice*, I thought sullenly. There were plenty of shade trees and even a water fountain for fresh, cold water in this little park-like area. I laid back in the grass, using Maverick for a pillow, and watched the clouds drift by until it was clear the sky was going to become one giant blanket of dark clouds.

A thunderstorm was set to roll in tonight, so even if this seemed to be a wonderful spot to pitch our tent for the night, I wasn't too keen on being caught out in the storm. Therefore, when one o'clock finally did roll around, we headed back down into the village to find the albergue that was supposed to allow dogs.

The young girl manning the front desk shook her head at me adamantly.

"No, no permite perros aquí," she told me.

"Pero, leí que…" I trailed off. It was clear she wasn't going to budge on this, no matter what I had read. "Bueno," I sighed. "Gracias." *Por nada*, I added in my head. I saw the girl surreptitiously looking at Maverick through the strips of plastic that counted as a door to this albergue.

I grabbed my pack from outside the door and took hold of Maverick's leash. He seemed to sense my mood and so he didn't pull me as we walked down the road. *What to do now?* I wondered. The sky had already changed to grey; the sun was no longer beating down. It was only one-thirty. The next town was about eleven kilometers away but it *was* the end of a stage. It would have more albergues than this small village. One of them would *surely* let us in…right? Before I really processed my decision, my feet had already taken us down the path that led out of Ventosa. There was no point in staying in that village for the night.

"Hola, Buen Camino," I greeted as we came upon two young girls just outside of town.

"¡Buen Camino!" they called back. "Is that your dog?"

Maverick was sniffing along the side of the road ahead of us. "Yeah, his name's Maverick." I fell into step beside the girls.

"Is he a German Shepherd?" one of them asked.

"Mhm," I nodded. "West German Working Line."

"He doesn't have the normal shepherd colors," the girl with blonde hair pointed out.

"No, he's a dark sable. It's pretty common in the working line."

"And you're walking the whole way with him?" the other girl questioned.

"That's the plan," I replied.

"That's brilliant! Are you walking on to Nájera tonight?"

"Well, I had planned to stay in Ventosa actually. The albergue was supposed to allow dogs, but they don't. So, yeah, I suppose I am walking on to Nájera now."

"Sorry to hear that. You want to walk with us for the afternoon? My name's Amy and this is Beth."

I smiled. "That would be nice, yeah," I admitted.

Suddenly, those next eleven kilometers didn't feel all that long. Most of the time we chatted, but sometimes we just walked quietly in each other's company. We talked about where we were from (near Cork, Ireland for them), what we did for work, what home was like, and what had brought us here. They tossed the stick Maverick kept bringing back to them and he would charge ahead for it, kicking up red dust before barreling back towards us in record time. The only time he paused was when a massive golden dog charged up to the fence beside the trail, barking nonstop. Maverick's steps only faltered for a minute, the log fallen from his mouth as he stared back at the angry guard dog. When he seemed to realize that the dog couldn't reach him, he picked his stick back up and sauntered on with a mocking pep in his step.

Just before Nájera, we came to a little park on the left that Maverick turned into while the girls made to walk straight on the road. A little yellow arrow pointed towards the park, indicating the Camino actually *did* cut through the green area that Mav had turned towards.

"Can that dog read signs? I swear he knows this route better than us," Amy gasped.

I laughed and shook my head. The boy was smart, but not *that* smart. He did have a knack for knowing exactly where trails twisted and turned, though. I suspected it was because he could smell where people walked most often and ended up following that on hiking trails. On the Camino, I'm sure he could smell hundreds of people that passed this same way every day.

The first hints that showed you finally reached Nájera, aside from the little park, were the broken-down buildings on the outskirts of town. One of which had the poem, "Pilgrim, who calls you?" graffitied on its side that faced the trail. All of us paused to glance at it, snapping pictures, but I stood there longer than Beth and Amy.

"Can you read it?" Beth asked. I nodded absently. "What does it say?"

"It's a poem. It's talking about the reasons for doing the Camino. That you aren't called to the Camino for the grand cathedrals, or the wine from La Rioja, or the seafood of Galicia, or fields of Castilla, or the people. Not Gaudí's palace, or Ponferrada's castle. That you see all of this as you pass, but there is a voice that calls you. That it can't be explained to you. Only the One Above knows."

"Huh, that's brilliant." The two of them stared a bit longer at the words, then walked on. I stood for longer still, soaking in the message. Something about the fact that it was painted on a broken-down building, on the outskirts of the city, with such a beautiful message just seemed to fit. In all the ways it shouldn't have, it just worked. Like it proved that something broken could still be worthy.

"Come on, Mav," I whispered down to him. He had hung back with me as the girls went ahead into the city. "Let's go find some food and a place to stay."

We had to pass through the slightly run-down, more modern side of town before crossing over the river Najerilla into Old Town. This part of Nájera looked as if it was built right into the cliffs behind it, which was fitting. The name Nájera actually came from an Arabic term meaning "town between the rocks." This town between the rocks served as the capital of the kingdom of Navarre until the kingdom fell to Castile in 1054. It has been an important stop along the Camino Francés for hundreds of years and had an abundance of albergues waiting to welcome pilgrims. It was my hope that at least *one* of those many albergues would take pity on us and let Maverick and I in for the night.

Amy and Beth, kind souls that they were, decided to tag along as we turned right over the bridge and went in search of a place that would accept us. Half an hour later, we had talked to five separate albergues, two *casa rurales*, and one pensión, and none of them would allow dogs. They were all very pleasant, but that didn't change the fact that Maverick and I were out of luck.

"You really don't have to stay with us. You can go back to that third place. That lady was really nice and it seems like a lot of pilgrims are there," I offered. I felt bad dragging them all over town. I was so tired and I was sure they had to be just as exhausted as I was. *Did we really leave Logroño just this morning?* It felt like it had been days ago.

"No, of course not! We're going to stick with you. Let's try that place that woman mentioned, Las Peñas? Even the locals said that one would be worth a shot."

"It's right at the edge of town, right?"

"I think that's what they said. We'll try there and if that doesn't work out, we'll come back and stay at one of the places near the river." The way she said it didn't leave room for an argument, so I had no choice but to nod my agreement. The three of us followed the Camino out of town until it was just a single road again with some houses scattered sparingly on the right.

"Are you sure we haven't gone too far?" Beth asked.

"I think I see a sign up ahead."

The sign in question hung from a building that looked just like any other house on this street but advertised this location as an albergue. I gave a shrug of my shoulders, it couldn't hurt to try, and left Maverick with Beth and Amy outside while I ducked in. The young girl at the front desk, probably the daughter of the owner, was delighted to say that dogs were allowed. Only, that was quickly followed by her saying that he would need to stay on the patio outside. The hope I felt rising in me was instantly crushed.

"Oh," I sighed.

"Quieres ver?" she asked.

"Uhm…" I couldn't very well say no to her offer of seeing where the dogs were supposed to stay. So I followed her out back to a miniscule brick patio that was fenced in with chicken wire. A tiny dog yapped at me from an upstairs balcony. It must have been the family pet. A couple more small dogs barely lifted their heads to look at us from their spot in the corner. There were little piles of dog poop, dried from the hot sun, littering the entire area. I grimaced.

"Muchas gracias por mostrarme. Pero, no, gracias. Mi perro nunca está sin mí. Nunca duerma solo." The young Spanish girl swiveled her head between me and the tiny concrete patio, clearly not understanding why I wouldn't just leave my dog here. The idea that Maverick never left my side was foreign to her. "Está bien," I tried to reassure her.

I left the girl and wrapped back around to the front of the albergue to find Amy and Beth seated on the sidewalk where I had left them. Maverick hopped up from beside Amy and tugged at the leash, yanking her arm forward as he saw me come around the corner.

"No?" Amy asked as I flopped down on the sidewalk beside her. I unclipped Maverick's leash from around his neck after I had taken it from Amy. He immediately bounded into the deserted street, eyes to the ground as he chased the shadows of birds in circles until they disappeared and he waited for a new shadow to swoop past.

"No. I mean, they allow dogs in the sense that dogs can stay the night out on their patio. But Maverick always sleeps with me. I would never just leave him outside without me. He'd freak."

I folded my legs under myself and leaned my palms back on the hot concrete. It was still warm from the sun that had been out this morning even though the sky was dark now. My brain was tired. Heck, my body was tired. While Amy and Beth had certainly made those last eleven kilometers pass by easier, it had still been a long day of walking. And now it was looking like we would have to tent out in the storm overnight.

"You guys don't need to stay with us. You can go grab a

bed somewhere else. Or here. I'll figure something out for me and Maverick."

I could sense the two friends looking at each other, figuring out their next move, even though I had already closed my eyes. I had the urge to cry, though I knew that wouldn't help anything. I just wanted one day to be easy. Just one day where we could be welcomed to a bed at the end of the day without a fight.

"¿Perdón?" An older man was leaning out from a balcony directly above us. "Vosotras juntas?"

"Pues…" I started.

"What did he say?" Beth asked.

"He asked if we were together."

"Oh, sí," Amy answered before I could do anything else.

"Tengo una habitación privada. Si queréis, el perro puede dormir en la habitación con vosotras. Por cuarenta euros."

"¿Es verdad?" I questioned in disbelief.

"What is he saying?" Amy hissed.

"He says we can stay in a private room with Maverick for the night if we all stay together. But really, it's okay if you don't want to. I know it would be more expensive than a normal albergue, you don't have to-"

"¡Sí!" Amy called up to him before I could even finish. I laughed.

"You're sure?"

"Of course," she said to me, and Beth nodded her agreement as they stood and dusted off their shorts.

"Thank you," I said, meaning it from the bottom of my heart. They waved me off like it was nothing. But it wasn't nothing. Not to me. It was *everything*. Because of their kindness, their selflessness, Maverick and I would have a roof over our heads tonight.

In the end, I paid twenty euros and Beth and Amy each paid ten for a beautiful room that had two beds in it. The man, who I later found out was the owner of the place, pulled a cot into what was typically a double room so that I had a bed to sleep on and Maverick was allowed in with us without bothering any of the other guests. We had a little balcony that looked out over the quiet street and a bathroom was just down the hall. I would have given fifty euros if he had asked. Maybe even more. I got to spend a night, in a bed, with my dog beside me and my two new friends, and I wasn't worrying about getting struck by lightning while I slept. What more could a girl ask for?

Colors of the Wind

Day Twelve: Nájera to Santo Domingo de la Calzada

22.7 km ~ 31,905 steps

July 1st

Maverick and I slipped out of the albergue as quietly as possible and took a seat on the curb so I could lace up my boots. The air was muggy, another result of the storms last night, and my leggings were a bit damp when I stood back up and donned my pack. The sun broke over the horizon as we climbed out of Nájera on a wide dirt track and cast an eerie glow through the fog, lighting up the vineyards we had just passed through. We dipped in and out of pockets of thick mist for the first hour of walking. At times, I would lose sight of Maverick even though he was never more than fifty yards ahead of me. The posts with yellow arrows loomed up out of nowhere, lining the path through more fields of hay.

It didn't take long for us to reach Azofra, the first of just two towns along this section of the Camino. As such, it made for a popular rest stop for many pilgrims. Even though the small outdoor tables were busy with pilgrims filling up on *tortillas* and *café*, I didn't recognize anyone. Since our side trip to Bakio, there were all new faces around us. It was clear that the people we found ourselves with now had been together since Saint Jean. Many of them looked to have found their "Camino families" already; those people you met and walked with for your entire journey. Some lifelong friends formed along the road. I suppose I could have been upset I hadn't found this yet, but I had Maverick. I had all I needed.

After eating yet another Spanish *tortilla*, my staple breakfast, and strapping Maverick into his booties, we set off on our own. It was another eight or so kilometers until the next town and according to the guidebook, there would be little shade and no water. As luck would have it, the day stayed overcast for most of the morning. If it had been clear, I'm sure we would have baked in the sun through the patchwork of farmland.

In the middle of all those endless fields, there was one little patch of grass with a tree on the right side of the trail. A gully between the trail and the tree was filled with water, likely from the rain last night, and before I could even think to stop him, Maverick was plopping himself down in the stream. The mud swirled around him where he had disturbed it, hiding the bright red of his booties beneath the surface of the water.

"Mave*rick*," I groaned, but I couldn't be all that mad. He was hot, that much was apparent. Even with the shade of clouds, he had to be roasting under his dark fur. I only wish he could have found a *cleaner* place to cool off. I could already smell the stench of the swampy water as I hopped down off the trail to rest under the tree with him. "At least let me take off the booties," I called to him. "Gross."

He plodded over to me and let me un-Velcro the shoes and yank them off his paws before taking off for the water again. "Ugh," I muttered, pinching one of the formerly red boots between the tips of my fingers and upending it. A stream of murky water poured out. "You did this on purpose. You didn't want to keep wearing them and knew if you got them wet, I'd take them off."

Mav tilted his head towards me to listen, then turned towards the sound of more pilgrims coming up the trail. They laughed as they passed by him. "He has the right idea!" one of them called.

"You know, if this path hurts your paws it's not my fault now," I grumbled to him once we finally resumed walking. "I put those booties on you to protect you. You just did not care. So I don't want to hear it if – Hey!" Maverick took off after a butterfly that had just fluttered across the trail. "You're not even listening to me," I huffed, trailing after him with a reluctant smile on my face.

Climbing into the hilltop village of Cirueña was like entering a different world. Just at the top of the hill, the dry fields below turned to the green grass of a picnic area where a group of young adults were refilling their waters and having a snack. We exchanged pleasantries, but nothing more than that. They didn't ask about Maverick, or comment about the nice weather, or anything at all. It was as if they had already formed their group of friends and didn't need another outsider. It was a decidedly cold response compared to how pilgrims typically acted along the Camino.

Suffice to say I didn't stay long at that rest area before I grabbed the end of Maverick's leash and followed the yellow arrows that led through town. Or what was meant to be a town. All of the houses, very modern looking houses actually, seemed empty. It was almost eerie how abandoned the whole place felt. Sure, the luxury golf course and country club here looked like it had some patrons, but aside from that? Cirueña felt like a ghost town. Except, when you think of a ghost town you mostly picture something old and broken down. This town was new and shiny and yet there wasn't a soul in sight. The Camino wound its way through barren neighborhoods that could have passed for modern suburbs in America minus the minivans and dads out caring for their well-manicured lawns.

Finally, we left the modern, lifeless town behind and got back onto farm lanes. Red poppies lined the edge of the trail again and blue blooms weaved their way through the stalks of wheat. This gave way to greener fields as we continued. In fact, as we descended from Cirueña, it looked like the old Windows2000 screensaver come to life. A young girl from Belgium fell into step just as I was marveling at the stunning view laid out ahead of us.

"Amazing, isn't it?" she said. I could only nod. "I feel like I'm walking through a painting."

"It definitely feels that way," I agreed. The clouds from the morning were just beginning to break up, revealing a light blue sky.

The last few kilometers to Santo Domingo de la Calzada flew by and soon enough I was standing in front of a hospitalera who was yet again saying that dogs were not allowed. I was quickly coming to realize that all the research I had put in before coming on this trek was proving to be useless. I didn't fight her on it, she was a shockingly stern woman and I was simply too tired to press my case.

I had known this would be a struggle – finding a place to stay with a dog. It was one of the main reasons so many people had warned me not to do this. I just had this false idea that I knew what I was doing before coming and it was quickly becoming clear that I did *not*. Yet again, I was being forced to admit that I had *no idea* what I was doing.

My whole life, I had been in control. I was successful. I had goals, aspirations, five-year plans. Since I was in kindergarten, I knew what I wanted to do in life. I wanted to be a zoologist and work with wild cats. When I was in high school, I signed up for all the animal science classes right from the start. I researched the best schools in the nation for zoology, applied early admission, and accepted a spot at Ohio State. Since I was five, I wanted to play lacrosse and so I did. I was on varsity by my sophomore year. All through school, I wanted to get the best grades and be at the top of my class. When I graduated high school, I was tenth in a class of over seven hundred students. My whole life, it had never occurred to me that I couldn't do anything I set my mind to.

It wasn't because I just had things handed to me. No. I worked for them. I practiced lacrosse all the time. I put in the extra effort on every project or report. I went the extra mile in everything I did. And each time, I was able to achieve what I had set out to do. That is, until my sophomore year at Ohio State. Until I was forced to admit that I had *no idea* what I was doing.

See, the thing about success is that it can be a mask. A Band-Aid. I had been so successful. So in control. Yet under the surface, I was spiraling. I had been for years. This sadness, this darkness, it was taking control of my life. I was splintering into a million pieces and for once I didn't have a solution or a plan. I had no idea how to hold myself together. Everything I had tried to fix it, to mask it, to bury it had failed miserably.

Last spring when I finally broke, everything still looked perfect from the outside. I had just aced an extremely difficult course on Organic Chemistry. I was on the board for Special Olympics at school. I was a member of multiple clubs and activities. I had a job and a full course load and some good friends. I was on track to get that zoology degree and work with wild cats, just as I had planned since kindergarten. Yet this thing that had been growing in me, this thing I had been trying so hard to tamp down and force into a corner, would not be silenced.

For the first time in my life, I had to admit to myself that I had no idea what I was doing. That I couldn't handle it on my own. That I needed *help*. If I had continued to ignore it and tried to pretend like my depression didn't exist, like it wasn't taking over my life, I don't know where I would have ended up. Maybe I wouldn't even be alive anymore. Because the very first step to healing, to making any progress at all, is to admit that it's okay to not know everything. It's okay not to be okay.

I've had plenty of practice admitting these hard truths over the past year. It appeared like the Camino planned to hammer home these lessons as well.

"Well," I said to Maverick now as we made our way up the street of Santo Domingo de la Calzada. "Another one bites the dust. If we're going to get denied at every turn, I would at least like to have some food and something other than water to drink."

I may have to accept that once again, all my carefully laid plans were going to shit, but there was no reason to be hungry while doing so. Maverick and I turned down the main road that the Camino followed and then off on a side street, wandering until we came across a small plaza with a bar that looked good. A decent crowd was filling the inside and spilling out to the tables in the plaza. A soccer match was on the TVs in the bar and one screen had been set up outside. The World Cup was in full swing.

"Puedo tener los croquetas y dos tés helados, por favor." I had no clue what a croqueta was, but the picture looked tasty. The waitress took down my order, letting me know it would be right out. I settled in next to Maverick at a tiny table and started looking up other places to stay in the city. We could handle this. We could pivot. Just like I had pivoted and found a new path after leaving school. I could find new places to stay along the Camino. *Psh,* I thought. *No big deal at all.*

"¿Croquetas?" a voice asked from behind me.

"Ah, sí." I turned and accepted the plate of *way* too many little fried things.

"¿Y dos tés?" she asked. I nodded but she still hesitated before placing the two cans of tea on my table. "¿Hay otra persona?"

"Uhm, no. Solo yo." I looked around, clearly noting there was no one else with me. Well, unless… "Y el perro, pero no necesita té helado," I joked.

"Entonces…¿los dos tés son para ti?"

Again, I looked around the table as if some second person might magically appear. "Sí…¿Tengo sed?" I said as a question. It was true, though. I was thirsty. I didn't realize it was a crime to order two cans of iced tea. They were tiny. I knew I'd want a second one. Just give me my tea, woman!

She tentatively placed the two cans and glasses down on the table with another strange look and then returned to the bar. *Sue me for not drinking beer or wine like every other person around,* I thought with a roll of my eyes.

I was already on my second can of tea when a little boy came toddling up to my table. He couldn't be more than two years old with a head of curly dark hair and he was making a beeline for Maverick, who was snoozing under the table. I could see the boy's parents hurrying to catch up before he could reach us. They caught his little hand just before he had a chance to grab Mav's tail.

Apologies poured from their mouths, but I just laughed.

"No, no," I told them. "Está bien. Le encantan los niños." It was true, not that he cared much for adults, but Maverick always had a soft spot for young kids.

"¿Verdad?" they ensured. I nodded with a smile as Maverick turned to look at the commotion. "Bueno, sé dulce, cariño," the mother chided, ordering the little boy to be gentle.

"Es muy guapo," the father told me. "¿Es un pastor alemán?"

"Sí," I agreed to his assessment of Maverick being a German Shepherd.

"Parece a un lobo, ¿no?"

"Ah, sí, un poco," I allowed. Many people had compared Maverick to a wolf before, so it wasn't too much of a surprise.

"¿Cuántos años tiene?" the mom asked from where she was kneeling beside her son, guiding his hand gently along Mav's fur while he lounged.

"Es un bebé. Solo tiene once meses."

"¿Sí? ¡Es enorme!" she gasped. I laughed. To me, Maverick never looked all that big. I guess I just never got over viewing him as a little puppy, especially with how he acted. But it was true he was grown now at almost a year old and weighed in at eighty pounds.

Their son had apparently tired of *el perrito* and was bounding towards the intersection as fast as his little legs could take him, so the parents called out a hasty *hasta luego* and *gracias* as they took off after him.

Maverick and I finished up at the bar and found our way to a pensión for the night. Or rather, the owner of the pensión found us. She was a nice lady, young, and ushered us into what looked like a building that was for sale. Although it wasn't the nicest of lodgings, the owner could not have been more pleasant, leading us to a room, happily stamping our credentials, and directing me to where she thought I'd be able to find dog food. It was a Sunday, so most places were closed, but she was sure the local grocery store would have something. I had a feeling we were some of her only tenants in the pensión and she was desperate to make us feel comfortable. Whatever the reason, I wasn't complaining. It meant we were a bit outside of the main part of Old Town, in an isolated room, but it was still a bed and a shower and a sink to wash my clothes in. For now, I had found a solution to one of our problems. I knew what I was doing, at least for the night.

However, the grocery store the woman had directed us to, mind you the *only* shop that was open this afternoon, did not carry the dog food Maverick had been eating. They didn't even have the small-breed version I had found in Estella. They did, however, carry some very unappetizing canned food. It looked like that was our only option for the night, so I bought a couple cans to mix with the last of his kibble and treated him to some vanilla ice cream as a compromise. Once again, it was the best I could do. Not a full solution, more of a Band-Aid to our problem, but I could only hope the next town would have dog food. Once again I was struck with those crushing thoughts of self-doubt, that I had no idea what I was doing.

I did my best to push them away by focusing on the town we found ourselves in for the night. Santo Domingo de la Calzada was actually home to a pretty well-known Camino legend that warranted a trip to the local cathedral. Inside, in a gilded cage inlaid into one of the towering walls, are two chickens. Yes…chickens. It's not every day that a cathedral is home to a chicken coop, but this cock and hen directly relate to a pilgrims' tale dating back to the Middle Ages.

According to legend, a young man and his family were passing through Santo Domingo de la Calzada on their way to Santiago and had stopped for the night. The boy apparently caught the eye of the innkeeper's daughter who attempted to seduce him. Being as devout as he was, on this religious pilgrimage, the gentleman is said to have refused her temptations. Of course, the woman was embarrassed by the slight and in retaliation, she hid a silver goblet among his belongings. Before the family could leave the village, she accused the young man of stealing and when he was searched, the silver goblet she had nefariously placed was found. Unfortunately, the innocent young man was hung for his "crime."

So…where in the world does a chicken come into this story? In those times, it was common practice for pilgrims to walk to and from Santiago. Of course, they would have to return back home and there were no trains or planes like we have today to zip them back. The young man's family did indeed have to pass through Santo Domingo de la Calzada on their way back home.

According to legend, when they arrived in town, they were shocked to find their son miraculously alive, still hanging from the gallows. The spirit of Saint Dominic, Santo Domingo, is purported to have kept the innocent man safe. The family rushed to the sheriff in an effort to get their son down. The sheriff, who was just about to start his dinner, listened to their story patiently. When they were finished, he claimed that their son was no more alive than the cock on his dinner plate. Apparently, at his words, the chicken jumped up from the plate and let out a loud crow. The sheriff rushed to the gallows to cut down the poor young man and gave him a full pardon. To this day, live chickens are kept in the cathedral as a reminder of the miracles that can occur along the Camino.

Miracles still occur on the trail. Or magic. It's not always big things like somehow surviving a hanging for months. Sometimes it can be something small, like the bubble of happiness and community that can be found in the most unlikely of places just when you need it the very most.

After visiting the cathedral and grabbing a small dinner with Maverick, some young girls invited us to the main plaza for some music. Apparently, one young Irish woman was walking the entire Camino with her cello on her back and she was going to be playing some songs tonight on the plaza. A troubadour band from Korea was also around with instruments to join in.

Even though it was almost nine at night, the sun was just beginning to set and gave a warm glow over the plaza as pilgrims came out to enjoy the community spirit. A French woman danced barefoot on the stone to tunes from the Jungle Book, while a girl from the US lent her voice to the cello player. Another Frenchman jumped in to sing a tune after that which a couple other French-speaking pilgrims were thrilled to add to. Some ladies from Australia contributed by snapping their fingers to the beat and Maverick let out a couple yips. He was just upset that the German man he had befriended to throw a stick had yet to pick it up to throw it again, but the gathering of pilgrims laughed, thinking it was his attempt to add to the music.

There was a buzz in the air that had nothing to do with the melody. It was something intangible but so prevalent. A feeling of community, of peace. Every single person in attendance, in dirty clothes, bandanas, some with shower flip-flops on, some still in their hiking shoes, had a smile on their face. It may not have been a miracle by most standards. No chicken came back to life...no human life was spared. But somehow, there was a sense of magic that could not be denied. It was exactly the sort of magic I needed.

Featherstone

Day Thirteen: Santo Domingo de la Calzada to Belorado

25.6 km ~ 35,973 steps

July 2nd

At six-thirty, we rolled out of the pensión and then out of Santo Domingo. As it turned out, most of the day would be spent beside a busy road, crisscrossing it to dip in and out of the little villages along the route before finally reaching Belorado. I felt almost sacrilegious to think this, but today was honestly a pretty boring stretch of trail. Of course, that's not to say everything went smoothly. No, no. That wouldn't be my way.

Apparently, six-thirty was a popular time for pilgrims to start their days. The first section of today's walk from Santo Domingo to the small village of Grañón was bustling with fellow pilgrims. We were lucky enough to come across many of the same people that were in the plaza with us last night. A few asked where we stayed, curious as to how a Camino with a dog worked, so I lamented about the difficulties we had been facing so far. It was nice to have people to share our problems with.

We also kept bumping into the older gentleman from Bilbao that we had first met on our way out of Logroño. I finally learned that his name was Txema and he was truly one of the sweetest people I had ever had the pleasure of meeting. The young girl who was walking with her cello and the girl who sang with her last night were also among the pilgrims we saw during this first stretch of trail. The cello girl had taken an immediate liking to Maverick last night but hadn't had much time to play with him since she had been performing for everyone. So this morning, she quickly became Maverick's new favorite pilgrim because she insisted on playing tug with his stick as we walked along together until Grañón.

The couple bars in that town were bustling with pilgrims getting breakfast and the large group of people we had been walking with made their way to tables to drop their gear and get some food. With everything so busy, and since I wasn't feeling all that hungry just yet, I made the horrible decision to continue on. *The next town was only another four kilometers or so away*, I thought naively. *That wouldn't even take an hour to get there.*

I waved goodbye to our companions and dipped out of Grañón, heading down the slight hill and into rolling fields that were blissfully away from the busy road. In fact, the landscape was once again looking very Windows2000 with its endless expanse of green patchwork fields. Before long, we came across a towering sign that welcomed us to the autonomous region of Castilla y León. We were officially leaving behind the wine country of La Rioja to enter the largest autonomous region of Spain. For the next 400 kilometers (give or take), the Camino would wind its way through this vast region. Over fifty percent of our time on the Camino Francés would end up being through Castilla y León, most notably along the famed (or infamous depending on what way you chose to look at it) *Meseta*. The region, anchored by well-known cities such as Burgos and León, also held important milestones of the Camino including *Cruz de Ferro* and the midpoint of the entire journey near Sahagún.

For now, we were treated to some more quiet time through green fields before we crossed back over the highway and into the village of Redecilla del Camino. Despite the guidebook's promise of a busy bar here, there was not a single thing open. My stomach grumbled angrily at me as we followed the yellow-ish strip of paving stones that cut down the center of the street through town. *Conchas*, or the patented Camino shells, decorated the paving stones at even intervals, bumping up from the stone to keep you on the right path. Not that there was any chance of you getting too off trail in a town of this size. In the blink of an eye, we were already out of town and crossing the highway again towards Castildelgado.

A cute wooden sign welcomed us outside of Albergue Bideluze with an arrow pointed towards Santiago, 544 km away, and one arrow pointed back to Saint Jean Pied de Port, 223 km away. It was the first time I had seen a marker showing how far we had gone. It was insane to think that just a few short days ago, we had been standing beneath a sign that said we had 790 km to go.

"What would be truly amazing," I said to Maverick, who was sniffing around the sign for the best place to lift his leg. "is if we could celebrate the fact that we've walked 223 kilometers already with a nice *tortilla* for breakfast."

But alas, this town was just as dead as Redecilla had been. What was with these villages? Didn't they love pilgrims? Pilgrims love food, at least this pilgrim does, and I was very much regretting the decision I had made earlier this morning to walk on to the next village.

Two agonizingly long kilometers later, we entered Viloria de la Rioja and my heart soared. Surely, there would be a bar waiting to serve a very hungry pilgrim here. I practically skipped my way into the heart of the village to find...nothing. *Seriously?* I grumbled internally. *Is this a joke?* I had gone through three villages now and each of them had been absolute ghost towns. Were they adorably quaint and desolate? Of course. But that did not solve my hunger.

An old pair of walking boots decorated a bench in Viloria with fresh blooms poking out of them. Apparently, boots made cute plant holders along the Camino. If I hadn't been so hungry, I would have smiled at the cute setup. As it was, it made me want to knock it over. Up on the right, a side street dipped off from the Camino that featured a wall completely engulfed by the thickest ivy I had ever seen. Not an inch of the original wall could be seen. The only break to the blanket of green leaves was a heavy, black, wooden door in the center of the wall. It looked like a door to a secret garden and was completely enchanting. Everything about these farm towns was adorable. Picturesque. But my rumbling stomach was having trouble appreciating the beauty. Instead, I stumbled through the last eight kilometers of the day's walk in a hunger-filled haze until the trail deposited us into Belorado.

The church was the first thing to welcome pilgrims to Belorado, looking as if it was built right into the limestone cliffs behind it. In fact, those cliffs had been home to hermits for centuries in ancient cave dwellings. They even have some modern residents. If you looked closely, on the left side of the church, you could see windows and doors carefully fitted into the limestone, indicating that there were indeed still Spaniards who made their homes there.

While I would have loved to stand in that little plaza and

inspect the church, dwellings, and various murals for hours, I was *starving*. And I had to pee. So really, there were much more pressing matters. I stumbled into the first bar I could find – a modern, almost fancy-looking restaurant that I felt completely out of place in in my sweaty, haggard state. The waitress didn't seem to mind in the least, offering me a blinding smile and helping me to choose something to eat before directing me back to a bathroom on the left. Maybe she was used to seeing hangry pilgrims every afternoon.

Only after I had scoffed down some food was I able to really take in the street art that Belorado was known for. Just across from the bar I was at was one of the largest murals I had ever seen. It spanned the side of a three-story building and was simple and delicate, done all in black and white, and full of sharp lines. A painted cabinet took up the center of the mural with two shelves that held various vases and bowls. On the right of the cabinet was an old man who was easily almost two stories tall. The artist had managed to perfectly capture the focus on the old man's face as he bent over a pair of leather boots to cobble on the soles. On the left side of the massive cabinet was an old woman who was just as large and life-like as the man. She was sewing what appeared to be laces onto a new shoe and her painted face had all the same intricate lines of age as could be seen on her husband. Her slumped posture told the tale of years of hard work, all somehow communicated in black and white strokes of a paintbrush.

Directly across from the ancient church built into the cliffs was a brighter mural painted with vibrant blues and golds that made it shine on the low wall between two signs that directed pilgrims to follow the Camino right. In this mural, a king stood in the center wearing a crown and breast-plate of gold, reading from a scroll. Behind him, a medieval army was waiting in the streets for his next command.

Maverick and I turned right past this mural, following the signs for the Camino through town. It was barely noon and after getting some food in me, I really didn't feel all that tired. Some sort of town market was going on in the main plaza here, so we weaved through the stalls, peeking at different things for sale and watching the locals go about their days. It was cool to take a look into everyday life in a place like this. It was abundantly clear in every town we went through that the Spanish were so much more laid back than most Americans and much more focused on community and family.

Our search for dog food also helped to show us more of what life was truly like in this corner of Spain. Following the suggestions of some vendors at the market, we stepped off the Camino and wound our way through alleys and side-walks in search of a grocery store across town. Once away from the Camino, the town took on a more genuine feel. The streets and buildings weren't shined to perfection for tourists and pilgrims to ogle over it. Instead, this side of town was populated by only locals pulling along their grocery trollies, teenagers goofing off on the sidewalks, and young couples walking arm-in-arm on their way to the market. It was a side of Spanish culture, the *real* side, that I never would have seen if it hadn't been for Maverick.

I had gotten a small of a sense of this true Spanish life before, when I had wandered to the pet store in Estella, or when I stayed in the pensión last night and went in search of dog food, but I really understood it today. Especially as I left Maverick tied to a lamppost outside the small grocery store and ducked inside in search of dog food. It seemed so *normal*, nothing like the pilgrimage. No, this was as normal as the daily life of the Spaniards who lived here.

There wasn't another pilgrim in the store. It was too far off the marked Camino for any other walker to come across.

Instead of being waited on and served dinners in an albergue or a café, I was just one of the locals out to pick up a couple items I needed for home. I liked getting to see this side of Spanish life. It made me want to live in this moment, in this town, for far longer than just one night.

Of course, just like last night, there wasn't any dog food other than the Spanish version of Friskies. I opted for a couple more cans of wet food like he had last night and checked out. Some locals were admiring Mav when I exited the store, and I chatted with them for a bit, telling them what breed he was and how he wasn't quite a year old yet. They were surprised to hear we were walking the Camino and wished us the best of luck before heading inside the store to complete their own shopping.

Now came the fun part of our days: trying to find an albergue that might let us in for the night.

At Cuatro Cantones, the hospitalero told me that I was welcome to have a bed for the night but Maverick would have to sleep in the garden. They had a very expansive back garden, complete with lush green grass, ivy covered walls, and an inground swimming pool. It was by far the fanciest albergue I had seen so far. Since there was so much space, I figured they might be open to letting me pitch my tent here.

That idea was quickly shot down. Apparently, my tent would "ruin the grass" so I would not be allowed to stay outside with Maverick. I set off in search of somewhere that would allow Mav to stay inside with me but didn't have any luck. In the end, I paid the eight euros for a bed at Cuatro Cantones and agreed that Maverick would sleep outside. My hope was that I could just set out my sleeping pad beside him in the garden and they wouldn't say anything. Surely a sleeping pad would not ruin their grass that badly.

It turned out that many of the pilgrims we had met last night were also staying at Cuatro Cantones. Some of them were planning to make a communal dinner tonight with ingredients they had gathered at the market. Many of them were enjoying the benefits of staying at an albergue with a pool. An Asian woman I hadn't met before and her young son, who couldn't have been more than six years old, were thrilled to meet Maverick. They insisted on being in charge of him when I went upstairs to dinner in the albergue's dining room. I happily agreed because Maverick seemed to be having the time of his life chasing his ball that the little boy kept throwing. By the time I returned from my own dinner, Maverick had also been treated to scraps from the communal dinner that was made in the kitchen. The Asian woman was sheepish when she admitted to giving him table scraps, but I only laughed.

"Seriously," I assured her. "That's more than alright. He hasn't been eating his normal amount of food the past couple of days. I'm sure he loved the treat. Thank you for taking care of him."

Even though it was nearing ten at night, the sun was still out when I finally unfurled my sleeping pad and unrolled my bright orange sleeping bag. A couple of the pilgrims I had met in the past day or two stopped on their way in from the pool. I swear, they were more upset than I was about the situation.

"What do you mean they won't let him inside?" one young girl from California asked.

I shrugged. "They said he could stay the night in the garden."

"So you're just going to sleep out here?" her cousin asked.

"Yeah. I'm not going to leave him outside alone."

"But you paid for a bed?" their blonde friend confirmed. I nodded. "What if you just sneak him in after everyone's asleep?"

I laughed. "It's really fine. I don't mind. It's not supposed to rain tonight, so I should be good." The three girls looked at me dubiously. "Really. I appreciate the concern, but we're good. It's actually pretty nice. The bathroom is right through there and the guy even said he'd leave it unlocked."

"Well, if you need anything, let us know," the youngest girl said. I thanked them and then they were gone, the door of the albergue clicking shut behind them. We were alone. Just us and the setting sun.

I laid down beside Maverick on my sleeping pad and stared up at the branches of the tree we were under. The sun was just beginning to dip behind the walls of the garden. I had thought I wouldn't be able to fall right asleep out here since it was still so bright, but I must have been more tired than I thought because the next minute, I was out cold.

Realize

Day Fourteen: Belorado to Agés

29.3 km ~ 41,210

July 3rd

A growl woke me up, vibrating through my chest, and I realized that Maverick was lying across me, his paws on either side of my neck, the full weight of him holding me down. I blinked my eyes open but everything was still dark. A sliver of light came from the back door to the albergue, enough for me to see Maverick's eyes looking past me to the door. He let out a deep bark.

"Maverick," I hissed, not wanting him to wake anyone. Even if they hadn't thrown us out last night, they surely would if we woke up the entire albergue before the sun had even risen. "Shhh."

He shifted on my chest and let out another low bark. I turned my head to see what he was looking at. A pair of young Asian ladies were waiting by the door to the albergue, clearly hoping to grab their clothes they had left out on the clothesline overnight.

"It's okay," I told them. "I promise he won't attack."

They shuffled forward, obviously doubting my words, and I laughed under my breath at Maverick's attempt to protect me. I had never known him to be tough or protective of me. He was only eleven months old after all; he hadn't grown into that role yet. But it was clear that staying outside without a tent to shelter us had changed him from baby to protector overnight.

I shoved him off me with a laugh and plopped the rest of the canned food into his expandable hiking dish for breakfast. He slurped it up with one eye on any pilgrims who dared to disturb our peace by coming into the garden to get their clothes from the line. At least it was an easy morning to pack up – just shoving the sleeping bag back into its sack and rolling up the pad. Even though it was only six forty-five when we slipped through the albergue and back out to the street, the shoe rack that had held all the pilgrims' shoes in the main room of the albergue was very sparse. Most pilgrims had clearly already left for the day.

We passed by one last mural on our way through the sleepy streets of Belorado, a vibrant one painted against a red wall, with shockingly teal trees, and an old pilgrim with a flowing white beard that would rival Albus Dumbledore's. Once out of the town, the rising sun behind us cast our shadows out far in front of us along the dirt track while little wisps of clouds blew on in the slight breeze. The first three towns of the day were barely a blip on the trail, tiny little villages amidst the sea of farmland.

We caught up to André, the German man I had dinner with last night, just after Espinosa del Camino. I lengthened my strides to match his. He was notorious on the Camino for being a fast walker. Amy and Beth had walked with him for a bit before I met them in Ventosa, and I remembered them telling me he was used to doing thirty-to-forty-kilometer days.

"So this is the dog then?" he asked upon seeing me with Maverick.

"This is the dog," I confirmed with a nod. It was rare that someone met me before they met Maverick. Two weeks into this trek, and I was still being referred to as "Maverick's Mom" by most pilgrims.

"He has much energy," André commented as Maverick dashed back to us, tossing his head side to side to swing the large stick he had found.

I scoffed. "That's an understatement."

We walked, or rather he walked and I struggled to keep pace, for a while in silence and then a thought struck me. "Hey, André?"

"Hm?"

"How do you hold up the number three on your hand?" I asked.

He looked at me for a moment and then held up a hand with his thumb, pointer, and middle finger extended.

"Huh, they really do make three like that," I muttered.

"What do you mean 'they?'" he asked me.

"Well, in a movie, there's this scene where an American is caught impersonating a German by holding up three fingers the wrong way. The Germans knew he was American because he held them up differently than any German would," I explained, referencing a scene from Tarantino's *Inglorious Basterds*.

"How do you hold up three?" he asked. I held up the first three fingers on one hand - pointer, middle, and ring. "Why would you ever do that?" André gasped.

I laughed and reached down to throw Maverick's stick for him absentmindedly. "It's how we count! One." I held up my pointer finger. "Two." I added my middle finger. "Three." I raised my ring finger.

"That makes no sense at all," he countered. "One." André extended his thumb. I cut him off before he could go further.

"You hold your thumb up for one? Seriously?"

"I thought everyone did." He bent to grab Maverick's stick this time and tossed it off to the left into the fields. Maverick's tail went boinging after it.

I shook my head. "Definitely not. So you do thumb and pointer finger for two?"

"Yes," André replied as if I was simpleminded.

"Wow. Fascinating." We both laughed at this useless bit of information about our respective cultures. Who knew something as simple as counting could be done differently?

A crumbling rock structure appeared just ahead of us on the right of the trail, so old and decrepit that a tuft of thick plants was growing out of the roof of it. "Do you know what that is?" I asked André. He shook his head. "I'm going to go check it out. You coming?"

"No, I am going to keep walking. Buen Camino," he said with a wave and a smile. I waved him off and Maverick and I dipped into a thin trail beaten into the wheat fields that lead to the structure.

We immediately dropped off the side of the trail into a ditch of sorts, the grasses up beyond even my head as I wandered towards the rubble of stone. All that was left was a small square of rock, almost like a single cell, with an arch that held closed iron doors. It really did look like a jail cell, the inside was bare and the rungs of iron barring the way had rusted over time. Despite looking so uninviting, apparently this heap of rock with the iron doors was once *Monasterio de San Félix de Oca*, or the Monastery of San Felices de Oca. Further, the founder of Burgos, Count Diego Porcelos, was laid to rest here according to the stone plaque to the right of the iron doors.

I could hear pilgrims passing by on the trail, not twenty yards from us, yet no one else stopped to explore the ruins or get a closer look. Not that there was anything *too* interesting to see here, but still. It was kind of funny how focused pilgrims could get on the end goal, whether that was making it to the next town, or the end of the stage, or simply all the way to Santiago. Not many liked to stop and smell the roses or dive deeper into the history along the way. It made these little discoveries even more special to me.

In a way, it reminded me a bit about how I had felt back home and how focused everyone is on their end goals. There's this endless pressure to keep your grades up and get accepted into a good college. Then you need to boost your resumé so you can score a respectable job. Go out on dates and meet new people until you find your soulmate and get married. All these milestones just waiting to be checked off in life. It had taken me a while to break out of that mold but even still, I was struggling with it.

As I said before, from the outside no one would ever know I was depressed before I came home from Ohio State. There was nothing that set off my depression. By all rights, I had no *reason* to have depression. I had the *best* family. I had absolutely wonderful friends. I had faced no trauma or abuse in my life – no triggering event. Many people don't realize that depression can't always be pinpointed to a specific event. I know logically, this can happen. Sometimes, the brain just doesn't produce the chemicals it should be producing. Or the receptors in the brain, for whatever reason, don't take in those chemicals that code for happiness and pleasure. So while there was no event and "reason" for my depression, it still came on insidiously. Looking back, I knew that if I had been paying attention or had been willing to admit it, there were signs of my depression starting when I was in high school.

I was still going through the motions, checking those all-important boxes society pushes on us all, but my brain had started to change. In the quiet moments, I was filled with self-doubt. I lost confidence in myself. My outward laughter and bubbly personality had become a mask, not at all what I felt inside. In college, I was able to bury those quiet moments for a long time. Freshman year was so packed with new friends, new experiences, and new places that I was able to push those dark thoughts away. When sophomore year rolled around, it became impossible to bury this thing that had been growing in me.

If I hadn't been so focused on the end goals we set in life, I may have been able to recognize my depression and could have gotten help so much sooner. Instead, I denied what was happening because I *needed* to stay in school. I *needed* to get that degree from a reputable university. I *needed* to party like a normal college kid and cheer along with friends at football games. I was the smart kid, the fun one. I couldn't drop out. I couldn't just hide in a dorm surrounded by a blanket of sadness and the most hopeless thoughts.

I pushed so hard to stay on track, to keep following those shining goals, that it almost killed me. Perhaps if I had stopped, taken a step back, and given time to all the little things that happen along the journey, things may have been different. It was high time I realized that these goals society set for people? They didn't mean a damn thing. They didn't determine if you were intelligent or kind or fun. You could be a college drop out and still be smart. You could stay single for your entire life and still be loving and compassionate. The end goal wasn't all that mattered.

Many pilgrims had not been looking forward to today's stage. It was supposed to be a climb from Villafranca de Montes de Oca to San Juan de Ortega. Personally, I was excited to have some change in elevation. The past days had all be quite flat. Either way, I made sure to stop in Villafrance at a playground of sorts that had a water fountain so that I could fill each of our water bladders for the upcoming climb.

I will not run out of water again. I will not run out of water. Maybe if I repeated this enough to myself, it would actually come true. As I was screwing on the caps of Maverick's water bladders, a woman walked up to the playground across from us. Very carefully, he stooped to rest her pack on the concrete wall and gingerly unbuckled and stepped out of it. That was when I realized it was no ordinary pack she was carrying. It was one of those massive ones that doubled as a baby carrier.

"Wow," I couldn't help but comment. "Are you walking the whole way with your baby?" She was now carefully unstrapping her toddler from the carrier portion of the pack.

"We'll see. It all depends, of course. We don't make it very far each day." She smiled at me as she set the little girl down, who immediately went running towards the playground.

I chuckled as she followed after the toddler. "And here people thought I was crazy for taking a dog."

"I've heard about you, actually. A lot of people talk about the pilgrim with the dog," she said with a laugh.

I smiled weakly. "I guess each scenario comes with challenges."

"True. I've been staying in private rooms in the albergues because I don't want to bother people if she cries at night." She steered her daughter away from the playground so she could give her some sort of crackers.

"Oh, yeah. I hadn't thought of that." *At least albergues allow you in*, I added in my head.

We talked for a bit longer, about the troubles with finding food for our respective "babies" and the kindness we had received from other pilgrims. It was nice to come across another unconventional pilgrim. But eventually it was time for me to move on.

It was easy to see why she had said they didn't make it very far each day. With so many breaks to let her daughter down from the pack to play, it could make for extremely long days if she tried to do a whole stage. At the same time, I had a feeling they had no problem stopping to smell the roses. They certainly were not the end-goal-oriented type of people. The thought made me smile.

Though this next section had been talked about as being a grueling climb, it really wasn't bad at all. The first section was actually quite nice with a pretty gradual incline, through tunnels of trees, and beside fields. The last bit of the climb even ended with a beautiful look back over all the farmland we had been walking through recently.

The terrain evened out, though it was still climbing slightly, and we were amongst the trees again, which was wonderful. Maverick was in heaven with all the sticks to be found – the bigger the better in his mind. Better to take off your kneecaps with as he charged by you, that is. But that's fine. As long as he was happy, right?

About an hour past Villafranca, we reached a hilltop monument for the fallen soldiers of the Spanish Civil War. The site apparently also marked the spot of many shallow graves of those who had been executed. It was an odd mixture to have such a somber area of remembrance paired with the elation of pilgrims finding picnic tables to rest on and catch their breath from the climb. Maverick and I unfortunately didn't stay long because he kept wanting to play with his stick and his exuberance did not seem to fit the atmosphere for the memorial.

Instead, we fell into step with a young man from Boston just as we left the monument. He was a quick walker, which worked out well because there wasn't much to be stopping to explore along this stretch. It was just a wide gravel path with trees on either side of us. I quickly came to learn that this man had been walking for almost forty days now. He started in Le Puy, France, another well-known starting point for pilgrims along the Camino Francés. Apparently, he had family in Santiago that he grew up visiting each year. According to him, it was high time he actually made pilgrimage to the town rather than flying in. After about an hour at his blistering pace, I bid him farewell so that I could give Maverick some water. Okay. *Maybe* it was partly because I needed a break too, but that was beside the point.

Luckily, Mav actually seemed to be drinking today when we stopped. Yesterday, he wasted more water than he consumed since I always ended up dumping out whatever he didn't drink from his bowl. Although, today he seemed completely fine. Fine enough to be chasing the shadows of bugs along the gravel, at least. It would be just as easy to chase the actual bugs in the sky, but for whatever reason, this dog really thought the shadows were real. I was positive it was only a matter of time before he jammed his nose into the dirt trying to catch one. At least it provided us both with some entertainment, because this stretch of the Camino was otherwise pretty bland. It seemed to be an active logging area, and the path we found ourselves on was definitely a gravel logging road.

Finally, we turned off that and onto a lovely, wooded path that angled down to San Juan de Ortega. There was a little stream that cut through the grass just to the right of the trail that Maverick bounded into before I even knew it was there. He had a knack for sniffing out water wherever he was and charging right to it. At least he had the decency to wait for my okay before he laid down in it or drank it. Once I saw that this stream was indeed clear, running water, I gave him the go-ahead and he plopped down immediately, tongue lapping up the cool water.

That was one thing I was extremely grateful for when it came to Maverick: his ability to wait for certain things. It wouldn't have been something I ever really thought of, but the fact that he waited before drinking different water was actually very important in a foreign place like this. What if it was gross, full of parasites I didn't know about? What if it had pollutants in it and he just started drinking without waiting for my command? Granted, I couldn't be entirely positive of any water source he drank. But if it was running water, or it looked clean, I'd give him the okay. I would do the same back home, why should here be any different?

After Maverick had refreshed himself sufficiently, we continued the next couple of steps into the small town of San Juan de Ortega, named for the disciple of Santo Domingo who did so much for the pilgrims in his time. *Small* might be an exaggeration when it came to the size of this village. Really, it was one single road, bordered on one side by the ancient monastery dating back to 1150 and open fields on the other. And… that was all. No, really, that was basically the only thing in this town. There was a bar just a bit beyond the monastery, along the same stone face, and then that was it. The road curved to the left, towards the fields, and that appeared to be the end of town. I wasn't even sure where I would inquire about a place to stay for the night. I could figure it out, sure, but right now I just wanted some food.

I tied Mav to a leg of a chair outside the bar and popped inside to order a sandwich. The egg and ham *bocadillo* was much larger than I had anticipated, but at this point in the day it was perfect. As I wasn't a huge egg fan, I pawned off most of that to Maverick, who eagerly scoffed it up. Of course, he couldn't be bothered with the carbs from the bread, but he was happy to share my ham as well. As we were eating, the woman with the toddler caught up and stopped at a table nearby. A few men who had been sharing a drink at one of the other tables laughed.

"Our two favorite pilgrims, in the same spot!" they called. "The baby and the dog!"

I caught up with the woman and she informed me that she was done for the day. She and the babe would be staying here in the parish for the night. I weighed my options. Technically, this was the end of the stage according to Brierley's guidebook. Which was a bit surprising to me since the town seemed so sparse. Typically, the end towns of each stage had plenty of amenities for pilgrims. I supposed this was an odd stretch between Belorado and Burgos. Going from Belorado all the way to the city would be too far for one day, but there weren't any major stopping points along the way.

Maverick and I crossed the street to lay down in the shade of some trees to decide our next move. I could stay the night here, at the end of a stage. Even if the one albergue here didn't allow us in, I'm sure I could find a place to pitch my tent nearby. There were plenty of open spaces here. Or I could keep walking. The next town, Agés, was only another three and a half kilometers away. There was supposedly an albergue there that accepted dogs. Plus, I still needed to find food for Maverick tonight. It was clear I wouldn't be getting any in this town. I didn't even think it had a grocery store of any kind here. That made the decision for me. We would be walking on.

The short stretch from San Juan to Agés started along the road, then turned into a wide track with plenty of trees for Maverick to weave in and out of. He definitely agreed with my decision. His boundless energy continued even as we exited the tree-lined path to a grassy area that overlooked the town below. Agés was laid out ahead of us, a cluster of red terracotta roofs in a sea of green grass and wildflowers. It looked like something out of a dream. The pale, dirt track that led down to town, stretching out under a blue sky with large, puffy, white clouds.

Even once we arrived in town, it was like a dream. Each building, though connected as one, was a slightly different color, separated from one another by wooden beams. Yellow, tan, white, beige, red, all in old, faded paint jobs over the concrete walls. It was like a storybook village, though a little bit run down, and entirely human. Potted plants decorated the stone wall of one building, perched on weathered stumps and slabs of wood, and surrounded a massive wicker basket full of loaves of fresh-baked bread. A tiny green towards the center of the village sported a unique wooden sign pointing to Santiago: 518km away.

El Pajar, the most prominent albergue in town, was one of the few buildings without an inch of peeling paint on its sunny, muted-yellow façade. I popped inside to ask about their supposed dog-friendly atmosphere.

The hospitalera was delighted to have me. In fact, she told me I could have my very own albergue for the night.

"¿Perdón?" I asked, certain that could not be right.

"¡Sí! Tenemos un otro albergue y nadie se queda allí esta noche. Es perfecto, tendrás todo el albergue."

"Uhm, bueno. Que guay." *Another albergue?* I thought. *We'll have the whole albergue to ourselves?*

The woman called another young man over and said he would take me to the other albergue, so I gathered up my pack and Maverick's and took his leash, following the man outside and around the back of the building. We crossed through the empty lot next to El Pajar and diagonally across the street behind it to a long building painted in a deep red but with the same black, wooden beams of El Pajar.

The man explained that they owned this building as well and had been working on it to open a second albergue, but at the moment it wasn't used much. Since I had a dog, it was the perfect place. We could have our own area that wouldn't disturb any of the other pilgrims. He led me upstairs to a room that had been recently renovated. It had a bunk bed, a window that looked out over the street we had just crossed and the back of El Pajar, and a dresser equipped with plenty of books. He pointed out the bathroom, told me when dinner would be held and where in El Pajar, and then continued back downstairs, leaving me all alone in the empty "lobby" of this albergue.

"Well, Maverick. Would ya look at this. Our very own albergue." Mav looked from me to the half-open door the man had just left. It was one of those big, barn-like doors that had two parts so that the bottom could remain closed while the top half swung open. "Come on, then. We have clothes to wash. And a shower to take. And a bed to rest on. This is *awesome*!"

After settling in, getting clean, and hanging my clothes out the window to dry, we went over for dinner in El Pajar. I wasn't expecting many pilgrims to be in this town, since it wasn't an end of a stage, but I was pleasantly surprised by the amount present at the communal dinner. There was an older couple, a couple of young gentlemen, and the cousins and their friend who we had just met last night in Belorado.

"Hey!" one of the girls called as I came into the dining room and took a seat. "You made it! We didn't see you when we left the albergue this morning."

"Oh, yeah," I smiled. "We made it. I must have already left."

"I still can't believe they made you sleep outside," her cousin mumbled bitterly.

"Well, to be fair, they didn't make me. I did pay for a bed. I just didn't use it," I laughed.

"Still. Where are you staying tonight, then? Not here?"

"Kind of. I'm actually in a place across the street that they own. We're the only ones over there. It's really nice."

"Wow," the blonde woman said. "From sleeping in a garden to having your own albergue. Talk about an upgrade."

We laughed and joked through dinner, and I made friends with the older couple I was seated beside, but once I had eaten, I faced a new predicament. Maverick was still without food and it was time for his dinner. I sought out the sweet hospitalera after dinner had finished.

"¿Perdón? ¿Tiene algo por el perro por la cena?" I asked. I wasn't sure what she might possibly have for Maverick to eat, but there wasn't a store in this tiny town, either. I was going to have to get creative. "¿O conoce una tienda donde puedo comprarle comida?" At the very least, she might know of *somewhere* that I could buy food for him.

She thought for a minute and made a face at me. "Pues, no lo tengo nada. Pero, hay un bar. ¿Podrías comprarle un bistec para cena?"

Hmm, that wasn't a horrible idea, I thought. It was probably the best option. A steak would be nutritious enough, right? "Es un buen idea. Muchas gracias, Señora."

Maverick and I trotted down the road, just a few buildings past El Pajar, and I ducked into the bar the hospitalera had told me of. There were all sorts of combo plates available for dinners. I scoured the options, trying to find one that would give him enough nutrients for the day.

Was this ridiculous? Yes. Did I have any other ideas for what to do tonight? No.

The woman behind the counter came to take my order. I found a combo plate with a steak and two fried eggs and asked for that without any sort of seasoning on it. "¿Y papas fritas?" she asked.

"Ah," I debated, knowing Maverick would probably not eat any French fries. But the combo plate came with them, so I might as well eat them myself. "Sí."

"¿Para beber?" she asked.

"Nada."

"¿Nada?"

"Sí, no necesito una bebida. La comida es para el perro," I told her. I had just eaten and drank plenty at dinner myself; I didn't need a drink.

"Es para…¿el perro?" she questioned dubiously.

I smiled sheepishly. She seemed to sense a losing battle and didn't question the food being for the dog anymore. She only sighed and shook her head, then turned to bring the order to the kitchen. A few minutes later, when she brought the food outside, she shook her head again, mumbling something about "el perro" under her breath.

I smiled at Maverick and cut his steak into pieces, mixing it with the fried eggs to make a delicious meal. "Eat up, kiddo. We walk to Burgos tomorrow."

God Undefeatable

Day Fifteen: Agés to Burgos

31.8 km ~ 44,903 steps

July 4th

Today was a holiday...I thought. It was hard to remember what day it was along the Camino. It never mattered one way or another. I would have totally forgot the Fourth of July if Amy and Beth hadn't asked about it when we stayed together in Nájera.

"Don't you have a holiday coming up?" Amy had asked as she sat on one of the beds across the room from me.

"I do?" I questioned. Then it had hit me. "Oh yeah, I do."

It was kind of funny when the Irish remembered my holidays better than I did. Although the Fourth of July was really just an excuse to party for most Americans. In my opinion, walking across Spain was certainly more interesting than spending today in a pool or grilling burgers and hot dogs.

"Happy Fourth of July, Maverick," I told him as I gathered our stuff from around the albergue this morning. *And that*, I thought, *is the extent of our celebration today.*

The little bundle of pilgrims who stayed in Agés last night all left town around the same time today, so Maverick and I ended up walking along with the older man I met at dinner last night.

"My wife had an issue with one of her ankles," he told me in explanation of her absence. "She's going to take the bus into Burgos this afternoon and I'll meet her there."

"Well, it's a good thing I caught you then. I can be your walking buddy this morning," I joked.

"I couldn't think of two better pilgrims to walk with." He smiled and reached down to scratch Maverick's head.

We kept each other company to Atapuerca, where we stopped at a cute little café to get breakfast. The three girls from last night were here for breakfast, too. I guess I wasn't the only one who missed breakfast at El Pajar. After catching up with everyone over our breakfasts, Maverick and I waved goodbye and continue on. We were able to enjoy the rest of the walk through Atapuerca just the two of us. This town was actually home to the oldest human remains ever found in Europe.

The archaeological site is still active today, and there was a large information center just off to the right. Of course, it was too early for anything to be open, and I probably wouldn't have been able to visit something like that with Maverick, but it was still very neat. To think that people were living here 1.2 million years ago was simply mind-blowing.

The trail turned left out of town and began to climb up through a scrubby area on a rough trail. It was actually a really enjoyable hike…until I spied some sheep off to the left.

A farmer was standing watching the herd, and I could see him directing two herding dogs around the animals. I unfurled Maverick's leash and clutched the handle just to be safe. It looked like the farmer was herding the sheep towards the trail. Luckily, despite Maverick seeing the sheep, he didn't make a sound. However, that didn't stop the herding dogs from responding to the sight of Maverick.

One let out a shrill bark and then started heading our way. At the other dog's bark, Maverick answered with a bark of his own and within a few seconds, the sheep were scattering all over the hillside. Many of them disappeared over the crest of the hill in the opposite direction the farmer had been herding them.

"Oh, jeez. Not good. Go, Maverick, go," I urged him on. Despite the herding dogs still coming this way, Maverick ignored them and began running up the hill with me, staying on the trail for the Camino. "I'm sorry," I mumbled under my breath as we ran. "I'm so sorry, Mister Sheep Man."

We ran the rest of the way up the hill, which topped out with the most incredible view. A massive cross was overlooking patchwork fields that eventually blended into the many sprawling buildings of Burgos on the right. After catching my breath from that sprint (and checking behind us to make sure an angry farmer wasn't coming after us) we started down the hill and into the farmlands.

The clouds were clearing out to blue skies, the threat of rain from this morning forgotten, as we passed through the small villages leading up to Burgos, skirted through the scrubby land around the back of the Burgos airport, and finally came to the outskirts of the city. I stopped at a café for Maverick to have a break in the shade and treated myself to an ice cream. Here, the Camino diverged. One route led along the road into the heart of the city to deposit pilgrims in front of the massive cathedral, while a second route led through a city park along the river. The thought of walking alongside the busy highway into the city with Maverick did not sound like fun, so it was an easy choice to take the river route.

Of course, this meant that Maverick *must* go swimming at every chance he found. So really, the last stretch of six kilometers took us far longer than it should have to complete. He plodded into the sandy dips that led to the water so he could pull out waterlogged sticks to bring to me. Once he found one that was approximately six feet long, he was satisfied enough to walk on. Both ends of the limb bounced as he trotted ahead of me on the empty, riverside path. But at the next sandy area, he abandoned his tree in favor of rocks. He dug at them under the surface, shoving his muzzle down to pluck a stone out and running over to where I was waiting to drop it by my feet.

"I can't throw that, you dummy," I laughed. He tilted his head, then bounced his front feet as if to encourage me. "It's a rock. It will sink." His only response was to whine and dance back and forth in front of me. "Fine. Watch."

I reached down, picked up the stone he deemed worthy from the countless others that littered the riverbed, and tossed it forward into the river. It immediately sank beneath the surface as he went crashing after it. His head swiveled back and forth, trying to see where it had gone, but to no avail. He shoved his muzzle under the water again, snuffling around for the specific rock. A couple minutes later, after multiple trials, he lifted his face from the water with a rock in his mouth. In a few bounds, he was back in front of me, carefully releasing the rock just beyond my boots.

"No way," I muttered as he backed up, giving me enough room to see the stone he put down. The same exact one I had thrown. I looked back up at him, his bright eyes staring at me intently. *You gonna throw it again, Mum?* They seemed to ask.

"You're insane. Absolutely insane." But of course, I bent down to grab the rock and threw it yet again.

As we continued through the busy riverside park, I kept Maverick on his leash and my eyes mostly turned to the river on our right as Burgos steadily grew across the water. I ended up staying in the park for longer than the guide had directed, all the way to Puente de Santa María which led across to Arco de Santa María. It looked like the entrance to a medieval castle more than just an arch. Set directly between two modern five-story buildings, it featured multiple turrets and magnificent full-body carvings of people of great importance to the city of Burgos, such as the city's founder, Diego Rodríguez Porcelos.

The arch, which was originally much more simple, had served as one of many entrances to the walled city of Burgos in the Middle Ages. It was only later rebuilt by Charles V, Holy Roman Emperor, in the sixteenth century to look as it did today. While it truly was awe-inspiring, hints of the massive cathedral beyond it were already visible from the bridge. One spire could be seen jutting over the arch, beckoning pilgrims and tourists alike to enter the old part of town.

Emerging from the arch, I stopped dead. I had never seen a more massive, intricately designed structure in my entire life. The tourists crossing the plaza looked like tiny ants beneath this cathedral's walls. There was so much to take in, my eyes didn't know where to look first. The colossal spire to the left that I had been able to see from beyond the arch? Or the octagonal tower towards the center that was topped with eight spires with elaborate stonework protruding from them? Or maybe the towering circular window inlaid with careful stonework, making it look like an enormous spider web? I could have looked at this structure for days and still been unable to pick everything out. Knowing this was built in the thirteenth century was simply unbelievable.

With my jaw still dropped in awe, I stumbled to a table at a café just beneath the imposing structure and ordered myself some *paella*. I was sure this restaurant was overpriced, and the *paella* wasn't the best I'd had since I'd been in Spain, but it meant I could stare at the cathedral the entire time that I ate. Every minute that I stared, I found a new thing to focus on. The attention to detail on this building was mind-blowing.

After I finished eating lunch, Maverick and I made our way to the western façade, the original main entrance I would assume, known as the Portal of Saint Mary. Three arches held three separate doors into the cathedral, with the center door being well over ten feet tall. Above that rose two identical towers, complete with glass windows. A giant rosette like the circular window on the other façade spanned between them, topped with carvings of the eight kings of Castile in individual arches. As if that didn't make this façade tall enough, atop the individual towers were twin, octagonal spires, which were what I had first seen from Puente de Santa María.

I had heard a rumor that cathedrals in the Middle Ages were built so large so that pilgrims could see them from far away while they were walking on pilgrimage. I'm not entirely sure if this was factual, but it was a fun thing to think about on the Camino. It would have been much easier to pick out these massive structures ages ago, before apartment buildings or cityscapes crowded them for attention. Even now in a modern era with new buildings surrounding this cathedral, it still had the ability to make you feel incredibly small.

After taking in the structure for as long as I could, Maverick and I weaved our way through the thick crowds in

Old Town towards a hostel I had booked in advance. I had found it in Brierely's guidebook by calling every place listed and asking if they allowed dogs until I finally came across this one. It wasn't the nicest of places, but that never mattered to me. I was just excited to be staying in one place for two nights. Tomorrow would be our first rest day since the side trip we took to Bakio.

After checking in and dropping our packs, we headed back out into the city on a mission. Maverick needed dog food. There was no way a city this large didn't have a place to get pet supplies. Our search took us back across the river to what was supposedly a pet store. At least, that was what GoogleMaps had told me. As it turned out, they only sold pet fish. I tried asking the lady who worked there where I could find a pet store, but she didn't seem to have any idea what I meant. After trying for almost five minutes to ask about where people get food for their dogs, or any other roundabout ways I could think of in Spanish to get her to think of a pet store, I decided to cut my losses. She clearly was going to be no help. I pulled up GoogleMaps again, typed in *tienda de mascotas* as well as *tienda de animales*, but couldn't find anything promising. I would just have to wander and hope we found something.

We passed the Museum of Human Evolution on our way back to the main part of town. Outside, there was a series of interesting statues that depicted the change from ape to man. In fact, our travels around the city in search of a pet store revealed that Burgos was home to *lots* of statues. We found one of a little girl with an umbrella that was a fountain as well, complete with water dripping from the edges of her umbrella. One depicted a man leaning against a pillar to read a large newspaper. One appeared to be a court jester with his hand on the shoulder of a little boy. And of course, the most famous statue that fellow pilgrims will know well, the haggard pilgrim with his staff seated just outside the façade of the cathedral that faces Plaza del Rey San Fernando where we first arrived.

While coming across all of these statues was delightful, it got me no closer to food for Maverick. So far, we had found a store for cheese, a store dedicated to different yogurts, what appeared to be the Spanish version of the Dollar Store, countless tourist traps, and even a store for sausages, but not a single pet store. I was just about to give up for the night when I turned up one last street and found a store. It was some sort of designer pet store, that had more frilly sweaters and dress up clothes for small dogs than they did dog food, but it was a pet store. I rushed inside, scouring the shelves for the Eukanuba dog food Maverick had been on that was supposedly available all over Spain. I finally waved down a worker when I couldn't find any.

"¿Perdón? ¿Tiene Eukanuba?" I asked her.

"Eukanuba? No, no tiene esa marca." I frowned. *Okay, so they didn't have Eukanuba.* Maverick would just have to eat a different brand. It wouldn't be the proper food-switching protocol for dogs, but we didn't really have options. I picked up a bag of large dog food this store did have available.

"¿Es esta una marca popular?" I asked her. If we were going to be changing food brands, I better be able to get it all over this country.

"Sí. Esa es muy popular," she agreed. I was doubtful.

"¿Entonces, esta marca es en todo del país?" I tried to confirm. With my luck, this would be some regional dog food that I wouldn't be able to find anywhere else.

"Sí," she affirmed. "Está disponible en toda España."

Satisfied, I bought the biggest bag of the food they had. Maverick was getting a double helping for the next couple of days to make up for what he had missed.

New Slang

Day Sixteen: Burgos

12.1 km ~ 17,111 steps

July 5th

What a beautiful thing it was to wake up late and not feel guilty about it. I didn't have to worry about it getting too hot during the day. I didn't have to think we were behind because we started walking late. It was nice. What was even nicer was that I was actually walking out of the hostel without a pack on my shoulders. I felt like just another citizen, taking my dog for a walk in the city, off to meet a friend for breakfast.

Trish had texted me last night saying that she had some problem with her foot and had been laid up in Burgos for a few days while Margie walked on without her. Although I was sad she had something wrong, I was selfishly thrilled I would be able to see her again.

She was already at the café we agreed upon last night when Mav and I made it to Plaza del Rey San Fernando. I took a seat across from her at the table and promptly ordered some *churros y chocolate*. I'd been in Spain for over two weeks now and had yet to try this delicacy. Growing up learning Spanish in the schools, it seemed like teachers were always telling us how great *churros y chocolate* were. The reality is…I found them underwhelming. They were *okay*. Not bad. But I wouldn't be falling over myself to talk about how great they were. They were just sugary dough sticks dipped in melted chocolate.

Trish and I caught up over breakfast. Apparently, the issue with her foot had turned out to be an infection of some sort and the doctor told to rest for a few days and not to walk on it. She felt bad holding Margie back, so she had told her to walk on, but she was itching to get back on the trail. Just as she was telling me about this, the woman with the baby girl who we ran into in Villafranca de Montes de Oca spied Maverick and I and came over to say hi.

"Oh my gosh," I called out, surprised to see her since I hadn't run into them since leaving them in San Juan a couple days ago. "How are you guys doing?"

She told me that everything had been going well and that they would be starting out from Burgos tomorrow on bikes.

"Bikes?" I asked.

"Yeah, my husband is over at the bike rental shop now to reserve ours," she said, nodding back across the square.

"You can rent a bike?" Trish asked, immediately intrigued.

"Yes! I thought it would be great because I don't think the Meseta would be a great idea with the little one. Too much sun and not enough places to stop. So we decided to rent bikes so we can pass through that section quicker, but not completely skip it. The rental shop allows you to rent a bike here and return it to their other store in León once you're through the Meseta. They even have a trailer to hook to one bike for the baby to ride in."

"No way," Trish said, and I could see in her eyes she was thinking of some sort of plan.

"That's a great idea," I told the girl, because it really was. The Meseta was a massive part of the Camino. Actually, it was a massive part of the country of Spain. La Meseta, which translates to *the plateau*, was just that. A high plateau that stretched nearly 81,000 square miles across the country, making up about forty percent of Spain. As for the Camino, it encompassed over two hundred kilometers from Burgos to Astorga, though many pilgrims really only worry about the stretch from Burgos to León, the two largest cities of the Camino. And worry they do. I had to admit, I was not immune to that worry as a pilgrim.

The reason so much trepidation came with the words *La Meseta* was because the landscape was so desolate. Known for being extremely hot and dry in summer and frigid cold in the winter months, La Meseta is a barren landscape. Cereal grains cover almost all of the Meseta that pilgrims walk through, with next to no trees or structures for shade. The towns, really just tiny villages, were few and far between. Though the walking wasn't difficult, since it was quite flat throughout the entire section, it was known to be a mental challenge. The towns tended to dip down in valleys off the Mestea, leading the eyes to see just one giant, seemingly endless expanse of flat land.

I'd heard that a lot of pilgrims opted to skip the entire section of La Meseta. Many took a bus from Burgos to León and continued walking from there. Others hopped a train between the two cities. And apparently, from what this woman was telling us now, many rented bikes to zip through this section much faster. It made sense. I remembered just how quickly the Camino passed for those Italian men I had dinner with in Belorado because they were on a bike. It was easy to do forty- or fifty-kilometer days when you were riding. It would allow a pilgrim to cross the Meseta in half the time it took to walk it.

"Well, there's my husband now. I've got to go. It was nice seeing you!" she told me. "And you Maverick." She smiled and reached down to give him a pat where he was lying next to my chair. "Buen Camino!"

She had barely made it back down to the main part of the plaza when Trish was turning to me. "A bike, hm?"

"You want to rent a bike?" I asked.

"Why not? I would probably be able to catch up to Margie. I won't be walking on my foot then. I'd just be pedaling. That's definitely better than walking, don't you think?"

I laughed and shook my head. "Do you think your foot can handle that? Didn't the doctor say you shouldn't be doing anything?"

She waved her hand at me like my concern was a fly she could brush away. "I'm sure it'll be fine. I think I'm going to check it out."

I raised my eyebrows and dunked another churro in the chocolate, swirling it around but not really interested in eating it.

"Where did she say the shop was? Somewhere across the river, right? I'm going to try to find it."

Trish continued to make her plans while we threw down enough euros to cover the bill and made our way towards the tourist entrance of the cathedral. "Alright, so Maverick and I are going to find this bike shop across the river. You go enjoy the cathedral. Take your time, it's really so cool. Don't worry about him, he's in good hands."

I reluctantly handed over his leash to Trish and he looked at me with doleful eyes. *Mum?* He seemed to say. *You're leaving me?* I clipped his collapsible water dish onto the handle of the leash.

"If he needs water, I'm sure it's easy enough to find a fountain. And here are his poop bags, but he already went this morning so you shouldn't have to worry about that. He's really obsessed with water, so he might try to tug you down to the river. I'm sorry in advance. You can just yell at him – he can take it. If you want to let him swim you can, though. Your choice. If you need to go into any stores or anything, you can just tie him to a lamppost or something outside, he just lies down, and-"

"Colby." Trish cut me off. "He's going to be *fine*. You'll be without him for maybe an hour. I promise he is in good hands."

I took a deep breath and looked down at him. His tail wagged back and forth a little bit, like he was asking if we were about to head out on a new adventure. I squatted down to his level. "Okay. You be good for Trish. I'll be right back, I promise, Nugget. I love you."

Trish laughed as I slowly backed away towards the massive arched entrance that opened on this plaza. "Don't forget to show your *credencial*. Special price for pilgrims," she called out to me before I got too far. Maverick looked at her, then back at me and whined.

I finally turned around, knowing if I kept looking back at him he would just want to come with me even more and that wasn't fair to Trish trying to control him. I could hear him whining from behind me and Trish soothing him, but I made it through the doors and into the gift shop area to get a ticket without a backwards glance.

Once inside, I showed my *credencial* to the clerk, bought a ticket that came with a map of the massive structure and a nifty, handheld speaker that would act as my own personal guide around the cathedral, and made my way further inside the building. There was so much to take in, it was impossible to know where to look. Luckily, there was a clear path to follow through the maze of chapels and alcoves. At each step, there was a new number to punch into the handheld speaker so the guide would explain what I was looking at. It was incredible, of course, but also very overwhelming. Plus, there were so many people milling about that it definitely did not feel like a place of worship. It felt much more like a museum. Which is fine, it was very interesting to learn about the history and all the artwork, but it was hard to imagine this as a place where people came to worship in the past.

Some of the stonework was so delicate it looked like lace. Other scenes were carved into the walls as if there were really cherubs behind the block of stone pressing forward to break free. Figures of apostles and griffins towered over me and entire chapels seemed to shine in gold. As if that wasn't enough to take in, if I craned my neck back a little bit, there was a whole other world to view along the immense arched ceilings. Gold brushed domes with individual paintings in every panel, or ribbed arches that held stained glass windows, and webbings of stone in the shape of flowers all decorated the spaces stories over our heads.

Even walking through the cloisters was stunning with the sunlight pouring in through the high, stained-glass windows. It would have been easy to spend an entire day in this cathedral and still not soak in half of what it had to offer. However, I had a dog waiting on me and I couldn't take all day. Eventually, I turned in my speaker and made my way back outside to the bustling plaza.

When I didn't immediately spot Trish and Mav, I decided to take a walk around the outside of the cathedral. It was so huge I had to take multiple different streets just to get up and around to the back side of it, which afforded even more views of the structure that I had yet to see. I had to admit, it was a bit nice to be able to do this without Maverick. He wasn't exactly the best on a leash because he always had so much energy and just wants to *go*. It was very relaxing to be able to walk around without him tugging me towards a pigeon or some shadows on the ground that he wanted to chase. But at the same time I missed him, even if it had only been an hour apart. So I headed back to Plaza del Rey San Fernando and there he was, eagerly staring at the door I had first disappeared into.

I smiled as I walked towards him, even though he hadn't seen me yet. Since I was across a busy plaza of people, it wasn't like I could yell out his name. But he must have smelled me because his head suddenly whipped in my direction and he tugged against his leash, pulling Trish a few steps forward. I hustled over to them before he had a chance to drag her to the ground.

"Was he good?" I asked.

She smiled. "He was perfect. Didn't pull at all." I shot him an annoyed look, wondering why he couldn't be like that when *I* had him on a leash. "Although, do you know how many people came up to me just to say 'That's not your dog. That's Maverick. We know who he is and he's not your dog.' He apparently has quite the fan club."

I laughed. "No way. Other pilgrims?"

"Apparently. I had to keep telling them I knew you and that I was just watching him so you could visit the cathedral."

"That's kind of awesome," I admitted. At least I knew that if anyone dared to try to steal him, other pilgrims would have our back. "Did you guys find the bike shop?"

"Yeah, I reserved a bike for myself! I should be all set to start pedaling tomorrow. Oh, and I asked if they had a buggy to rent for you and Maverick. They said that would be totally fine and that one was available. You'd just have to go reserve it yourself."

"Seriously?" I laughed. I wouldn't lie, I had definitely been thinking about it. I'd seen pictures of people biking with their pets in the little trailers hooked to the back of a bike. Granted, those were normally small dogs or cats, not eighty-pound German Shepherds, but still. It was a tantalizing thought if we could pull it off.

"Do you think he'll stay in it if you were to put him in?"

I looked down at Maverick, who was happily watching all the people in the plaza buzzing around us. "Honestly? I don't know. I would be inclined to say yes. He just lies down and doesn't move for entire plane flights or our time on a train. He seems to know when it's a situation he has to lie down for. Do you think he'll even fit in the buggy?"

Trish looked down at him, gauging his size. "I don't see why not. And they have saddlebags on the bike for all your stuff. You could just ship your pack ahead and keep what you need."

"Seems complicated," I added. Then I tipped my head to the other side, as if weighing options on a scale. "But I suppose I'm used to complicated with him at this point."

Our conversation was interrupted at that point by the arrival of the girl from Ireland who was walking with her cello and her friends we had met that night in Santo Domingo. "It's Maverick!" she called, rushing over to us across the plaza. "How are you guys?" she asked me.

I quickly made introductions between her, her friends, and Trish. "We're good. How have you guys been?"

"Oh, we're grand," she said as she bent down to ruffle Maverick's fur and then began play-boxing him so he tried to nip at her hands while she danced around him. "We just got here, actually. Have you been here long?"

"We got in yesterday. We're taking a day to explore the city before walking on tomorrow."

"Ah, walking on, are you?" Maverick grabbed a hold of one of her sleeves on her next assault and pulled. I heard a telltale *rip* of fabric and my eyes widened.

"Oh my gosh, I'm so sorry," I gushed, but Sarah waved me off immediately.

"Don't you worry at all. That was my fault, wasn't it Maverick?" she cooed. "I was playing rough; he just went along with me. So you're walking the Meseta, then?" She returned to her previous topic like there had been no interruption at all.

"Well…" I started, looking to Trish. "Maybe. We may be renting a bike and buggy, though. I figure it might be best for him to stay in the shade of a buggy if it's so hot."

"Incredible," she laughed. "You best take pictures of that. That's amazing."

"Are you not walking the Meseta?" I asked.

"I am," she replied, but then indicated to the small group of friends beside her. "But they're not."

"You're not?" I asked, directing my question to the blonde who had sung *Jungle Book* tunes with her in Santo Domingo. She shook her head.

"No. We're going to take the bus to León tomorrow."

"Ah, gotcha," I nodded. One of the many avoiding the lengthy Meseta.

"Well," Sarah said brusquely. "We better be checking into the albergue. Great seeing you! Good luck with that buggy!" And they were off, as quickly as they came.

Just moments after the group had departed, a procession of massive doll-like giants strode into the plaza. "What in the world?" I gasped. There were at least ten of them, each towering over ten feet tall, dressed up like kings and queens of all sorts of different nationalities.

"It must be noon," Trish said from beside me.

"Does this happen every day?" I asked in wonder.

"From what I've seen, yes. I think they're called *Los Gigantes*."

Families with small children were gathering around to see the huge dolls and to take their picture with them. "What are they for?"

"I have no idea," Trish admitted. "Will you take my picture with them, though?"

I laughed and took her phone to snap a picture for her. She insisted that Maverick and I take a picture with them as well and afterwards we set plans to meet for dinner by the municipal albergue and parted ways for the afternoon.

I stood in the plaza for a little while longer, debating what to do. A part of me, actually a large part, was leaning towards checking out the bike shop and the buggy. I knew it sounded ridiculous; it *was* ridiculous. But I was worried about the Meseta. It was going to be so wide open, with no shade, not many towns, no water supplies or trees or streams for Maverick to drink from or lie down in. It was supposedly gravel paths through the whole thing, so he would need to wear his booties all the time so his paw pads didn't become sore again. Which would be fine, but since it was supposed to be so hot, I was worried about him having to have the boots on the whole day. Dogs only "sweat" through their paw pads and when they pant. If I made him wear the booties the whole day, that would be eliminating one of his ways to let off heat. We'd have to walk very early in the mornings and be done by around eleven, because it would be getting very hot at that point. If that was the case, I wouldn't even know what to do in the afternoons. Most albergues didn't open until one.

Even if we did all that, I had a feeling I would get down and depressed again like that first week on trail and be absolutely miserable. I know the Camino wasn't supposed to be all rainbows and butterflies, but I would really not like to feel that shitty again. I would get so low I'd want to quit again and wonder why the heck I decided to do this trail. Then I would end up taking a taxi from some town to León, which would make me feel guilty for skipping part of the trail. As it was, I still felt guilty for skipping that small section between Los Arcos and Logroño.

So with all that running through my mind, I turned with Maverick and headed through Acro de Santa María, back out across the river, in search of the bike shop. It didn't hurt to at least look into the buggy.

I had my reservations about the bike as well. For one, it would be a hassle to rent and then find the place to return it in León. The whole thing about sending our bags ahead was a bit ridiculous. My most obvious reservation was definitely how Maverick would handle the buggy. I didn't even know if he would sit in it and stay, so this could all be for naught.

Even if he did sit and stay and enjoy it, I would still feel a bit guilty for not walking. As if I *should* be walking it because that made me a "true pilgrim." There was no real reason to prevent me from walking. It wasn't as if I have an injury like Trish does. I should be strong enough to walk the whole Camino.

These were the same "should" statements I always felt with my depression.

In therapy, they teach you how to reorganize your thoughts to be less negative. I learned that I made my depression worse by beating myself up for being depressed. It was a vicious cycle. I was constantly telling myself I *shouldn't* be depressed because there were so many people who had a worse life than I did. I told myself I *should* be happy and appreciative of the small things. That I *should* get out of bed, not just lie there. That I *should* go to the gym, or to see friends, or take a hike. Should, should, should. When you keep telling yourself what you *should* be doing or feeling, you're also telling yourself that the feelings you *are* feeling, the things you *are* doing are wrong or invalid. And that isn't the case.

My therapist taught me that there was nothing wrong with what my body was telling me. If I needed to take a day to rest, take a day to rest. If I was feeling sad, allow myself to be sad. Sit with those emotions and thoughts. Stop trying to tamp them down or push them away or say they're not what I *should* be feeling. There is no *should*. There's just what your body and mind need.

I tried to remind myself of this when debating on the bike. But all these worries were pointless if I didn't test it out and see.

I finally arrived at the store and tied Maverick out to a bike rack so I could go inside. It was a busy place, bustling with workers pulling bikes out from the back and setting them up or moving others out front of the store that were ready to go. I saw one bike being hooked up to a buggy and wondered if that was for the woman and her baby.

"Hola," I said to the room at large. A man smiled at me from behind the counter, so I told him that Trish had been here this morning to ask about my situation. "¿Mi amiga estuvo aquí y preguntó de una bicicleta por mí y mi perro este mañana?"

"Ah, ¡sí! La chica con el perro, que fantástico."

The man was so kind and took the time to answer all of my questions on the bike rentals and how it would work and if I could try it in the morning before agreeing to really take it. I definitely didn't want to just jump into it in the morning only to realize that Maverick was *not* having it ten minutes in and then not be able to undo my reservation.

In the end, the man told me everything would be ready

to go at seven tomorrow morning and that I could of course test it out around the block to see if it would work before paying for it. I signed the agreement to be there tomorrow, they took my measurements to set up the right size bike, and I waved goodbye feeling just a little bit optimistic for this next section. I had always been a huge proponent of the saying, "It doesn't hurt to try." I'd rather give this a try and if it didn't work, so be it. We could walk on. At least I would know I explored all my options.

After making our arrangements, I took Maverick for a walk down by the river again and let him go swimming. Plenty of Burgos residents were walking along the river paths during this beautiful afternoon, and I lounged in the grass to enjoy the day of rest as well. I tossed a stick for Maverick each time he brought it back to me and tried to avoid the water droplets he sprayed everywhere. Clearly, he did not fully comprehend the idea of a *rest day*.

When we headed back out to meet Trish for dinner that night, the streets were packed. According to the guidebook, the weeks on either side of June 29th, which we were in, was the time of Burgos' main festival, *San Pedro y Pablo*. Though I wasn't sure what this entailed exactly, or what it celebrated, it seemed to mean there was an influx of people in the city. We passed one concert in a plaza on our way over, multiple street performers, and many artists who could create spray paint masterpieces in record time. Perhaps this festival was why *Los Gigantes* came out each afternoon.

We eventually reached Trish and sat outside a pub for dinner together. She told me that she didn't think she would be ready to start biking tomorrow because her foot was really bothering her still, so she was extending her stay at the

AirBnB she had been renting. I definitely thought that was for the best, but the selfish part of me was sad. I had hoped we could bike together. Then again, this whole trip had been just me and Mav, so it wasn't like it would be much different tomorrow morning. I guess I was just feeling a bit of anxiety involving this whole bike situation.

Luckily, there wasn't much time to dwell on it. Besides a great dinner companion in Trish, fellow pilgrims kept passing by stop to say hi and ask about Maverick. I felt bad because they all seemed to know who we were, or rather who *Maverick* was, and I couldn't seem to remember anyone's names. It was uplifting to see how happy everyone got when they ran into Maverick, though. It made all the hard parts of this trip seem worth it. He had been bringing joy to my life for the past eleven months; it was nice to see him spread that joy to hundreds of other people as well.

Trish and I parted ways after dinner with a "Buen Camino," knowing this might very well be the last time we ran into each other along this journey. As I weaved my way back towards our room for the night, through all the activities in the street, I was struck with the idea that I should stay out and enjoy the nightlife. I should really be taking in the scenes of the city and soaking up as much as I could of the culture here. Once again, those *should* statements were creeping in. So instead of giving in to those, I accepted that I was *tired*. The Camino was amazing, but it was also draining. Even with a full rest day, I was ready to go to bed. Plus, Maverick wasn't exactly a city dog. It wasn't fun to constantly be tugging on his leash or fighting my way through crowded streets with a dog beside me.

So instead of wandering the town, Maverick and I turned in for the night. Screw what we *should* be doing. I packed up almost all of our stuff, leaving out the dog food to give him breakfast in the morning, and finally lay back in bed. Part of me was still dreading tomorrow, but there was no use worrying about it now. Whatever happens, happens.

You can also see the following pictures in full color on my website: colbymillsaps.com/books/conelperro/

Leaving Saint Jean Pied de Port on Day One

The (in)famous sign in Roncesvalles

Center portion of the pilgrim statue on Alto de Perdón

Puente la Reina

Looking up from the bottom of the steps in Fuente de los Moros

San Juan de Gaztelugatxe

Enjoying wine country in La Rioja

Always following yellow flechas (arrows)

Modeling somewhere between Agés and Burgos

Feeling like ants beneath the towering walls of Burgos Cathedral

Clip-clopping along la Meseta in booties

*Following more flechas, this one in the lovely town of
Castrojeriz*

Early mornings on la Meseta

Endless wheatfields can be pretty...sometimes

Halfway point just before Sahagún

Intricate details of the Astorga Cathedral

My favorite fountain along the Camino

The most magical morning at Cruz de Ferro

Leaving behind more than just a stone at Cruz de Ferro

Thriving in the mountains after leaving Cruz de Ferro

Alone with Me

Day Seventeen: Burgos to Hornillos

27 km ~ 37,640 steps

July 6th

We woke with the sun and slipped out of the hostel with all our gear this morning. The streets were eerily silent and empty compared to the mayhem that was last night. I was even able to let Maverick off his leash since there wasn't another soul in sight as we made our way through Old Town and towards the cathedral. To be honest, I wasn't even exactly sure where the Camino ran through the city. When I came in, I had walked too far through the park and crossed into Old Town through Acro de Santa María, which wasn't the marked route. And now I was on my way to the bike shop, which also wasn't on the main route.

We stopped in Plaza del Rey San Fernando one last time and I took a seat beside the bronze pilgrim statue just to take in the impressive cathedral one last time. The sun was just rising behind us, lighting up only the tops of the spires and the octagonal tower, leaving the rest of the stone in shadow. The parts of the cathedral the sun did reach took on a look of molten gold and it was truly a sight to behold, with no one else around to see it but myself and the street cleaner. Maverick certainly couldn't care less. He was currently chasing pigeons off the ground in the center of the plaza. They rose with a burst of squawking, disrupting the peace of the morning.

I sighed and slung his pack over my forearm again and called him back so I could take his leash and lead him over Puente de Santa María. We were the first people to arrive at the bike store. They still hadn't fully opened their doors when Maverick and I walked up, but the man that helped me yesterday came out and guided me over to a bike with a buggy hooked to it.

"What do you think, Mav? You want to ride in the buggy?"

He barely paid me any attention, clearly not under-standing what I had in mind for him.

The man unzipped the two sides to the buggy, which was really like a miniature tent on two wheels, and I pulled Maverick towards it by his leash. His paws stopped before getting in and he resisted going any further.

"It's okay," I told him. "Hup." His command to jump in didn't seem to sway him at all as he dubiously looked at the tent on wheels. I bent down and patted the inner surface of the buggy, which seemed a bit flimsy to me. "Come on. Hup up."

Finally, he hopped into the buggy…and promptly exited straight through the other side. "Maverick," I laughed. "No, you have to stay in it. Hup up." I patted the floor again, enticing him to get back in.

After a couple more attempts, where he bounced straight

through to the opposite side, we zipped one side of the buggy closed. "Come on, Mav," I pleaded. "Get in and stay in."

This time, instead of bounding into it, he tentatively raised each paw and stepped into the buggy, squishing himself into the small space. It wasn't exactly roomy, but he fit.

"See?" I told him. I was aware of the bike shop employee watching our whole experience with this and felt mildly uncomfortable, but I *had* told him it would be a trial-and-error event. "Isn't this fun?"

Maverick looked up at me, his ears pinned back in displeasure. I gave him a weak smile.

"So fun!" I tried.

He brushed past me and out of the buggy.

The employee asked if I wanted to test it out with Maverick in it while I biked. I urged Mav back into the buggy and he reluctantly followed my commands. But when I went to zip the door shut, he started to freak out like I had never seen him do before.

"Hey, hey," I soothed. "You're okay. It's fine." But he was having none of it. He burst through the door before it could be closed and sat defiantly on the sidewalk.

After another ten minutes of trying and failing to zip him closed in the buggy, I finally turned to the man, telling him this wasn't going to work. He had witnessed our failure, so at least he understood where I was coming from. I apologized profusely for having the shop go through the trouble of setting everything up for us. With a curt nod, he disappeared back into the store.

I looked down at Maverick out of the corner of my eye. He seemed to realize he was no longer being forced into the unnatural tent on wheels and his whole demeanor had relaxed, his tongue lolling out as he looked up at me happily.

"Oops," I muttered to him. "Well, there goes that idea."

By the time we finally started walking (since we would no longer be biking the Meseta) it was far later than I would have liked. I suppose I could have stayed another day in Burgos and wrapped my head around walking La Meseta, but I wasn't a city person. If I had stayed another day, I would have just continued to worry about what this section would be like. It was better to just go. Rip off the Band-Aid.

I didn't bother crossing back over the river because I knew the Camino came this way at some point. Instead, Mav and I stayed on the sidewalk closest to the river and I kept my eyes peeled for any yellow arrows or *conchas* that would denote the French Route. I finally spotted some signage for it just as we were coming up to another city park, and just like that we were back on trail. However, we didn't encounter any other pilgrims along the route until we were just leaving the city limits of Burgos when we came across a mother and daughter duo. They were enamored with the idea of walking the Camino with a dog and asked countless questions about how our journey had been going as we walked from the outskirts of the city to just before Tardajos together where we crossed the river once more.

I waved them on as Maverick and I dipped off the trail and down to the water. Maverick was thrilled to plunge into the deep pocket of the river we found ourselves at. And of course, he drank plenty because he much preferred running water to anything I poured in a dish for him. It was barely ten in the morning and the sun was already hot. We still had two more villages to pass through, which would hopefully have some shade and water fountains, before we climbed up to the Meseta.

Walking towards Rabé de las Calzadas on the paved road, we got our first glimpse of this infamous landscape. The

Meseta rose steeply out of the plains ahead of us with a rocky face that looked like it would make for a hard climb up before abruptly leveling off to a flat top. It was one thing to hear about what a plateau is in textbooks; it was another to see the very edge of one.

Rabé de las Calzadas was yet another tiny village along the Camino but it came with the last opportunity to fill up on water before Hornillos, so I made sure to top off my water bladder as we passed through. Just at the edge of town was a long, low building on the right of the trail with the most spectacular mural covering its entire side.

In various shades of blue, from the deep midnight used near the roof and for the closest mountains, to any icy shade used for mountains painted in the background, the entire façade was painted to depict a starry night above a massive lake ringed with mountains with a giant moon rising above the scene. In the center of the building there was a burst of light, the yellows and oranges bleeding out from the sun into the blue of the starry sky. Further along, the scene changed from cool blues to warm reds and yellows covering the building. More than one scene was painted on this side, with Genesis 1:31 painted in four separate languages along the top. The center image was one of two pilgrims meeting on a road through endless fields, with the fingers of God and Adam above them – the same from Michelangelo's famous "Creation of Adam" in the Sistine Chapel. Regardless of your religious affiliations, the murals were a stirring sight and gave hope for the journey through the Meseta ahead.

Weathered waymarkers pointed us along the trail, onward and upward. One had the words "Are you ready? Listen and Observe" scrawled on it. It was well-known that many found the graffiti along the Camino disheartening, but I appreciated these messages. Of course, not all the graffiti was beneficial and I was not a fan of useless scribbles or tags.

But a lot were messages of hope or encouragement for fellow pilgrims. This note, just at the beginning of La Meseta, was a good reminder that this next section had the power to be something wonderful. I knew so many pilgrims were leery of the Meseta, but it seemed the other half of veteran pilgrims had incredible experiences along this desolate stretch. I chose to take this as a reminder to be positive, and pushed on to the crest of the hill, finally looking out over what appeared to be a never-ending expanse of impressively flat land.

But there, all alone, was one singular tree. In the midst of so many grains and flat land, this one lush, green tree stood alone in the distance. There was something so simple about it that made it beautiful and something worthy of a picture.

After snapping a picture, Maverick and I ended up walking beside two ladies from Barcelona. We immediately fell into easy conversation in Spanish, chatting about all the typical introductory things along the Camino. Where we were from, what brought us to the Camino, all that normal jazz. Upon learning that one of their names was Verónica, I had to ask. "¿Viste la película *Verónica?*"

"¿La película del terror?"

"Sí, de Madrid," I confirmed. It was supposedly based on a true story from Madrid and had become one of the most popular horror movies this past year.

"Sí. Lo vi. ¿Tú viste? ¿Y no eres de España? ¿Eres de los Estados Unidos?"

This was a question I got a lot once I started speaking to others in Spanish, or in this case just being knowledgeable about some aspects of Spanish culture. People were shocked to learn I was from the United States yet I could speak a second language. They were shocked to find out I took an interest in another culture. Which says a lot about Americans and is pretty sad.

The majority of other nations are at the very least bilingual. It is commonplace to know their native language and English as well. Some know more than two languages. Yet Americans are known around the globe to speak only English. So when someone comes across an American who can actually talk to them in a different language, it is truly shocking to them.

The two women and I kept talking about *Verónica*, but eventually our conversation also veered to discuss this very topic of Americans lack of cultural knowledge. They asked about how I came to be so proficient in Spanish, and I claimed I really wasn't. I still struggled, I wasn't completely fluent, but I could definitely converse and manage myself here. I informed them that students in the US were required to take classes for a foreign language in high school, but that was about it, so most Americans didn't actually absorb the language or culture. In contrast, other nations begin teaching kids English in elementary school.

The three of us descended from the Meseta towards our final destination of the day, Hornillos, with Maverick leading the way. Just before entering town, we crossed a stream which Maverick immediately splashed into. I stayed with Verónica and her friend on the bridge, watching Mav plod through the water beneath us.

"Le encanta agua, ¿no?" her friend asked.

"Oh, sí. Es su favorita." I smiled. Maverick was digging at the clear water, attempting to paw a waterlogged stick to the surface. He shoved his muzzle under to grab the piece of wood and came up victorious.

"Qué hace?" Verónica asked, confused by his antics.

"Le encantan…" I paused. I really didn't know how to say *stick* in Spanish. But I felt comfortable enough with the two girls to ask them. "Cómo se dice *stick*?"

"Stick?" Verónica asked, mimicking my pronunciation.

"Sí, este." I grabbed the soggy stick Maverick was now presenting to me.

"Ohhh, ¡un pelo!"

"¿Pelo?" I asked. "Este es un pelo?"

"Sí, sí. *Stick*," she tried again. "Es un pelo."

"Perfecto," I smiled, happy to have acquired this new piece of vocabulary. It really was crucial when it came to living with Maverick in Spain. Forget *gracias, hola, por favor,* or *perdón*. With Maverick it was *sombras, pájeros, mariposas,* and now *pelos*. "Le encantan pelos."

Verónica and her friend laughed and then told me they were off to get a spot in the municipal albergue before it filled up. I waved them off, letting Maverick enjoy his time by the water. I hadn't put his booties on him today and he had just started to limp a bit as we were descending into Hornillos. Luckily, this was our planned stop for the night. An albergue here said they allowed dogs on their website, so I was pretty confident we would have a bed for the night.

Once Maverick was finished in the river and had dried off enough to be acceptable, we made our way the last few feet into town and found the albergue I had researched. It was one of the first things in town, so I immediately popped inside and rang the bell, waiting until a hospitalera appeared at the front desk.

"Hola, ¿quieres una cama?" she asked me with a smile.

"Sí. Pero, tengo un perro también," I informed her.

Her face immediately changed. "¿Un perro?"

"Sí. Permite perros aquí, ¿no?" It was more of just a clarification, since I actually had seen a website that listed this albergue for allowing dogs.

"No," the girl said adamantly, almost angrily. "No permitimos perros aquí."

"Pero, hay una página del web-"

"No," she cut me off again. "Lo siento, no tengo una cama para ti con el perro."

"Pues," I stuttered. "¿Es posible acampar en el jardín? Tengo una tienda." I tried. I would tent in the garden; I didn't need a bed.

"No." She didn't elaborate, just stared me down. I was so thrown off by her anger, I didn't know what to do. So instead of doing anything, I just stumbled back out into the hot sun and picked up Maverick's pack and leash in a daze.

Okay, I thought. They wouldn't allow us in. There were other places.

I stumbled up the single street that ran through town, still disoriented from how unpleasant the young woman had been, and practically ran right into Verónica and her friend again.

They must have been able to tell from my face that something was wrong because they immediately pulled me aside and started asking questions.

"Ven," Verónica said, demanding I come with them. "El albergue no tiene una cama, pero el hospitalero es muy amable."

The municipal albergue here was pretty small, so it made sense that it had already filled for the night. But maybe they had a back garden we could tent in, or would know of somewhere to tent, or had some ideas for me. I followed Verónica and her friend through the small plaza at the center of town and to the back of the albergue. Although the girls had claimed the hospitalero was kind, I wasn't getting that vibe from him. He was just as adamant that no dogs would be allowed here and he had no space. He advised that we look behind the church, that I could pitch my tent there for the night and no one would bother me.

I came back out and told Verónica the news. She smiled brightly and started around the back of the church, eager to check out where we would pitch our tent. Only…the back of the church was a concrete slope. I'm not sure where this man had thought I could pitch a tent, but it certainly wasn't here. Verónica and I stood with Maverick between us, looking down the hill that led down to a small playground behind the church.

"No es posible acampar aquí," I told her, stating the obvious.

"Pues, no es perfecto…" she hedged. I tossed her a look. "Bueno, tienes razón." I knew I was right. I just wish I wasn't. "Hay otros lugares aquí, ¿no?"

"Sí," I sighed. There were other places here, but I was just so tired. It was a hot day, I could already tell I had gotten a sunburn today, and I just wanted to lay down. I needed a nap. I couldn't believe it was just this morning we were in Burgos, back at the bike shop. It seemed like that was days ago. Plus, I was starving but I was too worried about where we would sleep to think of finding something to eat.

I told Verónica and her friend not to worry about me, that I would figure it out, and I trudged back down the road to a *casa rural*. These types of lodgings were typically more expensive, but at this point I was willing to go for anything. It was clear there was nowhere in this miniscule town that I would be able to pitch a tent. There weren't any green spaces, nothing other than concrete around us. I wasn't about to try to walk to the next town now; Maverick had started limping and it was so hot out that I would never subject us to walking at this time. So we were kind of stuck.

We made our way around the back of the *casa rural* and to what appeared to be a tiny bar. I asked the bartender if he knew where I could talk to someone about a room at the *casa rural* and he let me know that it was his house. Tentatively, I asked if he would allow me to rent a room for the night with a dog.

"Sí, claro," he said easily. "No hay un problema."

My breath whooshed out of me in a sigh of relief. If only I had come here first, I could have saved all that frustration and disappointment. The man plucked a key from a hook behind the bar and called his daughter over to lead us into the house. I handed over sixty euros, a steep price, but I didn't even care at this point. It meant we had a room out of the hot sun and could relax for the afternoon.

The man's daughter led us into the *casa rural*, which was a normal house. She showed us the upstairs, where there were two other bedrooms and a bathroom, and then left us in our downstairs bedroom. It was kind of strange, just staying in the bedroom of someone's fancy house, but so be it.

I dumped our bags in a chair in the corner and dug out my money and clipped Maverick's water dish to his leash. Then we headed back out the front door of the house and up the street to the bar in town to find some lunch. I was gone maybe an hour, probably less, and was so excited to come back and take a shower before collapsing on the nice puffy bed for a nap.

I pulled out the key the girl had given me and went to insert it into the front door of the *casa rural* when I noticed an old woman standing just inside the door shaking her head at me.

"Hola," I smiled, waiting for her to open the door for me. She just glared at me through the glass of the front door. *O-kay then...* I thought. *Bit odd.* I stepped forward to insert my key into the lock, since it was clear she wouldn't open the door for us.

"No," she barked, her voice harsh through the door.

"¿Perdón?" I asked. "Tengo una habitación aquí."

"No," she barked again.

"Lo siento, pero tengo la llave. Mi mochila está aquí. Pagué por una habitación." Clearly, she wasn't understanding the fact that I had a room here. I didn't even know who this woman was, but this was getting ridiculous. I waved the key in front of the window, proving I had the key to the place. All my stuff was in there. I had already paid.

"No. No perros aquí," she growled, still not letting me in.

"Señora, el hombre al bar permitió el perro aquí esta noche." At that, she suddenly turned on her heel and disappeared further into the house. I looked around us, confused where this formidable old woman had suddenly gone.

I finally stepped forward and inserted the key into the lock, letting myself back into the house and back to the room I had rented. Within a minute, the old woman's voice was back, accompanied by the man from the bar. I heard them coming in the back door through the kitchen and then they were at my room.

The man gave me a defeated look. "Lo siento, no puedes quedarse aquí," he told me.

"¿Cómo?" I asked. *No way.* There was no way he was stripping us of a place to stay after already allowing us in.

"Lo siento mucho, señorita. Pero, mi madre no le gusta el perro."

His mother?! *He was kicking me out because this bitch, his mother, didn't like Maverick? Was this a joke?* I took a deep breath. "Señor. Ya te pagué." He had to understand reason. I already paid for this room. There had to be some rule about not being able to take it away.

"Ven conmigo. Tengo tu dinero." He didn't leave it up for discussion. Instead, he turned and walked from the room and straight out the back door, heading for his bar. He left me no choice but to follow him. This was insane.

I gathered up our stuff and stomped out of the room. The grandma was standing in the kitchen with a smug smile. I glared at her as we passed, in my head commanding Maverick to growl at her. By the time I made it out to the bar, the man had sixty euros out of the cash register and passed them over to me across the bar top.

"Señor…" I tried one last time, not above pleading. He just shook his head.

"Lo siento."

"Pero…" I looked at the back lawn behind me. It was huge and was covered with soft, lush green grass. "¿Puedo acampar en el jardín con mi tienda?" He had to let me tent here. It was the *perfect* place for a tent. And we wouldn't be near grandma in the house. No one would be bothered.

"Lo siento. No puedes."

My jaw dropped, but no words came out. I seriously couldn't believe my luck. Now I was just angry. And annoyed. And tired and dirty and sunburnt. I stormed out of their backyard but then quickly lost steam. I had nowhere to storm *to*. I had nowhere to go. I collapsed on the sidewalk just outside the *casa rural* and Maverick whined from above me, clearly not understanding what was going on.

"Lay down," I snapped at him, even though I knew it wasn't fair that I was taking out my anger on him. He laid down beside me on a sidewalk with a groan.

An older gentleman came out from the bar of the *casa rural*. "What happened?" he asked.

An American, clearly not understanding the altercation between me and the owner. I forced back the tears that had been threatening to break free and looked up at him. "We're not allowed to stay there anymore," I sighed.

"But I saw you earlier. You paid for a room," the man said.

"Yeah. Apparently the guy's mom doesn't like dogs. So he kicked me out."

"Can he do that?"

"I guess so," I sighed. There wasn't much more I could do.

"Is there somewhere else you could try?" he asked.

"I've tried them all. The place I thought would allow dogs said they didn't, even though it's on a website that they do."

"I would show them that. They have to let you in."

I had been staring straight ahead at the empty, dusty road, but at this I looked back up at the man. "You have a point," I said.

"It's worth a try." With that, he turned and headed back to the backyard bar of the *casa rural*. I pulled out my phone and with a few clicks, I had found the website that said the albergue allowed dogs. There it was, clear as day, a little picture of a dog walking with the words "allowed" above it. Triumphantly, I stood from the sidewalk and marched the couple of steps down the street and back to the first albergue with Maverick sullenly tagging along by my side.

I barely made it in the door before the hospitalera behind the front desk sighed. "No permitimos perros, señorita."

"Espere," I pleaded, urging her to just wait a minute and give me a chance. "Mire por favor."

I held out my phone to her, asking her to just look at the information. She took it from me and scrolled, as if ensuring it was indeed their albergue listed.

"Es falso. No sé porque. Nunca permitimos perros. Adiós, señorita." She handed my phone back to me and swiftly disappeared out back again.

I wanted to scream. She had just read information and then said, *too bad, no*.

I left the albergue, made it about halfway up the street, and ran out of steam from my anger. I was just sad. I was defeated. And I couldn't go any further right now. My legs gave out beneath me and I collapsed down on the sidewalk again, this time across from the small, town plaza. I didn't have the mental power to think of a solution right now. At least this side of the sidewalk was in shade now.

"Settle in, Maverick," I mumbled to him, tying his leash to a strap of my backpack and positioning it behind me on the sidewalk. "We're taking a nap."

I laid back, the rock of the sidewalk warm from the sun against my back. My eyes fluttered closed, partly to sleep, partly to keep the tears at bay. I wanted to cry. I wanted my mom. I wanted to not be in this mess. My hand reached out and found Maverick's fur and I buried my fingers into it, holding onto the one solid thing in my life.

I was woken by the voices of two girls. My eyes cracked open to see them sitting on the other side of Maverick on the sidewalk. "Oh," one of them said. "You really were sleeping."

I blinked myself awake and pushed myself to sitting, noticing that the shadows now covered the entire street and stretched into the plaza across from us. "Yeah, I guess I was."

"Sorry to disturb you. We just wanted to see the dog."

"That's okay," I mumbled groggily. I wasn't feeling very rested and the reality of our situation hadn't changed.

"What's his name?" one of the girls asked.

"Maverick."

"He's so cute," one said, scratching him between the shoulder blades.

"Why were you sleeping out here?" the other asked.

"Because nowhere will let us in."

"Because of the dog?" I nodded. "That sucks. Does it happen a lot?" I nodded again, clearly not feeling very chatty, but they didn't catch the hint.

"What are you going to do?"

I shrugged. "Keep walking, I suppose."

"Really? To the next town?"

"Or somewhere that I can pitch my tent, yeah."

"Well, good luck. Thanks for letting us pet your dog."

They turned and headed back towards the municipal albergue, leaving me alone with Maverick.

I had no energy. The idea of walking again sounded horrible. But there was really nothing else to do, so I finally stood and gathered our packs up again.

At the very end of the village, a woman was sitting at a table on the right side of the road alone. "Hola, pilgrim," she smiled. She had a distinct Irish accent and a warm smile.

"Hola," I replied in kind, but couldn't put much feeling behind it.

"Are you okay?" she asked, instantly curious from my tone.

I paused in the street, looking forward to where we had to walk, then back to the woman at the table. "Yeah, I'm fine."

"What's wrong?"

"Just a tough day," I shrugged, not sure why I was admitting anything to her.

"Come sit with me. What happened?" And for some reason, despite my normal social anxiety, I actually took her up on her offer. I dropped Maverick's pack and my own and folded myself down into the chair across from her. Then I told her of everything that had happened today, from the bike shop debacle, to the albergue I had researched, to the concrete hill behind the church, the grandma, and then even going back to the other albergue again. She listened to it all without interrupting, just nodding or raising her eyebrows in disbelief at times.

"So I guess we're just going to keep walking now. I don't know what else to do," I finished.

"You have to stay here for the night. This is my café. We're going to have live music tonight. You have to at least stay and come for dinner and music. Maverick will be allowed in. I don't mind at all. Please, say you'll at least stay until after dinner."

"I don't know…"

"Oh, please? I have a garden, too. It came with the property, but I never use it. You could pitch your tent there if you want? I just have to ask my husband if it's okay. Would you do that? And then you and Maverick can come for dinner."

"Well…if you're really okay with us pitching the tent there…"

"Oh, yes! I insist! Just let me ask my husband. Wait here, I'll get you a scone to have while you wait." Before I could protest, she was off, dipping into her café and coming back out with a warm scone and jam and then disappearing again to presumably find her husband.

Within a few minutes, she was leading me across the street and through an empty lot to a walled garden. She unlocked the metal door set in the wall and led us inside. It wasn't much of a garden. The ground was hard and burnt, and there wasn't a lick of shade, but it would have to do. I certainly couldn't turn down this woman's hospitality.

"Make yourself at home. Dinner will be at seven. We'll have a place for you." She smiled and then slipped back out the door, heading back to her café.

I found a patch of the "garden" that didn't seem to have too much burnt grass on it, so it wouldn't poke through the bottom of my tent and stab me in the night, and I got to work setting up for the night. It was still so hot, but at least once the tent was erected it offered a little shade when I crawled inside. Of course, then I didn't get any benefits of a slight breeze, and the air was hot and stale, but that was better than roasting under the sun. Maverick chose to press himself up against the concrete wall in what little shade was there and I didn't fight him to join me in the tent. I drifted into an uneasy sleep out of pure exhaustion until it was almost time for dinner.

When we arrived at the café, it was packed with pilgrims. Someone was singing at the front of the room and each table was full, but the owner found me as soon as I came in the door. "You made it! Come with me, I saved a place for you."

I followed behind her, squeezing between the tables and through people who were up and about in the room to the far side just beneath the windows that opened out to the street. She introduced me to the table of pilgrims, none of whom I recognized, and then disappeared back into the crowd. My mind wasn't completely present, even though the food was delicious, and the table of pilgrims was friendly. The music for the night consisted of various singers and then Sarah with her cello as well. The traveling group of musicians from Asia were also part of the act, but at that point I was ready for bed and could barely keep my eyes open. Just as I was about to slip out of the main room and into the hall that led to the door, the owner caught up to me again.

"Colby! Wait a moment."

I paused with Maverick in the hallway, turning to her with as much of a smile as I could manage at this point in the day. "What's up?" I asked.

"So I just got some bad news." She made a face and I braced myself for yet another blow. "My gardener was just here. I let him know you were staying the night in the garden and he said you can't do that. I guess he saw a snake in the garden this morning and he doesn't want you to get bitten."

I sighed out in relief. He was just being overcautious. I was safe. A little garter snake didn't bother me. I chuckled, "Well, as long as it isn't poisonous, I'm sure it's fine."

She grimaced. "It is."

"What?" I gasped.

"It's a poisonous snake. You really can't stay there tonight.

I'm so sorry, I had no idea when I said you could go in there. I never would have let you if I knew. Please, be very careful when you pack up your things."

"I…uhm…yeah. Thank you for letting me know."

"I'm *so* sorry."

I knew she meant it and I didn't want her to feel bad. She had been so kind to me. So I just nodded and plastered on a smile and waved as Maverick and I went back to the garden. It was finally starting to get dark, but the air was still warm.

I dropped my pack outside of the garden and tied Maverick's leash to a strap. "Stay here," I sighed, not wanting him anywhere near the poisonous snake. Then I flicked on the flashlight of my phone and made my way back to pack up my tent. I couldn't stop the tears any longer. I was alone and exhausted and I just wanted my mom. I dialed her number and put her on speaker as I went to work breaking down the tent. I could barely speak through my tears, and she had nothing to say that could help me.

"Colb, you've got to calm down. You just have to breathe. Get your stuff as quickly as you can and get out of there and then we'll figure it out," she told me. I sniffled and cried some more. "It's going to be okay. You'll figure something out. You always figure something out. Did you finish packing the tent yet?"

"No!" I practically shouted through my tears.

I was a horrible person. My mom was being nothing but nice and yet I just kept snapping at her and sobbing. She was helpless, an ocean away, and I shouldn't have called. It would only make her worry more about me.

She stayed silent as I finished gathering my stuff up, but it was nice to know she was on the other side of the phone. Finally, I had everything together and met up with Maverick in the empty lot across from the garden.

"Are you out of the garden?" she asked me over the phone.

"Yes," I sighed, punctuated by a sob.

"I wish I could do something."

"You can't. I've got to go." I didn't, but I also didn't want to still be on the phone. I didn't know what to do, but I needed to move from this dusty lot. I was tired of sitting in the dirt crying. I stood, grabbing my gear but not even pulling it over my shoulder as I wandered back to the main street. The sun had fully set, twilight was fading to a dark night. I didn't have the slightest clue what to do now. Walk in the dark? Sit in the middle of the street?

I crossed to the opposite side of the street with Maverick and took a seat on one of the stoops to what looked like a very dark house. Maybe no one was home and they wouldn't mind a pilgrim sitting on their steps. At least I had made progress, right? This was definitely an improvement from sitting in the dirt. Maverick laid on the top step beside me and rested his head in my lap.

"¿Señorita?" The man and a little boy who had been playing ball in the empty street were suddenly standing directly in front of me. "¿Estás bien?"

I gulped down my tears and tried to brush them away before they could see them. "Ah, sí. Estoy bien," I lied. I was so far from okay.

"Pero, estás llorando," the little boy pointed out. He wasn't wrong, but I thought I had hid my tears better.

"Está bien. Estoy bien," I tried to convince them.

The boy's dad studied me for a second longer but I couldn't meet his eyes. It was a pretty bad lie and if I looked him in the eye it would be clear I had spent the past hour crying. "Eres la chica que mi esposa permitió acampar en el jardín, ¿no?" I nodded without looking up. "Un momento." He called his son to him and then disappeared down the street again. I really should start walking. I had napped enough today. Maybe I could just walk through the night with my headlamp.

Before I could stand, the owner of the café was back, this time with the man who had to be her husband and their son in tow.

"Oh, Colby," she soothed as soon as she saw me. She had such a motherly demeanor I couldn't help it, my tears started all over again. "Come on. Come with me. You're staying with us tonight." She wouldn't allow me to argue, just picked up Maverick's leash and my pack from the ground beside me and began walking. I followed blindly. "My sister just moved out last week, so it actually works out perfectly. The room isn't exactly cleaned out, but there's a bed. And you can shower if you want. We have hot water."

"You don't have to do this," I sniffled as I followed her up the steps of a place just next to the café, one stoop over from where I had been sitting. Her husband and son stayed outside, the little boy already toddling after his basketball again.

"Yes, I do. It's no problem at all." She pointed out a bathroom to the right at the bottom of a staircase and then led me up the stairs and into a small bedroom. "Here we are. Make yourself at home. I've got to get back to the café but please, let me know if you need anything at all. It'll all be okay."

She rubbed my arm, gave Maverick a pat on the head, and then she was gone.

I collapsed on the bed in a heap. I was disgusting, I knew, but I didn't have the energy to shower. I didn't even have the energy to get under the covers. Within a second, Maverick had hopped up on the bed and weaseled his way under my arm so he was the little spoon, my face pressed into his fur.

"I love you, Maverick," I croaked.

Better

Day Eighteen: Hornillos to Castrojeriz

24.3 km ~ 34,266 steps

July 7ᵗʰ

    I woke up far before the sun. Everything was quiet in the house around us and I would never dream of disturbing the family who had been so kind to take us in. I scrawled a note on a page in my journal and ripped it out, leaving it behind on the pillow with twenty euros. It would never be enough for the kindness they had shown me, but it was something. I never even knew the woman's name and she had taken me in. They say there are angels on this trek. I had definitely found one of them.

    I laced up my boots outside, on the same stoop I had been sobbing on the night before, and then we were off. There wasn't another soul in sight. The café was silent as we passed, the music and laughter that had been pouring out of the open windows late last night long forgotten. We climbed back up onto the Meseta in darkness and paused just as the terrain leveled out again. The endless wheat fields stretched out before us in the light of dawn that was just beginning. I dropped Maverick's pack to the dirt and pulled out a sack of his food, dumping it into his pop-up dish. I hadn't dared to feed him back at the house; it would have been far too noisy.

An older gentleman crested the hill and Maverick paused in eating his breakfast to glance at him briefly. "Buen Camino," he murmured softly. If the whole morning hadn't been so still and quiet, I wouldn't have been able to hear him at all.

"Buen Camino," I whispered back, not wanting to upset the peace of the morning. He continued on without pause, the crunch of gravel under his boots soon fading away. A strip of pink was just becoming visible over the wheat as Maverick finished eating, glowing over the valley we had just climbed out of. I collapsed his bowl and tucked it back into his pack, then double checked the straps on his booties now that there was enough light to see without a flashlight.

It wasn't yet daybreak, but the sky was light enough to see that the path we now walked on split down the center of two fields. On our left was dark green grass; on the right was golden wheat. It made an interesting contrast of light and dark in the dim light of morning. The only sound for the next hour of walking was the clip-clop of Maverick's booties along the gravel and the crunch beneath my own feet. He wasn't limping at all this morning, and I attributed that completely to the bright red boots. He had become accustomed to them at this point in the journey, not even changing his gait when I first put them on in the morning. He stood completely still, like a good soldier, any time I put them on his feet, too.

A Cross of Saint James marked our descent into San Bol, with its recognizable pointed lower limb and embellished top pieces. It stood atop a pole driven into a heap of rock on the side of the trail with nothing else in sight. We dipped down to San Bol, which really wasn't a village so much as a single albergue set back off the trail to the left, and then climbed back up to regain the Meseta.

The sun had finally broken free of the horizon to shine its light on the trail. The morning rays made for a beautiful golden glow, stretching our shadows out in front of us as we continued towards Hontanas. I knew the guidebook said the Meseta suddenly falls away to reveal this little town, but it really did appear out of nowhere. We were walking along this impressively flat stretch of land, with more barrenness spread out before us, and suddenly it just dropped off. And there, in the sudden dip, I could see just the top of the church. Getting closer, the town was revealed at the bottom of a steep, rocky slope. Aged waymarkers pointed pilgrims down and deposited us onto the main, paved road through the village.

Maverick and I passed by the chapel, the first thing I had been able to see of the town, and turned left into a café with a spacious patio area before we even made it to the heart of the village. I dropped our bags in a chair and bent down to unstrap Mav from his booties, giving him time to air out his paws before we continued on. Then I dipped inside, where it looked like they were still in the midst of all their opening duties, to grab a croissant and an iced tea for breakfast.

I pushed through the door back out to the patio, my hands full of breakfast, and saw a girl at the far edge of the patio looking positively terrified. She was as far from me as possible and when she saw me heading towards the table with Maverick, she let out a little shriek and sprinted the rest of the way to the door of the café, apron in hand. I glanced from Maverick to the far corner of the patio where the girl just was a second ago, then back to Maverick with my mouth half open in surprise. *What the heck was that?*

I was still looking between the two spots when a burst of laughter interrupted my confusion. I looked up toward the road where the laugh came from and spotted Tobiah. He had been at the same table as me last night in the Green Leaf Café for dinner and music, but of course I hadn't been all that chatty then. As I looked at him, I couldn't help but laugh, too. It was ridiculous.

"She really was that scared of Maverick?" I asked.

Tobiah shrugged and shook his head in amusement, then came off the road to sit with us at our table briefly. Maverick, oblivious to the stir he had created, continued licking his paws, only sparing Tobiah a glance as he sat down with us. He didn't stay long, instead continuing on with a friendly smile and a wave. Not another soul passed by while we had breakfast or while I was strapping Maverick back into his booties. It seemed we really were ahead of the crowd this morning.

Never wanting to pass up the opportunity to fill up on water, Mav and I set off in search of one of the many fountains this town was said to have. However, I could only seem to find one. I pulled out one of Maverick's water bladders from his pack and unscrewed the cap to fill it up. That's when I noticed the sign. Water from this fountain was not potable. AKA – don't drink it. So that was super helpful. It's fine, though. We each still had plenty of water.

Except...I realized something was dripping on my leg before we were even out of Hontanas. I opened up Maverick's bag, which I was carrying on my forearm, to see I never fully screwed the cap back on. And it was now empty. And the entire bag was soaked.

Nice. So not only was that water fountain useless, I had now spilled all the water we *did* have.

I took a deep breath and let it out slowly. This was fine. All was fine. It was only…ten kilometers until Castrojeriz. Lovely. Ten kilometers with little water.

Well, there was nothing to do but keep walking. So off we went, past the crudely sketched mural depicting the Camino Francés that told us there were 457 kilometers left to go to Santiago. We crossed over the road and started back along the dirt path. It wasn't even ten minutes before I heard footsteps coming up behind us and turned to see Tobiah.

"Oh, hey, you were still in Hontanas?" I asked as he caught up to me.. Mav swiveled his head back to see who I was talking to, then turned to hurry back to say hi to our friend.

"Yeah, I grabbed breakfast at another bar," he said in that easy Australian accent. I told him about my recent stupidity with the water bladder, and he offered a bottle of his own.

"Oh, no, we're fine for now. Just a stupid thing."

It was already growing warm, even though it was barely nine in the morning. Of course, this section of trail wasn't exactly helpful in keeping out of the heat. The landscape was mostly short, scrubby bushes with not much shade.

Maverick let out a frustrated-sounding bark and I craned my neck to see what had him in a mood. He was trying to grab onto Tobiah's walking stick each time he lifted it forward. "Mav!" I laughed, unable to keep the amusement out of my scolding. His head was tilted at an awkward angle, doing his best to wrap his jaws around the stick. "That's not your stick!"

Tobiah laughed and shooed him away, but Maverick was not one to be easily deterred. "Maverick, no!" I said more adamantly. I found another stick on the side of the trail and tried to tempt him with it. He went all of ten steps before he determined that Tobiah's walking stick was much better and returned to figure out a way to steal it from his hand.

"I'm so sorry," I groaned as Tobiah did his best to avoid Maverick's teeth trying to clamp down on the piece of wood. "Here, this might help." I unzipped Mav's pack as we kept walking, digging around through the still-wet contents until I located the pink ball I bought for Mav in Estella. "Maverick," I called, waving the ball in the air. His eyes immediately lit up and his focus was gone from the stick in an instant. I chucked the ball out ahead of us, and he was off at a sprint.

"Wow, that works," Tobiah laughed.

"I'm so sorry," I repeated emphatically. It wasn't often pilgrims had wooden walking sticks. Many used the new, lightweight trekking poles. However, each time we'd come across a pilgrim who did use a wooden walking stick, Maverick thought it was somehow for him. "He hasn't quite learned to differentiate between sticks for people and sticks for him."

Tobiah smiled, then tossed the ball for Mav who had just dropped it in front of his feet. "How old is he, anyway?"

"He'll be one on the thirteenth actually."

"You mean he's not even a year old yet?" he asked in shock. I shook my head with a smile.

Our conversation switched easily from Maverick, to what we do for work, to what led us to the Camino, and Tobiah's previous Camino as well. I found it easy to talk to him. Of course, it was easy to talk to anyone along the Camino, as I've mentioned before, but there was something different about Tobiah. Like he really was my friend before the Camino, or that he'd be my friend for long after. What I had originally thought was going to be a terrible ten kilometers with no water from Hontanas to Castrojeriz flew by with Tobiah walking with us.

We passed through the ruins of *Convento de San Antón*, a

massive structure built in the fourteenth century that spanned the road here but was really nothing more than a shell. I had originally planned to stop to rest when we got to San Antón, but there was nothing much to rest for. Of course, Tobiah and I took some time to admire the massive stone structure as we walked through it, with its arches that were easily two stories high. On the right, as we passed through, I pointed out the alcoves cut into the stone and told Tobiah that bread used to be left there for pilgrims in the Middle Ages.

Somehow, our conversation turned from the kindness given to pilgrims of old to the kindness we found now. I told him about our night last night and the Camino Angel that allowed us to stay in her house.

"Has it been hard walking with Maverick?" he asked.

I tipped my head from side to side, weighing out his question. "Honestly? Yeah. For the most part, it has been hard. The people of Spain really aren't all that welcoming to dogs, I'm finding. We've come across quite a few people who are scared, like that girl this morning who worked at the café. But a lot of the time, it just seems like they hate dogs."

"That's too bad."

I called Maverick back to us as we broke from the scrubby landscape we'd been walking in for the past hour and approached a road where a beat-up car was parked. An old man was sitting in the driver's seat with all sorts of tiny trinkets and stamps laid out over the dash and piled in the passenger seat.

"¡Hola, peregrinos!" he called out as we got closer. Upon seeing Maverick, a massive grin overtook his face. "¡Y un perro! ¡Qué fantástico! ¿Quieren una silla?"

"Ah, sí. Gracias, señor," I answered for the both of us, looking at Tobiah.

The man took our credentials, and Maverick's of course,

and popped stamps into each of them for us. Then he reached over and grabbed one of the trinkets that were littering his passenger seat. "Esto es para el perro," he said seriously. "Esto es un Tau. Es la cruz del San Antón, el santo patrón de animales. Es muy popular aquí," he told me.

"Oh, wow," I said, thoroughly touched by his gesture. "Muchas gracias, señor."

"Y para ti, también." He reached back into his car and pulled out another wooden cross, which looked more like a T than a cross, and handed it to me through the window with two strings to attach them.

Tobiah took a Tau of his own when the man offered it as I was bending down to tie Maverick's to the hook on his collar. "No hay muchos perros en el Camino," the old man told me.

I scoffed and straightened up. *Not many* was an understatement. There were no dogs on the Camino. "Sí, yo sé."

"Pues, Buen Camino a usted y su perro. Y Buen Camino a ti, también," he directed to Tobiah, who nodded with a smile as we turned onto the main road that led into Castrojeriz.

We hadn't gone very far before Tobiah interrupted the silence. "What was he saying?"

"He was really excited to see Maverick," I murmured, thinking about how we had just been discussing how unwelcoming Spaniards were to dogs just before we reached the man's car. "The Tau, the cross he gave us? It's the cross of San Antón."

"Like the convent we just went through?"

"Yeah. I guess San Antón was the patron saint of animals."

"Huh, interesting," Tobiah muttered before falling silent beside me.

The town of Castrojeriz was easily seen before us on the

hill with its ruins perched at the very top, but I wasn't
focusing on that. I was too focused on the strange coinci-
dence we had just come across. This was a pilgrimage after
all. And it was almost as if God had seen me struggling, had
seen me disheartened over the reception Maverick had been
receiving in Spain, and put that man in our path right when
we needed it most. The patron saint of animals. Pretty spectacular timing, if you asked me.

What was it that sign had said just as we started the
Meseta? Are you ready? Listen and observe?

Duly noted, I thought.

The Camino branched off the main road, blissfully
dipping into the shade of some trees, and wound its way
uphill to the town of Castrojeriz now. Once in town, it
followed a relatively flat street, with many streets that dipped
downhill branching off to the left. Maverick, in his tired
state, continued to drop his pink ball, which of course went
rolling down each of these side streets. After the third time of
me and Tobiah chasing after it down the hill like those
English people who chase the wheel of cheese down a hill, I
finally called it quits.

"You don't want to carry it?" I panted at Maverick after
trudging back up the most recent street to meet up with him
and Tobiah. "You don't get to have it then." I snatched up his
pack again and shoved the ball inside. Tobiah quirked a smile
and raised one brow at me, handing Maverick's leash back
over.

We walked up the street just a bit further and found a
water fountain with a bench conveniently placed beside it. I
practically skipped over to it to fill up Maverick's bowl for
him and fill my own water while Tobiah sat and took out a
guidebook. Once I was done filling, I took a seat beside him
and started untying my laces, toeing off each of my boots.

Because that's what you did on the Camino. You freed your feet from your shoes every chance you get.

As we were resting, the guy I met just before Agés who had been walking from Le Puy came up to us. He actually was at the Green Leaf last night, too and sat at the same table as Tobiah and I, so he nodded hello to both of us and stooped to fill his water. "Are you done for the day?" he asked as he took a pull from his water bottle.

"Uhm, I think so. I had planned to stop here. I just got here earlier than I expected." I wasn't even sure if it was eleven yet. I was feeling pretty good. And Maverick hadn't limped at all today. But knowing my luck, if I tried to go any further, something awful would happen. It was best to quit while we were ahead. Plus, there was supposed to be an albergue that allowed dogs here in Castrojeriz. Granted, I wasn't too keen on believing any of the things I had researched beforehand anymore, but it certainly didn't hurt to at least ask before moving on.

"Are you going to keep walking today?" I asked Tobiah, turning my head to look at him next to me on the bench.

"Yeah. I think I'll stop at Itero today," he said, glancing down at his guidebook. I frowned. Not that it really mattered, Camino friends walked on, stayed behind, passed you at all different times. Mav and I were definitely used to going it alone. But it made me kind of sad that Tobiah wouldn't be staying in the same town as us tonight.

"Just Itero? I'm heading on to Boadilla today. Plenty of time to make it there," the Bostonian bragged.

I looked up with a skeptical face. Then again, the man had been walking for over forty days now. Plus, I knew from the little bit of time I had spent walking with him how quickly he traveled. I had no doubt he'd reach Boadilla, a full nineteen kilometers away from here, in no time.

"Boadilla?" Tobiah laughed. "I don't know, mate. Seems a bit too far for me. You sure you're staying?" he asked me.

"Yeah, but I'll walk with you guys through town," I offered. I slipped my feet into my Chacos, officially calling it for the day, and tied my boots to my pack before slinging it back on. The four of us continued up the main road, which was still heading slightly uphill, until the narrow street opened up to the *plaza mayor*. On the right, a shop that looked like a mix of a sandwich store and a Camino gear shop was tucked beside the post office, town hall, and other cafés on a shady terrace with large stone pillars. Tobiah continued on here, and I bid him a melancholy "Buen Camino." Our friend from Boston popped in to get a sandwich but didn't even stay to eat it, ever eager to keep walking.

Maverick and I were officially on our own again. It was just after eleven, so none of the albergues were open yet and the sun was officially high in the sky and incredibly hot. I brought Maverick into the shade of the terrace and sat down on the stone with my back against one of the massive pillars. I could have been like a normal human and sat in one of the benches here, but it was kind of nice to have the cool stone of the floor beneath me. I reached forward and got to work freeing Maverick from his booties.

An old man smiled at us from a bench just a little ways down the terrace, and a toddler came up to tug on Maverick's fur. I waved his dad off when he tried to apologize. Maverick didn't mind at all. In fact, he just laid his head down on his paws while the little boy, who couldn't be much older than one, twisted and turned to get a better look at Mav's collar and the new Tau hanging from it. I twisted it around to show him the carved wooden charm.

"Es un Tau, ¿no?" I asked with a smile. The little boy

grinned back in that way only babies had and reached out a pudgy hand to play with it. The dad looked on with a smile, as did the old man on the bench. There was something nice about this. It was almost as if I was just another character in this sleepy village, like I belonged here with them. I hadn't felt that sort of feeling since Belorado.

After spending the afternoon people watching on the terrace, I made my way back down the main road to the albergue Ultreia and hesitantly walked inside. I wasn't expecting a warm welcome, certainly not after the ordeal that was yesterday. But the old man behind the front desk was positively thrilled to have me. He urged Maverick and I in, then directed us to a bottom bunk in the albergue. Never once did he lay down any rules for Maverick or try to force him to stay in the garden, which was spacious and sported a wonderful wash station for washing clothes, a stone pool to soak your feet in, and tables with large umbrellas. I could have lived in that garden alone and been content. But instead, we had a bed for the night, a warm welcome in every room but the kitchen for Maverick, and an invitation for a tour of the cellars (which apparently led all the way to the castle) later tonight.

I was in a state of pure shock as I sank down on our bunk in the large bunkroom. Other than Uterga, this was our first time in an albergue in a large room with many pilgrims. To say I was excited, especially after last night, would be an understatement. I had to sit for a while after the hospitalero left us just to take it all in. Then I headed out to the wash station to clean my disgusting clothes and hang them on the lines in the garden. Mav kept me company, trotting along the narrow hall of the albergue and out to the garden, where he chased the shadows of birds back and forth across the lush grass. I strung up my clothes along the line and made my back inside. After ensuring Maverick was pleased with the lion stuffed animal I had got him in Burgos and clipping his leash around the leg of my bunk, I lay back for a well-deserved nap.

When I woke up, more pilgrims were bustling all over the albergue so I decided to slip out of their way and go find something to eat. Just before the plaza, I ran into Verónica and her friend sitting at a table of one of the restaurants. They immediately waved me over and urged me to eat with them. I easily took them up on the offer, happy to see them again. It was hard to believe I had just met them yesterday. It seemed like whole days had passed since I parted ways with them after going to the *casa rural* because so much had happened after that.

I had just finished explaining everything from last night to them when out of nowhere, a violent storm rolled in. One moment, it was sunny and warm, the next the skies were black and hail was pelting down on us. Actual balls of ice were falling from the Spanish sky. A waitress sprinted out to grab our plates and usher us inside, but I had Maverick so I couldn't just barge into a crowded bar. I waved Verónica and her friend inside, saying I was fine as I attempted to dodge the hail as best I could. Which, quite frankly, was impossible. Mav and I did our best to squeeze under the skinny overhang of the restaurant's roof.

The girls hadn't been inside for more than a minute when the waitress poked her head out to usher Maverick and I inside. Apparently, ice balls falling from the sky warranted an exception to the "no dogs inside a restaurant" policy. Whatever the reason, I was happy to follow her into a rustic bar and join my friends at a table to finish our meal.

By the time we left, it was as if no storm had ever happened. The sky was blue, the street had already begun to dry from the blazing sun, and I could barely see the leftover hail. I had never seen anything like it before.

I parted ways with Verónica and her friend with a hug. "Si vienen a Barcelona después del Camino, necesitan quedarse conmigo," she reminded me with a smile. I had told them Maverick and I would be going to Barcelona once we finished the Camino in Finisterre and she demanded that I tell her once I was there.

I laughed. "Claro. Muchas gracias." She kissed both my cheeks and waved goodbye as they headed the opposite way from my albergue.

Once back at the albergue, the communal dinner was just wrapping up and the pilgrims who were staying the night were lingering in the dining room, trickling back to the dormitory, or getting ready to head down to the cellar with the hospitalero. Those still in the dining room urged Maverick and I to join them. I tried to hang back by the doorway, not wanting to push my luck with a dog in the room where everyone ate, but so many of them wanted to ask about Mav and our journey so far. Luckily, I was spared from the limelight when the hospitalero came in and announced it was time for the tour. He asked if Maverick could stay in the dormitory while we headed down, so I tied him back to the post of my bunk and gave him his stuffed lion again. Then I rushed back to join the small group heading down to the cellar.

According to the hospitalero, the tunnels we were now in were constructed centuries ago. In fact, some of the stones that formed the walls were from the first century, placed there by the Romans. The large space just beneath the albergue was a spectacular wine cellar, which our gracious hospitalero allowed us to sample some of, but what was really interesting was the tunnel. Apparently, it used to run from the castle at the top of Castrojeriz to the church at the bottom of the town. It had been designed as an escape route for emergency situations centuries ago. Over time, parts had caved in, but they were excavating it bit by bit to this day. To walk the length of that tunnel when it was open would have been astounding.

Originally, when I had been looking through my guidebook before actually embarking on the Camino, I had planned to take the walk up to the castle when I stayed in town here. The thing about those sorts of plans is that you don't realize just how tired you are by the end of the day on the Camino. There was no way I was trekking up to that castle now. Sure, I said I could have kept walking earlier today, but once I decided I was staying here tonight? That was it. These feet were done walking for the day. Kudos to any pilgrims who actually tacked on the extra hike up to the castle. I'm sure it was super interesting and the views must have been delightful. This pilgrim, however, really enjoyed her afternoon nap.

After the tour of the cellar, my eyelids were starting to droop again. I thanked the hospitalero once more for the kindness he'd shown to me and Maverick, and the interesting tour, and headed to the now-dark dormitory. Maverick had managed to completely destroy his stuffed lion in the half hour he had been left alone. The animal's poor head was hanging on by just a single strand of rope.

"Really? Really, Freak Reek?" I asked him, dangling the misshapen piece of cloth and rope. "You really had to rip him to shreds already?"

He looked up at me, eager for me to throw it. As if I would do that in a crowded albergue. "No," I whispered to him, conscious of the fact that some pilgrims were already sleeping. "It's night time. Go to sleep, goon." I shoved the remains of Lion in his pack and slipped into my sleeping bag on my bunk.

With one last forlorn look at his pack where Lion just disappeared to, he recognized it was time for bed and awkwardly shimmied his way onto the bunk and on top of my sleeping bag. The metal creaked noisily under his weight as he laid his head on my chest.

I stoked the top of his head, rubbing his velvet-soft ears. "Night, kiddo. Love you."

Until the Sunrise

Day Nineteen: Castrojeriz to Boadilla

20.5 km ~ 28,908 steps

July 8th

It was cold this morning as Mav and I slipped out of the albergue as silently as we could. Since we never got the opportunity to stay in an albergue like that, I definitely didn't want to be one of those pilgrims who got up super early and made a ton of noise that woke everyone else up.

I gently pulled the door shut behind us as we made it out to the dark street and slipped my feet into my boots, but didn't bother lacing them up yet. Mav and I continued on to the plaza, where I stopped by the fountain. There, I dished out his breakfast for him to eat while I filled up our waters for the day. Then I slipped his booties on his paws, tied my own boots, and shrugged on my pack. The clip of my chest strap seemed to echo in the empty plaza this morning as I buckled it.

We left the village of Castrojeriz behind while it was still dark and the only thing I could see were the orbs of Maverick's eyes when he looked back at me in the beam of my flashlight. Once it finally started to lighten up, we'd already made it almost five kilometers and the climb back up to the Meseta loomed ahead of us. There were puddles in the gravel path we followed and once the sky was light enough to see, I could tell there were dark clouds all around us. It must have rained again last night, but the stiff breeze this morning was doing its best to push the storm away.

We veered left and began the steep climb up. As a former athlete and current coach for lacrosse, the first thing I could think about this slope was that it would absolutely *suck* to run hill sprints on this. I wondered if Castrojeriz had a soccer team or something that had to run this for practices. That would be brutal. Because I was dying and I wasn't even close to running. I was more like a snail heading up this hill. Maverick kept looking back at me as if I was wasting his precious time.

"Listen, your mom only has two legs and is clearly very out of shape," I gasped at him as I caught up to him at a curve in the trail. His tongue lolled out of his mouth in a doggy smile. I put my hands on my hips and sucked in more of the crisp morning air while the breeze attempted to shove me off balance. Clouds billowed by us, so close it felt like I could reach up and touch them now that we were so much higher than we had been just minutes before. The sun still hadn't broken the horizon behind us, but there was a golden hue just above the haze. A swath of flat farmland stretched between where we were perched now and the tiny hill in the distance that was Castrojeriz. I could just barely make out the silhouette of the castle from here. Maverick whined, urging me to keep walking and stop sight-seeing.

I took the turn after him that curved around this massive

hill and continued angling upward. Birds were starting to wake up all around us, adding their morning songs to the otherwise quiet air. Finally, we reached the flat top of La Meseta.

"Oh…my god," I huffed out to Maverick. "Thank God we didn't keep walking yesterday. This would have killed me." Mav looked at me with what appeared to be a pitying glance, then went off to sniff around the rest area up ahead. "Right then," I groaned. "Onward."

Though this flat top of the Meseta seemed to stretch out endlessly, within minutes the ground fell away again to reveal a patchwork of green, brown, and golden fields below. The view was stunning under the blue light of dawn. But if we were being brutally honest, it seemed a bit rude to make us hoof it up that steep incline just to drop back down again within minutes. *Ah, well*, I thought. *Such is Camino life.*

After pausing for a mini photo shoot with Mav (thanks to my handy-dandy tripod and remote clicker for my phone) we started down the steep, cement road on this side. It grew darker once we had dropped back down to flat ground since the Meseta was now blocking the rising sun behind us. But the wind had died down and most of the clouds had drifted away. Just a light breeze was rustling the wheat beside us as we walked along the empty trail. Sunflowers dotted the edge of the path, little spots of sunshine among the tall grasses and wheat.

We saw our first pilgrims of the day right as we were about to enter Itero. They looked to be just starting out from the old albergue here that had been built in the thirteenth century. We waved hello to them and crossed over the river Pisuerga, which formed the boundary of the province of Palencia. In ages past, this river used to be the boundary between the kingdoms of Castilla and León, which now are joined as the one autonomous region.

We followed the river into the almost industrial-like town of Itero. I was excited to stop for breakfast, since it was just after eight and we had already been walking for over two hours. However, not a single thing was open. It was like a ghost town. Sure, there were bars and cafés in town, but not one of them showed any signs of life. My stomach growled sadly as I trudged along the empty roads.

It wasn't even that early. Where was everyone? Hadn't pilgrims stayed in this town last night? Where was Tobiah? Where was the *food*? Maverick looked up at me and I realized I must have let out a pathetic little sigh without even knowing it. I really needed to start keeping food in my pack for these times I wasn't able to find breakfast.

So instead of stopping for a rest and food in Itero, Maverick and I walked on. The nice shade we had found by the river on the way into town was a thing of the past. We were back to the open farm country, with not a tree in sight for hope of shade, and the sun was beating down. It was clear Maverick was starting to get hot, too. When he smelled water, he immediately perked up.

"Oh, no," I called ahead to him. "*Hier*." I could see he was torn, wanting to run towards the water, but then also having a direct command from me. He planted his bootie-covered paws on the dirt track and waited for me to catch up. I immediately bent down and grabbed hold of his leash. This wasn't just a river we were crossing on a thin metal bridge. This was a man made canal, one of the many in the region that allowed for such a dry place to be thriving farmland.

We came up to it and Maverick tugged to get closer, but I held tight to his leash. The cement sides of the canal sloped steeply into the murky water. I knew if Maverick tried to get close enough to reach the water to drink, he would inevitably slip in. I didn't think I would know any way to get him out of that short of having to go in myself and then getting myself out would be a nightmare. Plus, the water looked like it was moving deceptively fast. And it was so dirty, there was no way to tell how deep it was, or what was within it. The whole thing screamed of disaster if Maverick had tried to cool down in that water.

"Sorry, Bud," I told him as he looked longingly at the stream as we crossed over to the other side and hesitated to keep walking away from it. "That's not for swimming."

I refastened his leash into a loop that hung around his neck once I was sure we were far enough away from the canal that he wouldn't be tempted to turn back. His head drooped dejectedly. *I feel that, kid*, I thought. The wheat fields that had been so beautiful in the morning sun were becoming quite monotonous. My stomach was growling now, and I was definitely feeling the fatigue of walking without eating anything for so long. Plus, I could feel the sun burning into every inch of my exposed skin.

"Hey, Reek." He perked up at my voice, walking directly beside me now in the shade of my shadow. "Want to play I Spy?" His booties clip-clopped along the gravel in response. "Okay, cool. I'll start. I spy with my little eye…something green." I waited in silence for his answer. He paused just ahead of me and looked back. "Oh, did you say that tree way over there? Yeah. You're right. Okay, your turn." I waited again.

"Something brown?" I asked him. "Is it that hay bale? Mmm, yeah good one. I spy…something green." Maverick's bootie kicked ahead a pebble. "Did you say the bush? Yup. You got it."

And so went our time across the Meseta. Safe to say I was pretty close to losing it by the time we reached a small rise that had a few trees to rest under. Maverick was just beginning to look like he was limping, and I was exhausted myself, so we collapsed into the dirt together.

Mav had already lapped up a whole bowl of water when a young Spanish guy we had been bumping into now and again since Burgos turned off the trail to come sit in the shade with us. I felt bad because I still didn't even know his name and I had actually had a handful of conversations with him. Although, they always left me a little confused. I thought my Spanish was pretty good but whenever I talked with him, he always used words I didn't know. Regardless, it was nice to see a friendly face, if only for a little while. He ended up walking on while Maverick and I continued to lounge in the shade.

When we did eventually pull ourselves back onto the trail, the last four kilometers into Boadilla were grueling. I'd developed my first pain of the Camino: an odd pain from my ankle up the inside of my calf that hurt if I turned my foot inward at all. Which, granted, I shouldn't be doing, but still. The sun continued to be absolutely brutal and Maverick was so hot and tired that he was basically stepping on my heels the whole way into Boadilla. Plus, there were all these little black flies around and they kept buzzing straight into my eyeballs. I know I shouldn't complain, because there had been no bugs the entire journey so far, but they were really starting to annoy me. So when Boadilla finally did come into view, I had never been happier.

We stopped at the very first bar I saw as we came into town and I rushed inside to get some food. The woman running the place was from London and she was easily one of the nicest people I'd met on this journey so far. She told me that she had six Belgian Shepherds and before I could even respond, she was offering scraps of food for me to bring out to Maverick and filling up a pail of water.

"A friend of mine runs the albergue in town and I'm sure he'll let you stay with the dog. But if he doesn't just come back here. I have no problem at all with you guys staying here if you're okay with it. I know it's not an albergue or anything, but it would be a place to stay. Just let me know," she told me with a smile.

I spent the next couple hours hanging out on her patio, eating a *tortilla Española* and drinking iced tea. When it was late enough that the albergue would be open, I bid the woman farewell and walked the rest of the way into town, easily finding the albergue she said her friend ran. The man there was just as welcoming. He offered me either a room in their adjacent hotel or a mattress in the lobby of the albergue. He said he couldn't let us stay in the actual bunkroom, just in case some pilgrims were adverse to dogs, but he had no problem letting us use the spacious common area just outside the two bunkrooms.

"Es perfecto," I agreed happily. Being able to be in a regular albergue again? Surrounded by fellow pilgrims? I'd take it. Plus, this place was amazing. There was a giant mural on one wall as you came into the garden, which was full of blooming flowers and lush grass, and a kidney-shaped swimming pool in the middle of it all. It was like a real oasis in the middle of the dry farmland we had been walking through all day.

The hospitalero took down my information, then stamped both Maverick and my credentials, and led us back across the garden to a separate building. The common area of the albergue was a long, narrow room, with doors to two separate bunk rooms on the back wall and couches on each side of the room. The man directed us to the left side, where he pulled out a thin mattress and laid it on the ground. "¿Está bien?" he asked doubtfully.

"Sí, sí," I replied emphatically. It might not seem like much to him, but it was an upgrade from the sidewalk we napped on in Hornillos or the windy churchyard in Monjardín. "Muchas gracias, señor," I told him for what had to be the fiftieth time. He accepted the thanks and pointed out the two separate rooms available to shower in and wash my clothes, told me when the communal dinner would be, and returned to check in other weary pilgrims.

I had already showered, washed my clothes, and was grabbing a snack at the bar here when Trish pulled up on her bike. "Colby!" she called out happily. "You're staying here for the night?"

"Oh my gosh, hi!" I waved her into the garden.

"Woah, this is great!" she admired, taking in the pool that was quickly filling up with pilgrims. "Do you think they'll let me stay with my bike? Or are they already full?"

"I don't see why they wouldn't let you stay with the bike. The hospitalero is right through there if you want me to go check in with you," I added, nodding towards the office area. Maverick happily greeted our friend and trotted inside with us to talk with the hospitalero. Apparently, while I had been busy getting all my ducks in a row for the day, the albergue had filled up. But there were still a few rooms open across the street at their hotel.

"Could I still come hang out in the garden here with you if I stay there?" Trish asked me. I translated the question for the hospitalero, who claimed that was perfectly acceptable. "Then yeah, I'll take a room there!"

Trish squared away her payment, got her credential stamped, and I relayed the information of where she can store her bike for the night. "I'll meet you back at the pool in a little bit!" she called with a wave, heading back out of the garden and to the hotel. Back outside, I tied Maverick to a shady tree with his long leash and took a spot on the side of the pool with my feet dangling in the water while he chased butterflies.

"Oh my gosh, is that Maverick?" A voice asked from near the entrance to the garden. I looked up from where I had been relaxing to see a girl coming towards us with another young man in tow. I was certain I had never seen them before, but somehow they knew who Maverick was.

"Uhm, yeah, it is," I said from my spot by the pool. I pulled my feet out of the water so I could stand and walked over to Maverick. He was oblivious to the new attention, too intent on trying to catch a shadow as it raced across the grass.

"Do you mind if I pet him?" the girl asked, finally reaching us. "I was wondering when we were going to catch up to you guys." I must have been giving her a blank look because she quickly realized I had no idea who she was. "Oh! I follow him on Instagram! I knew we weren't too far behind you from the pictures he posts each day."

"Oh," I laughed. "Well, okay then." I'm not exactly sure what else to say to that. What *is* the proper protocol for meeting people who follow your dog's Instagram account? It had happened to us once before on this trek, when I had been sitting on the side of the trail just after Puente la Reina. A young man from China had come up to us and asked if he could take our picture because he followed Maverick on Instagram. That had been the day I cried more than I walked, so I really hadn't bothered to make much of an answer but sure enough, that night Maverick had been tagged in a new post on the social media platform. I hadn't a clue what the man had written, because the caption was all in Chinese characters, but I was going to assume it was something nice that had nothing to do with my puffy eyes from all my tears that day.

Luckily for my socially awkward self, I didn't have to worry too much about the interaction with this young couple. They were completely enamored with Maverick and Maverick only, who couldn't care less about them. "Sorry," I said to them. "It's nothing personal. He just really doesn't care for other people. Unless you've got a ball or a stick, he's pretty uninterested."

"That's okay." The girl smiled and straightened up from crouching down in an attempt to pet him. "I'm just happy we were finally able to run into you guys. It's been so fun to follow along with your journey!"

"Oh, thanks," I mumbled awkwardly. We exchanged typical Camino pleasantries, and then they walked away to go hop in the pool. I chose to take a seat with my back against the tree Maverick was tied to, happy to sit back and watch everyone else. Trish had arrived and was sitting with her feet dangling in the water, talking with a few men who were sitting on the opposite ledge of the pool. She seemed to have regained her groove again since I had last seen her in Burgos. It was nice to see her having a good time here.

It wasn't too long before the previously cloudless sky suddenly grew dark and out of nowhere, a torrential rain started. It was almost exactly like last night in Castrojeriz, only this time the storm came without the hail. And instead of crowding into a bar, everyone crowded into the common area outside the bunkrooms on the opposite side of the room from where my gear and little mattress were set up.

There was a group of young people staying here tonight that were clearly extremely close. They'd been walking together all the way from Saint Jean Pied de Port and while they were entertaining to listen to, it was clear they'd established their Camino Family and were not looking for any new members. It reminded me of the group I ran into near Cirueña.

"Uhm, Colby?" Another pilgrim came over and interrupted a story the little group was telling. I looked up from my spot on the tile floor. "Your bed is...floating," the girl told me.

"My bed? Is…floating?" I asked her, sure I'd heard her wrong.

"Uh, yeah. You're sleeping on the mattress over there, right?" she asked. I unfolded myself from my spot on the floor and walked towards our bed for the night…only, the other half of the common area had become a series of rivers across the tiles.

"Oh, yikes," I breathed.

"Yeah…" The girl agreed, looking between me and the mattress that was indeed floating in a few inches of water. On the plus side, I had put our packs on top of the mattress earlier so they looked relatively dry.

I braced my hands on my hips and tilted my head to one side, assessing the situation, then I laughed. "This would happen to me."

"I'm sorry?" the girl asked, clearly not getting what was funny about this situation. A few of the other pilgrims had also come over to see how bad it really was.

"It could be worse," I told them.

"Do you want me to get the hospitalero?" someone asked.

"Nah," I waded forward and plucked out our packs. "I'll tell him at dinner. For now, I'm just going to move my stuff."

The group of us having the communal dinner here had to wait out the storm a little while longer, then sprinted across the garden to the main building and the dining room there. By the time we were finished with the delicious home cooked meal, the storm was long gone and the sun was already coming back out to dry everything. The hospitalero followed us back over to the bunk room to assess the damage and could not apologize enough for my soaked sleeping arrangements. I laughed it off and tried to assure him that it was really fine; no damage was done. Really, the floor was already dry, but I could tell he still felt horrible. He found another mattress for me, this one not sopping wet, and apologized another hundred times before I was finally able to usher him out of the room. If only everyone we encountered along this journey was as nice as he was.

Reek and I set up our bed again, in a drier corner, and then headed out to explore the little town on an evening walk. Most pilgrims just stayed in their albergues for the entire afternoon, socializing with others or reading or napping, but if I wasn't too exhausted I had come to enjoy taking evening strolls around each town we stayed in. Most of them were so small it only took a few minutes to explore the whole town, not just the parts we saw along the Camino's path. It also gave me a chance to decompress for the day and a time to call my mom and check in. These evening walks just before bed tended to be around the same time she was getting out of work back home, so it worked out well to fill her in then. Plus, Maverick was always up for a stroll even if we had walked for miles already.

Tonight, I told her about the beautiful sunrise we had seen this morning and the sunflowers (because she loves sunflowers), and about the town with nothing open for breakfast, and then we laughed about my flooded bed. She told me about how her day at work went and what was going on back home, as if I wasn't half a world away all alone with just my dog.

"I wish you were here," I told her for what had to be the millionth time this trip.

"Me too," she said, and I could tell she was smiling through the phone.

"Alright, I guess I'm gonna go to bed now," I said, even though the sun was still high in the sky here. I swore it never set before ten at night.

"Make sure it isn't floating again," she laughed.

Don't

Day Twenty: Boadilla to Carrión de Los Condes

33.1 km ~ 46,588 steps

July 9th

The darkness of this morning was almost suffocating. I'm not sure why it seemed so much darker than any of the other mornings we'd started before sunrise, but it really did. Boadilla was quiet as we left town and trudged through the black farmland towards the canal. I kept Maverick on his short leash just in case he snuck towards the water without me being able to see him. Luckily, by the time we were walking along Canal de Castilla, the horizon was ablaze with a deep orange strip that was reflecting off the still waters beside us.

Our first stop of the day came barely five kilometers from Boadilla in the industrial town of Frómista. It definitely boasted more accommodations than Boadilla had, which explained why it had been listed as the end of a stage, but I was happy we had spent the night in the town before. This place felt more like a city and less like the quaint, Spanish villages we'd come to know and love along the Camino. However, I was infinitely grateful that it did indeed have plenty of cafés to stop at for a bite of breakfast.

The trail was already busy, with plenty of pilgrims who stayed the night here grabbing breakfast before hitting the trail. There were also a few familiar faces trickling in from Boadilla, too. Unfortunately, today's stretch didn't look all that promising. From Frómista on to Población de Campos, the Camino stayed right beside the busy road on what was referred to as "sendas." Apparently, these were supposed to be a great infrastructure of the Camino, giving pilgrims a dirt path beside the road rather than just the shoulder of the highway. Regardless, it still meant we were walking on a hard, gravel sidewalk essentially, with no shade in sight.

On the plus side, there was an option to take a more scenic route as we left Población de Campos, which would eventually go past a river, so I was looking forward to getting to that point. I stopped for a brief bathroom break in town before Maverick and I followed the flow of pilgrims along the trail. The guidebook instructed us to stay right just before the stone bridge over the river outside of Población de Campos in order to take this optional route, and I was just about to do so when a man stepped into my path from the edge of the bridge. He wasn't exactly well-kempt, but I held back any judgment and pulled Maverick closer to me, since he was still on the leash.

"Perdón," I said, averting my eyes from a sort of tube that was protruding from his neck. His breath wheezed in and out as if he was on a ventilator and while it shouldn't have bothered me at all, it was a bit unnerving.

"No puede pasar," he croaked in a grating voice.

I lifted my eyebrows in a mix of amusement and exasperation, still averting my gaze from his face. *Did he really just say that? You cannot pass? What is this, Lord of the Rings?* "Lo siento, señor, pero vamos por la ruta alternativa del Camino."

"No," he croaked again. "El Camino es así." He pointed me over the bridge where the two other pilgrims we had been behind were walking further away from us.

"Sí, pero hay una ruta alternativa del río y quiero andar esa ruta para mi perro."

"Camino es así." He gestured again to the road route, his breathing apparatus wheezing aggressively.

I gritted my teeth to avoid snapping back at him. I realized I was clearly not going to get anywhere with him, so I made to just step around him, but he moved to block my path. "Señor," I snapped, taking a step back because he was suddenly in my personal space. So much for not snapping. I wasn't able to get another word out because he suddenly had my shoulder in one of his hands and was spinning me towards the main route of the Camino. I ripped myself out of his grasp, not even registering if any other words came out of his mouth, and took off across the bridge. I couldn't believe he just grabbed me. I couldn't believe he wouldn't let me go on the alternate route. Who the heck *was* this man?

But I was more shaken than angry, and I found myself glancing over my shoulder to ensure that he somehow wasn't following me. I was sure I'd be able to tell if he was from the wheezing of his breath and that tube, but still, I was thrown off. I practically ran up the main Camino route until I was only a couple steps behind the pair of girls who had passed by earlier.

"Sorry," I gasped out to them once I was close enough.

"Are you okay?" one of them asked.

"Yeah, fine, just…sketched out." They looked to me for more. "That man by the bridge, did you notice him at all?"

"Not really, why?" the other said.

"He said I couldn't go on the alternate route. Kept trying to make me come this way. And then he grabbed me."

"He grabbed you?!" she asked in outrage.

"Yeah, I'm fine, it's fine, just strange is all."

They both looked about as alarmed as I felt when he grabbed me and made room between them for Maverick and me to walk. "Well, you're welcome to walk with us. That's not right. Should we tell someone?"

"I mean, who would we tell? I'm not going to call the police on him just because he freaked me out." They seemed doubtful, but it was nice to know that people who I had never met before would have my back. He obviously couldn't have been too dangerous, because I had full confidence in Maverick's ability to protect me and judge the people we encountered and he hadn't reacted to the man at all. Regardless, the whole encounter had been strange.

Mav and I walked the rest of the day surrounded by other pilgrims, but never stayed with anyone for too long. It was quite the uninspiring stretch of Camino, being basically a sidewalk the entire time. The only saving grace was that there were plenty of little villages along the route, making it so there was at least a little change in scenery and a chance for some shade and fresh water every couple of kilometers.

By the time we reached Villalcálzar de Sirga, I was eager to just be done for the day. Although I could see the church from the road with its interesting circular window, I decided against turning up the side road to visit town. I had passed through four other towns at that point directly along the route, and Carrión was only five kilometers further, so I chose to just stay on the *senda* and bypass Villalcálzar. I would regret that decision later, when I actually looked at the guidebook again and saw that the church was a "must-see" of the Camino and the town was home to one of the more famous pilgrim statues along The Way. At that moment, though, I was too bored by this stretch next to the busy road to care all that much.

"Hey, Pilgrim!" I heard a voice call out from the road beside me just after the turn off for town.

I looked up and smiled as I saw Trish bike into view on the road beside us. "Well look who it is," I joked. "The bicigrina."

There was always some contention between the biking pilgrims and walking pilgrims, though I'd never fallen into any animosity relating to it. Of course, when you're sweaty and exhausted on the dusty path and the bikers come up behind you with their happy little bell and zip right by, it was a bit disheartening. "Buen Camino" always seemed to come out as more of a grumble from the walking pilgrims to the biking pilgrims. But of course, Trish was no true bibigrina.

She hopped off her bike and walked it over to the *senda* where I had been walking. "How's your day been?" she asked, reaching out to bop Maverick on the head after he came running back to us to show her his stick. If nothing else, today showed me how well-trained he was. For the majority of the day, even though we'd been right next to a highway of sorts, he hadn't been on the leash. He stayed on the *senda*, his booties clip-clopping away, always within a few yards of me and always checking in with me.

"Meh," I answered honestly. "I meant to take the river route today, so this has been kind of sucky. How's the foot?" I asked her.

"Not too bad. The bike definitely helps. Although, it really does hurt your ass. I even got the nicest seat cushion, but it's not helping too much. What happened with the river route?"

I laughed at her honesty. Never one to hold back, this one. Then I relayed the run-in with the sketchy man by the bridge and what had brought us to this roadside route. "But we're almost there."

"Well, I'm glad you're okay. That guy sounds like a creep. You're lucky he didn't do anything else. I take it you're staying in Carrión de los Condes, then?"

"I figure we have to. There's nothing else for another seventeen kilometers after that. We'll start as early as possible and get that out of the way before it gets unbearably hot. That's gonna be a rough stretch."

"Yeah, I'll be happy to be on the bike for that." She grinned at me sheepishly. "Do you know where you're staying tonight?"

"Not yet," I admitted. "I planned to call every place in the guidebook until someone allows dogs. And if not...well, I'll figure something out."

We walked for a while longer together, Trish pushing her bike beside me while we chatted comfortably. Eventually, though, her foot started bothering her and I urged her back onto the bike. There were only a couple more kilometers until Carrión. I would be there soon enough.

"Meet for lunch when you get into town?" she asked.

"That would be perfect."

She agreed to text me when she got there and found a good place to eat, then wheeled her bike back onto the shoulder of the highway and mounted it with a slight wince.

"Damn seat," she grumbled, but immediately slapped a smile back on her face. "See ya in a bit!" And then she was gone, buzzing away down the slight incline into town.

Mav and I passed through the outskirts of town, first by the monastery and a museum, and then to a busy intersection just before what appeared to be Old Town. I was paused beside a bar to check the text Trish had sent me with directions on how to get to the café she had chosen for lunch when I heard my name called. Maverick turned to the sound of the voice as well. I scanned the patio of the bar until I found Tobiah lounging on a bench of what appeared to be a bus stop here.

"Hey! How are you?" I eagerly headed over to join him.

"I'm alright," he said in that rich Australian accent, but something seemed off. "How's the pup been doing?"

"He's good, we're good. What are you doing over here?" I asked, looking around at what I was now sure was a bus stop.

"I'm all done. I'm gonna grab the next bus that's heading to León and then get the train to Barcelona from there and head home."

"Home?" I asked, stupidly repeating what he just said. I heard him just fine, I just wasn't ready to believe he was leaving the Camino.

"Yeah, I spent the night throwing up. I'm just not feeling well and my head's just not in it."

"Oh jeez, I'm so sorry. Are you sure you should leave, though? What if-"

I didn't get a chance to finish my thought though because a group of Asian pilgrims had completely surrounded me and Maverick at that point. "Do you mind if we take his picture?"

"Can we pet him?"

"What's his name?"

"Are you walking the Camino with him?"

"How old is he?"

"What kind of dog is he?"

I blinked rapidly, turning from Tobiah who just chuckled weakly, back to the group who had descended on us. "Uhm…yeah, sure. His name's Maverick."

There was only so much I could take of all the attention, though, so after a few minutes I tried to make my escape. "I'm so sorry, but I'm actually late to meet a friend." It wasn't even a lie. "It was nice meeting you." *That* might have been a bit of a lie, but I had to get out.

"Tobiah, I–"

"Go," he cut me off, waving a hand good-naturedly. "My bus will be here soon anyway."

I hesitated, not sure what to say. "Are you sure?"

"Go meet your friend. And Buen Camino." He smiled and I returned it, but it felt weak.

I turned down the sidewalk and made my way to the restaurant Trish had sent me. She was seated at a table on the sidewalk and I made my way over to the empty chair across from her, pouring out some water for Maverick in his dish and picking up the menu.

We chatted over our pasta and I came to accept this was most likely the last time I would see Trish. She would pass me tomorrow on the bike and then be far ahead. In a day or two, she would be in León where she'd meet up with Margie again and they would walk the rest of the way to Santiago together.

"Do you ever try Booking.com?" Trish asked as I pulled out my guidebook after we had finished eating and began looking up the different albergues here in town.

"I haven't, no," I admitted. I hung up yet another call after trying one more of the numbers listed in the guidebook and getting told they did not accept dogs.

"You should check on there. I think you can check off an option for pet friendly."

She helped me weed through the rest of the places in town to stay and then I finally succumbed to her suggestion. Maybe it wasn't very "pilgrim" of me, but I needed a place to stay tonight. There was no option to walk on to the next town today. The next closest town was seventeen kilometers away.

"There's one place that allows dogs, but it's kind of expensive," I told her.

"Does it look nice?" she asked.

"Yeah…"

"So splurge. You guys definitely deserve it."

I wavered for a moment longer and then clicked down on the "reserve" option for fifty euros. It was outside of the main part of town, just over the river by the San Zoilo monastery. Trish and I parted ways with a hug and a Buen Camino and I walked off in search of the random place I had found.

Maverick and I made our way slowly through Old Town, taking in the sights of the bustling area with its narrow streets and busy shops. We crossed over the river on the bridge out of town and I followed the map on my phone that led us to…a neighborhood? I looked up and down the street around us. This didn't seem right. These seemed like actual homes of citizens of Carrión, not anywhere someone would stay.

"Hola, peregrina," a voice called out to my left. Two men were smiling at me from a sidewalk. "¿Estás perdida? Los albergues están por allí." One gestured back over the bridge and to Old Town helpfully and I could tell they were both genuinely concerned and wanted to help a wayward pilgrim. I crossed the street over to them and figured I would ask their advice. Maybe they knew of this place I was trying to find.

"No estoy perdida," I informed them. At least, I didn't *think* I was lost. "Estoy buscando por este lugar." I lifted my phone to show them the place in question.

"¡Ah! Sí, yo lo sé. Es en esta calle. Ven." With a smile, he led me just a couple blocks down the street and pointed me to an inconspicuous door, looking just like any of the other well-kept townhouses in this neighborhood. "Aquí. Buen Camino, señorita."

"Muchas gracias, señor." I waved goodbye and slipped into the building and into a beautiful, modern entryway. Signs directed me to the lobby upstairs and I hesitantly made my way up, feeling way too dirty for a place such as this. But the woman at the front desk in the office didn't bat an eye at my appearance. She just confirmed my booking and led me and Maverick back out the door and down the street to yet another house. Once inside, I had to fight to keep my jaw from dropping. We had apparently rented an entire condo for a night. Not only did it have a full, modern kitchen and a living room, there was a massive skylight over the king-sized bed that made the whole space sunny and welcoming. But the best part? The bathroom. It was easily the size of my entire bedroom back home, with the centerpiece being a jacuzzi tub that could sit four.

I wasn't one for baths, but even I couldn't pass up this opportunity. Equipped with a waterfall feature, bubbles, and even an underwater lighting system, this tub was by far the fanciest one I had ever seen. I had thought this place was expensive when I booked it but I was really starting to think they should charge more. I would easily pay fifty euros just for the chance to use this tub. Is this why so many people like to relax in a hot bath? Because I was certainly beginning to understand the allure of it.

"Mmm, Maverick?" I sighed happily, sinking down in the lounge-chair that was molded into the tub. He perked his head up from his spot on the bathmat beside me. "Thanks for being with me. If it wasn't for you being so difficult, I'd be in an albergue with thirty other pilgrims right now."

Only Love

Day Twenty-One: Carrión de los Condes to Terradillos de los Templarios

27.5 km ~ 38,797 steps

July 10th

When I woke, there was no light filtering through the giant skylight above me. The sun wouldn't be up for at least another hour. I rolled over and checked my phone. Since there was such a time difference, I was used to having messages from people back in the States when I woke up in the morning. The only notification was a Facebook message from Tobiah. After going for a walk around town last night and exploring down by the river with Maverick, I still hadn't been able to stop thinking about Tobiah and how he said he was leaving the Camino.

So I had looked him up on Facebook. Surely, there weren't all that many people with the name Tobiah. Lucky for me, that logic was sound, and it hadn't been hard to find his profile and send him a message just to make sure he had arrived in León safely. I had done my best to convince him to stay on the Camino and just take a few days to rest in León, but it seemed my attempts had failed. I clicked out of the message he had sent saying he was indeed flying home and went to work gathering my gear from our spacious apartment.

I probably could have set out earlier this morning, knowing how long this stretch was going to be with no stops and little shade, but I was never all that great at waking up when I meant to. So we slipped out of our apartment and onto the road around six this morning. The fancy hotel where we ate dinner last night was dark as we passed by it this morning. I smiled, remembering how they had made an exception for me to eat out on the patio with Maverick even though it had been closed for the night. Even though the other guests on the indoor patio had been tourists used to luxury, they had all taken an interest in Maverick and many had come out to sit by us and chat while we ate our meal.

We skirted by the quiet, imposing façade in the dark and out through the last of the half ancient, half modern city. The last structure of town was a run-down gas station with one car running in the lot. I called Maverick over to me quietly. Not that he actually *was* much of a guard dog, but at least he looked like one. He was still a big baby, but other people didn't know that. I spied the outline of another pilgrim a little way ahead of us and hurried to catch up. Safety in numbers, and all that. I slowed my steps as I came up behind him, not wanting to look like a weirdo, and fell into step with him.

"Buen Camino," I murmured with a smile, not wanting to speak too loudly in the early morning.

"Buen Camino," he returned happily. He had a lined, weather-beaten face that lit up in a grin when he saw us. "He has boots!" he exclaimed as Maverick thumped along ahead of us in the dim light.

I chuckled. It had easily become pilgrims' favorite thing about Maverick. Inevitably, everyone who came across us had to ask about the boots. "Yeah. His paws get irritated on the gravel of the paths, so the boots protect him from that."

"Amazing!"

And just like that, the old man and I fell into easy conversation that lasted the next seventeen kilometers. I learned he was from Taiwan and got a history lesson that lasted he first five kilometers we walked. All that he told me, I had been ignorant of before. There unfortunately aren't many classes in school that cover the history of Southeast Asia and their different colonizers.

I was grateful for the company and the interesting conversation. I had always loved history and I loved learning new things, so it was a welcome distraction from the monotonous route today. About halfway through the stretch from Carrión to Calzadilla de la Cueza, there was a little mobile café that the man wanted to stop at for breakfast and coffee. I agreed to stop with him, even though I had a muffin tucked away in my pack and hated coffee. We had already walked ten kilometers and it didn't hurt to take a break.

While he headed to the little food truck in this grove to order his food and coffee, I took a seat in the dust in front of Maverick and pulled off his booties. He licked at his paw pads and between his toes once they were free of the confines of the heavy fabric. I took one of his front paws into my lap and began to massage the pads of it for him while he licked at the other.

The man from Taiwan laughed from above me and I saw that he was sitting at the picnic table now, sipping his coffee. "When you have a son, I think you will love him more than the son," he chuckled, gesturing to Maverick as I moved on to the next paw to massage.

"He is my son!" I laughed. It was true. Maverick was like my little child, and this journey had certainly served to solidify that.

A woman from France named Rose was also at this pitstop and had been watching from the table next to us. I first ran into her when she was dancing to the music in the plaza in Santo Domingo. Since then, I've bumped into her a few times. She was staying in the same albergue in Boadilla with us as well. Every time I've seen her, she's had a smile on her face. Like she couldn't be any more content than she was right at that moment. Like she was soaking up every single thing the Camino had to offer. Her energy was contagious.

"You know, I had a daughter," she said now, and I turned to look at her. Her smile was dimmer now, nostalgic. "I lost her when she was three." I gasped in shock, not at all expecting something so tragic. "The bond between you and Maverick? It reminds me of what I had with my daughter."

Tears sprang to my eyes and I was at a loss for words. She turned her gaze from Maverick to me, and I could see tears in her eyes as well.

"We can all see it. The connection you have. It is inspiring. You can feel the love he has for you. And the love you have for him. We all can feel it. It reminds me of the love I had for my daughter. It brings me joy. Seeing you and Maverick brings us all joy."

I swallowed hard. No words could ever fit this moment. The woman blinked a few times, clearing her eyes of the tears and the memories of her past and when she spoke again it held just as much meaning, but it was lighter. "Every time I see him, I am happy. He brings so much love and joy to all of us pilgrims. You know we all love you two. If you need anything, we will all be there for you."

"Thank you," I croaked. "So much."

As we all made to leave the café and head back out on the trail, I strapped Maverick back into his booties and slung my pack over my shoulders. I made to grab his pack from the table, but the woman beat me to it. "Let me carry it. We should all pitch in to help with Maverick. He brings us all joy; it is only fair that we all carry his stuff."

I laughed. "No way. You don't need to do that."

"I want to," she insisted.

"It's really okay. That's heavy. Plus, it stinks," I admitted. It was true, when Maverick was wearing it and would lay in mud puddles or he would get wet, the pack inevitably began to smell.

"I do not mind." She smiled. "Just for a little while."

In the end, I agreed to let her carry it for a little while, but I made sure to take it back within the first couple kilometers we were back on the road. She walked a bit ahead of us, humming along to the music in her headphones while Maverick chased the butterflies ahead of her and the Taiwanese man and I brought up the rear of our little group. I smiled to myself as we walked. Maverick snapped his jaws on thin air, yet again missing a butterfly, and pilgrims just ahead of him laughed at his attempts. The sun was shining, but it hadn't begun to soak into my skin yet. The company was great, and I was on a high from our luxurious night before. What was supposed to be a dreaded section of desolate land and no stops had somehow become one of our greatest times on the Camino thus far.

When we did finally reach Calzadilla de la Cueza, there seemed to be a celebratory feel among the pilgrims who were there. Many were lounging at outdoor tables, or on benches with bare feet, while others were grabbing food from the cafés just off the trail. My little group and I took up residence at one of the outdoor tables and then headed inside to order some well-deserved lunch. Before long, both my companions were ready to keep walking. There were only another six or so kilometers to the end of the stage, so I wasn't in a rush to leave now.

I waved goodbye to my friends and Maverick and I settled deeper into our resting spot at a shady café table, enjoying the time to stretch our feet outside of our boots. I took out my journal and wrote about our morning while I picked at my *tortilla Española*. After about an hour of resting, I stood and tapped Maverick's leg so he would lift his paw for me. I slipped each of his feet into their bright red booties, then laced up my own boots.

"Looks like it's just you and me, Freak. Last six kilometers of that day! Are you excited?" Maverick whined in agreement before tugging me forward to the trail. I laughed and allowed him to pull me through the tiny town and back out to farmland.

We hadn't been alone for more than a few steps before someone called out to us. I turned back and saw it was the young Spanish boy that I could never seem to remember the name of. "¡Hola!" I called back in greeting, waiting for him to catch up. Since we were out of town again, I looped Maverick's leash back around his neck and clipped it for safe-keeping. He trotted ahead of us on the trail as the boy and I kept pace behind him.

"¿Cómo estás?" he asked. I filled him in on our morning and how great it had been, then asked about his own morning. I realized that we had never really had a long conversation before now. We always seemed to bump into each other and then be on our separate ways. This was the first time we had ever walked any distance together.

"¿De dónde eres?" I finally asked him. It was normally one of the first things you asked another pilgrim, where they were from, but our brief chats had never gotten that far.

He told me the name of a small town I had never heard of before.

"¿Y dondé es eso?" I asked, trying to figure out where that town might be.

"Oh, es en el norte de Italia."

"¿Italia?" I clarified, fighting to keep my jaw from dropping.

"Sí, Italia," he laughed. "¿Por qué?"

"¡Pensé que eras de España!" I said incredulously. This whole time I had been referring to him as "that Spanish boy" in my head and he wasn't even from *Spain*?

"¿Verdad? ¡Qué fantástico! No pienso que mi español fue tan bueno."

"No, es muy bueno," I assured him.

"Muchas veces, no recuerdo las palabras en español, entonces uso palabras italianas."

I turned to him in shock and laughed out loud. "¡Claro!" No wonder I hadn't been able to understand so many of the words he used when we had talked in the past. It wasn't that they were Spanish words I had never heard before; they were Italian words! "Pensé que esas palabras eran palabras españolas que no sabía."

The boy laughed at that. "No, son palabras italianas. Lo siento."

We walked on to Ledigos together in easy conversation. I had grown more comfortable using Spanish in the past weeks, but I felt so much freer talking to him because I knew he wasn't perfect, either. It took about an hour, but I was able to pick out which Italian words he used now and would call him on it. Sometimes I would help him remember the word he wanted, sometimes he'd help me with the word I was thinking of. By the time we were in Ledigos, I was picking up on how he still pronounced his 'H' in words and the different lilt of Italian that managed to sneak in.

"¿Paras aquí?" I asked, motioning with my head to a bar in town.

"No. Voy a continuar a Terradillos ahora."

"Bueno, hasta luego." I waved my goodbye and dropped my pack on a table before heading inside to use the bathroom. I wasn't necessarily hungry, so I bought an ice cream just so I didn't feel bad for only using their bathroom and headed back out to Maverick. We sat for a moment and I chatted with some locals about doing the Camino *con el perro*, and then we were on our way again.

It wasn't far from Ledigos to Terradillos de los Templarios, and despite running right alongside the busy highway, the path was hidden between two hedgerows of brilliant yellow flowers. They were so thick you couldn't even see the cars zipping by just on the other side. Naturally, I had to pause for a photo op. I plucked my little tripod from the pocket on the side of my bag and set it up with my phone, dropping our packs to the dust beside the setup. Of course, when we saw other pilgrims approaching in the distance, I hastily packed up my things. Listen, I may be a weirdo and have my own picture-taking ways, but I didn't need others to judge them.

As I went to sling on my bag again, I noticed my sun hat dangling from the same spot it was in every other day. I think I had only worn it one day on this entire journey... Day One. Knowing my mom would be disappointed if I didn't at least *pretend* I was trying to protect myself from the hot, Spanish sun, I unclipped it and slipped it over my head. Then I took a selfie, actually smiling as a result of this very pleasant day, and sent it to her as proof that I was being responsible.

Mav and I continued on the *senda*, passing by the first albergue on our way into Terradillos. The building for it was set back from the path with a sweeping green lawn that stretched all the way to the Camino. A few pilgrims who had been lounging outside called out a greeting to us as we passed and I waved a response. According to my (never accurate) research, the one other albergue in town was supposed to accept dogs. If it didn't, Maverick and I were doing fine today. We could walk on to the next town if need be.

Terradillos de los Templarios was a sleepy little town, made up almost entirely of dirt buildings. The hot sun that scorches this part of Spain has allowed the inhabitants here to make their own brick by baking the clay of the earth found here. The result is crude buildings the same color as the dust beneath our feet with shoddy wooden roofs and window shutters. Despite the busy highway we just veered off of, it felt like this little village hadn't been touched by modern times.

The hospitaleros were happy to allow Maverick and I a place to stay. They just asked that I book a private room in order to avoid any issues with other pilgrims. The extra price of a solo room was easy for me to pay if it meant we actually got to stay in an albergue with other pilgrims. As much as last night was luxurious, I'd much prefer the community that came from staying in an albergue.

As we were getting shown to our room, Verónica and her friend were making their way from one of the dormitories down the hall. "Colby!" she called out excitedly. Maverick's ears perked up and he tugged on the leash in her direction. "¿Cómo estás? ¿Maverick está bien? ¿Cómo fueran?"

Her questions after our well-being ran into each other as she bent down to scratch Maverick's head. I laughed and managed to assuage her worry for us but told her that I would have to catch up with her after I got settled into my room. The poor hospitalera that had been leading me to my room was still patiently waiting out our reunion. Verónica sheepishly apologized and told me to meet her out on the patio for some lunch whenever I was ready.

Even though we weren't in one of the dormitories with other pilgrims around us for the night, it really didn't matter. I still used the communal bathroom while Maverick waited alone in our private room. I was able to wash my clothes and hang them out to dry. I ended up spending most of our afternoon on the patio of the albergue with Verónica and her friend, as well as many other pilgrims. While we were out there, I even ran into my *Italian* friend again. He and the young girl he was often walking with were both staying in this albergue for the night as well. He invited me to have dinner with them and watch the World Cup game that would be on tonight. Since I didn't have to worry about Maverick, because he'll be happily passed out on the bed in our private room which I have a key to, I was even able to accept the offer.

For one of the only times on this trip, I ate a leisurely dinner inside with the boy and two other friends he had made along the way. We laughed over how I had thought he was Spanish and the differences I was able to pick up on in his accent now. Both of the other girls were from Italy as well, but they weren't fluent in Spanish like he was, so he acted as a translator between us throughout the meal. Luckily, Italian is so similar to Spanish that they understood a lot of what was being said, and I could pick up quite a bit of what they said in return, but it was nice to have him to clarify things as well.

After dinner, I left them in the little sitting area of the albergue watching the rest of the soccer game and Maverick and I went out for a stroll around the small town. I still wasn't exactly sure what my plan for tomorrow would be. But I was learning to be okay with that. I had to keep reminding myself that this Camino was not at all what I had planned and that's *okay*.

Despite trying to accept this, trying to remember that things go off the rails but that doesn't mean I'm a failure, I still got so upset in Hornillos because my plans were being ruined again. Of course, it didn't help that I was exhausted. This whole journey was exhausting. It might not seem that way, but it really strips a person down to their core and I definitely broke that day. If I was being honest, I'd been breaking a little bit every day. But maybe that was the point of all this. Maybe we had to break to build back stronger.

Halfway Gone

Day Twenty-Two: Terradillos de los Templarios to Sahagún

18.2 km ~ 25,515 steps

July 11th

After all my thinking last night, I had decided to just do a short day today. I had been putting so much pressure on myself to be what I thought was a real pilgrim for this whole journey. I beat myself up for not staying in the pilgrim albergues every night. I beat myself up for taking a private room or a hostel rather than pitching the tent I had in my pack. I still kicked myself for taking that taxi from Los Arcos to Logroño. But what I came to the conclusion of last night was that this was *my* journey. No one else had this Camino. No one else knew exactly what it was like to walk this Camino I was walking with Maverick. And I was allowed to do it any way I needed to.

With that thought in my head, I planned to walk on to

Sahagún today, which was only thirteen kilometers from Terradillos de los Templarios. Sahugún was thought of as the unofficial "halfway" point along the Camino. I would spend the night there and then take the train from there to León the next morning. Maybe it wasn't the conventional pilgrim route, but I would do it. There were only three more stages between Terradillos and León, totaling to a little over fifty kilometers of walking that we would be skipping.

If we were to take the traditional route, every one of those fifty kilometers would be directly beside a road on the gravel *sendas* that we hated so much on the way into Carrión. If we took the alternative scenic route, which I had planned to do in advance, it would mean little to no shade, and very few spots to fill up on water. With the heat of the days recently, that sounded miserable at best. If I had been all alone, I would have grumbled and kept on walking.

However, this wasn't only my own Camino. This was Maverick's Camino, too. I made a promise to both him and myself before we started this journey that I wouldn't make a single decision without his well-being in mind. The idea of almost twenty-five of those upcoming kilometers being in the scorching sun with no shade or water was in no way okay for him. Add in the fact that on the gravel of the paths here in Spain he would have to be wearing his booties the entire time, it made the thought of that stretch feel like a death sentence. We had been doing okay recently. Maverick hadn't limped since Hornillos. I hadn't cried since then. That was a win in my book. There was no reason we had to subject ourselves to something so unpleasant.

With this reasoning, we took a late start from Terradillos this morning. Of course, late for us meant we were still on the road by eight. There had been talk of a storm rolling in this afternoon, so a lot of the pilgrims we had stayed with planned to leave early this morning in an attempt to outrun the storm. I hadn't been all that concerned, knowing I was only walking to Sahagún. Plus, there had been quite a few intense storms lately, but they always came late in the afternoon. We had yet to be caught in one.

However, the dark clouds up ahead did not look promising as we left Terradillos and weaved along farm roads on our way through the little villages of Moratinos and San Nicolás. I stopped to grab some breakfast in Moratinos while the skies were luckily still blue here. The group of Aussies we had met in Boadilla were also getting breakfast, so I nodded a hello to them but didn't chat much. Though they did always seem to be having a good time, they still gave off that vibe that they weren't looking for any tagalongs. Plus, me being the social-anxiety-ridden human that I am, I wasn't about to insert myself into their conversation at all. I could barely speak up in a group of my own friends. I was much better at one-on-one settings.

Maverick and I sat for a quiet breakfast together, and then meandered around the bodegas across the street from the café. They reminded me of little hobbit homes, bumps in the earth with cement casings to doors that led into the ground. Supposedly, these bodegas were perfect for storing wine in the cool earth. Some of them looked like they were actually homes, though. Others were more rundown, the doors not adorned with shells set into the concrete or tile nameplates. Either way, they were interesting to see and even more interesting to wonder about what they looked like inside.

The wind was picking up and the blue skies we had been lucky enough to walk under so far this morning were quickly clouding up, so I urged Maverick on and we continued down the wide farm tracks and onto the next little town. I paused just long enough to fill up our waters and poured some in a dish for Maverick to drink. The wind was whipping the wheat around in the fields beside us and the storm clouds had grown to fully block out the sun.

"Well, Maverick," I said to him as I waited for him to finish drinking. "I'm gonna go ahead and say that storm is coming sooner than the forecast predicted."

The group of Aussies caught up to us just as I was folding Maverick's dish back up and clipping it to his pack. They exchanged pleasantries in their boisterous way as always. I silently wondered if any of them had ever had a bad day along the Camino. Surely, they've been super tired one day. They definitely had faced blisters. One of them had to know how to frown.

"Where you walking to today, mate?" one of the boys asked me. I stirred myself from my thoughts and focused on the group of them, seeing they had fallen into step with me.

"Oh, just Sahagún. What about you guys?"

"Not quite sure yet. We just go until we get tired. Figure we'll have to brave the storm at some point."

"Right, right. Seems like it's gonna start raining at any time."

I tagged along with them for a little while, but really they walked kind of slow. Or maybe I was just used to walking faster since I typically walked by myself with Maverick leading the way. At any rate, I ended up walking a bit ahead of them until I couldn't really hear them behind me anymore. The sky had become a scary shade of black by that time, which made for great contrast against the bright yellow flowers lining our path yet again. At one point, we passed a sign that looked like it had been painted by a little kid hanging from one of the wire fences.

"We are all broken," it said in green paint; all capital letters. "That's how the light gets in!" What looked like an attempt at red and blue flowers were painted on the corners of the sign.

"No way," I muttered in disbelief, looking from the sign up to the sky and then back again. Did I really just spend last night thinking about how much this Camino had been breaking me, if only to put me back together? And now this sign in the middle of nowhere? If anyone wanted to talk about waiting for a sign, here it was. Quite literally. I didn't care how religious you were, God was definitely present along The Way of Saint James.

The path weaved back to the side of the highway after that and we could glimpse Sahagún in the distance. Which was a blessing because the first drops of rain were just starting. I looked both directions, ensuring now cars were bearing down on us, and Maverick and I dashed across the highway onto the alternate route to Sahagún. The path dropped off the side of the road and was a bit sheltered, but I could still hear the rain starting to pitter-patter on the leaves of the trees above us. I shrugged out of my pack and started to dig into it. I knew I had a poncho in there somewhere. Somewhere at the *very* bottom because up until now, I hadn't had any need for it.

I heard the distant *splash* of Maverick. He had bounded off the trail in the direction of the river and from the sounds of it, he had found it. *Of course he had to go swimming.* I continued rifling blindly through my pack until I felt my fingers connect with the poncho and fought to pull it out without dumping the rest of the contents on the ground. I buckled everything back up and slipped the pack over my shoulders again, then yanked the poncho over everything as best I could.

"Maverick!" I called as I fought to get the snaps of the poncho buckled under my arms so it would actually stay in place. I heard him crashing up the embankment from the river and a second later he appeared, shaking off the excess water.

I paused from my attempts with the snaps. "Seriously?" I grumbled, narrowing my eyes at his booties. "You went swimming with the booties on, kid? Why? Why must you be like this?" The rain was really coming down now, the path already becoming like a little river. I knelt and made quick work of the straps on his boots, slipping the sodden fabric from his paws. I had to upend each one to let out a puddle of water. "You're the worst," I told him. I had no doubt these would smell atrocious tomorrow.

I looped the straps of his booties around his pack so they wouldn't be soaking everything that was inside and decided to call it quits on getting the snaps to buckle on my poncho. I couldn't quite reach them and as it turns out, Maverick wasn't the most helpful companion when it came to these sorts of tasks. The whole lack-of-opposable-thumbs thing was really a downfall.

We set off down the trail in the pouring rain and within seconds, Maverick was on my heels. I stepped aside, giving him room to pass on the trail, but he sidestepped with me. I walked a couple steps forward and his wet muzzle rubbed against my bare leg. After a few more yards of this, I finally paused and looked down at him. He shuffled closer, pressing himself to my side. "What is wrong with you?" I asked.

He looked up at me and blinked, the rain getting in his eyes as he tried to see my face. He positioned himself closer to me, ensuring the poncho covered as much of him as it could from where it flowed off the edge of my pack, then blinked some more. "You've got to be kidding me," I laughed.

I took a few more steps forward while I kept my eyes on him, watching as he shuffled to stay under the poncho. "You're really hiding from the rain? Are you serious right now?" Maverick tilted his head as he listened to me, his eyes blinking away more rain. "You do realize you were the one who just went swimming in the river, right?"

I stepped forward again and his paw bumped against my boot as he struggled to stay as close as possible. I shook my head at him. "You know that's water, too. The same stuff that's coming from the sky. You're already wet!"

In response, Mav shook himself off right next to me, soaking my legs. I growled back at him. "There's no difference! Stop being such a baby."

And yet, he stayed on my heels as we splashed our way over a little stone bridge and to the hermitage at a bend in the trail. The rain wasn't quite so strong at the moment, so I paused to take in the odd structure ahead of us. It stood in the middle of the clearing in front of the tiny chapel here. Two pillars of what looked like sandstone, about fifteen feet apart, each with a carving of a man facing the other on the insides, with words carved into the base of each pillar. I stepped forward to get a closer look at the inscription.

Sahagún, centro histórico de la Orden de Cluny.

"Huh," I said aloud to Maverick. I tilted my head to the side in an effort to get a better look at it. The d's did look more like o's and the e's like f's, which was kind of funny because it made *de* look like *of*, which is what it meant here. Regardless, I still couldn't make sense of it. I had no idea what the Order of Cluny was.

"Well, Mav. I'm just gonna say this marks the center of the Camino Francés. Sound like a plan to you?" He gave me a sad look from beside the base of the marker, the top of his head soaked through with rain now.

The Aussies caught up with us again, agreeing that this was the halfway marker for the Camino. We took turns taking pictures of each other while we stood between the two pillars, but the rain was picking up again and all of us were eager to keep moving. The sooner we got to town at this point, the better.

Within minutes, it was a full on torrential downpour and the wind was aiming the rain sideways into our faces. Maverick was doing his best to stay hidden beneath my poncho, but that was flapping about in the wind since I had never managed to get those snaps to work.

"Do you want me to help you with that, mate?" one of the guys called over the wind and rain. I looked over my shoulder as he jogged the couple steps to come up beside me.

"Oh, yeah, if you wouldn't mind I would appreciate that so much." I hadn't even finished talking when his friend had taken the other side and snapped it into place as well. "Wow, thank you," I said emphatically, already feeling a huge difference and not getting soaked.

"Not a problem."

"I guess this is one of those times I wish I had a human companion to help out with things," I joked.

"Yeah, I wouldn't suppose he's all that helpful with things," one of the girls laughed.

My answer was cut short by a crack of thunder that sounded like it came from directly above our heads. Maverick hugged himself closer to my legs. My eyes widened in shock.

"Well that's fun," the other girl muttered as we hurried forward. A streak of lightning lit up the sky in front of us, slicing down to the field ahead of us on the right. Not a second later, the echo of thunder rumbled again.

"Alright mates, double time." The group of us splashed along the path, jumping at each boom of thunder. The storm raged around us and the lightning seemed to be striking closer and closer, but there was nowhere to go. We were in the middle of a field. After what seemed like forever, we came to the underpass just before the city and ran towards it for cover.

"Fun stuff," one of the guys panted as we all huddled in the tunnel. Maverick shook out his fur, spattering the rest of us but we were all so soaked by that point it didn't even matter.

"Do you think it'll blow over soon?" a girl asked.

I peeked out at the sky, black as far as I could see in any direction. Another slash of lightning lit up the world and I backed under the concrete again. "Doesn't look like it," I muttered.

"We should keep going. At least to get into town and to a bar or something."

"It can't be too much farther 'til we reach one."

"Alright. Together then?" All of us looked around at each other, then donned our hoods again and set out as one to brave the storm again.

The streets of Sahagún were more like rivers as we splashed back and forth across them, trying to find overhangs that would shelter us for one second or another. We finally found a large one in front of a *farmacia* and we huddled there for a while, debating our next move. We had yet to pass a single bar or café, or even another pilgrim. They were clearly smarter than us and had found shelter already. That, or they were stuck in this awful storm on that open stretch after the city. That would definitely suck.

"¿Perdón?" A woman popped her head out of the pharmacy. "¿Necesitáis algo?"

The Aussies looked at each other and then back to the woman. I stepped in. "Ah, no. Lo siento. Pero, la lluvia…" I gestured out at the deluge in explanation for us crowding the steps in front of her shop. Because…*was that hail?* I looked back again. Oh no, that was *definitely* hail coming down now.

"Sí, entiendo. Pero, no podéis bloquear la puerta. Hay un bar por allá." She pointed down the street directly in front of us, effectively shooing us from in front of her establishment.

"Gracias, señora. Lo siento."

"Está bien. Buen Camino, peregrinos."

She dipped back inside the store, shutting the glass door on the whipping wind and rain behind her. "There's a bar over there, she said." I glanced down at Maverick, who was the saddest wet dog I had ever seen. "Come on then."

We looked both ways, then darted across the road and onto the side street, plastering ourselves as close to the buildings as we could to try to ward off the rain and hail. Within a couple blocks, we came to the bar she had told us about. If it hadn't been raining so hard, we probably would have been able to see it from the steps of the pharmacy. There was a covered patio where we dropped our sopping bags and finally felt some relief from the storm. There were so many pilgrims inside, the windows were beginning to fog up.

Well, I thought to myself. *I guess we found where everyone else was waiting out the storm.* I unfurled Maverick's leash from around his neck and hooked him to the leg of one of the empty plastic chairs on the patio. Not that he was going anywhere. He had promptly curled himself into the tiniest ball he could, with his nose tucked under his tail, and was already asleep now that he was sheltered from the rain. I shook my head at him and pushed into the crowded bar just behind the Aussies.

While they shoved their way to the bar for a hot coffee, I descended down the steep stairs inside following signs for a bathroom. You took your breaks whenever you could get them on the Camino. My companions were still waiting for their hot drinks when I made it back upstairs and to the bar. I had noticed from the postings along the stairwell that this place was also an albergue, so I figured it wouldn't hurt to ask if they allowed dogs here.

Once there was a break from customers, I caught the attention of the barista. "¿Permite perros en el albergue?"

"¿Perros? No, lo siento. Pero, conozco una pensión que permite perros en la ciudad."

She gave me the name of another place that was further into the city and I thanked her profusely before forcing my way back out to Maverick. He looked up at me with sad eyes, as if I was going to tell him we had to start walking in the rain again. "I'm sorry, bud. I never thought of needing a towel for you."

Whether he understood what I was saying at all didn't seem to affect him much. The fact that I had taken a seat on one of the slightly wet chairs outside with him was enough and he rested his nose back under his tail, satisfied we weren't heading back out into the downpour. I pulled out my phone from the hip pocket of my pack and pulled my guidebook from its plastic bag to look up the name of the pensión the woman had given me. It was listed just after all the historic information about the city and I dialed the number there just to ensure they did indeed allow dogs before trekking there in the rain.

I had just hung up with a very dull-sounding man, although he did say dogs were allowed so I wasn't complaining, when the Aussies emerged from the bar again. They all had giant grins on their faces, the fact that they were soaked to the bone and probably cold as well didn't seem to be fazing them.

"Hey, pooch. You gonna keep walking?" one of the boys leaned down to scratch Maverick's wet head and he raised an eyebrow at him lazily.

"Oh, no," I answered for Maverick. "We've found our place for the night. We just have to actually get there now."

"Right on. Well, Buen Camino to you guys. We're off."

The whole lot of them were slipping back into their packs, fitting their ponchos back into place. "You're walking on now?" I asked, eyeing the steady rain still pouring down. Granted, the thunder and lightning appeared to have passed, but it didn't exactly look like great walking weather right now.

"Yeah, don't see why not. We're already soaked. It makes no difference now."

I raised my eyebrows at their logic. *Sure*, I thought. *Sounds great.* "Well," I said instead. "I'll walk with you as far as the hostel I've got."

Maverick got up sullenly when he realized we were moving and we set off with the group through the streets of Sahagún. It wasn't long before the awning of our hostel appeared, luckily, and we waved goodbye to the exuberant group.

We dripped our way into the lobby of the pensión and up to the front desk. I could tell just from one look at the man behind the desk that he was the one I had just spoken to on the phone. His expression was blank as he stared Maverick and I down from behind the high wooden desk. "¿Tienes una reserva?"

"Sí," I replied to his monotone question. "De Colby. Con el perro."

He clicked a few things on his computer, eyed our dripping forms, and then grabbed one of the keys hanging from the hooks on one wall. "¿Credencial?" I slid my passport over to him and then Maverick's as well. He raised a brow at me.

"Es por el perro. Su credencial," I explained.

"¿En serio?" he deadpanned. I grinned sheepishly. He let out an extended sigh and pressed down a stamp on Maverick's credential as well. Then he slipped out from behind the desk and motioned for us to follow him up the stairs and to our room. He left us at the door without a word.

I watched his back retreat down the stairs and then turned to Maverick. "Pleasant, don't you think?" I muttered to him. He whined and pawed the door in front of us. I inserted the key and turned the lock, pushing the door open to let us into a tiny box of a room. There was one cot that didn't look at all inviting, a television that was about the same size as my phone screen, and one small window. But at least there was a tiny bathroom attached to it.

I dropped our wet bags on a chair that was at the foot of the bed and ducked into the bathroom, coming out with one of the rough towels I found on the rack. "Come here, kiddo." Maverick happily trotted the two steps to me, since that was about as much as you could move in here, and shoved face-first into the towel. I laughed as I wiped it down his back, scratching along his spine and all over his head. He spun in a circle after the first pass, then dove in again for another brush down. "Better?" I asked once he was satisfied with his drying. He responded by hopping up onto the cot, which creaked under his weight.

"Well then. You nap. I need a hot shower."

Waves

Day Twenty-Three: Sahagún to León

July 12ᵗʰ

The rain had blown out by the time I had finished showering yesterday afternoon, so we ended up spending the whole day exploring Sahagún. It was a great example of a medieval city. I was sure there were modern parts of the city as well, but from what we saw of it, it was as if modern-day had simply inserted itself into buildings of the past. Veterinary offices and pharmacies were tucked into buildings made of the same brick as the crumbling San Benito abbey. Of course, there were countless sights to take in, most impressive to me was the Church of San Tirso with its stately arches and impressive tower all built from the mudbrick this area was known for. The style of much of the older architecture here actually was heavily influenced from the Moors that had occupied Spain before Christian times. In fact, the architecture of San Tirso is Mudéjar, which is a unique combination of Islamic art and Christian styles.

Sahagún proved to be more than just churches and history, though. We also walked past more modern things, such as murals that took up entire walls and depicted pilgrims, horses, a starry night, and more. Some even featured poetry from Emily Dickenson translated to Spanish. But despite all our venture around the city…I had yet to find the dog food Maverick needed. He had just enough for breakfast this morning, but we were officially out now. I had found plenty of supermarkets, and even vets offices were here that carried Hill's Science Diet, yet I couldn't find anywhere that carried the brand we had switched to in Burgos.

Luckily, our train to León was scheduled for eight-thirty this morning. León was a big city, at least as big as Burgos. I was sure we could find food there. Even though I had made the decision to train ahead and tried to accept it, I was still struggling with feeling like a bit of a failure. However, knowing how small most of the towns along the Meseta were, I knew we wouldn't find any dog food between here and León if we continued walking. So this little hiccup actually made me feel a little bit better about taking the train.

Mav and I stopped at a café to grab breakfast before heading just outside of town to the train station. It wasn't much of a station, more like a big, empty, dirt lot and a little ticket house by the open platform. I had already purchased my ticket from Renfe on my phone last night, so I didn't need to talk to the attendant. Maverick was fitted with his vest, the patches of "Emotional Support" on each side standing out against the red. Other than the ticket takers in Logroño, I hadn't faced any issue with Maverick on the trains we had taken so far so I hoped this would be no different.

We took a seat on the concrete of the platform as we waited for the train to arrive. Soon enough, a couple other pilgrims had joined us. Seems there were quite a few that had had enough of the Meseta. It wasn't long before the locomotive screeched to a stop in front of us. Of course, Maverick wasn't even fazed by the bursts of air as it finally came to rest before us or the high-pitched squeal of the metal on metal of the rails.

I picked up his pack and urged him to a stand, then climbed on behind the other pilgrims in the last car. We took a seat at the very back even though there were no other people in this compartment at all. I just liked to be in the back with Maverick, it felt more out of the way if anyone had an issue with him. And then we waited. And waited. The train still didn't move. I looked out the window, wondering if we were waiting for any passengers that might be running late, but there was no one else in sight trying to reach the platform in time.

The connecting door to the compartment ahead of ours flew open with a rattle and a man in a Renfe uniform came striding down the aisle. It happened so quickly, so out of the blue, that I didn't even register that he was talking until he was halfway down the aisle.

I realized he was talking to me, because there was clearly no one else in this car he could have been talking to, but my eyes widened as I looked around helplessly for someone else. He came to a stop with his hands on his hips about two feet away from us and glared at me, clearly waiting for something. "Uhm…" I cleared my throat, not ready to speak since I had no idea what he even said. "¿Cómo?"

In his anger, he was speaking so fast and aggressively that I picked up about every other word. Enough to get that dog on train equals bad news. I'm sure there were also a few choice words thrown in for color, but I chose to ignore that.

"Ah, sí," I tried as calmly as I could, pulling my phone out. "Pero, él es un perro de apoyo. Tengo permisión de

Renfe por él." I pulled up the email from Renfe again; the one that denoted they would indeed allow Maverick onboard since he was a Support Animal. I turned the phone for him to see and reached for my letter from my therapist. I had a feeling this man would require every bit of proof I had. Only, he didn't look at the phone.

His words came out in a rage again and he began to move around me, so that he was at my back, forcibly moving Maverick and I down the train car and towards the door we had come in. From what I gathered, he didn't give a shit about my proof…and that was putting it nicely.

"Señor, tengo un correo electrónico de Renfe. Le dijo que es posible que mi perro me acompañe." I tried again to show him my phone, this time over my shoulder because he was still behind us, urging us down the aisle. If I didn't walk on my own, I was sure he would have taken the chance to shove me forward.

At this point, he wasn't even bothering to respond to me. "¡Señor!" I gasped, coming to a halt and whipping around to face him at the stairs to the door. "¿Qué es tu problema?" I finally snapped, then realized that definitely wouldn't be winning me any favors. "Tengo una carta de Renfe. ¡El perro es permitido en el tren!"

"¡Es mi tren y no está permitido! Los perros no son permitidos en ningunos trenes."

"¿Su tren?" I scoffed before I could stop myself. "Por favor. Es un tren de Renfe y Renfe le dice-"

"Soy el conductor y es mi tren. No perros en mi tren." His tone brooked no argument and if I hadn't scrambled down the stairs at that moment I had no doubt he would have pushed me down them and straight out onto the platform. Maverick scuttled ahead of me, clearly bewildered by all the shouting and the general furious aura this man exuded. His leap down onto the platform yanked me forward and I stumbled. By the time I had righted myself and turned back to continue my conversation with the man, the metal door slid shut in my face.

"¡Señor!" I yelled, but I could already see him moving back up the stairs and into the connection train car. "¡Señor! ¡Espere!" I called, following his form as he moved down the compartments of the train. Maverick jogged to keep up beside me as we strode down the platform beside the train. "¡Señor! Por favor, ¡escúchame!"

The train gave off a blast of the whistle and without further ado, the wheels started turning. I stood in shock, watching as the last few cars of the train slowly chugged by us. The conductor, that horrid man who we had just dealt with, was seated in the last car. He looked down out of the window with a glare in our direction. I looked back up at him with a hollow expression. And just like that, the train was gone, moving down the tracks at increasing speed.

Maverick whined from beside me, not understanding why I had suddenly gone still and silent. When I didn't respond, he tugged at the leash, trying to follow the shadow of a bird that had just swooped by. Just like that, he was onto the next adventure. Only, it wasn't that easy for me.

I yanked back on his leash, tugging him into position next to me and he looked up at me in shock. I wasn't normally so rough with him and I knew it wasn't him I was mad at. I didn't even know if I was mad. I didn't know *what* I was at that moment, but it wasn't okay.

I sank down onto the closest bench, awkwardly perched on the edge because I couldn't even be bothered to take off. Rationally, I knew this wasn't the end of the world, but I wasn't thinking rationally. All I could think was that I had never been treated so poorly by another person before. That man had absolutely no reason to treat me and Maverick so disrespectfully.

I felt a tear drip off my chin and fall onto the dusty earth and I realized for the first time that I was crying. I suppose I was used to crying all the time. I used to cry when I was at Ohio State every day. That's a depression perk – you can cry over anything. You can think you're doing great, that you're having a good day, but the littlest thing can change that in an instant.

I had thought we were doing well since Hornillos. I thought I had made the right decision today. We would take the train to León to avoid another spiral into my depression. I had felt it coming on, that's why I had been trying so hard to be positive and convince myself this was the best move. And look how that had turned out for me?

My chest shook as my tears came harder. What was I supposed to do now? The train wouldn't allow us on. Only seeing eye dogs were allowed on buses from what we had learned in Bilbao. Even if Maverick was allowed on a bus, I didn't even know where we could find one to take us to León. I didn't want to walk those next couple days. I had fully convinced myself of that recently. There was no way we'd make it between here and León. It wasn't just about Maverick and how he would be too hot or right next to a road. It was about me. It had been about me this whole time, but I had been trying to pretend it wasn't.

I wasn't strong enough. I was the one who couldn't walk on. I needed to train, not just Maverick. What did that say about me? That I was too weak for this journey? That I shouldn't have thought I could do this? I wasn't the fearless person so many liked to believe I was. I wasn't confident and capable. I was weak and tired and depressed. The depression was winning today. From one rude encounter, I was reduced to a sobbing mess on a desolate metal bench. Maverick nuzzled at my foot but I couldn't even see the top of his head through my tears.

"¿Señorita?" I vaguely registered a voice. "¿Señorita? ¿Qué es el problema? ¿Qué pasó?"

I turned to see another man in uniform, but his outline was blurry through my tears. He stayed a few feet away from me, like I was a wounded animal that might lash out at any moment. I rubbed at my eyes, trying to clear away the tears so I could see, and hiccupped. I didn't really feel like talking to anyone right now, but it would be incredibly rude to just ignore this man who was simply asking about my well-being. "¿Cómo?"

"¿Qué pasó, señorita?" he asked again.

"El conductor. N-no permitió mi p-perro en el tren. Pero-" My voice hitched through another sob. "Pero t-tengo una c-carta de Renfe." I swallowed and looked away, aware that barely any of my words would be discernible through my tears. I really was pathetic. I was a grown adult. I should be able to get over this and move on, figure out my next steps.

"Ven conmigo." The man tipped his head back to the little building by the platform and started walking in that direction. When he saw that I hadn't immediately stood to follow him, he stopped and motioned again. "Ven."

I shuffled after him, eyes on the dirt. Maverick padded along beside me, not bothering to tug on the leash for once. We stopped outside the ticket window and waited for the man to take his post on the other side. "Eres una peregrina, ¿no?" he asked. I nodded weakly. I didn't feel like much of a pilgrim at the moment, but I was supposed to be one. "Y, ¿adónde ibas por tren?"

"A León."

"Bueno. Me lo imaginé. Un momento." Apparently it was quite common for pilgrims to train from Sahagún to León if he had anticipated this. His fingers clicked along on the keys of his computer and then a whirring of a printer started.

He grabbed the printed paper and looked up at my tear-stained face. "Es verdad es la decisión del conductor para permitir los perros en el tren," he admitted to me. So the conductor had been right, then. He *did* have the authority to kick us off his train despite my letter from the train company. "Pero, nunca he conocido un conductor que tenga un problema hasta ahora. Ojalá que no tenga un problema con el próximo conductor. Aquí está un boleto del próximo tren. Sale a la una."

He handed a paper ticket for the next train across the counter to me, but I hesitated to take it. "Es tuyo," he encouraged and I finally reached forward to take it. When I still couldn't form a reply, because I was still too numb, he urged me to go get something to eat. To sit and regroup. I had four hours before the next train was supposed to come, and even then, like he just said, there was no guarantee we would be allowed on.

When it was clear to him I could only sniffle in response, he began to pluck away at his computer again. I finally looked up. "¿Señor?" He paused and looked back at me with a small smile. "Gracias," I hiccupped. "Por todo."

He gave a small nod, seeming to realize this was about more than just the ticket. "De nada, señorita. Buen Camino, peregrina. Y *perro*grino."

I managed a watery smile at that, then Maverick and I turned and headed back towards town. We found a bar to sit outside of because I didn't have any heart in me to walk around the city to kill time. And I cried some more. I cried because I felt like a failure. I cried because I had to rely on the kindness of others to help me through this Camino. I cried because it was Maverick's birthday tomorrow and this

wasn't what he wanted to be doing. What had I been thinking? What if he was absolutely hating this?

A German pilgrim I had met in Boadilla stopped when
he saw me crying outside the bar and sat down with me. I'm
not sure I got more than five words out between all my blub-
bering, but he must have sat with me for at least an hour
while I poked at the risotto I had ordered so the bar wouldn't
kick me out. In the end, there wasn't anything he could do
for me, so after he had finished his beer, he reluctantly
moved on after laying a hand on my shoulder and giving it a
squeeze and Mav and I were alone again. We lingered at the
bar, while I sniffled intermittently, until it was time to get
back to the station for Try Two of getting on a train.

There wasn't a single issue on this train. We climbed on
just like every other passenger. Each car was so full on this
train, so not like the morning's train, that we ended up
outside the very last car on the metal landing by the door
with a few other young Spaniards. Luckily, this made it easy
to hop down when we pulled into the station in León and
escape before the throngs of other passengers trying to exit
onto the platform.

The pensión we were staying at was located pretty close
to the cathedral, on a busier street, but it was small and could
be easily missed as it was wedged between flashy stores. I rang
the bell from the street and was buzzed into the building
immediately. We climbed the tight stairs up to a door that
had a plaque with the pensión's name and rang the buzzer for
that as well.

A man came to the door a second later with a grin that
took up his whole face and he ushered us inside, immediately
gushing over Maverick. Inside looked more like an apartment
than a hostel at all, but I had come not to expect much when
it came to the places we stayed in Spain. They were all so
different from the sprawling motels or hotels of America that

it was best just to go in with no expectations at all. Not that either place was better or worse; they were just very different.

This pensión definitely had a family feel to it. The man introduced me to his wife as he showed me around. He explained how they had two miniature pinschers, so they *loved* dogs, although Maverick was much bigger than they expected. Then he also waved to his mother who lived here as well and was out hanging the laundry. Our room was small, more like a bathroom than a bedroom actually. It had tiled floors and sported a bed under a window that opened out to a view of the inner courtyard of the building, so it really just stared across to another window. There was a miniscule stand-up shower in one corner and a sink, but no toilet. The hospitalero explained the toilet was in a separate bathroom across the hall.

He gave me a recommendation for a nearby park to take Maverick to but seemed to recognize I wasn't in the most talkative of moods. With a little half bow and a reminder to let him know if I needed anything at all, he left us.

I sank down onto the cot and looked at Maverick. He folded himself into the tiny amount of open floor between the bed and the sink and looked up at me with curious eyes. *Mum?* He seemed to ask. *You good?*

I shook my head at him. "I'm just tired, Nug," I told him. I was exhausted, body and soul. He crawled up on the little cot with me and laid his head on my chest as I laid back. My hand absentmindedly came up to his head and stroked his fur there and eventually I drifted off to sleep.

I stayed in half-sleep-half-wake daze for most of the afternoon. I had no energy to get up and explore this great

city. Had no desire to see the towering cathedral or run into
any other pilgrims. Couldn't even muster the energy to write
in my own journal. But Maverick was out of food and that
was a necessity. So eventually I pulled myself out of bed and
hooked his leash back to his collar. He immediately perked
up and spun in a circle, his claws tip-tapping against the tile
in excitement to be moving.

I asked the hospitalero if he knew of any nearby pet
stores and he was confused by my question at first. When I
explained that Maverick was out of food, understanding
dawned on him. He told me of multiple vets that were
around. "Pero, ¿no hay una tienda de animales aquí?" I
asked.

"¿Tienda de animales? Pues…Creo que hay una en
Carrefour."

"¿Carrefour?" I asked.

"Sí, el centro comercial."

"Ah…bueno." He directed me towards the mall of the
city and I thanked him before heading down the stairs and
back out to the busy streets. I didn't necessarily want to go to
a mall, because I had no idea how I'd make that work with
Maverick, but if there wasn't any other option…

Armed with GoogleMaps, we wandered the city in search
of somewhere other than the mall. In the end, we ended up
outside the sprawling modern mall. It looked even bigger
than any malls we had at home. I had become so used to the
small mom and pop shops and village stores along the
Camino, the giant building was a bit of a shock. As was the
McDonald's across the street. I felt so out of place in my
sweat soaked, dusty clothes and dirty-caked boots.

I stood at one of the entrances with Maverick by my side,
just staring at the automatic doors. An old woman walked in
and the doors slid open, revealing the shiny floors inside and
a blast of A/C hit us. Then the doors slid shut behind her

again as we stayed immobile outside. Couples passed through the exit, laden with shopping bags from various stores. Still, we didn't move. A man pushed past us from behind, jostling my shoulder, and muttered a "perdón" before passing through the doors as they slid open for him. Maverick looked up at me from my side, not understanding why we hadn't moved.

I finally tore my eyes from the doors and looked back down at him. "You can't come in," I told him. There was no way a mall would let him in. I hadn't even thought to bring his Support Animal collar or his vest, not that it would have made a difference. Support Animals didn't even have access to shopping centers back in the States. There was no way they would here. Maverick whined. "I know. I don't know what to do. You need food."

I looked back up at the massive building, multiple stories tall and blocking out the sun. The highway roared behind us. I weighed my options. We had come all this way, nearly a five kilometer walk to this mall. I wasn't just going to turn around and head back. But I hadn't been able to find anything else, not with the food he had been on since Burgos. There was no way I wanted to switch him to another food brand, with no time to get acclimated to it *again*. I needed that same brand. This was the only place I could get it.

I looked back down at Mav. "I leave you outside of the little stores I go into to get food along the Camino. This is no different, right?" He tilted his head at me, raising his eyebrows in that way he had. "Ugh, I know. It's very different. But we have no other options, kid." His head tilted the other direction. "There's a little shady spot next to that post. I'll be super quick. It will be fine." I was definitely trying to convince myself more than him at this point. "Okay. Let's go."

I strode over to one of the posts outside the doors and looped his leash over it, then looked around. There were people walking in and out, but it wasn't *that* busy. And really, they had to know I'd be right back for him. No one would just steal a dog. *Right?*

"Okay. I'll be right back. Don't move." I started to back away from him and he tilted his head again, not knowing what I was doing. "It's fine. You'll be fine. I love you. I promise I'll be right back."

I finally turned my back on him and headed towards the door that opened in front of me with a swish. I looked back over my shoulder and saw Maverick at the end of his leash, staring after me longingly. *Right back*, I mouthed to him.

I sped up my steps, weaving between the slow mall walkers around me and scanning the storefronts for a pet store but didn't see anything. This was the strangest mall I had ever been in. But luckily, there was a sign that showed which departments were on which levels. I practically ran over to it and skimmed it, finally locating *tienda de animales* on the fourth floor.

Fourth floor?! Not good. I looked back up at the map, seeing where on the fourth floor it was. Of course, it was on the opposite side of the building from my little "you are here" marker. There was no way. I couldn't leave Maverick outside for all that time. I just couldn't. Not in a place like this. Decision made, I strode back out of the mall.

Maverick was laying beside the post he was tied to, his eyes glued to the automatic doors. As soon as I emerged from them, he jumped up, his tail wagging like he hadn't seen me in days. I gave him a weak smile and bent down to pet him once I reached him. "I'm sorry," I murmured. "I'm sorry I left you out here. And I'm sorry I didn't even come back with food for you. But it's all the way across the mall. I can't. I can't just leave you here."

He wagged his tail and turned in a circle, not at all bothered. I sighed. I had to get him food. "I could run," I told him, glancing at him out of the corner of my eye. He stood and stared back at me. "Yeah. What if I just speed walk and run to the pet store, grab the food, and run back? That couldn't be more than ten minutes. It would be fine. You were fine out here when I just went in." His tongue lolled out happily. "Okay, stay. Be good. I'll be right back."

I stood again and this time I didn't look back. I had no time to waste. I hustled through the doors, down the mall until I could find a side stairwell that was kind of sketchy but I didn't have time to grumble about it. I took the stairs two at a time until I reached the fourth floor, which in Europe really just was the third floor since they labeled the ground floor as one, and pushed out of the stairwell. I was in some sort of hardware store, or at least the hardware section of some store. I took stock of my surroundings so I would know how to get back and then ran through the store, slipping between shelves and shoppers as quickly as I could.

Finally, I rounded a corner and saw the bright colors of the pet store. I sprinted towards it, scanning the aisles until I could find the dog food and then hurrying towards it. My eyes skimmed over the different brands, searching for that one the girl at the pet store in Burgos had said was so popular.

"¿Necesitas ayuda?" a boy's voice asked. I turned to face him and immediately asked him about the brand. "Ah, sí. Aquí."

He pointed me towards a small selection of it. "Muchas gracias." He turned to leave then, but I called out again. "Espere. Este marca…¿es muy popular?"

"¿Esa marca?" He scrunched his nose. "No, no es popular."

I grumbled under my breath after he walked away. Of

course it wasn't popular. That lying little… No use in being upset over it now. I had found what I needed and now I had to get back to Mav. I was just about to head to the register when the toy aisle caught my eye.

Not five minutes later, I was skidding out from the automatic doors, panting from my run back down to the exit. "Maverick?" I called, and immediately panicked when I didn't see him right away. A group of white-haired ladies shuffled towards the entrance and suddenly there he was, peeking around them until he was fully in view. He hopped up from where he had been lying and tugged at the leash, tail already wagging.

"Mavy!" I rushed towards him and swallowed him in a hug as I dropped to my knees. "I'm so, so sorry. I'll never leave you outside a mall again, I promise."

Never one for public displays of affection, he tolerated my love for only a second before wiggling free from my arms and shoving his nose into the plastic bag I had dropped. "Hey!" I shooed, pulling the bag from his nose. "No, those are for your birthday. You have to wait to open them."

He whined in protest and tried to reach his nose even higher. I ruffled his fur between his ears. "Alright, kid. Let's go eat some dinner."

Poetry

Day Twenty-Four: León

July 13th

"Happy birthday, Mavy boy." I pulled out a blue, squeaky ball from the plastic bag and he eagerly took it from my finger. "I can't believe you're already a year old." I uncovered a rope monkey and Mav immediately abandoned the ball in favor of this new toy. "It seems like just yesterday I was waiting for you to be born." I pulled out the last present I had bought him at the pet store yesterday, a Nylabone, and he dropped the monkey to try this new one.

I stretched, finally getting up from bed while he enjoyed all his new presents. While he played, I took a shower in the itty-bitty stall here in the room and then washed my clothes in the sink. There wasn't much room to dry them, so I did my best to droop them over the windowsill. I didn't have much faith that they would actually dry since this window didn't get much sun…or a breeze. Really it was kind of a waste of a window.

I sighed as I rubbed the towel through my hair and then threw on the last set of clean clothes I had. After a day like yesterday, you didn't just go to bed and wake up all better in the morning. That's not how depression works. Once that mood has wormed its way in and taken hold of you, it was hard to shake. So I was still not feeling very cheery, but it was Maverick's birthday. I would do my best to make it a good one. Plus, we had a rest day in a beautiful city. We might as well make the most of it.

Around eleven, after Maverick had eaten breakfast, we wandered out so I could find some food of my own. We made our way towards León's cathedral, one of the largest along the Camino. Unfortunately, it was undergoing some restorations on the front façade. Between the two impressive towers was covered with what looked like giant poster paper that showed a picture of what the façade has looked like for hundreds of years and what it will be once the restorations are complete. While the white cover-up certainly took away from the beauty, there was still so much to see and the massive structure was still so impressive. It didn't seem quite as sprawling as the cathedral in Burgos, but it came very close.

I found a café right across from the entrance to the cathedral and left Maverick at a table while I went in to order breakfast. I had just sat down to eat when a blonde woman came up to our table.

"Oh my gosh!" she gushed. "I'm so glad to see you guys! I've been thinking about the two of you. How are you? How has everything been going for you?"

"Oh," I said with wide eyes. I quickly recovered and stood to return her hug. "Hi, yeah, we've been hanging in there. Do you want to grab some breakfast with us?"

It was only polite. She clearly was thrilled to see us but for the life of me I could not remember who she was. Maybe she had been a part of the group who had started out from Saint Jean at the same time with us? Or she could just be someone who was following along with our journey on social media. It wouldn't be the first time we had run into someone like that. The least I could do was offer her a chair at our table. I would take all the positive people in my life I could get right about now.

"If you wouldn't mind my company." She smiled and pulled out a chair, patting Maverick between the ears as she did so. "I'd love to share breakfast with you. Are you having a rest day today in the city?"

"Yeah, actually. It's Maverick's birthday so we're going to just relax and enjoy it."

"No way! It's my birthday, too!"

I smiled, maybe my first real smile in over twenty-four hours. "Happy birthday. What a great place to spend your day."

"I thought so, too." She paused to order a café con leche from the waiter and a croissant and then turned back to me. "How old is Maverick turning today?"

"One."

"His first birthday! Oh my! But he's so well-behaved. I would have sworn he was older. And so big." She looked down at him and began speaking directly to him in a puppy voice. He paid attention to her for approximately five seconds before he saw a pigeon trying to approach our table and his focus was torn away.

"Sorry about that," I laughed as he *harrumphed* and laid back down after successfully frightening away the bird. "He doesn't care too much for most humans."

"Just his mom, then. I guess that's all that matters." Her

smile seemed to radiate a sense of peace and I found myself smiling back without even thinking.

Over breakfast, we talked about all the ups and downs of Camino life each of us had faced so far. It hadn't even been a month and yet it felt like we had been out here forever. Even though she seemed to have everything together, and seemed the epitome of peace and happiness, she admitted that even she had moments where she didn't know why she was doing this.

"I suppose it really is a mirror for life, don't you think?" she asked.

"What do you mean?"

"You get it all. In just one journey. Just a few short weeks. You experience happiness and pain. You form friendships and lose them. You experience growth and you shed your past. And it's all shoved into this one moment. This one walk. And yet, you get it all."

"Yeah," I agreed quietly. "It really is."

We went our separate ways after breakfast. She was off to do some shopping to find herself a birthday present and Mav and I were off to explore Old Town. We had seen more than enough of the bustling, fast-paced modern side of León on our quest for dog food yesterday.

"Hey," I called just before she disappeared around the corner of the building. She turned back to face me with a smile. "I'm so sorry but I don't remember your name."

"Oh, how rude of me! It's Joanne. It was so very nice to meet you guys. I hope I'll see you again along the way."

Before I could respond, she was gone, disappearing between a throng of tourists. So I hadn't met her before, then. She must have been following us somewhere on social media. Perhaps one of the Camino Facebook pages I had been posting updates on. There were so many supportive pilgrims, past, current, and future that had reached out to us through that platform.

We chose to explore the sights of Plaza Regla first. Of course, I had to pose Maverick for a birthday photo op in front of the block letters that spell out *León* here. Then I tried to make sense of the memorial statue that featured twenty handprints. I have since learned that it is in honor of the hardworking men who built these massive cathedrals all those centuries ago. This particular cathedral, officially known as *Catedral Santa María de León*, was almost entirely completed in the thirteenth century. Apparently, it is built on the site of what was once a sprawling Roman bath complex.

I decided to take Mav for a walk around the exterior of the building and I was starting to doubt that it was actually that much smaller than the cathedral in Burgos. It seriously would take at least a half hour to walk around the whole thing. But it was so built into the city that we ended up wandering down cobbled side streets and exploring the alleyways that surrounded it.

If I thought the front façade was impressive, it was nothing compared to the back. Sure, the towers were imposing, and maybe the centerpiece would have changed my mind if it had been on display, but the back of the cathedral demands to be admired. Particularly, the sharp angles and countless windows. The delicate-looking buttresses took my breath away. There was even a single chair placed alone on the wide sidewalk, like a bench but just for one, to view this rear masterpiece.

After a sufficient amount of time spent gaping at the limestone, Mav and I discovered a little ice cream shop in the neighborhood behind the cathedral. "Birthday ice cream?" I asked him. He wagged his tail in excitement, having no idea what I was talking about but knowing the tone of my voice sounded promising. I hooked him to a leg of a chair outside the shop. "One minute."

I headed inside the shop, which was so dark it took a minute for my eyes to adjust to the gloom after spending the morning in the bright sun. I spied a woman by the cash register, just to the left of the ice cream display. "Hola," I called out. "¿Cómo está?"

"Bien. ¿Y tú?"

"Bien, bien." I stepped up to the glass display. "¿Puedo tener una copa de chocolate y una copa de vainilla?"

"Claro." She bent to scoop the ice cream into a bowl and I realized she was going to put both scoops in the same dish.

"Oh, lo siento. Necesito dos tazas. Una para la vainilla y una para el chocolate." She paused and looked up at me. "Sí, porque es para mi perro."

Now she really stopped. "¿Para el perro?" she questioned.

"Sí," I smiled. She continued to stare at me blankly, so I continued. "Y, pues, perros no pueden tener chocolate, sabe…"

"Mmhm," she mumbled, clearly thinking I was unwell. She went about dishing up the vanilla in a separate bowl, though.

"Y es su cumpleaños. Él le *encanta* helado," I told her, but at this point I had no idea why. She had already written me off as crazy, so I might as well go all out.

"El perro…¿le gusta helado?" she asked dubiously as she rung in the two ice creams.

"Oh, sí. Es su favorito," I answered emphatically, handing over the required euros.

"Pues…feliz cumple a su perro," she offered with a forced smile.

"Muchas gracias, señorita."

I made my way back out to Maverick happily. "Look

what I got you! Birthday ice cream!" He stood from beside the chair I had anchored him to and his nose perked up when he saw the cups I was carrying. I gently placed the cup down, but he was already devouring it. His tongue was so aggressive, I had to wedge the cup between my feet as I sat so it wouldn't move every time he tried to lick it.

Not five minutes after I had sat down, and Maverick was long done his birthday ice cream, the same young girl who had scooped our ice cream poked her head out the door. She stepped out and I realized she was carrying a large bowl in her hands.

"Realmente le gusta helado," she murmured when she noticed his already empty dish of ice cream beside my sandals. I looked up at her and laughed. Yeah, he really did like it. "Tengo agua," she admitted, showing me the bowl. "Para el perro. Si lo quiere."

I smiled even wider. "Sí, muchas gracias." I'm sure he would love some water to wash down that ice cream. "Está bien," I told her when I realized she still hadn't stepped forward to put the bowl down. She probably thought, like many people we had passed in León in the past two days, that because he was so big he was somehow dangerous. It seemed like the only dogs I ever saw in the city were small breeds. She finally placed the bowl about two feet in front of Maverick and then with a sheepish wave, she ducked back into the store.

I lifted a brow with a small smile to myself. I may be biased, but there was something about Maverick that, for the most part, could bring out the best in people. Rude train conductor not included. We wandered around a bit more after that and stopped in a park to play ball so that Mav was tired by the time I went to see the inside of the cathedral.

I found a quiet, shady side street just beyond the

entrance to the cathedral and hooked his leash around a lamppost. I set up his water dish with some fresh water beside him. I hadn't felt comfortable leaving him outside the mall. And I never would have left him alone outside the Burgos cathedral, or even the one in Pamplona, but for some reason it felt safe here. As if this corner of the city was for the pilgrims and no pilgrim would ever bother Maverick.

"Okay, you're good. I won't be long. I'm just going to look around and be right back." He looked back up at me expectantly. "Oh, you're right. Here," I passed off the Nylabone I had for him. "Be good." He laid down on the cobblestones with the bone between his paws and watched as I turned the corner and into the gates before the cathedral.

I showed my pilgrim's passport at the entrance to get the discounted admittance and passed through the massive stone arches. There was a hushed feel to the inside of this cathedral, not at all like the one in Burgos. Of course, it was just as awe-inspiring in terms of its architecture and the attention to details. The ceilings alone were impressive and some columns were adorned with wrapping vines and carved grapes so life-like you'd think you could reach out and pluck them.

More than anything, the stained glass throughout the entire place was simply breathtaking. Even though the stone inside seems cold and grey, the light pouring through the stained glass – much of it dating back to the thirteenth and fifteenth centuries – gave the whole place warmth. Maybe not in temperature, but in a welcoming feeling.

I knew I couldn't take too much time inside, because I didn't want to leave Maverick for long, but I felt so much more at home in this cathedral than in the one in Burgos. I wasn't a Catholic, and I couldn't see anyone actually prac-ticing in either of these monstrous cathedrals, but this one definitely seemed to be focused more on religion. I suppose over the years, the cathedral in Burgos has become more of a museum than a place of worship. At least, that's what it felt like to me when I was inside it.

Here, I could actually feel the true purpose of the place. Maybe it had to do with the light from the stained glass. Or maybe it was something more, something different about this cathedral. Whatever it was, it set me more at peace than the maze that was the Burgos Cathedral. Luckily, it was indeed much smaller than the one in Burgos, so I was able to take a tour of the interior of this cathedral and still make it out to Maverick within a few minutes.

He was still chewing on the Nylabone when I came around the corner. "Mavy," I called, and he immediately abandoned the bone to find me. "Wanna go explore some more?"

I unhooked his leash from the lamppost and picked up his bone and bowl, tucking them away. We spent the rest of the day wandering the old parts of León that I had ignored yesterday. In our rambles, we came across what seemed to be a sinkhole in a sidewalk. However, it had revealed what looked to be some sort of foundation beneath it, with stone and brick being revealed by archeologists.

I paused and looked around, though no one else seemed to be paying the scene any mind. The hole dropped about ten feet beneath the sidewalk, right in the middle of a busy area, and people were bustling around the site as if this was normal. Maybe in Europe it was, I guess. But I certainly wasn't used to sinkholes revealing remnants of past cities anywhere in my neck of the woods back in New Hampshire. I guess that's what happens when you build cities on top of cities for centuries as they do in Europe. Who knows, this could have been some Roman house. The cathedral supposedly sat over old Roman baths so it wasn't out of the realm of possibility.

Our adventures for the day took us past the important

sights of the city, including Roman walls that still stood intact, Guadí's *Casa Botines*, the *Palacio de los Guzmanes*, and the Basilica of St. Isodoro. The city is clearly full of architectural gems, but it's also full of plenty of parks that we romped around in as well.

After my conversation with the worker in the pet store yesterday, I was sure it would be next to impossible to find that particular food again. Then again, it seemed pretty impossible to find pet stores in most places. However, veterinarian offices have become more popular in recent towns. And they all seem to carry Hill's Science Diet. I ducked into one on our way back to the pensión for an afternoon nap and ended up buying a bag of the food. If I was going to change Maverick to yet another food brand, I was going to do it the right way.

When we got back to our room, I poured a mixture of the two different food brands into one of his sacks of food. Then I prepared a second mixture, weaning him more to the Science Diet in his other food sack. And yet I'm left with half a bag of pure Science Diet. I sit back on the cot since there's nowhere else to go in this room.

"Huh. Well." I looked to Maverick, who has been watching the whole endeavor intently, waiting to catch a stray kibble that fell during any of the transfers of food. He quirked his eyebrows at me impatiently. "I'm not just going to throw out a half a bag of food. Do you know how hard this has been to find? This stuff is gold, *gold* I tell you!"

Maverick snuffled the food sack I had just sealed up in response. "Guess we find a way to carry it all. But that, my friend, is a problem for tomorrow."

He sighed in agreement then laid his head by my feet. One eyebrow popped up and his eyes looked up at the food bag one more time as if it would magically drop another kibble.

"Tomorrow we keep walking," I told him. I could hear the trepidation in my own voice. "It'll be fine. It'll be good. Right?"

He didn't respond.

The Reason

Day Twenty-Five: León to Villar de Mazarife

24.3 km ~ 34,336 steps

July 14th

I groaned and covered my eyes with an arm, though there wasn't much light to be hiding from in this little hostel room. It was just the fact of the matter. I didn't want to get up. I felt like I was going to be sick. Maybe if I just stayed here another day…

Maverick stirred on the floor once he realized I was awake. He must have gotten hot in the night and hopped off the bed. His stupid little head perked up and cocked to one side as he looked at me. I couldn't believe he was a whole year old now.

"You want to walk?" I whispered to him. He boinged up, right onto my chest on the bed and I grunted while I half-heartedly tried to bat him away. "Alright, alright. Get off me. You want breakfast?"

At that, he bounced back to the floor and spun around, waiting for me to dish out some of the food he had been staring at so longingly yesterday when I had divvied it up. I poured out as much as would fit in his little, pop-up bowl. The less I had to carry, the better. But it didn't make much of a dent in the overall weight.

I packed up everything I had been attempting to air out on the windowsill (mostly Maverick's awful-smelling booties) and sighed, looking around the shoebox we had called home for the past two nights. There was nothing else to stop me from leaving, but I had no desire to go. I'm sure all of my nausea was a result of dread, or anxiety I suppose, but I was still denying that I had anxiety. I was just not at all looking forward to getting back onto the trail. Not after how we had left it just a couple days ago.

I knew if I didn't just rip off the Band-Aid and leave now, I could put it off forever. So off we went. The sun was just starting to rise as we reached the *Parador* and cast a beautiful golden glow on it. The massive stone building was once the Convent of San Marcos and stretches across the entire plaza. A weary pilgrim in the form of a bronze statue sits just before it, leaning his head back against a pillar to rest with his shoes off as he faces the intricate, stone façade. Now, the building has become home to a lavish hotel. In fact, it's the very one featured in *The Way* where Martin Sheen's character splurges and pays for him and his companions to spend the night in luxury.

After admiring all the intricate details in the stone façade and how the light was casting shadows along the whole building during its slow rise, we began the long slog over the river and out of the city. This was not the León we had explored the past two days. It was not the bustling metropolis that housed the mall or the train station or the fancy shops. Nor was it the jaw-dropping, old world architecture that filled the heart of the city. No, this was just industrial suburbs, plain and simple. It was run down, gritty, and the side that no tourist pamphlets would guide you to. Yet the Camino ran straight through it all, along the sidewalk just beside what was sure to be a busy road once the rest of the population woke up for the workday. If it even was a work-day. I had no clue what day of the week it was anymore.

Maverick stayed attached to me as I held his leash throughout the morning. On an industrial sidewalk such as this, I didn't want to take any chances, even if he had come to learn the command "sidewalk" over the past few weeks. Plus, the litter of broken glass and other objects in the alleys deterred me from taking him off-leash.

The yellow arrows criss-crossed us over the highway and through the first "town" of the day, though it really was still just a suburb of León. We had caught up to other pilgrims already, and even bumped into Sarah and her friend as we came up to them where they waited for traffic to pass on the highway.

"Maverick!" she called in her Irish accent as she caught sight of us coming up behind her. Her blonde friend from before, the one I would always just know from singing the *Jungle Book* songs with her, turned to face us as well. She offered a smile.

"Oh, bugger it. We have to cross now. Come on," she urged. There was a break in the rushing traffic on the highway and we dashed across the pavement to the other side. Once there, she turned to me with a wide smile. "How have you two been?"

We exchanged an awkward hug, thanks to her cello case and my large backpack, not to mention the bag of dog food and Maverick's pack I had dangling from one arm. "We've been alright. How have you guys been?"

"Oh, grand! Wasn't León just magical? I loved it." I

nodded my agreement as we came up to the little roadside café here. I planned to stop and eat the banana I had bought last night and look through the guidebook to make sure we chose the right upcoming route.

"Are you stopping for breakfast?" I asked the girls. They shook their heads no.

"Already ate this morning. Best to keep going," Sarah said. "It was great seeing you guys again! Buen Camino!" With one last pat to Maverick's head, they were off, continuing down the sidewalk past the cafés.

I gave a wave and turned towards the shaded patio area, blocked off from the road by cement barriers. I had just stepped into the place when a voice called out to me from one of the tables. "There you are!"

I turned to see an older man with a wide smile standing up from one of the tables in the center of the patio. I was sure I had never seen him before in my life. "Here I am?" I replied doubtfully.

He laughed and began to make his way towards me and Mav. "You don't know us, but we've been following you and Maverick's trip through your posts on the Camino Facebook page! Please, come take a seat with me and my wife."

"Oh! Uhm, sure, of course," I fumble through my words, ever the eloquent speaker, and followed him as he weaved his way back to their table. Joanne, the woman from yesterday's breakfast, was seated there with his wife and waved as I came closer. I smiled at a familiar face and attempted to return her wave, but my arms were too laden with bags.

"Think you have enough stuff?" she laughed from her seat at the table.

"Life with Maverick," I muttered back, dropping the large plastic bag that held his half-full dog food along with his pack onto the cement beside their table. I started to shrug out of my pack when the man's wife spoke up.

"It's so nice to finally meet you two!" she cooed. I looked up to return her smile before unclipping my pack and digging in to find the banana I had stashed there. "We've been following along with your trip this whole time, but we didn't know if we'd ever run into you. You've had quite the journey so far! You've had us both in tears multiple times!"

I looked back up in time to see her husband nodding in agreement. Luckily, I had located my banana and had the stem between my teeth in order to have my hands free to get Maverick's water out. It prevented me from needing any sort of response to that. It was sweet, really it was. And they were so nice. But I wasn't exactly sure how one was supposed to respond to being told you made people cry. I'm sorry? You're welcome? I didn't mean to? None of it seemed like the right answer.

"It's true!" the man said, sparing me from thinking any more on it. "You write so well; it draws you right in. We feel like we've been walking right beside you this whole time. You've written a book?"

I finally had finished taking out Maverick's water, pouring it into his collapsible bowl, making sure he was secured to the leg of my chair, and had pulled it out to sit. "Oh, yeah, I have. Nothing Camino related, it's a fiction book, but yeah, I've written a book." Not that my current stammering was any indication that I was some compelling writer.

"Have you really?" Joanne asked from beside me. I managed a nod around my bite of banana. "That's amazing."

I lifted my shoulder in a shrug. J.K. Rowling I was not. It wasn't all that difficult to self-publish on Amazon when you put in the effort. Regardless, the group of us got to talking about writing and how I had been updating the group on me and Maverick's endeavors along the Camino.

"You should write a book about this once you guys finish," the man's wife said. I had yet to learn their names.

"Maybe," I allowed, but internally I wrote it off. I wasn't one for nonfiction writing. A few Facebook posts was one thing. I wasn't sure I would manage an actual book. I had planned to blog while out on the trail and clearly, that hadn't happened. The idea of a book seemed to be a moot point, but I nodded along with their ideas. Eventually, the couple made to head out.

"I know we don't exactly know each other, but I want to give you a hug," the man said, standing by the table before they left.

My eyes widened, because I was never really a hugger, but I found myself standing nevertheless. His arms enveloped me like a father would and held on for an extra beat. Oddly enough, I felt completely at ease. "Thank you," I whispered.

He pulled away and gave me a small smile. "Buen Camino."

The day suddenly didn't seem all that bad anymore. I took out my guidebook to consult the alternate route while Joanne finished her breakfast. She was also planning on taking that route today, so we agreed to walk on to Villar de Mazarife together, another thirteen kilometers from where we were now.

Once she was done with her breakfast, the two of us shrugged into our packs and made for the alternate route. I unhooked Maverick's leash from the chair leg, keeping him close as we crossed back over the highway and onto a less busy road. It wasn't long before this pavement faded to the gravel farm tracks we had become accustomed to.

"I just have to stop to put on Maverick's booties," I told Joanne, dropping his pack and the bag of food to the red earth and causing a cloud of dust to go up. "You don't have to wait for us if you don't want to."

"Of course I'll wait!" she said easily. "Not a problem at all."

I called Maverick back from where he had been romping ahead of us, happy to be away from the bustling highways and the concrete jungle of city life. He would never make a good apartment dog in a big city. I made a face as I pulled his booties out from the bag. The whole thing was starting to smell at this point. Joanne laughed from above me.

"That bad?" she asked.

I sighed as Mav came to stand next to me and lifted his back leg for me. "It's because he's obsessed with water." I pulled the red bootie up towards his hock and then pulled the black strap so it was tight in place. Then I tapped his front shoulder and he lifted that front paw, eyes scanning the horizon for butterflies to run after. "So when he insists on lying down in whatever water he finds, and he has his booties on, they get soaked." This bootie I pulled towards his wrist, then made sure the foam pads were in place so the fabric wouldn't rub on his fur, and strapped him in.

I stood and moved around to the other side of him because Lord knew he wouldn't be the one to move for me. "Wet bootie, stinky dog, you can imagine how that turns out."

Joanne laughed, watching me make quick work of the last two booties. As soon as I was done, Maverick was off. He had just spotted the shadow of a bird on the ground up ahead. "They don't seem to faze him at all," she commented.

"No," I agreed. "He walked a little funny the very first time he wore them, but ever since then he doesn't even notice them."

"Why do you put them on now?" she asked.

It was a question I had gotten quite a bit now since he had worn them through most of our Meseta experience. I probably would have wondered the same thing, since I hadn't anticipated him needing to wear them for anything but hot tar on this trip. Turns out, we never even walked on much hot tar. "The gravel actually bothers his paw pads. I hadn't thought of it before we started, but it makes sense. The little pebbles dig in and if he goes without booties on it for too long, he develops a limp."

"Well, it's a good thing you thought to bring them along."

"Definitely." I shifted his food bag yet again, then decided to just hug it to my stomach. I had gotten used to sticking my arm through his pack at this point and having that just dangle over my forearm, but the extra bag of food was a bit of a nuisance.

"Do you carry this much food for him all the time?" she asked now.

"No. Actually, it's been really hard to find food for him. I actually had to change his food while we were in León, and that's why we have so much now. I'm trying to switch him over the proper way, by slowly incorporating it with his old food. Which means I've got about two full bags right now."

"I can carry a bag if you want!" she quickly offered.

I shook my head immediately. I hadn't said it to make her feel bad. "No, it's okay. It's really not too terrible." And it really wasn't.

Although the sun was beating down on us since there wasn't a cloud in the sky, and there was no wind to be had today, and this stretch of the Camino was starting to rival the Meseta with its open expanses and no shade, it really wasn't all that bad. We had a friend today. One who was kind, and interesting, and gave off a sense of peace I didn't quite know how to explain but was grateful for nonetheless.

We talked about everything under the sun on those thirteen kilometers. We talked about family and I gushed about how grateful I was for mine. How my mom was my best friend, how my brother and I had never been in a fight, how I would always look up to my dad. We talked about history and she added her insight into some of the things we had passed along the trail that I had no idea about. She explained how she, too, had a love for history and stopped at every little thing along the way just like Mav and I had been doing. We talked a bit more about writing. And we even talked about depression.

"So why'd you come out here? I can't believe I haven't asked that yet, because that's the first question anyone seems to ask and it's completely slipped my mind with you," Joanne laughed just after we had stopped and filled our waters at a fountain in Chozas de Abajo and were on our way again through open fields. "We just seem to be able to talk about anything, I never thought to ask."

I smiled and it was on the tip of my tongue to say because I had learned about it in Spanish class and leave it at that. It's what I had told plenty of other pilgrims. I had learned about it through Spanish and decided that I would walk it someday, and now just seemed like the right time. But it was more than that of course. Just like when people would ask why I left Ohio State and I would answer that it wasn't the place for me or that I didn't like it. There was more to the story than that. But this was the first time I felt like I could admit that out loud to someone other than my family. Maybe I had grown on this journey. At the very least, I was finally coming to grips with the person I was.

"I…was suicidal," I said. My eyes stayed straight ahead, watching as Maverick dove his nose into the red dirt, yet again missing a shadow. He shook it off and spun in a circle, eager to find it again. I could feel Joanne's eyes on the side of my head, had heard her sharp intake of breath, but I didn't turn to face her. "I dropped out of college because I wanted to kill myself. And it didn't get better. I ended up in a ward because of it."

"I…had no idea," she breathed, finally breaking the silence between us. The only sound was the crunch of gravel under our boots. No wind rustled the shrubs beside us on the trail. "I'm so sorry."

I flashed her a smile, finally turning to face her, but quickly looked back down at my boots. "It's fine. Really," I said. It was my go-to response. *Fine* is a really funny word in the English language, when you think about it. Is anyone ever really *fine*? What does fine *actually* mean? Because it certainly never means what the dictionary intends it to. "I'm on better meds now. I have Maverick. It's okay."

I wasn't sure who I was convincing, her or myself. For a while there after the ward, I really did think I was better. Did it do the trick like it was supposed to? Heal me while I was in the inpatient ward? Definitely not. I begged and pleaded until they let me out of that place against their will. I actually had to sign a paper before they released me, saying I was leaving against their professional opinions in case anything were to happen.

After that little stint, I had been better because I was so happy not to be locked in *there* anymore. It hadn't healed me the way it was meant to, but it had made me happier for a bit. The medicine the psychiatrist at the ward had prescribed me started to work. My perpetual numbness to the world had worn off a bit. I thought I was better.

"So this was my way to kick depression once and for all," I told Joanne now. "I thought if I came out here, something I had wanted to do for years, and completed the pilgrimage, it would show that I was really over my depression. They say miracles happen out here. I figured by the end of this walk, I would have released all that sadness. Somehow learned how to feel things again other than hopelessness."

The crunch of the red dirt beneath us was my only answer for a while. "You speak as if you've realized this isn't the case," she prompted.

I quirked a half-smile in her direction. "It's not, is it? We said that yesterday, right? The Camino has its own magic, its own plan. Because God is out here with us. This is, at its heart, a Christian pilgrimage, is it not?"

"It is."

"We can have all the plans in the world, but in the end they don't matter. I think that's what the Camino's meant to teach us all along, don't you agree?"

"That your plans don't matter?"

"Yes and no. Not that they don't matter I guess, but that it's not always about what you *think* you need. I couldn't just *think* myself out of depression. I couldn't just *say* it was gone and have that be so. Just like I couldn't decide what this journey was meant to be before I went on it. We figure it out as we go. Not everything is in our control."

Joanne was silent again. Maybe I made no sense. Maybe my words had no direction at all. They probably didn't, because I clearly didn't have it all figured out. For some reason, she made it seem like I could just spill my innermost thoughts to her, though. She wouldn't judge.

"You know," she said finally. "You don't talk like you're twenty-years-old."

I laughed. Just a little snort of amusement at first. But then I couldn't stop and soon enough we were both cackling, the only sound splitting the still air out here, no other pilgrims in sight on this alternative route. "You know, maybe that's why I don't make many friends with people my age," I said once we had finally gotten ahold of ourselves. "Maybe that's why Maverick's my best friend."

Joanne knocked her shoulder into mine. "I think you're doing just fine."

Boulevard of Broken Dreams

Day Twenty-Six: Villar de Mazarife to San Justo de la Vega

34 km ~ 44,975 steps

July 15th

I had been determined to start today with a better mind-set. Yesterday afternoon, Joanne and I stopped in Villar de Mazarife for some food and the hospitaleros there were so nice Maverick and I ended up staying the night. Joanne pre-booked all her sleeping arrangements, so she had to walk on to the next town after we finished eating, but we had made a plan to meet there in the morning. I told her how Maverick and I started very early most days to beat the heat, so we should be arriving at Villavante by eight-thirty or so. We had a solid plan. I felt happy for the first time in days when I went to bed last night. All was well.

Except, I woke up this morning and immediately felt like I was going to throw up. Maybe it hadn't just been anxiety yesterday morning. Maybe I really was sick. Or I could just have drunk some bad water somewhere along the way. Whatever the reason, there was no way I was walking at that moment. I shot Joanne a text saying I wasn't feeling well and wouldn't make it to her on time. She was probably still sleeping, but she would get it when she woke up. Then I groaned and rolled back over. Maybe the next time I woke up I wouldn't feel like absolute garbage.

No such luck. The sun was streaming through my window when I finally pulled myself into a sitting position. Joanne had answered, saying it was no problem at all that I was running late and she would be happy to wait for me. I left the text open as I went to the communal bathroom and brushed my teeth, hoping that might make me feel less nauseous. I dished out a heaping serving of breakfast for Maverick and sat back on the bed, looking down at my phone again.

If Joanne was waiting for me, I had no choice but to start walking. The thought made me want to cry. Which was really stupid. What happened to all that positivity I had been feeling yesterday afternoon? Where had that gone? Instead, I sullenly slipped my feet into my boots and laced them up. I packed the banana and the few granola bars I had bought at the little market in town into the side pockets of my pack. Then I slung it onto my back, slipped Maverick's red one over my forearm, and hefted the still half-full dog food bag into my arms as if it was a toddler. The plastic shopping bag had been ripped during our walk yesterday, so now I had no choice but to hold it to my chest with both arms wrapped around it.

"Come on, kiddo. We've got ten kilometers til we get to Joanne." We snuck out of the albergue unnoticed. There hadn't been many pilgrims here last night and most had probably left for the day already.

The stretch of ten kilometers between Villar de Mazarife and Villavante was a *long* ten kilometers. You wouldn't think that it could be possible for some kilometers to feel longer than others, but it really was. And this ten was a killer. There was nothing to look at. We were on a paved road the entire time, but no cars passed us. The only company we encountered in that whole ten-kilometer stretch was a herd of cows.

I hadn't even been paying enough attention to know there were cows in the fenced paddock beside us until Maverick's hair began to stand on end. I raised my eyebrows at where he trotted ahead of me, a log protruding from his mouth. "What's your issue?" I asked.

A low growl came from his throat, and his hackles raised as he stared past the barbed wire fence to our left. I followed his line of sight and saw a grey cow looking back at us. In the distance, there was a whole herd of them. I turned back to blink at him slowly. "You're growling…around your log?" In response, he *woof*-ed, only it came out muffled around the wood. "Now you're barking around the log. Right, of course."

The log clattered to the ground on the side of the road and Maverick launched into a full-out bark. I looked around us hastily, but there was still not a soul in sight. Regardless, I hushed him. "Shh," I hissed. He paid me no mind. "Maverick, stop." His barks continued and I looked up to see three grey cows standing at the fence next to us, staring at him curiously. "Maverick, no."

The pounding of hooves caught my attention again and I looked beyond the three cows staring us down to see the whole herd was on the move. Only, they were moving *towards* us, not away. *What in the world?*

I kicked Maverick's log that he had discarded in an attempt to gain his focus. "Mav, come on. Get your stick. Let's go." The whole herd was still on its way to the fence.

The front runners were already lined up, watching us walk along while Maverick continued to bark. It appeared that they found him the most amusing thing in the world. One let out a low *moo* and Maverick's barks picked up in intensity.

"Maverick, *no*," I practically shouted. "Aquí. *Now*."

With one last growl and what sounded more like an *arf*, he finally picked up his log again and hurried to catch up to me. The rest of the herd had made it to the fence and was watching us walk away from them sadly. Some clopped along beside us, trying to keep pace until their paddock cut off.

"You can't bark at cows," I muttered at Maverick. He tossed his head, the log thumping from side to side and then paused to look at me. "No. Bad dog," I told him. He continued to smile up at me around his log because nothing in my voice actually sounded upset. I was more on the brink of laughing than scolding. It *had* been comical to see all those cows running towards us. Although, I'm sure the farmer wouldn't have been too pleased with a dog barking at his herd.

Maverick's log bumped my thigh as he finally gave up trying to get me to throw it and trotted on ahead of me. His fur was finally laying flat on his back again. "You're a nut," I sighed, hiking his bag of food up higher in my arms.

I ended up tweaking something in my knee after that, before we reached Villavante, and I texted Joanne to tell her to walk on ahead. I would catch up with her sometime, but I didn't want to hold her up any longer. I slowed my pace, no longer needing to reach the next town at a certain time, and limped along the last four or so kilometers to town. Although Maverick had briefly distracted me with his antics with the cows, I still wasn't feeling well. My nausea had never really disappeared and now my knee was bothering me and to put it frankly, I wasn't in the Camino spirit today.

Even the seemingly endless fields of sunflowers just before Villavante couldn't brighten my mood all that much. They brought a spot of brightness to the otherwise dull landscape, but I didn't have it in me to fully appreciate them. Instead, I snapped a couple pictures as we walked by and kept plugging along.

Maverick was definitely bored by my slow pace and the way my feet were dragging, so I dug around in his pack until I found his pink ball and threw it for him. Of course, that resulted in me having to bend down to pick it up every five seconds when he dropped it at my feet. So by the time we made it to the bridge into Hospital de Órbigo, I was about ready to keel over. I felt like I was going to be sick at any moment. I knew I should eat something but I had no desire to. I was exhausted as if we had finished a whole day even though we had walked just fourteen kilometers so far.

We paused just before the sprawling bridge. There was a small river at the start of the bridge that passed through two arches, but after that? Well, after that there was really no longer a point for such a long bridge. With twenty arches of varying sizes, this medieval bridge spanned over two hundred meters from start to finish. Apparently, when it was built back in the thirteenth century, the Órbigo River hadn't been held back by a dam. Now, most of the bridge is over flat earth which looked to be an athletic compound, or a place where a circus might be held.

The real interest in this bridge, beyond being excessively large and old, comes from the story of Don Suero Quiñones. Don Suero was a knight from León in the fifteenth century who fell in love with a lady, Lady Leonor, who unfortunately did not return his affections. Like any reasonable man would do in response to such a rejection, Don Suero chose to shackle himself with an iron collar every Thursday to show his imprisonment to love. When this was apparently not a big enough gesture of devotion, he asked the king if he could hold a tournament to joust any knight who dared to face off against him on the long bridge in Órbigo.

For some reason, King Juan II agreed to this ridiculous idea and so in 1434, Don Suero posted up on this lengthy medieval bridge, iron collar and all, and faced off against anyone who dared to pass. He also had nine comrades who agreed to help in this jousting endeavor. Probably so he could sleep or eat. As this happened to be a Holy Year, there were many pilgrims walking The Way. Apparently, the solution for not having to joust against Don Suero Quiñones or his comrades was to drop a glove and then ford the river below rather than using the bridge. In the end, Don Suero defeated three hundred opponents and then made pilgrimage to Santiago to give thanks for his success.

If you think this tale is ridiculous (and you'd be right) it's even more ridiculous to think Don Suero also succeeded in impressing Lady Leonor with his feats and went on to marry her the year following his tournament. And if the name *Quiñones* seemed familiar to you as well, there's a good reason for that. Just over eighty years after the tournament on the *Paso Honroso,* or Honorable Pass as it came to be known, an author chose to write extravagant tales inspired by our lovesick Don Suero. This author's name was Miguel Cervantes, whose famous work, *Don Quixote,* has captured readers' attention for centuries.

Thankfully, Maverick and I were able to walk along the Honorable Pass unscathed. I wouldn't have had the energy to ford a river in my current state, let alone joust a knight. In fact, I had barely enough energy to make it over the two hundred yards to the other side of the bridge. I spied a rock wall of a little patio just to the left over the bridge and started depositing all my bags on it. I just needed to sit. Or lie down. Lying down would be nice. My stomach felt like it was revolting against itself. Luckily, there was shade here so I poured out some water for Maverick and looped his leash around the strap of my backpack. Then I boosted myself onto the wall and collapsed. My giant pack didn't make the greatest pillow, but it would do.

After napping for close to two hours on the wall, I finally shuffled down the main street through Órbigo in an attempt to find an albergue that supposedly allowed dogs. I had learned not to have any faith in my research, though. As it turned out, the albergue in question was beautiful. And they did indeed allow dogs, but only on the patio.

"Ah, Bueno. Está bien," I sighed. Of course, it was too good to be true.

"¿Señorita? El patio es muy agradable. ¿Quieres verlo?"

Did I really want to see their patio? No. But did I follow her out the back doors to the cute space regardless? Of course. I didn't have the energy to say no. The patio really was nice. It looked like a hipster hangout, or a trendy café. Even if it had been the Taj Mahal, I still would have said no. Maverick wasn't sleeping outside in some strange place without me. "Es muy bonito," I told her honestly. "Pero Maverick nunca duerme sin mí. Está bien. Muchas gracias, señorita."

She gave me an odd look. Another Spaniard confused by the fact that Maverick and I were never separated. I peeked my head into a couple other albergues on our way out of town, but in every one, I was told they would only allow Maverick on the patio. There weren't many other options coming up. The next closest town had only one albergue listed in my guidebook and the town after that had just two, so my odds weren't looking great. But there was nothing for us here in Hospital. We might as well try to push on to the next town. It was only three kilometers away. I swallowed down my nausea as best I could and gathered up all my bags.

Maverick happily snuffled ahead on the dirt track. The trail remained by the road, at times crossing over it, at one point climbing a little hill before rejoining it in Villares de Órbigo. I wasn't one to have my phone out while we were walking, other than for taking a million pictures, but I pulled it out as we climbed up the scrubby hill and shot off a text to my mom.

If I ever tell you I want to walk the PCT, remind me of this time. It sucks.

Her laughing emoji response pinged back within a minute.

I let out a sigh and looked around us again. Yeah, dry, cracked earth and scrubby, prickly bushes were not my cup of tea. I could do without the hot, California vibes. Plus, the heat definitely wasn't helping me feel any better today.

We shuffled into Villares de Órbigo. If I hadn't been feeling so crappy, I probably would have said it was a cute village. As it was, I needed a bathroom and to see if anywhere might possibly let us stay. I tied Maverick to a tree in the plaza so he had shade and made my way towards the one bustling bar here. Oddly enough, it seemed to be mostly locals here. I wasn't used to seeing a busy bar with normal people instead of sweaty, dirty pilgrims. The nicely dressed patrons shot me odd looks as the hostess directed me to a bathroom in the back.

After spending enough time in the bathroom to ensure I wasn't actually going to throw up at that moment, I made my way back to the front and found the same girl so I could ask her where the albergues were in town. It was after one o'clock, but I hadn't seen anything else open. She directed me across the plaza to the only place in town. Of course, the adorable albergue here in Villares adhered to the same policy as the albergues in Hospital. The man was more than happy to have Maverick and I stay, but Mav would have to be kept outside.

I finally returned to the shady spot by the tree where Maverick was and sank down beside him. He wagged his tail lazily but didn't even bother to stand up. He must have known I didn't plan on moving any time soon. "It's just so tiring," I mumbled to him as I leaned back until I was laying with my head on his back. He wasn't the most comfortable pillow, but it would have to do. My eyes drifted closed.

"I need to try to call the albergues in the next town." Maverick shifted under my head in response. "I don't want to call another albergue. I hate phone calls." He shifted again, clearly not appreciating his newfound role as a pillow.

"Can you call them?" I turned my head slightly so I could attempt to see his face and peeled open my eyes. He stood up, sending my head crashing to the dry earth. I groaned. "Rude! You could have just said no."

He whined and pawed at his pack, clearly thinking because I was talking to him that meant I wanted to play ball with him. I rolled my eyes and sat up to dig my guidebook out of the top pocket of my pack. There were only two places to stay listed in Santibáñez de Valdeiglesia. Perfect. That meant fewer phone calls for me.

I punched in the first number. "Hola. ¿Permite perros en el albergue?" I asked sullenly. I had lost the ability to inject enthusiasm into my voice today. I just wanted to curl up into a ball.

"¿Cómo?" the girl on the other end of the line asked.

"¿Permite perros?" I tried again. I was never great at rolling my r's, but it had never been much of a problem before.

"¿Pero?" she asked.

"Perros," I tried to correct. "¿El animal?" Still nothing. "¿Permite animales en el albergue?"

"Ah, *perros*," the girl enunciated perfectly. I rolled my eyes at her tone, not that she could see me. Maverick thought I was looking at him again and made another swipe at his pack. He whined and tilted his head at me, clearly asking me *Mum? Can we play?* I returned his look blandly. *No*, I said with my eyes.

"No sé," the girl's voice spoke in my ear. How could she not know if they allowed dogs or not? Didn't she work there? "Puedo comprobar."

She took down my cell number in order to call me back once she checked to see if dogs would be allowed and promptly hung up. I guess that meant I could take a mini nap while I waited for her call.

After ten minutes (I never claimed to be a very patient person) I determined we might as well walk on. There was another albergue in Santibáñez de Valdeiglesia. If this place didn't say we could stay, I'm sure the other one would let us in. Right?

I laughed aloud to myself. Maybe the heat and my nausea was making me crazy because that would most likely *not* be the case. Maverick looked up from beside me and gave me a strange look. Yeah, I was definitely losing it. Oh, well. It was only two and a half kilometers more.

"Let's go, Freak Reek," I told him. I hefted his heavy pack back onto one forearm and cradled the food bag like a baby. "Onward."

We climbed out of Villares de Órbigo. I'm sure if I were to go back and do it again, it wouldn't be much of a hill at all. But at the moment, it felt like Everest. We passed a fountain that was set into a stone wall and I stopped to fill our bladders, even though that would make both Maverick's and my packs heavier again. There was graffiti on many of the stones that made up the façade of the fountain, but it was actually all motivational and nice. Now, I know a lot of pilgrims hate all the graffiti along the Camino on the different waymarkers or signs, but the majority of it is uplifting messages, so I don't see too much of a problem with it. In fact, I've kind of enjoyed it up until this point.

Among messages in languages I couldn't read, the largest one just under the spigot read *Be Here Now*.

"I can't really be anywhere else, now can I?" I asked the rock rhetorically. One to the left of the spigot stated *Just Breathe*. "How prophetic. Like it's that easy. I'm breathin' alright," I grumbled at it. *Would you look at that?* I thought to myself. I had become just another one of the Camino graffiti haters.

My pessimistic cloud followed us into Santibáñez de Valdeiglesia. It was even more of a ghost town than Villares de Órbigo. There were no lively townsfolk hanging around here. The albergue I had called ahead to was one of the first buildings as we came into town. I dropped Maverick's food and pack onto a bench outside with a resounding *thump* and tied his leash around it. "Wait here," I sighed before stepping into the entryway of the albergue.

"Hola," I called. There wasn't another soul in sight, which was actually reassuring. It wasn't like they could turn away a dog on the grounds that he might bother other pilgrims if there were no other pilgrims. After a moment, a young girl appeared through the back door to a garden.

"Hola, peregrina," she smiled as she came to the front desk. "¿Necesitas una cama?"

"Sí, pues, llamé antes porque tengo un perro," I told her, though I could tell from her voice she was the woman I had talked to before about staying with a dog.

"¡Oh!" she exclaimed, realizing I had walked here without

waiting for her return call. "Sí, sí, sí. El perro puede quedarse en el jardín. ¿Está bien?"

I blinked at her slowly. Was it possible for blinking to be tiring? Because at this point, it took effort for me just to do that. No, that wasn't okay. Maverick wasn't going to stay in the garden. "¿Es posible acampar en el jardín con mi tienda?" I asked. If they had a garden, maybe they'd allow me to pitch the tent and use their facilities. I wouldn't say no to a shower right about now.

"Uhm…no." The girl shook her head at me slowly. She didn't seem too sorry about her denial, though.

"¿Podemos quedarnos en una habitación privada?" I'd pay extra for a private room at this point. Even if there was no reason for it because this albergue did not have a single other pilgrim staying in it tonight.

"Lo siento, señorita. El perro solo puede quedarse en el jardín."

"Bueno. Gracias." I turned to leave, clearly not getting anywhere with this hospitalera.

"Señorita," she called before I could leave. "Qué vas a hacer?"

"No sé. Caminaré," I deadpanned. It was the only plan I had for this whole trip, right? To just keep walking.

"Pero, no hay nada por diez kilómetros," she scoffed. As if I didn't know that. As if I thought some other place may pop up on this next desolate stretch.

"Pues, no puedo quedarme aquí entonces no tengo ninguna una otra idea." For some reason, I thought that might make her pause. Maybe she would reconsider for us. As she had so kindly pointed out, there weren't any other albergues between here and San Justo de la Vega. But no. She just let me walk out without another word after that.

Enjoy having no pilgrims in your albergue, I thought bitterly as I slumped onto the bench next to Maverick. He lifted his head for a second off the dusty sidewalk, then rested it on my foot. What I had said to the girl was true; I had no other ideas but to keep walking. I might as well see what we were up against for this next stretch.

According to Brierley, the next ten or so kilometers were supposed to be "serene" and "naturally beautiful" including dry riverbeds and trees. "That doesn't sound so bad," I mumbled to Maverick. His ears perked at the sound of my voice, but he didn't get up. "Trees are good. Trees give shade. We like trees," I told him. "And riverbeds. Sure, they're dry, but those are always good. Serene is nice. We can do this."

I knew Maverick didn't need any convincing to keep walking. This was all an attempt to make this seem possible for myself, but I still wasn't completely convinced. Although, the guidebook did seem to think this was a beautiful stretch. I could do this. I hadn't thrown up yet. I could make it another ten or so kilometers. Besides, there was supposed to be an oasis of sorts about six kilometers in that might have food or drinks for us. At the very least, it would be a place to rest. I could make it six kilometers. That would only be another hour and a half of walking. With that positive thought in mind, Mav and I set out towards Astorga.

Let me tell you, Brierley is a big fat *liar*. There was nothing delightful or beautiful about that stretch from Santibáñez de Valdeiglesia. It was desolate and hot and grueling. Did I mention *hot*? Because I was led to believe there would be shade and trees along this section and that was a straight up lie. Instead, Maverick and I baked in the sun through the entire walk from Santibáñez de Valdeiglesia to San Justo de la Vega. Plus, it didn't even have the benefit of being flat like the Meseta had been. Granted, the hills weren't steep but in my exhausted, nauseous state, they could very well have been the death of me.

At least Maverick was enjoying himself. He finally

succeeded in catching a butterfly in his mouth. I'm sure it was just an accident, because he still hadn't realized that chasing the shadows on the ground didn't actually get him any closer to the real butterfly. Yet somehow, he ended up with one poor butterfly between his jaws. I raised my eyebrows at him as he attempted to spit out the papery wings. He looked like he had just tried a spoonful of peanut butter as his tongue lapped fruitlessly in an attempt to get the taste out. As comical as it was to watch, I didn't even have it in me to laugh.

I wanted to cry. Actually, I didn't think I had enough energy to cry. I was too numb for that right now. We'd been walking for well over an hour and I felt like we'd gotten nowhere. At least we were starting to see some trees. Not that they were shading the path at all, but there were some trees off to the left of the trail now. I could barely muster the energy to be excited about that, even though Maverick had taken to bringing me sticks he found from them.

My feet stuttered to a stop at the base of the biggest hill yet. I couldn't even quite see the top. It wasn't steep, but I just did not think I could do it. I really was that exhausted. The thought of this hill had stopped me in my tracks.

Just one more step, I told myself in my head. My lead foot lifted and stepped forward. *Okay, good. Another.* I started up the incline, keeping my eyes trained on Maverick. He was waiting in a shaded part off to the side of the trail about halfway up the hill. "One more," I mumbled. Maybe if I said it out loud, I could actually keep going. "Just another step."

I reached the shaded spot Mav had found and I couldn't do it anymore. I couldn't keep going. I dropped his plastic bag of food to the hard earth and his red pack quickly followed suit. I sank to the dirt without even taking my pack off and leaned back. Maverick sniffed around his bags and looked at me out of the corner of his eye. Whatever he saw on my face must have told him not to bother me, because he curled up by my feet without even attempting to give me a stick to throw.

I let my eyes flutter closed. This was pathetic. I was pathetic. I was lying basically in the middle of the Camino and I couldn't even make it to the next town. Had pilgrims ever been this tired before where they had to sleep in between towns because they couldn't physically make it to the next town? Probably not. Most people would be smart enough to recognize their limits and stay for the night in the previous town rather than push on.

I vaguely wondered if I could spend the night here. I could pitch my tent here, right? Who was going to stop us? Well, I guess we would have to go back down to the base of the hill. This wouldn't be the best place to try to pitch a tent since it was such an incline. I think there was even a little stream down at the bottom of the hill. That would be good. I had some water purifying tabs. We were about out of water at the moment, so I would definitely need that. I didn't have anything to eat, though. Not that I was hungry. The uneasiness in my stomach had kept me from eating all day. I knew I needed to eat something, but I just couldn't find it in me to care at the moment.

Once again, I wanted to cry. But what was crying going to do for me? Nothing. It wouldn't magically transport me to the next town. It wouldn't somehow make food appear. I took a deep breath and gulped back my tears. Maybe if I just laid here for a while, I would get enough energy to keep going. I could take a nap here and when I was feeling better, then I could make it to Astorga. Well, probably not Astorga. But I could at least make it to the next town, San Justo de la Vega. I could do that. That would be my plan. Make it to San Justo de la Vega. Just after a little rest.

I didn't actually fall asleep there in the dirt. I lay there for what had to be close to an hour before I rolled myself back onto my feet and pushed on. Just at the top of the hill, not three hundred yards from where Maverick and I had been lying in the dirt, was the oasis described in the guidebook. It was even better than I could have imagined. Apparently, a man named Davíd lived here and served all the weary pilgrims that walked past. It wasn't an albergue, and I was told the structure didn't have electricity or running water and yet it easily became my favorite place along this whole trek.

Tarps were draped for shade around a pretty, rock garden. Stumps held platters of apples, peaches, oranges, bananas, pears, and kiwis. There was a cooler full of watermelon that I headed for straight away. Wooden pallets were covered with blankets to make couches and hammocks were strung up where there were trees.

There were plenty of other pilgrims milling around, lounging on the various seating arrangements of the garden. I couldn't believe I was so close to this beautiful place and didn't even know it. I immediately scoped out a shady spot for Maverick and I to lay down and snatched a few more pieces of watermelon. It wasn't the sweetest I'd ever had, but it was so juicy that it instantly became the best watermelon I had ever tasted. I hadn't realized how thirsty I was until now. All of our water bladders were empty, so I sucked on the rinds of the watermelon slices for every last drop of juice. I must have looked like some sort of mad woman.

Even though we had just been resting for almost an hour, I took my time at this oasis, too. By the time I gathered our stuff to hit the road again, it was almost six p.m. At best, I still had another two and a half kilometers to go before we reached San Justo de la Vega. If the clouds rolling in were any indication, there might also be a storm brewing tonight so I knew I really should get a move on. I shoved some euros into the donation box and Mav and I headed back onto the hard, dirt trail.

Maverick found a huge stick to carry along as we pushed through the last of the farmland towards Astorga, trotting along without a care in the world. As if we hadn't been walking for over thirty kilometers already. Once again, there was no shade in sight and even with my sun hat on, I could feel the back of my neck burning. You'd think it wouldn't be so hot now that it was later in the afternoon, but that sadly wasn't the case. Finally, we made it to *Cruceiro Santo Toribio.* Here, a large stone cross, easily fifteen feet tall, stood as a monument to fifth century Bishop Toribio of Astorga. Supposedly, the bishop had been exiled from Astorga and it was here he fell to his knees and looked out over his beloved city one last time.

I, too, felt like falling to my knees in this spot. Only, I wasn't in exile. I just wanted to lie down. The view out over Astorga in the distance was divine...and daunting. There was no way I would ever make it another six kilometers to that city. I was hoping against all hope that somewhere in San Justo de la Vega would let us in. I truly had no idea what we'd do if there wasn't a place for us to stay there.

Mav and I started our way down the wide, paved road towards town. It was a steep descent, but at least it wasn't on loose rocks. The sure footing allowed me to go as fast as I could because the clouds above us were definitely storm clouds. With my luck, we'd be caught out in another thunderstorm. Despite my haste to get to town, I did still make one last stop at the base of the hill we ran down. There was a water fountain just to the right of the path. It was a small fountain next to a statue of a pilgrim. He was a mix between a modern pilgrim, with sturdy walking boots and cargo shorts, and the pilgrims of old who were often depicted with a gourd to carry water in. This statue was raising the water gourd above its head, angling it back into its open mouth for a drink.

It was so well-carved, I could pick out every detail on the pilgrim. The folds in his clothes, the straps of his pack, the way his shirt was tucked unevenly into his belt, even the laces on his boots were perfectly depicted. But what made this statue so incredible was its connection to the water fountain right beside it. When I pushed the fountain to get water, water also poured from the pilgrim's gourd into his open mouth, dripping down the buttons on his shirt and down to his belt.

I laughed for the first time all day and a smile broke across my face as the water trickled down the pilgrim. The muscles in my cheeks felt stiff from disuse today, or maybe I was just that caked with dirt and sweat. I pressed for water again and more streamed out from the gourd.

"Do you see that, Nugget? Isn't that awesome?" I called to Mav, where he was sniffing at a nearby bush. He came trotting over, ignoring the fun stream of water from the pilgrim's gourd, and instead lapped at the puddle that had formed by his feet.

We didn't stay at the fountain for too long. The dark grey clouds hurried us along and onto the sidewalks of town, leading us into San Justo de la Vega. It was a pretty industrial area, the first one we'd come across since leaving León, and definitely was lacking the Camino vibe that many of the small villages seemed to thrive on. I peeled off the main road to the first hostal I saw. It was a mix of a bar, a restaurant, and a hotel and the woman at the front desk accepted Maverick and I without blinking an eye.

Thank you, Lord, I sent up a prayer as I handed over my passport so she could fill out my information. She asked if I'd like to stay in the albergue or the hostel. I hadn't even realized this place *was* an albergue, but I jumped at the cheap price. Once she finished with her paperwork, she led me outside and around the back of the hotel/restaurant building to another small building.

Inside was a bunk room on one side, where one other pilgrim had taken up residence, and a bathroom and showering area on the other side. I thanked the woman profusely and she waved me off like it was nothing. To her, it probably was nothing. She didn't know what my day had been like. She had no idea how much of a blessing this was to me.

I weaved my way between the bunks, which were tightly packed in the room, to the far corner away from the other pilgrim and dumped all our bags on the bed. I would have loved nothing more than to lay down right now and sleep, but I knew I needed to shower first. If I laid down for even a minute, I knew I wouldn't get up again. So I looped Maverick's leash around a bed post, took out my showering necessities, and headed towards the bathroom end of this building.

I placed my quick-dry backpacking towel and all-in-one soap on the edge of a sink and decided to use the bathroom before I showered. Only, when I came out of the stall, the one other pilgrim was standing by the sink. I hesitated and smiled at him awkwardly. "Hola," I tried.

My one word set him off. The next second, he was tearing into me so quickly I didn't even have time to figure out what language he was speaking. I thought it was Spanish? Maybe it was Portuguese? Whatever it was, I could only understand every third word, but his message was clear. He was not okay with Maverick being here.

I tried to reason with him. I told him that it wasn't his decision to make. That the albergue was allowing us to stay. I told him that we would stay on the other side of the room. No matter what I tried to say, the man did not care. If he hadn't been making me so upset, I would have found the situation comical. Me, about to get in the shower, and this man berating me about my dog who was currently sleeping under a bunk bed. As it was, I had been pushed past my breaking point today. I was caked in grime and sweat. I had barely eaten a thing all day. I was physically and mentally drained. Everything on my body ached from the tips of my toes to my wrists. And I could *not* take one more thing.

Without even bothering to listen to the end of this man's latest tirade, I turned on my heel and stormed out of the bathroom area. Maverick stood as he saw me making my way toward him; the man still spitting out angry words at my back as I walked away from him. I shoved my soap and towel back into my pack and slung it over one shoulder, gathered up Maverick's pack and his bag of food, and picked up his leash. The angry pilgrim had fallen silent behind me, a solid twenty feet away because God forbid he get too close to my *vicious* dog. I glared at him as I stormed past and out the door.

Maverick and I stomped our way back into the restaurant area of the hotel and found the same kind woman at the front desk. "Hola," I bit out, then took a deep breath in an attempt to calm my frustration. It wasn't her fault the one other pilgrim in the albergue was horrible to us. "Es posible tener una habitación en la pensión? El hombre en el albergue no le gustan perros."

Bless her soul, she didn't even question me any further. She just handed me over a room key and led me up to the room on the third floor. Was I slightly bitter that I was now paying more for an individual room rather than staying in the albergue? Sure. But after everything that had happened today, I was just happy to have a bed and some peace. I wouldn't have wanted to stay in the albergue with that man, anyway. It was like the train conductor from Sahagún in pilgrim form. No thank you.

So once again, I pulled out my towel and all-in-one soap,

only this time I headed to my own private bathroom. Maverick hopped up on the bed and watched me as I disappeared into the next room. By the time I had finished showering, he had already passed out with his head on one of the pillows.

"Baby," I muttered with a shake of my head. I pulled on the clean clothes I had in my pack and slipped into bed beside him. I knew if I laid my head down, I would be out within a couple minutes. I should really think about getting food first. Or planning what we were going to do tomorrow. Or making calls to albergues in one of the next towns to see where we could stay tomorrow night. But instead, I threw one arm over Maverick and curled into him.

"Just a quick nap," I mumbled into his fur.

Rivers and Roads

Day Twenty-Seven: San Justo de la Vega to Astorga

7.35 km ~ 10,365 steps

July 16th

Last night was actually really nice. Contrary to what I told Maverick, my nap was very long. At least that didn't pose much of a problem since dinner is always such a late affair in Spain. By the time I made my way back downstairs to the dining room, there was only one other table of patrons. Some of the staff were out on the deck of the dining room and they urged Maverick and I to join them out there and watch the World Cup with them while we ate dinner. It almost felt like we were at a bar with friends.

Even though it was a nice evening, my stomach was still bothering me after my nap so I barely choked down any food for dinner and I woke up feeling queasy yet again. I planned last night that we would just do a short day today. I would call every single place listed in the guidebook between here and Rabanal del Camino to see if somewhere would allow dogs. Then I'd just walk to wherever that place was. Only, not a single hospitalero would accept me.

Not only was I frustrated at being turned down on every phone call, but the people were having trouble understanding me just because I couldn't roll my 'rr' in perro. Up until yesterday, I hadn't faced any issues with this but apparently I was incomprehensible now.

I threw my phone down on the bed after calling the fourteenth place and getting another, resounding "no." Maverick lifted his head from eating breakfast to see what the commotion was all about, but when he realized it was just me throwing a mini tantrum, he went back to eating. My stomach rolled again and I laid back on the pillows to stare at the dingy ceiling. It wasn't the nicest of hotels we found ourselves in, but the welcoming staff more than made up for it.

Well, there was one last thing to try. So much for being a real pilgrim.

I reached out blindly for the phone I had just tossed and pulled it towards me again, swiping over to my Booking.com app. After plugging in the filter that said "pets allowed," I loaded up any nearby lodgings.

One. There was one place in Astorga that would allow pets. And it wasn't cheap. Forget the thirty euros I had paid to stay here last night. This was more like a price you would expect of a typical hotel. I sighed and dropped the phone back by my side again and debated my options. I felt like crap still. Whether it was a flu, or bad water, or whatever else, I wasn't feeling any better today than I had yesterday. And I was well aware of how miserable it had been to walk feeling like that, so I wasn't too keen on the idea of walking very far today. The four kilometers or so to Astorga was doable, but beyond that? I knew it would be stupid to even think of walking past Astorga today. So my options were to stay here in this pensión for another night or to walk on to Astorga. If I walked to Astorga, I could try to pitch my tent somewhere or I could pay for the expensive hotel.

I groaned once more and reached out for my phone again.

———

It was another scorching day as Mav and I set off along the main road through San Justo de la Vega. Since I had allowed myself a chance to sleep in and then spent all that time calling different albergues, it was already ten thirty as we made our way over río Tuerto and towards the outskirts of the city. I paused to admire some cute Camino graffiti (apparently I wasn't in a hating mood like I had been yesterday). It featured an unamused face with a jaunty top hat spray painted in neon green on the concrete and it brought a smile to my face. What *didn't* bring a smile to my face was the asinine pedestrian bridge that crossed over the railroad tracks just outside the city.

I stuttered to a stop just before the ramp and looked up and down the tracks for another option, but no. This was it. Now, don't get me wrong. I am all for being handicap accessible. Definitely. But this? This was insane.

Instead of a ramp going straight up, then leveling out as it crossed the tracks and declining to return to ground level on the other side, this was a labyrinth. Painted an ostentatious shade of green, the bridge rose parallel to the railroad tracks at a barely-there incline for at least twenty yards, then cut back the opposite way as if it was a stairwell, and again rose at a slight incline for another twenty yards. All in all, it was four levels with switchbacks before it reached a flat stretch where it crossed the tracks. Only then, you needed to wind your way back down four levels of ramps on the opposite side.

Mav and I rounded the last corner, entering the flat stretch over the tracks, and he happily scampered ahead. Then he paused and looked back at me as we turned to head down the first incline. "I know," I groaned to him. "This is absolutely insane. Whoever designed this needs serious help."

As we rounded the next switchback, some graffiti on one of the iron posts caught my eye. *Buen Camino to everyone. Except the person who made this bridge.*

A laugh broke free and I clapped a hand over my mouth. Maverick looked up at me in confusion. "Amazing," I mumbled. "That's amazing."

The next short stretch to the city center wasn't pleasant. The main part of the city was actually on top of quite the hill, and the sidewalks were much steeper than the ramps we had just used to cross those train tracks. It took all my energy to slog up the sidewalk. Even with Maverick pulling me along with his leash, I was like a dead weight. It was a good thing I had splurged and chosen to stay the night here. There was no way I could have walked any further today.

Lucky for me, this city was full of all sorts of little wonders from the moment we crested the hill. One of the first sights we came to was the Roman Plaza just off of Plaza San Francisco. The ruins, which have been carefully excavated and seem to still be undergoing some archeological work, were right beside the road. A pavilion sheltered them from the weather and walkways allowed any curious passerby to get a birds-eye-view of the ancient Roman home.

I turned off the sidewalk and coaxed Maverick to come with me. There were plenty of signs around, both in Spanish and English, so it was almost like an open-air museum. I'm a huge nerd when it comes to Roman history, so getting to read about the different rooms of this house, and the way they were equipped with different water temperatures even way back then, was amazing to me. The most impressive part of the ruins was definitely the mosaic floor of the reception room. Apparently, the mosaic was called an *Orpheus* and was massive, composed of hundreds of tiny terracotta tiles to make up scenes with birds and bears and plants. To think it was made back in the first century and still is in such good shape today is simply mind-blowing.

Aside from the Roman ruins, Astorga is well known for its chocolate. In decades past, the city was a center for chocolate production and now boasts a museum dedicated to the history of their chocolate-making. While I didn't intend to visit the museum, I did take the time to grab some chocolate from a shop just across from the Roman ruins before we continued on. There seemed to be a lot of pilgrims taking a rest day in the city, and as we sat outside a café to drink some water, lots of familiar faces called out a greeting or stopped to say hi and ask how we were doing. On the plus side, I was able to tell them all that Maverick had been doing great. Since we got food in León, he had put some of the weight back on. He also seemed to be handling the heat like a pro lately. Of course, I hadn't been doing too great as of late. One woman told me that she and her husband got a stomach bug just the other day and they'd been staying here in Astorga for the past few days to rest up. Apparently, I wasn't the only pilgrim feeling under the weather.

Mav and I continued our leisurely stroll through the city towards the cathedral. We passed through two more plazas (it seemed there was another one around every corner) before the street opened up to the Plaza Catedral. It was stunning. The whole plaza was stunning with its artful planters and trees throughout the open space, but most important were the buildings flanking it. Gaudí's *Palacio Episcopal* was the first building that caught my eye. It truly did look like a castle, with four towers, multiple turrets, and narrow, artfully placed windows set into the methodical granite faces.

The building was originally designed as a palace for the city's bishops after the previous palace burned in 1886. The bishop at that time was a huge fan of the famous architect Antoni Gaudí, best known for his various works in Barcelona, the most recognizable of those being La Sagrada Familia. Gaudí drew up the plans for this *Palacio Episcopal* and they were quickly approved. Today, the building is a museum about the different routes and roads that converge in the city. Of course, El Camino de Santiago is a prominent feature of that.

While I would have loved to go inside and explore, I didn't like the idea of leaving Maverick outside and I knew I was already going to have to do that once if I wanted to visit the cathedral here. Which I did. Not to be overshadowed by Gaudí's work, the cathedral here, *Iglesia de Santa Marta*, was just beyond that palace on the far side of the plaza. Something about it drew me in more than any of the other cathedrals we'd seen so far. Maybe because it was huge, but not so massive that it was impossible to take it all in. Maybe because the reddish hue of the stone on the two towers of the front façade seemed warm and inviting. Or maybe it was the impressive details carved into the entry arch of the front doors. Whatever it was, I *needed* to see more of this cathedral.

The woman who checked my pilgrims' passport and handed me my ticket offered to hold my pack for me while I explored the inside. I thanked her for the offer, but I typically left my bags with Maverick if I left him outside. Which made me wonder...

"¿Es posible que mi perro espere afuera?" I asked her. She seemed nice enough. If I gave her a heads up that I was going to leave Maverick outside, maybe she'd let him stay inside the gated area of the cathedral grounds.

"¡Claro! Puedo vigilarlo si quieres," she told me happily. No random Spaniard had ever offered to keep an eye on him for me before. I almost got teary-eyed from her kindness.

"Muchas gracias, señora," I gushed.

With the assurance that she had an eye on Maverick while I was inside, I looped his leash around one of the iron fence posts that separated the front area of the cathedral from the road, and made my way to the entrance.

This cathedral was even brighter than the one in León, though it didn't have the beautiful stained glass that León had. Instead, it was simpler. The massive columns that stretched up to the vaulted ceilings weren't ornately carved with different leaves, vines, or fruits. These were just plain, ribbed stone that towered over me as I craned my neck to see everything. There weren't many people in this cathedral, only a handful of other pilgrims and tourists milling about, so it didn't feel like it was a museum. Instead, it was the first big cathedral I'd been in that still felt like services could be held here.

I was able to truly take my time exploring this place of worship. I checked out each alcove and marveled at the golden altarpiece that was three stories tall and bursting with colorful carvings before finally making my way back outside to Maverick. The girl inside the tourist office gave me a wave as I unhooked Mav from the fence post. I smiled and waved back, mouthing *gracias* to her from afar. She flashed me a thumbs up before turning to help a customer.

"Come on, kiddo. Let's go find our fancy pants hotel room." I slipped his pack back over my forearm, hefted the bag of food back into my arms (though it was getting lighter by the day), and slipped his leash over my wrist so we could make our way back through the streets in search of this hotel.

It was only a few blocks away from the cathedral, and it was insanely fancy. The man at the front desk had to be older than my grandfather, but he was easily the happiest person I had met so far on this trip. "¡Hola! ¡Peregrina! ¿Qué tal? ¿Qué tal?" he greeted with the biggest smile. He was almost bouncing with energy.

"Ah, bien, señor. ¿Y usted?"

"¡Muy bien! ¡Y un perro! ¡Qué fantástico! ¿Tienes una reserva?"

"Sí, de Booking," I told him. "Soy Colby Millsaps."

"Ah, perfecto. Está aquí. Pero, la habitación no está limpia ahora. ¿Puedes esperar un momento en el jardín?"

I told him not to worry at all; I knew I was early. It was barely one o'clock now and I was pretty sure I wasn't supposed to check in until two, but I just wanted to lie down. We'd barely done anything today and I was dead on my feet. After the little old man took down all my info, and happily stamped both Maverick and my credentials, he directed us to the garden out back and some iron lounge chairs with poofy cushions on them. Within a minute, the man was back again, this time with a rawhide treat in one hand for Maverick, and multiple cans of soda precariously balanced in the other hand for me. I had to fight back a laugh at just how overwhelmingly *nice* this man was.

Even when I turned down his offers of the soda, since I never had been a soda fan, he still left them on a nearby table for me in case I changed my mind. Once Maverick had demolished the bone, he came back again to play fetch with him while the room was still being cleaned. In any other situation, I would have felt awkward for coming so early and having to wait for my room, but the man made me feel right at home here. Even the maids that passed by smiled and patted Maverick.

Once the room was clean, the old man showed us to it

and then waved goodbye. The room was more like an apartment; it was so spacious. Of course, it's nothing like the place we stayed in Carrión, but it had an old-world charm to it. Plus, the bathroom was huge and had a nice, deep tub that seemed to be calling my name. I dropped our bags unceremoniously at the foot of the bed and wasted no time in filling the tub with warm water.

After soaking my tired muscles, and fishing Maverick's pink ball out of the depths of the water each time he dropped it over my shoulder and into the tub, I curled into a ball in the middle of the huge bed. I knew I should be out exploring the town, but I was exhausted. If anything, the bath had made me even more tired. So I gave in to my fatigue and took a nap.

After that, Mav and I headed back out in search of a laundromat where I could dry the clothes I had washed in the sink here. Since our room only had one little window that looked out onto the main road, I couldn't exactly dry them there.

Just that small excursion wiped me of my energy again and we returned back to the hotel for another nap. By the time I woke up again, it was already eight p.m. and I was frustrated. I was frustrated with myself more than anything. I was in a beautiful place. Astorga is an incredible city with so much history to explore. But instead of taking it in, I had spent at least seventy-five percent of my day sleeping. I'd wasted it. If I had to take a rest day, I should have at least been taking in the local culture.

I was frustrated because I didn't feel like a "true pilgrim." I had yet to stay in one of the big, municipal albergues with a bunch of other pilgrims. I hadn't cooked a communal meal with others. I hadn't groaned about the snoring pilgrims or the ones who woke up early and shined their lights on everyone and made a lot of noise, because I hadn't experienced that. I felt like I was cheating the experience by staying in a place as nice as this. Or the one in Carrión. A "true" pilgrim wouldn't stay in such luxury...would they?

"Nugget?" I called for him where he was curled up at the foot of the bed. "Do you think we're *true* pilgrims?"

He let out a big sigh in his sleep.

"Well...maybe we are. Maybe it's all about perspective... right?" He flopped over onto his side and looked back at me. "I mean, we've had our fair share of hard times. We've slept in the tent a couple of times. We slept in that garden in Belorado. We've cried in the dirt plenty of times. We carry the same pack and shell as any of the other pilgrims. Sure, our packs are more dog food than excess clothing, but it's still the same. It doesn't make us any better or worse than other pilgrims. Just different."

Mav huffed in response and snuggled closer to his pink ball.

Whether he agreed or not, I knew I was right. Everyone's pilgrimage was different. Mav and I have struggled enough along this trip. I should be able to take this night, where we had an amazing place to stay, with people who loved Maverick, and simply *enjoy* it. We deserved that much. I can choose to be thankful even though I've been feeling under the weather lately. Neither of us have sustained injuries. We haven't been forced to stop our trek. We're still walking. We're still making our way towards Santiago. Just because we do it in a slightly different way than others doesn't mean it's wrong. I needed to stop holding myself to these invisible standards. There was no *right* way to do this pilgrimage. I needed to accept that our way was going to be different from others. I needed to throw out the idea that I have to conform to some ridiculous idea of what a pilgrim *should* be.

We are exactly who we are. For better or worse, this was our Camino. And we *will* make it to Santiago.

All In

Day Twenty-Eight: Astorga to Rabanal del Camino

23.7 km ~ 33,390 steps

July 17th

Even though we were getting a bit of a late start this morning, no one else was up and about at the hotel as we left our room. Well, most people who stayed in this place probably weren't pilgrims. And most tourists didn't tend to wake up early. Regardless, I was a little sad to slip out of the hotel without saying goodbye to the sweet old man who had taken us in so kindly yesterday.

The street outside the cathedral was crowded with pilgrims this morning. I stopped to take in the structure one last time. It really was my favorite cathedral we had seen so far. With the morning sun, the red hue of the stone seemed more prominent. But Maverick wouldn't let me pause for too long. He tugged on the leash and pulled me back around, facing forward on the Camino that stretched ahead.

For the first time in the past couple days, we were joined by another pilgrim as we walked. He was a Canadian man and he talked *a lot*. Maybe I'd just become so used to walking alone for most of this trek that it seemed strange now to have that solitude disrupted. Of course, it was nice at times. I really enjoyed walking with Joanne the other day. Or when we walked that stretch with the man from Taiwan. For the most part, though, I'd come to enjoy the times where it was just Maverick and myself. So the constant chatter of this man for the first hour of our walk from Astorga was slightly grating.

"I'm going to stop for coffee here. You want to stop with me?" he asked as we came to the first town.

I blinked out of the haze I had been in as he droned on about his job back in Canada. "Hmm?" I asked. Then I saw the café he had nodded his head towards, packed with pilgrims. This was the first time in a long time I was walking on a normal schedule with others. Apparently, there was a pilgrim coffee hour and we were smack dab in the midst of it. "Oh, no, sorry. I think we'll keep walking. I try to get most of the day done before it's too hot. It was nice meeting you, though!"

"Buen Camino." He waved us off as we scurried through the end of town and back onto the dirt track through more scrub land beneath some power lines. Did it make me a bad human for basically running away from this man? Maybe. But as Maverick and I walked on, with just the sound of the gravel crunching under our boots, I smiled to myself. I had come a long way from feeling all alone like I had on that third day from Zubiri when I thought the Camino was all about meeting new people and finding your Camino Family.

My Camino family was Maverick. Turns out, that's really all I needed.

It didn't take long for my stomach to rumble, reminding me that I may have skipped the first breakfast stop to escape the overly talkative Canadian, but I really needed some food. Luckily, whatever stomach bug I had been battling for the last few days seemed to break overnight and I had my appetite back. Mav and I stopped in Santa Catalina de Somoza so I could get a tortilla Española. I might have had my appetite back, but that didn't change the fact that I had been eating the same thing for breakfast for the past three weeks.

I picked at the egg and potato dish with my fork and shoved another bite in my mouth. Then I stabbed another bit onto the fork and held it out to Maverick. "Want some?" I asked.

He lifted his head at the sound of my voice, and then stood when he saw the offered fork. Of course, he had to sniff it to make sure it was something he would deign to eat. I rolled my eyes at him. "You're just a prima donna. It's egg. You like egg." I waved the fork enticingly. His tongue stuck out and tentatively teased it from the prongs of the fork before he chewed thoughtfully. I let out a big sigh and waited for his judgment. "Good?" I asked.

Once he had swallowed, he stuck his nose forward again, sniffing for more. "Perfect," I smiled. I stabbed some more of the quiche-like breakfast and held it out to him. He scoffed it down with a bit more enthusiasm this time. I finished off the iced tea I had ordered, my staple drink besides water for this entire journey, and Maverick licked my plate clean, and then we were off again.

The next four kilometers from Santa Catalina to El Ganso were beside the road, but only one or two cars passed by us so it really didn't feel like it was all that bad. Of course, there were still barely any trees for shade, but it was a cloudy day and it wasn't as hot as our days on the Meseta. Mav and I plodded along at a leisurely pace, only encountering a few other pilgrims as we went. We must have left most of them behind at that first town when we chose to keep walking.

As we came into El Ganso, I made a conscious effort to slow down and really take everything in. I had been so wrapped up in how miserable I was the past couple of days, I felt like I hadn't been properly soaking up everything the Camino had to offer. The buildings in El Ganso were definitely of a different style than we had gotten used to seeing along the Meseta. Instead of the mud style we had seen, or even bodegas, these houses were built completely of stone. None of it was uniform nor did it appear to be held together by any sort of cement. The stones just seemed to be stacked together to make walls that somehow didn't topple over. Big rocks, little rocks, some as small as pebbles. Long flat stones, thick square ones, some as big as cinder blocks. They were all piled to make homes and businesses, with holes where wood was placed around a window or an old wooden door was set into the rock.

Unfortunately, many of the structures had fallen into disrepair. In fact, most look abandoned. A row of what once must have been stone houses were all missing their roofs on the right side of the road and trees were growing right up out of the gaping openings. It seemed like the majority of these stone cottages in Ganso were roofless.

"Colby!" I was pulled away from my perusal of the new architecture when I heard my name called. Outside the one bar in this town, the Cowboy Bar as it happens, was Rose. My face broke out into a smile just at the sight of her and I hurried over to give her a hug.

"Rose! How have you been?" I was so incredibly happy to see her again. I hadn't even realized how much I had missed her.

"Wonderful," she said in her soft French accent. "How is Maverick? He is looking great. How are you?"

"Good, good. He's been doing really well lately."

The thing about Rose was that just being in her presence could fill a person up with hope. It was amazing how some people in this world just seemed to radiate light. There's never an explanation for it, but it's a beautiful thing to witness if you're ever lucky enough to meet a person like that. I've only met a handful of such people in my life, but Rose? Rose may be the brightest light of all. And now knowing the story of her love for her daughter? That just made her all the more remarkable. To think that she had endured such loss and could still be so strong was truly an inspiration. It gave me a bit of hope for myself.

Not that I had faced tragedy like Rose had. But she gave me hope that I could be a source of light for others even when I felt hollow myself. That just because I had depression, it didn't stop me from spreading love or being an inspiration to others battling through dark times.

Rose invited me to take a rest with her in the Cowboy Bar, but I really had no reason to stop at the moment. I wasn't hungry, and Mav and I had just taken a long rest under a shady tree just before town. I let her know I would be stopping in Rabanal, though so we agreed to meet up there.

Leaving Ganso, an older man fell into step with us. "Hello! You're walking with your dog?"

"Hola," I returned and smiled at him. "Yeah, this is Maverick."

"Well hello, Maverick," he cooed. "Have you been walking the whole way?"

"Since Saint Jean," I replied.

"That's amazing! Has it been very difficult?"

"Yeah, we've had our hard times."

"I can imagine. Are you planning to make it all the way to Santiago?" he asked.

"That's the goal."

"Incredible. I've only been walking since Burgos and I'm just loving it. It is such a beautiful trek, don't you think?"

"It definitely is," I smiled.

"I'm from the Netherlands. And you? Are you American?"

"Mhm."

"Lots of Americans out on the trail. I've met quite a few. And many people from Germany, too. Actually, quite a few pilgrims from Asia as well. Have you noticed that?" he asked.

"Yeah, I have." Maverick glanced back at me over his shoulder but didn't come back to join us. *Traitor*, I thought to myself. *Can't he see I'm trapped here?*

"I was surprised to see so many. I expected more from Spain, but there are still quite a few. Have you met many people from Spain on your walk?"

"Uhm, yeah a few."

The older man nodded. "Nice people, Spaniards. Everywhere I've stayed is just so welcoming. I guess they have to be since it's their job. To welcome pilgrims. But it has just been so lovely. Don't you agree?"

I raised my eyebrows. I did not agree, actually. Then again, I was an anomaly on the Camino. Not many Spaniards were used to welcoming pilgrims with dogs. I hadn't seen the same hospitable side to them. But I wasn't in a very talkative mood today. As nice as this man was, I really just wanted to walk on in silence today. That clearly wasn't going to happen any time soon. "There are some really nice hospitaleros," I ended up saying.

"And the food!" he gushed. "Oh, the food is incredible. Just last night I had the best dish. To be honest with you, I don't even know what it was," he laughed. "It was delicious, though. I just can't seem to remember all the Spanish names."

He seemed to expect my response so I mumbled an, "mmhm."

"It's the same with all the little towns. I can't keep them straight in my brain. I lose track of all the towns I walked through."

"Yeah," I replied when I realized he was waiting for me to say something again.

Much to my dismay, I managed to be trapped in conversation with this man for the next four kilometers. Now, there was absolutely nothing wrong with the gentleman. In fact, he was quite nice.

"You know," he said at one point during our time together. "I've walked with so many different people. And some of them just talk *nonstop*. It's crazy. Sometimes, you just want to walk along in silence. Just take in the peace and quiet of the trail. But they just *keep talking*. I have nothing to say to them, so I just keep saying 'yeah' or 'mmhm' and yet they don't even catch on! They just keep going! Isn't that crazy? You would think they could take a hint."

I choked over a laugh and my feet stumbled in the gravel.

"Are you okay?" the man asked.

"Oh, yeah," I coughed, keeping my eyes trained on the ground. If I met his eye now, there was no way I wouldn't break out in laughter. Did he not understand I had been doing the same thing to him for the past three kilometers? "Just, uh, tripped over a rock."

"Oh, boy! You've got to be careful about that. I met a man from France who tripped over a rock and ended up twisting his ankle. He had to take the bus to León, it was so bad. I also saw a girl from Italy who…"

I tuned him out, choosing instead to look out over the farmland. After another kilometer or so we finally came across a tree by the trail and I paused. "Hey, I'm gonna stop for a little while. Give Maverick a rest in the shade," I told the man.

"That's a good idea. He would probably like some water I bet. Well, I think I'll continue on, if that's okay with you."

"It is!" I said quickly. I hoped it wasn't too quickly, though. "If you want to, I mean. I don't want to hold you back, but I like to rest in the shade when we find it."

"Of course, of course! It was so nice walking with you. Buen Camino!" He waved as he headed on.

"Buen Camino!" I sank down at the base of the tree and rested my back against the bark. A massive sigh passed through my lips and Maverick paused in drinking his water to give me a side eye.

"I know," I groaned back at him. "I'm a horrible person. But you weren't much of a help! You could have distracted him with a stick or something. Been cute. I don't know."

Mav's eyebrows quirked, but then he turned back to his bowl of water. I let my head flop back against the tree. "No wonder we don't have a Camino Family. I'm just antisocial. And you don't make things any easier, you know." I turned my head to look at him again. He had already abandoned his water dish in search of a stick.

"Aren't you going to rest?" I asked him. He trotted back to me with a stick hanging from his mouth and promptly dropped it by my feet. His booties tapped back and forth in front of me. I stared back at him for a moment, unamused. "Of course not. Why would you ever rest?"

I reached for the stick and then pitched it out into the

scrubland beside us and pushed myself back up to standing. "Alright, then. Let's keep going. We're supposed to cross a river soon."

Yet again, I am here to say John Brierley is a *liar*. According to his guidebook, we were supposed to be able to "refresh ourselves" in some "cool mountain waters" somewhere just before Ranabal del Camino. We found no such thing. There were no cool waters to be had. No "refreshing" to speak of. Instead, we found a rather steep incline up some shale as we headed towards the next village.

It wasn't all bad. I was actually happy to be doing some climbing. It seemed like we hadn't done much real hiking in ages with all the flat Meseta walking we had been doing. Plus, there were more trees around here. We came up on a couple who were walking pretty slowly through the incline. I had seen them a couple times since León actually. They were easily recognizable because of the baby they had with them.

"Hola," I called in greeting as we caught up to them from behind.

"Hey," the woman smiled at me over her shoulder. "How are ya?" Her English accent was endearing and although she looked tired, she was always smiling. Her husband waved his greeting and then focused back on their toddler, making sure the little one didn't tumble on the steep stretch.

"Doing well. How are you guys today?" I asked them as I fell into step with her.

"We're doing pretty good. It's a really nice day today."

"Yeah, it really is," I agreed. The slight breeze was great and it was amazing not to be dripping sweat for the first time in weeks.

"How has it been walking with a dog? I keep seeing you and thinking how cool it must be to have a dog with you."

"It's definitely different. Overall, I'm grateful I have him. He makes things a lot harder, but I couldn't imagine it without him. It must be the same for you guys, too. Right?"

"For sure. Having him with us changes everything, but it's good. I really think it brings the highest of highs and the lowest of lows, if that makes any sense."

I nodded emphatically. "Oh, it definitely does. Not that a dog is the same as a baby of course, but I definitely feel the same way. It's like everything is heightened. If something doesn't go well, it feels so much harder. But when things are going good, it's even better to be able to share it with him."

"Exactly!" She grinned. "I know we're blessed to be able to share this experience with him. And whenever we have good days, they're amazing. It's so great to watch him take in everything we see. It gives a whole new perspective on things. But you're very right with the bad times. It feels like the end of the world," she laughed.

All I could do was nod, but she nailed it. I could definitely attest to feeling like it was the end of the world when I couldn't find food for Mav. Or when we got turned away a million times. Or plenty of other times. However, he also made this journey so much better. At this point, I couldn't even imagine how I would be able to do this if I had been completely alone.

"What made you want to do this with a baby?" I asked her after we had walked in silence for a little while, both of us thinking back on all the memories of the past few weeks.

"Well, we met while I was backpacking in Romania," she said, indicating her husband up ahead. He was following behind the toddler, ensuring he didn't fall, but the little boy didn't even know he was there. He was too focused on trying to keep up with Maverick. "Then we spent our honeymoon backpacking around Thailand for about three months. I actually found out I was pregnant while we were still there. I guess you could say it's our thing." She smiled at her husband's back at this. "It never occurred to us *not* to take him backpacking once we had him."

I grinned at her story. It sounded perfect to me. What a beautiful life to live. "That's amazing. What a way to grow up for him." I noticed her husband saying something to the baby up ahead, but I couldn't make out the words. "So does he speak Romanian and English, then?"

"Yeah. Some words he knows only in Romanian now, some just in English. We talk to him in both."

"Well, he's already ahead of most Americans," I laughed.

As much as I loved walking with them and getting to know them better, they really did walk at quite a slow pace. I guess that's one downfall to walking with a one and half year old. Their little legs can only go so fast. So before long, I had to wave goodbye to them and Maverick and I continued on at our own pace. I could hear the little boy calling out "Doggy! Doggy!" from behind us for a few more minutes before his voice faded into bird song.

It wasn't much further to Rabanal del Camino where we met up with Rose again at a little garden across from a café. She was just stopping for some lunch and to spend time with me before continuing on to Foncebadón where she planned on staying for the night. I would go with her, but I had found a place that allowed pets on Booking.com here in Rabanal. It wasn't listed in the guidebook as a place to stay, but the listing on the app made it out to be an albergue. I wasn't sure what to expect exactly, but at least I would be guaranteed a place to stay for one of the few times on this whole journey.

Now that I was over this whole "what makes a true pilgrim" kick, I had no qualms about using Booking.com. I would book my way across the rest of this trail if I had to. Well, pending prices at least. I wasn't trying to stay in fancy places and spend all sorts of money. Of course, I wasn't opposed to pitching the tent, either. As long as we didn't get caught in any more nighttime thunderstorms.

Rose and I found some comfortable chairs in a shady corner of the garden by the main road through Rabanal so we could people watch as pilgrims passed by. The garden was set up as an oasis of sorts for pilgrims with all kinds of different seating areas and big, puffy cushions that were like couches. It even had a resident calico cat that Maverick was very interested in. We settled into easy conversation as if we'd known each other forever, not just bumped into each other a few times along the trail.

I was recounting Maverick's recent success in catching a butterfly to her when I heard "Doggy!" shouted from the road. I turned to the sound with a smile to see the toddler coming up the road, his pudgy little arm outstretched to point at Maverick.

"I love it whenever you walk by us," his mom laughed as she came into the garden and tossed her bag onto one of the open tables near Rose and I.

"Why's that?" I asked.

"It's the fastest we can ever get him to walk for the longest amount of time!"

"It is true," her husband added. "He walks by himself for the next ten minutes saying 'doggy, doggy' trying to catch up to you again."

Rose and I burst into laughter. "Good boy, Maverick," she cooed with a pat to his head so he dropped his ball by her feet happily. She leaned over and launched it further into the garden for him. The cat glared at the rocks he kicked up in his tear after the ball.

"Well I'm so happy we can be of service," I told the couple as they settled into some lounge chairs in our shady corner. Over the course of the next hour, I truly felt like I had a Camino Family. And what a family it was. I'd be willing to bet most pilgrims didn't find a dog, a baby, or a cat to be part of their Camino Family all that often. This was quite the difference from the past few days we'd been having.

Of course, nothing on the Camino lasts forever. Rose eventually headed on to Foncebadón and the couple with their baby went off to check into their place for the night. Like us, they had booked in advance because it wasn't always easy to find lodging with a baby. They said they tried to get a private room at most places they stayed so that he didn't bother any other pilgrims, so they were staying in what sounded like a *casa rural* for the night here in Rabanal.

Mav and I took a tour of the little town before going in search of our place for the night. There wasn't much to the town, but I'm sure most pilgrims didn't look beyond the main road that the Camino followed through each town. It was nice to dip into the side streets. We even found an over-grown picnic area complete with tables and chairs made from logs and stacked together like the old school Lincoln Logs I used to play with as a kid.

The buildings of Rabanal were in the same style as the ones in Ganso, all stone of varying sizes stacked methodically on one another, but they weren't in such a dilapidated state. Some of the more well-maintained buildings looked like they may have actually used cement to hold the rocks together, ensuring the structures didn't fall apart like others had. Not all were so well-made, though. There were still some cottages that were roofless, just as the ones had been in Ganso. Rock walls along some side streets were so overgrown I could barely see them through the overhanging grasses and hay. But there were also well-maintained walls dividing different orchards from one another and different farmers' fields.

After seeing what was almost every inch of Rabanal del

Camino and falling in love with the quiet village, Mav and I turned in search of the place where we were to stay. A man just a little older than myself seemed to be the only one working here, and he spoke English so well I had a feeling he wasn't a native Spaniard. I had heard of plenty of little albergues opening along the way by former pilgrims who couldn't seem to stay away from the Camino after their treks. I wondered if this man was one of them. The hostel, or albergue, wasn't large and looked just like another house on a side street from the outside. It was only a few rooms with a common room on the first floor and two communal bathrooms and to me, it was perfect.

There was never any question of if Maverick would be allowed to stay or not, and the hospitalero stamped his credential with a smile, admiring all the previous stamps he had collected thus far. He gave us a quick tour of the place, showed me where I could wash my clothes and a place to hang them outside, and said there was a little market just down the street if we needed anything, then left us to our room.

I was riding a high from such a perfect day. The weather had been divine. Rabanal was an adorable village. We had an amazing place to stay for the night. Why hadn't I been using this Booking thing for the whole Camino?! I plugged in the town we intended to walk to tomorrow and booked us a place right then.

"There," I said triumphantly to Maverick. He lifted his head from chewing on his blue, squishy ball that had been a birthday gift to look at me. "All set for tomorrow. We've got a place to stay already. This is so *cool*!" I practically squealed at him. He jumped up from the floor, catching on to my excitement. "We know exactly where we'll walk tomorrow. We have a place to stay at the end of the day. You still have plenty of food, and it's not even breaking my back to carry it anymore. I don't feel sick today. And tomorrow we get to leave our stones at Cruz de Ferro!"

His tail wagged back and forth, though he had no idea what any of that meant. I doubt he even knew that in his pack, he had been carrying a rock from home to lay down at the foot of the Iron Cross tomorrow. It was a pilgrim tradition. At the highest point of the Camino, Cruz de Ferro stood amongst a pile of rocks. Each pilgrim was supposed to carry a stone with them to lay down at the foot of the cross once they got there. It symbolized the burdens we all carried that we wished to lay down on this Camino. Of course, for every pilgrim that rock would mean something a little different. It was a part of the Camino I had been most looking forward to. I hoped to get there for sunrise tomorrow, which would mean we had to start out very early to make the final climb to get there through Foncebadón.

It also meant we should grab some snacks to have for breakfast, since I doubted anything would be open that early in Foncebadón to pick up on our way. "What do you say? Want to check out the little market with me, or do you want to stay in the room while I go?" Mav squished his blue ball in his jaws in response. "Yeah, I didn't think you'd want to stay. You know, by the end of this we're really going to have some separation issues, aren't we?" He spun in a circle as I grabbed his leash from the bed and then ran to the door of our room once I hooked it on him.

The market was just a stone's throw away from the hostel and it had a mix of locals and pilgrims hanging out at some tables that were on a little patio just outside the door. "Alright, wait here." I hooked Maverick's leash around the leg of a chair outside and then ducked through the hanging plastic that counted as a door in so many places in Spain.

I loved going into different markets in these small towns. Of course, some were geared to pilgrim things. But a lot of the ones I had been in were really just corner stores, almost like convenient stores in the US. Only, it was mostly fresh things since everything people ate here tended to be fresh each day. Which meant I was grabbing a couple of bananas rather than some granola bars. I was just looking in the cooler to see if they had any iced tea I might want to bring with me in the morning when I heard a bark followed by a *crash* and then a *clang* of metal scraping against paving stones and what I thought was…hissing?

I sprinted out of the store, the bananas still in my hand. "Maverick?" I called before I was even fully through the plastic. I scanned the little patio where an old man had clearly just been startled up from a chair and was looking towards the back corner. The metal chair I had hooked Maverick to was tipped over and dragged halfway across the patio. There he was, tail between his legs, at the far corner from where I had left him.

"Maverick!" I gasped, rushing towards him. At the sound of my voice, he whipped his head around and scampered towards me to meet me in the middle of the patio. Other customers who had been in the shop had come outside to see what all the commotion was about at this point, too, including the store clerk. "What happened, baby?" I asked him, checking him over quickly to see if there was anything wrong.

"¿Qué pasó?" I heard the clerk ask from behind me.

"Fue un gato," the old man who had been startled from his chair answered. He turned to me now. "Un gato lo atacó."

"¿Atacó?" I gasped, redoubling my efforts to check him out. A cat *attacked* him?

"No fue malo. Fue principalmente una sorpresa para él."

Maverick growled beneath my hands as I checked him out and I followed his line of sight to see a black cat on the rock wall at the back of the patio. Its fur was all standing on end, making it look like a giant, black cotton ball and it hissed in response. "Shh," I cooed. "It's okay. I'm here. You're fine."

Though his growling didn't stop, I was able to lead him back towards the door to the store by his leash. He wouldn't fully turn around with me – couldn't take his eyes off the little black devil in case it decided to launch again, I'm sure. I grabbed the chair he had pulled with him in his haste and brought it back to the table it had been at, a good ten yards away. Then I went about fixing the other tables and chairs he had managed to disrupt.

"Okay, I have to leave you for one more second." He finally looked back at me with wide eyes, like he knew what I was saying and was *not* okay with that plan. "I know. You're going to be fine. Just one second. I need to pay for this stuff." At that point, the other customers and the clerk for the market had all returned inside the store, but I still had the bananas in my hand. "One second, I promise." I bent down and kissed his head, then secured him to a sturdier post this time. Perhaps a tin chair wasn't the best thing I could have tied him to.

"Lo siento, señora," I apologized to the clerk as soon as I reached the checkout counter.

"No fue nada," she brushed off. "Su perro, ¿está bien?"

"Sí, fue solo un gato. Todo está bien. Gracias."

"De nada. Buen Camino, peregrina," she added as I ducked through the door. Maverick was already straining towards me when I emerged again and I quickly unhooked him from his post.

"I told you it would be fine. I'm right here. Let's go back to the room before you get traumatized by something else," I laughed. He glued himself to my side, for once not yanking me forward while he was on his leash. "Baby," I muttered with a laugh.

. . .

Mav was happy to lounge in the room while I washed my clothes and took a shower before we braved heading out one more time so that I could find something to eat for dinner. We ended up at a different albergue right at the entrance of town where we ate with two older ladies, each Spanish teachers back in the States who couldn't get over the fact that I was walking with a dog.

After our meal, we were enjoying a leisurely stroll around town one last time before turning in for an early night when Maverick yanked on the leash *hard*. His bark boomed over the empty street and he charged towards the corner of the barn we were passing at the time.

"What are you *doing*?" I demanded, trying to yank him back, and my arm back into its socket for that matter.

Out of the corner of my eye, I caught the back end of a cat whipping around the corner of the barn. "Oh, good lord," I sighed. "So this is how it's going to be now, huh?" Mav's low growl vibrated through the leash and up my arm. "Stop that," I hushed. "It's just a cat. It wasn't even the same cat! See?" I pointed out the cat, scared out of its wits on the stone wall, as we came to the edge of the building.

Maverick let out a new chorus of barks. "Stop that!" I commanded. "Mavy, *no*." The cat hissed in response, its whole body arching and white and black fur standing on end. Mav barked back louder.

"Alright, let's go." I hauled on my end of the leash, tugging him down the next side street and away from the cat. An old couple out for an evening walk looked at us curiously.

"Lo siento. Es el gato. No le gustan gatos." I shrugged in a *what are you gonna do?* manner. They side-eyed us for a little longer, but then disappeared down the road.

"You're ridiculous," I hissed down at Maverick, but I couldn't help it. I laughed instead. I couldn't stay mad at him. "You do realize you live with two cats at home, right?" He trotted beside me, head held high, tail arched in a semi-circle, the picture of alert. I pinched the bridge of my nose in response. "Right then. Not a fan of cats now. Noted."

Drops of Jupiter

Day Twenty-Nine: Rabanal del Camino to Molinaseca

31.2 km ~ 44,009 steps

July 18th

I slapped my hand blindly at my phone, finally connecting with it and turning off the quiet alarm. I didn't want to wake any other pilgrims, even if we were in a private room. The place was pitch black despite the windows being wide open. I groaned softly and glanced over at Maverick. He was sprawled on his back, his two front paws stretched out in front of him, his back legs kicked straight up in the air. I blinked at him slowly.

"Huh," I muttered. "I see you're still really torn up about that run in with the cat yesterday."

He stretched his front paws a little further, then flipped over onto his stomach, his tail already wagging wildly at seeing me awake. He crawled forward until he was on top of my chest, pushing me down into the mattress, and proceeded to smother my face in kisses.

"Okay, okay, I'm up," I groaned as I tried and failed to turn my head away from his slobbery tongue. "Ugh, enough. That's gross." Of course, I was laughing as I said all this, but I did eventually wriggle free of him and stood to reach for the light switch. The room immediately lit up, the only blip of brightness in the whole town probably.

I flipped my wrist so my watch would light up. Four thirty-three. Wonderful. It's about seven kilometers between Rabanal and Cruz de Ferro, and it's a climb seeing as the cross sits at the highest point along El Camino. So if I wanted to make it for sunrise, we had better start walking soon.

In the light of our room, I gathered up the rest of my clothes that had been drying overnight and packed away Maverick's toys and now-empty breakfast dish. "Come on," I whispered, flicking the switch as I pushed open the wooden door to the hallway.

He clomped his way down the stairs, never one for subtly, and I tried to shush him but it was no use. He was already waiting by the door when I made it down the stairs, looking back at me through the morning gloom. The streets of Rabanal were empty of pilgrims this morning. It seemed we were the only ones in this town crazy enough to get up in time for sunrise at Cruz de Ferro. Anyone else who planned to be there for sunrise was sure to stay in Foncebadón like Rose was.

The stars were beautiful as we left the village behind and started to climb on the dirt trail. With not a hint of light pollution for miles, it was as if they were right in front of us. Like if we walked a bit more, we'd be able to reach out and touch them. And the air was finally cool and fresh, the kind you only found in the mountains. I hadn't realized just how stifling the air had been along the Meseta, even in the early mornings. It lacked that crispness; that hint of spontaneity that said the weather could change at any moment.

We had walked about three kilometers, all of it a steady climb, before I could see anything beyond the light of my flashlight. To my left, far away, I could just barely make out little blips of light. Maybe that was Astorga in the distance, back in the valley we had left behind. A tinge of violet now rose from the earth, lightening the sky just barely enough to make out the shadows of trees beside us. Another ten minutes and the violet had turned to indigo. A sliver of orange sat like a hat over the lights in the distance, promising the sun's arrival. But when I looked back ahead, not to the east and over the valley, all was still dark. Maverick's eyes glinted back at me in the beam of my flashlight and I hitched my pack higher.

In the lightening morning, I was able to make out the road just beside us as we came towards Foncebadón. It was just about six as we made our way into the tiny village. If I had thought Rabanal was a small town, it was a city in comparison to Foncebadón. Yet there was something about the mountain hamlet that called to me. It was run down, that much was certain. Many of the buildings, from what I could make out, were falling apart or just dingy. Instead of the stone structures that had been so popular from Astorga to Rabanal, it seemed like everything here was made of wood. I suppose that made more sense because there were trees around for the first time in ages. They could actually afford to make structures out of wood here.

I unclasped Maverick's leash so I could hold one end of it as we came into town because it looked like farm animals had the run of the town. I didn't need him charging after a chicken at six in the morning and waking up every person in town with his barks. A few pilgrims were outside, lacing up their boots and slipping into their packs as we made our way up the main road that wound up the mountain.

"Buen Camino," they murmured in whispers as we passed. Even though first light had come and flashlights were no longer needed to see, it was still too early to speak above a whisper. Or maybe that was just because this whole area demanded a kind of reverence, a silence of sorts. There was the feeling of something heavy in the air. Something important.

The trail got busier as we made that last steep ascent towards Cruz de Ferro. For the most part, it seemed like everyone understood the feeling of the gravity in this place. Most pilgrims were not keen to make conversation as we passed them heading up. Instead, nods of "Buen Camino" were exchanged. Although, there was one group of young adults that appeared to have missed the unspoken memo of this sacred place. They laughed and joked on their way up the mountain, bumping their shoulders into one another in an attempt to knock each other off balance on the loose stones.

Even though my legs were burning from the last six kilometers of climbing, and my lungs would have enjoyed a break, I pushed myself faster so I wouldn't be stuck amongst that group for long. Maverick was happy to take the lead. If it was up to him, I'm sure we would have been running for the last kilometer. The trail continued up, then turned to the right with the road, and then finally turned once more and there it was. Cruz de Ferro.

In all actuality, it looked a bit like a telephone pole sticking out of a mound of rocks. But at the very top was the iron cross from which it got its name. There were a handful of pilgrims already there as we made our way forward along the path that led up to the cross, but everything was silent aside from Maverick's booties against the hard packed dirt. Two pilgrims were kneeling on the rocks at the base of the cross, another was leaning against the fence that stopped just before the pile of stone, his head bent in prayer.

Rose stood from where she had been sitting cross-legged on the stones and nodded a hello but that was all. Without speaking, we both knew we needed some time here in this place alone. This was something that needed to be done on your own.

I stood at the base of the pile of stones, just staring up at the cross against the lightening sky. I thought about everything we had gone through to get here. The hard days. The sweat and tears. The fun. The amazing pilgrims we had met along our path so far and the kind Spaniards who had taken us in. I thought about the people who had turned us away, the ones who had scorned us. It all led to this. Of course, the Camino wasn't over yet. But this spot? This moment? Seemed just as important as Santiago would be.

My eyes dropped from the iron cross, down the pole, to the pile of rocks and Maverick. He was standing at the base of the wooden pole, just staring at me. He hadn't made a sound. For once, he wasn't whining or bothering a fellow pilgrim to throw something for him. Even he recognized the depth of this moment. The energy of this place seeped into him as well and he stood silent, watching me take it all in.

Then I finally mounted the hill of stones, carefully picking my way over the rocks that hundreds of pilgrims had left before me. Some had writing scrawled on them. Others had paper notes wrapped around them. Some had been painted, others left plain. Some were large, almost the size of a loaf of bread, and I couldn't possibly imagine carrying that this whole way. Then again, I was carrying Maverick's pack laden with food so there really wasn't all that much of a difference. But most of the stones were small, some as small as a quarter, but mostly the perfect size to fit in the palm of your hand.

I reached down to my hip pocket and drew out the stone I had been carrying there for the past twenty-nine days. It was smooth under my fingers, the grey-green worn down from the battering of waves. I had taken it from the beach back home because it looked almost like an emerald when it was wet. But dry, it was just a dark greyish color. I squirted some water from my drinking spout onto a finger and rubbed it across the surface, bringing the green to life. There was something so simple about it that had called to me. Like there was beauty in something that was so worn down, that looked so plain. It was proof that sometimes you just needed to look at something in a different light to see it for what it truly was.

I knelt in the rock at the base of the cross and without prompting, Maverick laid down right in front of me so he was between me and the wood.

"Lord," I murmured in a whisper only Mav could hear. "May this stone, a symbol of my efforts on this pilgrimage, that I lay at the foot of the cross, weigh the balance in favor of my good deeds some day when the deeds of all my life are judged," I recited. "Let it be so."

I brought the stone to my lips and pressed a kiss against the cool surface, then placed it on the pile of rocks between Maverick's red bootie and my knee. I unzipped the small pocket at the top of Maverick's saddlebag and pulled out the heart-shaped rock a friend had gifted to us just before the journey. "Mavy?" I asked him. He turned his head to look at me but didn't move. "You want to put down your rock?"

I held the white stone out for his inspection, which he snuffled at daintily. His nose left a wet imprint on it and I smiled. "Let it be so," I repeated, placing his rock beside my own.

I wasn't ready to get up yet. I still had a lot to say to God in this place. There was a lot that that little stone was symbolizing. So instead, I stayed bent over in prayer, my knees digging into the stones beneath me uncomfortably, and yet I barely even noticed it. Maverick laid his head across his front paws, the red of his booties shining like a beacon in the rising sun.

"Lord, I don't think one little stone is suddenly going to fix all my problems," I told him in my head. "I know it's not. But if it was possible, I'd love that stone to be a symbol of my depression. I would love to lay down my depression at the foot of this cross and never have to pick it up again. I would love for this to be the moment when I start feeling truly alive again. Like I *want* to live again. I know it's not that immediate. But I'm learning to have faith. I'm seeing what You're doing out here. I'm seeing how everything has its place. Everything has its time. So I guess I want to say thank you, Lord. For keeping me alive all this time, even when I didn't want to be alive.

"I don't know why You did it. I don't know why I'm still alive. But I know there must be some reason. I just hope You can help me to remember that. Help me remember to live.

"And I want to say thank you. For Maverick. For everything that he is to me. For allowing me to have this journey with him. You have taught me so much through him. He's taught me how to bounce back. He's taught me that sometimes, a long nap is just as good as a long walk. He's taught me to find the joy in the little things, like chasing a butterfly. He's taught me to push through the hard things. He's brought me out of my comfort zone. So thank you, Lord. For everything. For bringing us here. For reminding me to live."

I opened my eyes to see Maverick with his head still on our two rocks. I touched them one last time with my fingers, then pushed myself to a standing position. I felt empty, but not in a bad way. I felt empty in the way you feel when you finally put down that heavy bag you've been carrying. Like I had let go of a weight I hadn't realized I was holding.

I turned to make my way back down the mound of stones and Rose came forward to meet me halfway. Without a word, she folded me into a hug. We held each other for a long time and when we pulled apart she kept my hand in hers, tears in her eyes. Maverick jumped up, though I had never seen him jump up on people before, and balanced his paws on our joined hands. Rose laughed through her tears.

"He knows," she said. "He knows."

We retreated to the little park area off to the side of the trail and sat together, just staring up at Cruz de Ferro while the sun rose in the east, turning the wispy clouds that were drifting past the cross to a pink hue that resembled cotton candy. Rose took the time to smoke a cigarette. I munched quietly on my banana. And Maverick romped around the grassy area with a stick, trying to entice any pilgrim who came near to throw it for him.

At the sound of music blasting from a speaker and shouting, Rose and I turned to look down the trail to see a group of teenagers making their way towards the cross. Clearly, they were not of the same mind that this was a sacred place. It was almost as if it was an entire high school field trip bearing down on us. I glanced over at Rose, who shared my look of horror. She stubbed her cigarette out in the dirt and tossed it in the trashcan nearby.

"I think that is our cue," she grinned at me slyly.

"Onward then," I responded, slipping my shoulders back into the straps of my backpack and buckling the hipbelt. I hauled Maverick's pack into my arms. "Let's go, kiddo."

Rose smiled at my name for him and then we were off, making our way out of the grassy rest area just as the teenagers reached us. One of them was literally carrying a portable speaker to blast the music. I fought down my frustrations and took one last look at Cruz de Ferro before we dropped down and rounded a turn in the trail. From our position on the far side of the cross, the sun had just crested the mound of stones. Pilgrims standing atop the pile were silhouetted against the blazing rays. The cross stood out pitch black against the gold of the sun. And it. Was. Perfect. There couldn't have been a more perfect last look at such a sacred place.

The great thing about walking with Rose was that I really didn't have to walk with Rose. I meant that in the sense that while yes, we walked together from Cruz de Ferro on to Manjarin, words weren't needed. We didn't walk step for step together. Sometimes Mav and I found ourselves way ahead of her. Sometimes she passed us. Yet it was still comforting to know we were together for this stretch of time.

With the morning sun making the entire landscape seem golden, we walked through the short mountain grasses and over rocky terrain and for the first time in weeks, I felt truly at peace. Maybe it had something to do with laying down our stones at the foot of the cross, but I knew it was something else. It was the mountains themselves. I had missed the mountains. It might seem incredibly simple, something I should have already realized, but I think I was having my very own Camino Epiphany. Because I am truly *happy* in the mountains. I can breathe. I feel *alive* in the mountains.

Just over a year ago, I had felt trapped. Sure, I had enjoyed the parties and the friends and going out while I had been at Ohio State. But I needed something else, something I couldn't get there. I could never get out of that concrete jungle of Columbus. And if I did, everything was flat. It was flat for *miles*. Just endless corn fields. It made me feel like I could run forever and not get anywhere. Just run and run and run and still be in the same exact place because it all looked the same. In a way, maybe the Meseta had made me feel those same things. Wide open, flat spaces didn't make me feel free. They made me feel trapped.

I took in a deep breath now and it was perfect. The mountain air filled my lungs and my hand reached out to brush the grasses as they were waving in the breeze. Everywhere we looked was more mountains, as far as I could see. They weren't rocky and bare like the higher summits in New Hampshire. No, they were more like the mountains we had crossed in the Pyrenees with fields and farm animals grazing in them, looking like white dots against the patchwork of different grasses. Hedgerows of shrubbery divided fields, and short, hardy trees were speckled along our route. I hadn't realized how much joy just seeing *trees* could bring until this trip.

Truly, the day couldn't have been more beautiful. The kilometers passed with ease, dipping down steadily along a ridgeline of sorts. The trail was narrow, much more of a hiking trail than the wide farm tracks we had been used to as of late, and it wove through the green mountain shrub and past beautiful wildflowers. The violet buds seemed to blanket entire sections of the mountain, somehow managing to grow amongst the rock and turning the whole landscape purple for stretches. The breeze was perfect, and even with barely any clouds in the sky, I wasn't sweating. In fact, I even pulled my long-sleeved shirt back over my t-shirt for a while. What a beautiful thing it was to have a chill.

Acebo appeared out of nowhere. We were walking along,

declining steadily, and then all of the sudden the black tops of roofs popped up ahead of us, prompting a steep drop down to the village. Mav and I half ran, half scrambled our way down and onto the pavement of the single road through town and turned into a patio for a rest and some food. Being the first real town in almost ten kilometers, it made for a popular rest spot for pilgrims.

Two different bars stood across the street from one another, vying for pilgrims' attention. We filled our waters and joked with other pilgrims who were lounging about the patios, their boots forgotten beside them as they attempted to stretch out their feet. It seemed not everyone was as excited about the rough terrain and mountain weather as I was. Maverick amused the masses by bouncing back and forth across the pavement, darting after the shadows of birds as they swooped by in search of pilgrim food scraps.

After about an hour or so of rest and refueling with some delicious food, Mav led the way through the narrow streets of Acebo. While we had seen plenty of other pilgrims in Acebo during our rest, we hadn't happened across Rose again. Maybe she had passed through town when I was inside getting food. Maybe she had stopped to rest somewhere behind us. But we didn't see her again. Instead, we set off alone for this next stretch from Acebo, just me and Mav once again.

The buildings were close together, made with stone bricks carefully placed and held together tightly, unlike those stone buildings we had seen in the villages leading up to Cruz de Ferro. Some seemed to be more cement than rock, but all were well made and even if they did look empty, they weren't in danger of falling apart. Many of them sported terraces, or little balconies made of rough wood from their second stories and the combination of stately stonework with rough wooden posts and railings was somehow charming and unique.

It didn't take long before we left the stone buildings behind and were back on mountain trails again, winding our way down to the next town of Riego de Ambrós. This village was decidedly less populated than Acebo had been, but still adorable. Stairs that were a mix of stone and turned to wood led up to various wooden balconies here that gave the whole town a more natural feel, like it had been built right up out of the mountains with the materials that had been available. There was maybe one bar for pilgrims in town, but it didn't look like many stopped here.

Mav and I paused outside the stone chapel of San Sebastián to enjoy the shady church grounds and fountain here. If I hadn't already booked a place ahead of time in Molinaseca, I would have thought this was the perfect place to pitch our tent for the night. *Wow*, I thought to myself. *I must be feeling better if I'm thinking of pitching my tent so happily.*

After exploring the church, I came back out to the grassy knoll under a tree where I had left Maverick and flopped down next to him. "What do you think, Nugget?" I asked him while I stared up at the green leaves over us. He dropped his stick on my chest and danced back out of reach, waiting for me to throw it. I grabbed it without looking and tossed it behind my head. "It's perfect, isn't it? We love the mountains," I sighed. Maverick came skidding to a halt beside me again and deposited the slimy stick back on my chest.

"Oh! It's a dog!" a voice interrupted me. I sat up straight, the stick sliding from my chest to my lap, and Maverick dove forward to scoff it up again. My eyes landed on a pair of bicigrinos by the fountain in front of us, their bikes leaned against the stone wall while they filled their waters. "I didn't realize who you were talking to," the woman laughed.

"But then we realized the dog was yours," the man added with a smile. "He is yours...right?"

Upon seeing they were discussing him, Maverick trotted over to the wall to say hi and plopped his slobber-covered stick on the top of the rock wall in front of them. He took a little hop back and glanced back up at them expectantly. I raised my eyebrows at his antics, then turned back to the pilgrims. "Yes, he's mine. For better or worse," I added with a laugh.

"Oh my, you brought us your...stick? Is that what this is?" The woman bent forward to grab it but paused with a laugh. "This isn't much of a stick for a big dog like you," she told him.

She was right. The stick he had found was no longer than my finger, more a sliver than a stick, but I'd be lying if I said that was the smallest fragment he had ever brought me. Nonetheless, she obliged and plucked the wood from its pool of slobber and tossed it out over the grass towards the church. She must have noticed our packs laying by the base of the tree, because she took her eyes off Maverick to turn back to me. "You're a pilgrim?" she gasped.

I nodded, not really sure what else I was expected to say to that. "With your dog?" the man clarified.

"Yeah."

"Where did you guys start?"

"Saint Jean," I replied.

"Oh my goodness. So how long have you been out here?" she asked while her husband took up the task of throwing the stick for Maverick.

"Uhm, just about thirty days now."

She blinked in shock, unable to answer right away. "That's impressive," her husband filled in. "I can't imagine. And with a dog. Wow."

"Ah, right," I nodded towards their bikes. "Bikes definitely make it go by a bit quicker. Although, I can't say I envy you when it comes to going up hills."

The woman's laughter greeted me and her husband smiled, too. "Yeah, well, the downhill parts seem to make up for it," he said.

"Oh, of course. Then today must be a blast."

"It really is."

"Well," the woman said, reaching out to pet Maverick's head while he was bent over his stick. "It was so nice to meet you and…"

"Maverick," I filled in for her.

"Maverick," she smiled. "It was great meeting you guys. Best of luck to you both. And Buen Camino."

"Buen Camino," I waved as they strapped their helmets back under their chins and mounted their bikes. Soon enough, they were bombing down the road and disappeared from view. Maverick watched them go with a tilt of his head, then snatched his stick back up from the rock wall and trotted it back to me.

"That could have been us, you know. If you had just sat in the dang buggy," I told him seriously. His head tilted to the side, his dark amber eyes flicking down to the stick he had placed on my lap and then back up to my face. To the stick, then back to my eyes. I laughed and shook my head. "Nah, that never would have been us. We like walking too much."

I brushed his stick from my lap, which sent him skittering across the grass to find it, and stood to grab our bags. The next stretch down from Riego de Ambrós was steep and wet, even passing through a boggy river area that Maverick *loved*. It was here that we came across a woman walking with her two daughters who were both under the age of sixteen. I ended up staying with them and chatting for the rest of the way to Molinaseca because they loved Maverick so much.

They were from Madrid and decided to walk a small portion of the Camino while they were on a break from school. For the most part, we talked in Spanish, but when the older daughter wanted to practice her English, we switched into that as well. They told me all about their school system and I shared about where I taught as a substitute and answered any questions they had about Maverick, of course. Eventually, I bid them a Buen Camino just after we crossed the bridge into Molinaseca together.

"¿No quieres comer algo?" the older daughter asked me once more just as we reached the busy street through Molinaseca.

"No, gracias. Quiero encontrar un lugar para que Maverick nade," I smiled.

She and her sister grinned back at me. "Le encanta el agua, ¿no?"

"Oh, sí," I said conspiratorially. Although, I didn't think he would be welcomed with open arms by all the children wading in the river just beside the bridge. I'm sure I could find something a bit further up the river where we wouldn't disturb anyone else with his splashing.

"Buen Camino, Colby. Y Maverick," the mom said. She purposefully drew out Maverick's name, just as I had done when I first told it to them. It sounded more like *Mab-er-eek* in a Spanish accent. The Spanish pronounced their *v*'s with a *b* sound, so I always had to enunciate clearly when introducing him to Spaniards. More often than not, they somehow forgot how to pronounce *Mabereek* within a few moments of meeting us and would then refer to him as *Never*. My thought was that *never* was one English word with a *v* that they were well-acquainted with so they somehow just came to that when thinking of Maverick. Of course, I had never asked directly so I could be completely off base, but I was sticking with that theory.

"Buen Camino," I nodded back at the little family, waving goodbye to them as they continued down the street and disappeared into the crowds of pilgrims pouring out of cafés and bars along the road.

"Alright, Freak Reek. Let's find you a place to swim." He whined in response, tugging on his leash towards the steps that led down to the beach-like area many locals were slashing in just under the wide arches of the stone bridge.

I found a way to turn left and wandered along until we came to an opening by some restaurants that had a low stone wall separating it from the lush, green grass edging the river-bank. "Come on. Hup," I told him as I hopped over the wall myself quickly, not sure if we should be doing this and not wanting some restaurant worker to come and scold us. Mav didn't have to be told twice. He leaped over the stone wall in one bound and plunged forward into the river in the next.

I laughed, but hurried him along. "Come on, keep going," I urged, walking up the bank so we would be out of sight of anyone from the restaurants or those splashing down by the bridge. Maverick happily plodded along up the river, following me around a bend and up river until I reached a little tree to plop our bags under. There was a stone wall at our side, blocking us from view of anyone in the town, and we had curved far enough up stream that no one from the bridge could see us. It was like our own private oasis. So with a contented sigh, I sat on the bank of río Maruelo and dipped my feet into the refreshing water.

Maverick scrambled up and down the riverbank, chasing the butterflies back and forth through the grass, diving to snap his jaws at any that came close enough. I laid back and listened to the sound of the flowing water and closed my eyes, letting the sun warm my skin. The grass was soft under me, the perfect place to rest at the end of a perfect day. Every so often, I'd give Maverick the command "drink" and he'd dutifully abandon his attempt to catch butterflies and plop himself down in the river to lap up more water. It only would last a moment before he was up again, tearing off after another shadow, water droplets flying.

"I could stay here forever," I mumbled to him sleepily.

Take Me to Church

Day Thirty: Molinaseca to Cacabelos

27.4 km ~ 38,610 steps

July 19th

Light was pouring into our room by the time my eyes
fluttered open this morning. I *may* have accidentally slept in
until eight thirty. Which was understandable seeing as I got
very little sleep the night before and even though yesterday
had been amazing, it was still a long day of walking.

The place we stayed in last night was more of a *casa
rural* than anything, but it was wonderful. It was like an old
farmhouse, the main floor all open-concept with rickety
rocking chairs and couches to lounge in. In the end, I think
only one other family of pilgrims was staying here with us
and aside from running into them as we checked in, I never
saw or heard of them again. Although Molinaseca is indeed
a bustling town, we aren't all that into crowds and packed
bars, so we explored the lesser traveled side streets last night

and found a nice place to eat dinner by the river. Rain ended up rolling in later in the evening, so I was very pleased to have a dry bed and roof over our heads for the night.

Unfortunately, today's stretch looked like it's going to be a lot of road walking and through a city area that could be tricky to navigate if we weren't paying careful attention to any yellow Camino markers. On the plus side, the weather seemed to be beautiful again as we started out of Molinaseca. It would have been rough if I had slept in so late and it was a sweltering day, but maybe (hopefully) those blistering days were a thing of the past now that we're through the Meseta.

Aside from one short section, the trail from Molinaseca to Ponferrada remained entirely on a roadway and dipped through the desolate hamlet of Campo before dropping down to the industrial major city. If I had come to the epiphany that I felt truly alive in the mountains yesterday, today really solidified that fact. I was reminded of just how much I disliked cities.

I have since seen various pilgrims tout Ponferrada as one of their favorite stops along The Way. I'll give them the fact that this city was rich in history. Most importantly, it was home to the *Castillo de los Templarios*, the castle built in the twelfth century for the Knights Templar. It's the dominating structure of the city, or at least of what I saw of it, and it was indeed impressive with vibrant red and white banners of the Order dangling from the castle walls.

Maverick and I opted for a quick breakfast break just beneath the towering ramparts. I would have liked to check out the inside of the castle, but I doubted they would allow Maverick in. And to be honest, I didn't feel comfortable leaving him alone in this city. While the castle was nice, the overall feel of the city to me was a bit sketchy. Rundown and grimy. Almost like a forgotten industrial city. It was the first time along the Camino where I didn't feel completely comfortable in a town.

We had passed through some busy places so far, large cities like Burgos or León, but I had never felt uneasy in them. I wasn't looking over my shoulder as a lone girl, worried about being followed. I wasn't nervous about putting down my pack for a moment to go into a store. I didn't worry (too much) about leaving Maverick outside to go into a cathedral. Maybe this was just my own naivety, but there was a feeling of peace on the Camino no matter where it passed through. You felt safe amongst other pilgrims.

I knew this probably sounded strange to someone who hadn't walked the Camino. In fact, many fellow pilgrims might say I was being stupid and Rule Number One is never leave your bag unattended. Hadn't I learned anything from that scene in *The Way* with the gypsy? However, this was just how I felt. Maybe there was an added assurance of, "Oh, no one is going to steal my bag if I leave it here because a German Shepherd is standing over it." I could see how my position was a little different than most. My point was, Ponferrada did *not* give me this same, safe Camino vibe. I had zero desire to linger here.

After breakfast, Mav and I passed the castle, then continued on through the city and turned down to *Pons Ferrada*, or Iron Bridge in Latin, over the río Sil which gave the city its name. I suppose it made sense that this felt like such a gritty, industrial city. It was originally built up around the iron ore and coal business that was lucrative in this area. Apparently, this bridge had been made of iron since as far back as the eleventh century.

We crossed over it and then detoured onto the river route. I was all set with cities and pavement and sidewalks, so if I could escape that, even just for a moment to walk through a city park, I would take it.

Maverick enjoyed romping through the grass, finally nice and soft in contrast to the burnt, brittle grasses that was all we knew on the Meseta. He even splashed in and out of the river whenever there was an opening for him. We didn't pass all that many other pilgrims in the riverside park, but there were plenty of Ponferrada citizens making use of the nice morning for a stroll through the trees and gardens of the park.

The next nine or so kilometers were easy yet unremarkable. Leaving the main city behind, we passed through an underpass that had been turned into a whimsical mural for the town of Compostilla. An animated painting of the Knights Templar castle was featured on the concrete walls as well as little wooden signposts indicating Ponferrada behind us and pointing forward to Santiago. It was the first time I'd seen Santiago mentioned like that. As if it was the next big city we were going to come to. I paused in the tunnel, staring at the painted wooden signs. *Santiago is the next city we'll come to.* After being out here for thirty days, the knowledge that we were so close was strange. Like it couldn't quite be real. And yet it was. In less than three hundred kilometers, we would be walking into the cathedral in Santiago.

For now, the small chapel in Compostilla would have to be enough. For some reason, I really enjoyed the little church as we passed by it. There were no ornate carvings on the building at all, no stone figures guarding the door or adorning the entryway. Yet there was something calming about the white-washed color of the plain façade. It reminded me of Hozier's song "Take Me To Church" oddly enough. As if this could be the very church in question.

Maverick turned back to look at me, his head quirked at the sound of my voice. I smiled and picked up my pace, easily following him along the neat sidewalk. "Take me to church," I sang to him since we were the only ones out here.

"I'll worship like a dog-" I reached out to poke his side and he jumped away, catching on to my playful mood. "At the shrine of your lies. I'll tell you my sins and you can sharpen your knife."

Maverick let out a playful *arf* and scampered away in search of another stick to occupy his mouth.

We continued like this through the other tiny towns that made up the suburbs of Ponferrada. The first few were starkly modern, not at all like the tiny farm villages of the Meseta or mountain hamlets we had recently passed through. Instead, they looked more like any suburban neighborhood back in the states. I found myself craning my neck, looking for a soccer mom with a minivan to pop out at any moment as we passed through Columbrianos.

Since we had a late start, it was already past noon by the time we were coming into Fuentes Nuevas and the sun was starting to get hot. Luckily, Maverick had discovered what I assumed were little irrigation canals for the fields between towns. Along the roadside, the little canals were no more than a foot wide and he had found that if he laid himself down, he fit just perfectly.

Which was a good thing, too, because I really didn't want to put his booties on him today. Recently, they had started to rub just above his paws where the straps secured them and were beginning to form little sores on his legs. I was hoping we would be able to have a few days where he didn't have to wear them. Between most of today's walk being on pavement, and the canals providing him a way to cool off his paw pads if the tar got too hot for him, it really was the perfect situation for us.

He grinned up at me from his spot in one of the canals, the water pouring around him because his fat butt was taking up almost all of the space. His goofy expression with his tongue lolling out one side seemed to say *look what I found,*

Mum. Isn't this great? I laughed at him and shook my head in response, but when he went to drink some of the water, I quickly redirected him.

"Nope! Sorry, no drinking. I don't know what kind of run off might be in that from the fields. You can lay in it and walk in it if it's next to the road. But no drinking." He looked up at me out of the corner of his eye, his little reddish-brown eyebrow quirking up. Then he immediately went back to pawing at the water as it poured from one canal that ran up the length of the field into the canal that ran parallel to the road we'd been walking on. I raised my eyebrows in return and drew in a deep breath.

"So this is what we're doing now, huh?" I asked him. He didn't respond, just redoubled his efforts to attack the water, now using both his front paws to dig at it. "What are you even doing? There's nothing there. Come on, loser. Walk along in your canal," I laughed.

At the sound of my retreating footsteps on the pavement, he looked up to see I was leaving him behind. With a quick hop, all four legs were back in the canal parallel to the road and he scampered towards me, water droplets flying as he went. I shook my head in amusement and looked back up at the road we were on. A young woman was walking towards us, just a local out for an afternoon stroll from the look of it. And beside her was a massive, black, shaggy dog. Laughter poured from my mouth unbidden and she looked up to see what had caught my attention. When she saw where Maverick was walking, her laughter joined mine.

"Es la agua," she laughed as we got closer. "Le encanta agua."

"Oh, sí, yo sé" I smiled. Her shaggy dog just so happened to be making his way up the road towards us in the same manner as Maverick, all four paws plodding through the irrigation canal.

"Es guapísimo," she told us just as they passed. "Buen camino."

"Muchas gracias." I smiled.

"You hear that, Nug?" I asked him after we had put some distance between us and the girl with her dog. "You is *hand-some*." He popped out of the canal just so he could grab a branch, complete with a bushel of leaves at the end, and ran it over to me. "Yes, I see your stick. Alright, go, go," I urged him, tugging on the stick for a moment before releasing him. He boinged ahead on the pavement happily, the leaves dragging on the asphalt and making a rustling noise in the otherwise still air.

The two of us stopped for a quick lunch in Fuentes Nuevas before continuing through the final five-ish kilometers to Cacabelos where I already had booked us a bed in a hostel. Since the day had indeed gotten quite warm, I made sure to soak Maverick's cooling collar in a fountain before we left town and slipped it over his ears. I smiled at him. "You look like the wolf from *Little Red Riding Hood* again," I told him. "My, my, what big ears you have." He looked up at me from under unamused eyebrows. I giggled. "What big teeth you have?" I tried again.

He shook himself out, the cooling collar falling back around his neck so his ears shot forward into their natural position, then he grinned at me. I scowled back. "You're no fun. Come on then, Little Red."

The next stretch was actually beautiful. I hadn't been expecting it, but much of the path went through vineyards. We hadn't been among wine country since we were in La Rioja region, and in the time that had passed between then and now, the growing season had been in full swing. Now, instead of miniscule seeds just beginning to form into green grapes like we had seen back in La Rioja, these vines were beginning to grow heavy with grapes. Of course, they were still all green, most no bigger than an average marble, but it was cool to see how much growth had occurred while we had been walking. I was sure the vineyards we had gone through before were in much the same state as these.

And in front of us, making up the entire landscape past the vines, was a wall of mountains. We were coming for them and I could not wait. After the slog through the city and suburbs today, I was more than ready to start another climb into the mountains that divided this region from the final region we would walk through: Galicia.

Since Maverick and I were really the only pilgrims out here, we took our time through this section of the trail. We played, and explored the vines, and took goofy pictures with my tripod and remote control. We took the time to just genuinely enjoy where we were, right at that moment. Maybe that graffiti I had been hating on near Hospital de Órbigo hadn't been all that off. *Be here now.* I understood it now.

We climbed a little incline out of the vineyard area and passed what must have been a farmer's house. Or at least it must have been at some point in time. It didn't look like anyone was living there now. And yet there were kittens!

"Oh my goodness!" I cooed, immediately dropping to my knees in the red dirt and outstretching my hands. "Hello, sweet babies. What are you doing out here? Oh, there's your mama. Hi, mama. Aw, see? She'll come say hi to me."

The two adult cats who were with the little group of kittens were still skeptical of me, so I found a little twig in the gravel and started to move it back and forth in front of them, finally enticing one of the adults to pounce on it. The kittens, much as I tried, would not get closer than two feet from me. I had been so distracted by cute, baby cats, I completely forgot about Maverick for a second.

"Mavy?" I called out, turning away from the cats. *Where was he? Why wasn't he right next to me?* And then I saw him.

Still at the crest of the hill as if he hadn't taken another step since we had made it to the top and spied the kittens. "What are you-" I cut myself off. "No way," I laughed. "You're scared of them, aren't you?"

He looked at me. Then quickly turned his gaze back to the kittens as if he couldn't take his eyes off them in case they suddenly launched.

"Oh, my gosh. They're kittens, Nug. They're more scared of you than you are of them." *Woah,* I thought to myself. *When had I become my dad?* That had always been one of his favorite sayings if I had ever been afraid of something in the woods. I smiled at the reminder of him and refocused on Maverick. "Come here, you big baby."

I tried to coax him forward, but he took three steps and then wouldn't come any closer.

"Maverick," I groaned. "It's fine. We don't have to keep playing with them. We can just walk by."

I made to walk away from the dilapidated building and the kittens, but Maverick didn't follow. "Mav, come." I finally commanded. He wouldn't avoid a command.

With his eyes still locked on the group of cats, he took a couple tentative steps to the right, making sure to keep a wide berth between him and them. Just as he was about even with them on the trail, his hackles raised, and he growled. The mother cats arched into a hiss in response. Just like that, he was off, sprinting the rest of the way to my side and then peering around my legs back at the cats...who hadn't moved an inch.

I burst out in laughter. "Oh. My. God," I laughed. "You're *insane.*" I couldn't help it; I couldn't stop laughing. Mav looked up at me from my heels like *I* was the crazy one.

"Oh, yeah," I told him in a mock deep voice. "Big, tough guy over here. Watch out for that *vicious* German Shepherd."

I'd like to say the last couple kilometers of the day were uneventful and full of bliss. But that wasn't the case. There was a little mobile café about halfway between Camponaraya and Cacabelos. It sat at a dip in the trail in a beautiful, wooded section. No, really, there *were* trees in this part. Unlike so many other times the guidebook told us something would be shady. It was even right beside a little stream. And being later in the day, where we had just been walking through the open areas of the vineyards, Maverick was very excited to go swimming in that little stream.

However, the couple that run the mobile café also had dogs. Big dogs. Who apparently did not like other dogs. As Maverick went to dart into the river, the two dogs came running over to intercept him. It all happened so fast, there wasn't much to be done. A snap of jaws, a snarl, and I was panicked. I screamed for Maverick to *go*, just wanting him out of that situation, and bless his soul, he listened.

Forgetting the river in a flash, we ran past the café and back onto the trail. I glanced behind us to make sure the dogs weren't following, and saw the owners had each of them in hand now. While they hadn't done anything to stop their dogs from attacking mine, at least they had the decency to stop them from chasing us. I quickly checked over Maverick, making sure no skin was broken, nothing was amiss, and then hustled him on so we were out of view of the café.

Once we were far enough away, I stopped again and dropped his pack to the dirt. "Are you okay?" I asked him, bending over and running my hands methodically across his body again. Already, he was acting like nothing out of the ordinary had happened, and I was just giving him a massage. He leaned into my touch and his tongue flopped out of his mouth happily, but my hands were shaking. I took a deep breath in.

"Are you sure you're okay?" I asked him shakily. "They

didn't get you? You're okay?" Mav squirmed out of my hold
and turned around to face me, then shoved his face in mine,
licking up my chin. I didn't even have it in me to bat him
away. I hadn't realized how much that had affected me until
now, when we were far enough away and I could process.

"I'm so sorry," I sobbed, and he licked up my cheek this
time. "I'm so sorry. I never should have let that happen. I'm
so sorry."

He kept licking, finally so overzealous he tried to hop in
my lap and sent us both tumbling backwards into the dirt.
"You're really okay?" I asked again, this time from my spot in
the dust. He scampered away from me and came back with a
stick and dropped it on my legs. I took another deep breath
in and looked him in the eye. Truly, you would never know
anything had happened at all. He looked no different, his
expression one of pure joy. Just waiting for me to throw the
stick. I sighed.

"Let's just finish this day, okay?" I told him. I stood and
grabbed his bag again, dislodging the stick from my lap in
the process. He shoved his nose into the dirt to snatch it up
again.

We walked on to Cacabelos; Maverick completely oblivious to my state of turmoil. It had been no one's fault. Those
dogs were probably there every day and never encountered
another dog. Why would they? People didn't bring their dogs
along on the Camino, that much was clear. And for good
reason. Should I have had a leash on Maverick? Maybe.
Would that have made a difference, though? Probably not. I
guess I would never know. I could keep going in circles in my
mind about it, or I could let it go. Clearly, Maverick had
chosen to let it go. Perhaps I could take a note from him and
just move on.

By the time we came up to the nice, little rest area and
fountain before Cacabelos, I was in a much better mood. The

fountain here ran at a continuous trickle, so I slipped off my pack to fill my water bladder and then turned to Maverick. "You want some water?" I asked him. He cocked his head to one side. "Come here, then. Hup." I patted the stone basin with my hand and he looked at it questionably. I smiled. There was plenty of water in the basin he could drink from rather than me filling his bowl. I just wanted to see if he would do it. "Hup." I patted the stone again and then in one motion, he sprung up.

Somehow, he managed to balance all four paws on the lip of the stone basin.

"Maverick!" I laughed. He looked at me in question like *isn't this what you wanted?* After another minute of teetering on the edge with just a disdainful sniff at the water, he leaped down none too gracefully. I shook my head in exasperation. "We have *got* to differentiate between just putting your paws up on something versus fully jumping onto something."

He just grinned at me from the stone bench he had just jumped up on. I eyed him warily. "No, that is also not what I asked you to do," I deadpanned. I couldn't keep a straight face for long, though. My grin took over and I reached out to ruffle his fur. "Let's go, kiddo. Time to find our place to stay."

The hostel I had booked was right at the start of Old Town and it was *amazing*. It looked like it had just been renovated to be pilgrims' lodging and every inch of it was spotless from the place to do your laundry on the second floor terrace to the room we have. I just booked a single bed, because that was an option. It was supposed to be in a shared room with three other beds, but we ended up being the only pilgrims in the room so we had a giant bedroom and attached bathroom all to ourselves. If Maverick wanted his own bed for the night, he could have it. And with these hospitaleros, they really would be fine with that.. They had given him the run of the entire place. Of course, I wasn't just going to let him off leash in their dining room on the main floor or through the halls upstairs, but I seriously didn't think they would mind even if I did. They simply adored him.

So he plodded outside to the balcony with me while I did laundry and hung out with me, looking out over the main street through Cacabelos and down on the pilgrims eating at the outdoor tables below us. I ended up walking over to lean against the railing beside him, taking in the town as well. It was funny. Today could have been awful. In fact, it kind of *was* awful.

I mean, all in all, we walked twenty-seven kilometers today. That's a long day. And it had gotten hot. *And* we had been walking through a city and on sidewalks for most of the day – all things I hate. The icing on the cake was definitely the dog attack, though. Yet here I was Smiling. At peace. If this had been a week ago, I doubt that would have been the case. Somehow, some way, we were different now. Maybe even...stronger.

It was a combination of things, really. Maybe it really did have to do with laying down that stone at Cruz de Ferro. Maybe that really had shifted everything just a bit inside of me. But it was more than just that. The fact that the weather was so different now definitely helped. I really believed that the heat of the Meseta affected us more than I consciously thought it did. It sucked the energy right out of us. Every day had been exhausting simply from how hot and dry it was. So the cool, fresh air of the more mountainous region was helping things immensely. It gave me a clear head for one. I also think a lot of it came from this new discovery of using Booking.com. Once I got over that idea of being a "true" pilgrim, and allowed myself to book ahead, it certainly made things easier. For the first time, I wasn't wondering where we would spend the night. If we'd even *have* a place to spend the night. The uncertainty, and the countless denials, took more of a toll on my mindset than I would have liked them to.

More than anything, though, it was the fact that we'd been walking for an entire *month* now. Thirty days. We'd been out here, just the two of us, figuring it out as we went, for thirty days now. So, yeah, maybe part of it had to do with the fact that we were just now getting a hold of this kind of lifestyle. Maybe it was the weather. Maybe it was whatever happened at Cruz de Ferro. Maybe it was the knowledge of a place to stay each night. Whatever it was, whatever combination of things, this whole Camino thing?

It wasn't so bad anymore.

I looked down at Maverick next to me on the balcony, watching the sun go down while the laughter of fellow pilgrims drifted up to us from the dining room and sidewalk tables below. "We got this, Mav." He tore his gaze from a pigeon he had been eyeing in the plaza across from us. "We do. Me and you. We've got this now."

You can also see the following pictures in full color on my website: colbymillsaps.com/books/conelperro/

Enjoying the cooler weather we found after la Meseta

Never pass up a chance to cool off in a good drainage canal

Views of the Valcarce Valley from the alternate route

Quiet moments after the steep climb up to O'Cebriero

Some peaceful miles through the mountains.

Officially only 100 km left before Santiago

One of the many holloways we walked through in Galicia

*Giving some love to pilgrims of the past just before
reaching Santiago*

Entering the city limits

Only slightly different than the sign we saw in Roncesvalles

Forty days later and we had finally arrived

I wouldn't have wanted to do this with anyone else

What it looks like to lug around Maverick's food

Still basking in embarrassment as we crossed Ponte Maceira over the río Tambre

*Sometimes he walks by my side instead of chasing
butterflies or fetching sticks*

*One of the many stone markers we followed throughout
the entire Camino*

On the wild shores of Muxía.

Swimming together in Finisterre

And just like that, our journey has come to an end

Sunset from the end of the world

Mykonos

Day Thirty-One: Cacabelos to Las Herrerías de Valcarce

32.3 km ~ 45,534 steps

*July 20*th

Alright, there was one con to having a nice place to stay at night…I never wanted to get out of bed in the morning. So even with the best intentions to start walking nice and early, Mav and I didn't end up leaving the hostel until eight. Which I suppose wasn't such a big deal anymore because the days weren't brutally hot anymore. It wasn't so much of a problem if we ended up walking through the afternoon.

Was this how normal pilgrims had felt the whole time? They could get up whenever and walk throughout the day and not even worry? I looked down at Maverick as we made our way through the tight streets of Cacabelos. He was trotting along without a care in the world, loving the slightly stormy weather that was hanging in the air this morning. *Well*, I thought to myself, *he certainly made things different.*

We passed by the beautiful murals of Cacabelos one last time, stopping again to admire the one that featured a pilgrim and his German Shepherd looking out over some vineyards. "Look, Nugget," I told him again, even though I had already pointed it out to him when we explored town last night. "It's me and you. Well, if I was a man. And if you were black and tan; not sable. So, really, it's not me and you. But kind of."

Maverick turned to look up at me, then followed my finger where it was pointing at the vivid, likelike mural. Not seeing anything of interest, he continued down the main street without waiting for me.

Leaving Cacabelos behind, the Camino followed the main roadway into a valley up ahead. Even though it was still early, it was a bit nerve-wracking walking along such a busy road that the cars seemed to be flying down. Luckily, within an hour there was an option to turn off the asphalt and onto a wide farm track.

We rested for a little while on some benches just off the main road as other pilgrims passed by. For some reason, I wasn't feeling that great. Even though the past few days had been wonderful, I felt *off* today. Which wasn't the best day to be feeling that way. I had hoped to do the Dragonte Route today.

Once we reached Villafranca del Bierzo, there would be a split in the trail. Three separate routes diverge just after the village, with all of them coming back together just before the steep climb into O'Cebriero. Of these routes, there was the main Camino which followed the N-6 highway through the valley. That one looked like a nightmare to me. For one, I hated walking along a busy road. I *especially* didn't like walking along a busy road with a dog. Then there was the

Pardela Route, or as Brierley called it, the "scenic route," which turned off from the main road and angled right, up into the mountains that formed one wall of the Valcarce Valley. And then there was the Dragonte Route.

This last route was *not* attempted by many pilgrims. Most pilgrims liked to take nice, flat, road walks. The Dragonte Route was none of that. Listed in Brierley's guidebook as the "remote route," the guide did a pretty good job of scaring off prospective pilgrims. As well as my mother. She knew I planned to do the Dragonte Route before I even left and she was none too pleased with the idea.

"Why can't you just take the regular route? Where there will be other people around. You can pass through towns and people will know where you are," she tried to reason.

"It's *mountains*," I had pleaded in return. "It'll be just like hiking here. I love mountains. And we'll have been doing so much flat stuff up until then, it will be so nice to climb again!" She had looked at me doubtfully. Then she looked down at her own guidebook again.

"It says here it's *steep*. That's not good," she had muttered.

I rolled my eyes. "The *valley* is steep-sided it says."

"Right. And you're going to climb up and down that? For no reason?" I stayed silent as she perused the guidebook some more. "It's listed as *remote*. What if something were to happen? What if something happened to Maverick? No one else will be out there. There's no towns or places to stop at. It sounds like a bad idea."

"It's just like when we hike here! It's no different," I reasoned.

"Not well waymarked," she quoted. "Obscure. Overgrown. Total climb of over six-thousand feet!"

I had just raised my eyebrows at her. "We hike over four-thousand feet all the time. We just did Washington. That's over six."

"I don't like it."

"We'll see when we get to that point. Who knows what it will be like by then and what I'll want to do," I had told her.

Only, we had now reached that point. And I still didn't know what I wanted to do. Honestly, the guidebook did make me nervous about it. It said all the things my mom had told me. It definitely made the Dragonte Route seem like a terrible option. I knew deep down it would be fine. I was used to hiking, and from the description, it was just like a mountain trail in New Hampshire. If I wanted to split hairs, true hiking in the White Mountains was exactly the same. There were remote trails most hikers didn't take. Some were overgrown. Hikers had to plan to be without resources for an entire day. This was nothing new.

Yet for some reason, I was filled with trepidation as we left the red clay of the vineyards behind and neared Villafranca del Bierzo. The clouds were gradually starting to break up, but it was still grey and dreary as we came into the medieval hamlet. The air still felt like it was holding back a storm that could be unleashed at any moment.

Mav and I dropped into the first café we came across in Villafranca, which was bustling with pilgrims eager to head out for the day. If their plan was to make it all the way to O'Cebreiro for the evening, there was still another twenty-nine kilometers to go. I still hadn't solidified our plans for the night since I still wasn't even sure what *route* I was going to take. I knew there was a place in Las Herrerías that would allow dogs, because I had already looked into it on Booking.-com, and I figured this was where we would stay. It would all depend on how tired we were, though. And which route we ended up choosing. Either way, I didn't plan on making it to O'Cebreiro today. That would have been a distance of over thirty-five kilometers no matter what route we chose. So that was a hard pass in my book.

I had gotten plenty of snacks for the day at a grocery store last night, just in case we really did end up doing the Dragonte Route, but I decided to stop here for a good breakfast regardless. Since the café was so busy, two gentlemen joined us at our table while we were eating and plotting our next move.

Once they were seated, their first questions circled around Maverick. Then they turned to asking what route we were taking for the day. It seemed everyone was well aware of the many options today.

"I had planned to do the Dragonte Route, but I don't know," I hedged.

One of the men raised an eyebrow. "That is supposed to be a very hard route," he said.

I nodded. "So they say. I just don't know if I'm feeling it today. And also, I wouldn't want to be caught up there if it does end up raining."

"Yes, the weather does not look good. That is probably not smart." I looked up, past the village and towards the mountains. The tops were still shrouded in grey clouds that hadn't burned off yet. "You should ask the waitress. She will probably know about the weather."

I dropped my gaze back down to look at the man who had spoken. "You know, that's probably a good idea. Thanks for that."

I stood and made my way back into the café where the waitress was entertaining some locals by the bar. She was more than happy to offer me some weather insight for the area, going so far as to say she would warn against anyone doing the Dragonte Route today. If it rained, the trail was sure to be slick and it would be miserable. So with my decision made for me, I headed back outside to prep for our next leg.

I slipped Maverick's pack over his head and he waited

while I clipped it into place. It was the first time he would be wearing it since we had walked to Pamplona. I had been carrying it on my arm ever since. But we were almost out of food at this point so it was pretty light and quite frankly, I didn't feel like carrying it while we hiked actual mountains today.

The other pilgrims eating at the tables outside were all watching us curiously. I did my best to ignore their stares until one of the men we had eaten with spoke up again. "So you will do the Pradela Route, then?" he confirmed.

"Yep," I told him, giving Maverick's pack a tug to make sure it was in place and secure. I smiled just from knowing I wouldn't be carrying it today. Maverick immediately shook himself, the red saddlebags flopping about, and then stared up at me expectantly. He was ready to be walking again. "I figure that way we still get some mountains, and a nice hike, but won't be up there too long if the weather turns bad."

"Why do you not just walk the main Camino?" his friend asked me.

I grinned. "You sound like my mom." A couple nearby pilgrims who had been listening chuckled. "We like the mountains. Plus, it's not on a main road all day."

One of the men tipped his head back and forth as if he was weighing out the options. "For me, I will stay on the road," he said. "Buen Camino, peregrina."

"Buen Camino," I answered.

We wound our way down through Villafranca del Bierzo, which was an adorable little village. I would have loved to have spent the night here last night. Not that I hadn't thoroughly enjoyed Cacabelos, it's just that this mountain hamlet seemed so quaint and charming, too. All too soon, we were through the village and to the split in the trail. The road we'd been walking on out of Villafranca continued straight ahead, but on the right a separate waymarked path diverged and climbed up a steep, cement incline.

"Alright, Mav. Onward and upward as we love to say." I looped his leash into the handle of his backpack so that I had easy access to it and let him take the lead up the steep ascent. Just a few steps in, we passed a small note of Camino graffiti on the back of a metal sign. *Santiago is not there. It is in you.*

I stopped for a moment to stare at the simple message, complete with a yellow arrow pointing us up. It would be easy to just brush past this message. Say it didn't mean anything, or it was too confusing. But I think it made a really good point. I think a lot of pilgrims could take that message to heart. I think even *I* should take this message to heart.

A lot of pilgrims came out here with a goal. Something they expected to achieve while they were here. Maybe they were walking for clarity on some problem they faced back home. Or perhaps they were walking to gain back a sense of self after a divorce or escaping from some toxic environment. Some walked to quit a bad habit. I had set out to end my depression, hadn't I?

We all set out with some idea of what the Camino would be for us. We all thought that after eight hundred kilometers, we were going to reach Santiago and whatever we had been expecting would suddenly come to light. That was simply not the truth. Just like this message said. Santiago wasn't just a place. It was something in all of us. It was on us to change the things we needed to change. It was completely our own will that was going to bring about a change, or the strength to quit whatever we need to quit, or even to gain back the will to live. That's in us. Santiago is *in* us.

The *Ruta Pradela* was everything I could have ever wanted and more. It was a steady climb, but nothing too strenuous. Within minutes of starting out, all of Villafranca del Bierzo was laid out beneath us and the views only got better with every step. The trail was mostly overgrown, not at all like the well-beaten thoroughfares we'd walked on this whole journey. Instead, grasses tickled my bare calves as we walked on, little yellow wildflowers waving in the breeze. The path hugged the very edge of the mountains, so for almost the entire walk we had a clean view down into the valley below and back to Villafranca. Not a single other pilgrim was on this route, which made it all the more special. Although, I'm sure my mother would not be very happy to hear that.

Looking back to Villafranca, it was almost as if the town was like a reservoir, held back by a dam at the very mouth of the valley. The buildings, all built tightly together in the village, appeared like the surface of a pond that slowly grew skinnier as the mountains rose up on either side of the valley until only the highway marred the greenery. Just one, grey squiggle cutting through the floor of the valley, just like a river would.

With one last look over the valley, Mav and I followed the overgrown path further into the mountains. The scenic route had beautiful views over the valley, lots of shade as it wound through woodland, and even passed by some fields that were surrounded on all sides by the forest. There was only one town along the entire alternate route, and judging from the locals' shock at seeing me and Maverick, I doubted many pilgrims ever used this trail.

After stopping to chat with the owner of the one bar in town and a few of the locals who were all interested in seeing what I was doing with a dog on the Camino, we began our steep descent to the valley floor. All too soon, *ruta Pradela* joined back up with the main Camino. The dirt track down was so steep, I ended up running most of the way down to Trabadelo with Maverick hot on my heels. I'd never been much of a runner, despite playing so many sports all through high school. Running was always used as a punishment in the sports I played, so I suppose that's reason enough to dislike it. Yet running down that slope from Pradela to Trabadelo it felt just like I was flying. I'm aware how silly that might sound, but it was true. With the mountain breeze, and the sun that was fighting to break through the clouds, I felt just like a bird would as we raced down that mountain.

The mountain path spit us out right behind the church in Trabadelo, just after a cemetery in the woods. It felt every bit the entrance to the hills where outlaws were rumored to have hidden out in years past. Maverick and I shoved our way through the overgrowth and hopped over a low rock wall to emerge back on the asphalt road running through Trabadelo. Though the guidebook touted this as a bustling village with plenty of amenities, there really wasn't much at all. It was more run down than anything, with many of the buildings for sale.

I took the time to stop and fill our waters and grab an ice cream at the only open store in town before we dropped back down to the main road which the Camino followed through the valley. While the Pradela route had been wild, silent, and solitary, this route was the complete opposite. Until this point, the Camino had never been so aligned with such a busy road. Sure, we had followed the main roads before, but they had never had as much traffic as this one. And in the narrow Valcarce Valley, there was no room to have the Camino trail separated from the highway. So instead, we criss-crossed the asphalt at different points, making sure to sprint across when a car wasn't bearing down on us, and hid behind cement crash barriers for much of the next kilometers. Apparently, this was less traffic than what used to travel on this road. A second free-way, the A-6, has been elevated above the valley floor. We passed under some of the massive overpasses on our way through the valley. Frankly, they were quite an engineering marvel even if they weren't all that pretty in their cement glory.

Luckily, this highway walking was pretty split up once we finished the first four kilometers after Trabadelo and reached La Portela de Valcarce. From there on, we were able to dip into a village every kilometer or so. Even better, most of the villages had access to the río Valcare. Each time we came to some river access, Maverick made sure to charge ahead and plop himself down in the clear mountain water.

We weaved in and out of the villages of the valley, enjoying the stone architecture and abundant flowers. It seemed like most pilgrims were opting to spend the night in Vega de Valcarce. As far as Camino villages went, this was a perfect place to stay. If we hadn't already booked a place in Las Herrerías, I would have been tempted to stay here with many of our fellow pilgrims. As it was, we played in the river here for a while and shared some of the croissants I had bought the night before. Despite Maverick's normal hatred of carbs, he enjoyed having a nibble of the croissant each time I went to take a bite.

It was already after four when we left Vega de Valcarce and made the final winding climb towards Las Herrerías. Thanks to the mild weather in the valley, and the fact that the sun didn't bake the earth so much in this part of Spain, we could walk all day without a problem. Well, that wasn't entirely accurate. After over thirty kilometers of pretty strenuous hiking today, I was more than happy when we finally reached our place for the night.

Tonight's bed was a bit more pricey than I would have liked. The place we were staying was kind of like a *casa rural*, but we didn't end up in the main building where there looked to be more rooms. Instead, we had our own mini apartment of sorts with its own entrance, bathroom, and porch complete with a hammock to lounge in. The property was spacious, surrounded by trees and grass for Maverick to explore, and it was just before the main village of Las Herrerías, so it was much more secluded than a place in a village would have been.

Surprisingly enough, I kind of liked that about it. After a day that felt much more wild, much more off the beaten path than so much of the Camino had been, this felt like the perfect end to the day. With most pilgrims staying in Vega de Valcarce or continuing on to O'Cebriero if they were really ambitious, it appeared there were no other pilgrims in the area at all. Even when Mav and I went for an evening stroll to explore the village of Las Herrerías, we didn't come across another pilgrim.

Instead, we made friends with the people who ran and worked at the place we were staying for the night and enjoyed a huge spread for dinner, including a massive salad featuring the goat cheese that was so famous in this valley and a giant steak. It was probably the fanciest meal I had eaten this entire journey. I had become quite used to *tortillas españolas*, bananas, and various pilgrim menus making up most of my diet. But after a day in the mountains, with just the snacks we had bought for our day of hiking and the ice cream I had gotten in Trabadelo, this meal was heaven. In fact, the whole day had been pretty close to perfect.

Wild Things

Day Thirty-Two: Las Herrerías de Valcarce to Triacastela

34.5 km ~ 48,494 steps

July 21st

I woke up early and my first thought was that I was cold. *Cold.* I hadn't been cold in a long time. Yet, there was a chill in the air and when I peaked my head outside to our porch, a heavy mist was shrouding the entire valley. For the first time on this entire trip, I wished I had a sweatshirt in my pack. I shrug on my one long-sleeve shirt over my t-shirt and am thankful that my one pair of leggings were clean for today's hike and off we go.

As we headed out through the sleepy hamlet of Las Herrerías, I could see both Maverick's breath and my own puffing up in the cold morning air. I'm sure we would warm up as we started the climb, but first we had to stop to take in the cute, little waterfalls in the river and the adorable tree grove at the start of town which had a tree that looked to be covered in…paper? I turned into the rest area to take a closer look while Maverick scampered over to the nearby pool of water. A wooden plaque at the base of the spindly tree read *What are your dreams?* Hundreds of tiny strips of paper were wrapped around and tied onto the branches. Beside it, a little table held scraps of paper and pens to write your dreams on and some twine to attach them to the tree. I smiled and went to turn away, ready to be on our way towards O'Cebriero, but then I paused.

What *was* my dream?

It was simple really. I stopped and reached for a pen and scrawled in blue ink *To be happy*.

How was that a dream, right? It was too vague. Too easy. But not for me. It would always be my biggest dream. I had spent far too long being numb to the world. I wanted to know what happiness felt like again. True, loud, bold happiness. Not the happiness I faked because I knew it was expected of me. I wanted to *feel* it when I laughed. I wanted to understand that feeling of happiness that caused a smile to form on my lips. It was such a simple thing. Yet it would be something I'd work every day to have.

With a barely-there smile, I tied my dream onto the little tree and then called to Maverick.

"Come on, kid. We've got a long day ahead of us."

We passed through the rest of Las Herrerías, by the horses that pilgrims could rent for the day to ride up to O'Cebriero, and by more cows. Luckily, Maverick refrained from barking at these ones. Just after the village, the climb began. In less than nine kilometers, we had to gain over 2,000 feet of elevation to get to the crest of these mountains and the village of O'Cebriero, the gateway to Galicia.

The trail started out wide at a moderate grade and then we dropped down a bit before starting a brutal climb up to the village of La Faba. The trail became just a tight tunnel through lush greenery, with damp dirt beneath our feet. I had never seen so much green before. In contrast to the burnt grasses we had come to know so well this past month, walking through this tunnel of trees felt like a walk in a rainforest.

It was still early when we reached the little mountain village and we hadn't seen another pilgrim yet. As I gasped in air after the steep climb, Maverick wandered around sniffing the slate grey rock that all the buildings of the hamlet were made of. No bars were open, no stores to welcome pilgrims so early in the morning. Instead, I pulled out our last mini croissant from my pack and munched on that while I filled our waters up again just to be safe for the next stretch of climbing.

We had left the forest behind after La Faba. For the rest of the way up to O'Cebriero we were treated to the most incredible views back over the Valcarce Valley and beyond. Today stayed cloudy so we weren't treated to a spectacular sunrise, but dawn had broken to reveal soft hills of green pastures spread out all around us. Coming from New Hampshire where the mountains are all covered in trees until the higher elevation where they turned to granite mountaintops, the patchwork of fields at such high elevations was awe-inspiring for me. Mav and I continued up the narrow farm track, pausing every few seconds so I could catch my breath but also so I could take in the views.

Just after Laguna de Castilla, we climbed one final steep ridge to reveal the massive stone marker alerting us of our entrance into the autonomous region of Galicia. Galicia is so very different than other parts of Spain with its own language and culture. Dating back to the Iron Age, the area of Galicia was home to Celtic people known as "Gallaeci" and despite Romans, Moors, and Visigoths over the years claiming control of the area, the traditions of this first culture remain to this day. The extremely verdant, rainy nature of the region paired with Celtic traditions such as the music led by bagpipes and grey stone buildings gave more of an Irish feel than a Spanish one to Galicia. Safe to say, I was thrilled to be entering this last region of our pilgrimage.

Just after the massive stone marker for the region, we came up to our first of the stone pillars that count down the kilometers left until Santiago. **160.948** this one read. Less than two hundred kilometers and we would reach the cathedral. On a trek of eight hundred, we were down to the homestretch. We turned and made our way along the ridge into the hilltop village of O'Cebriero which plunged us headfirst into Galician culture.

Even though it was already ten a.m. when we arrived, the temperature hadn't even risen above fifty and a damp chill hung in the air. Celtic music was playing from the speaker at one of the bars in the center of the village, and a little shop was open displaying different swirled art that were certainly Celtic. Every building was made of tightly packed slate, some even with thatched roofs. One of the first buildings we saw upon entering O'Cebriero was a *palloza*, a traditional building dating back to pre-Roman times that is used in some villages to this day. This *palloza* had been converted into a museum to highlight the unique building structures.

Maverick was allowed to dip inside with me, so we headed in to check out what it was all about and get out of the dreary, cold weather for a bit. *Pallozas* were known for their round or oblong shape with low, slate walls and thatched, conical roofs. They honestly looked like little, haphazard, hobbit houses to me. The inside was bare except for a fire crackling in the center of the massive room with a huge pot for cooking over it and hard benches surrounding it. Apparently, whole families would live in these buildings along with their livestock. The strong smell of wood burning was familiar to me, making me think of my own wood stove back home, and I relished the chance to warm up.

We didn't stay inside for too long because my stomach was grumbling too loudly, reminding me I hadn't had breakfast yet and it was past ten now. I hooked Mav outside a bar on the corner of the village center and left my bags with him before making my way inside. It was just as warm and woodsy in here as it had been in the *palloza* as I made my way down to a sort of basement where the main pub was. Though the area was known for *caldo gallego*, a traditional soup that was meant to warm you from the inside out, I opted for a piece of an empanada that I spied in one of the cases on the bar and took it back outside to eat with Maverick.

He peeked up at me as I came back into the raw air and took a seat on one of the high stools around the round table here. I poked at the empanada then looked back down at him. "It's tuna," I told him. He cocked his head. "*A tún,*" I clarified with Spanish for him, as if that would help. "I know. What was I thinking? Tuna empanada? Sounds terrible, doesn't it?" He blinked his deep brown eyes at me.

I pursed my lips and looked at the empanada again. It wasn't at all like the empanadas we thought of in America. Nor was it like the ones I had in Guatemala when I was down there visiting friends this past winter. Instead, it was more like a slice of a pie. The barista had even asked if I had wanted it warmed. Apparently, an *empanada gallega* was very different from a Spanish empanada. I cut off a bite with my fork and tentatively bit into it.

"Oh, my god," I breathed out to Maverick. He looked up at me again. "This is actually amazing." I shoved another bite in my mouth and poked at the remaining piece of pie with my fork, trying to lift up the flakey top to see the filling better. "What do you think is in this thing?" I asked Mav. "Is that...tomato? Maybe some pepper up in here? Hey, you want a bite?"

I cut off a piece for Mav and held it out to him. He sniffed it for just a second before scarfing it down and looking to me for more. "I told you it was good. Forget the tortillas, this is a new go-to. But no, you can't have more. This is my breakfast, sorry."

After polishing off my plate in record time, we headed out to explore the rest of the little village that was easily becoming my favorite stop of the Camino. As much as I had loved last night's stay in our own fancy apartment-like place, I kind of wished we had pushed on to here. Or that it had somehow worked out for us to spend the night here as well, because I would totally live here if given the chance. The mountains all around us? The adorable village of stone? The *delicious* food? I was in love.

We wandered across the center of the village towards the stone church, *Santa María Real*, which is supposedly the oldest standing church along the Camino Francés. It was built back in 836 and still holds services to this day. I tied Maverick to a bench outside so I could go have a look around. The clerk stamped my credential as I entered and offered a candle to light, but I waved him off. Instead, I mingle with the few other pilgrims who are here to take in the plain, spacious interior.

Just beside the church, Maverick and I took a look at the bust of Don Elias Valiña Sampedro. Well, I took a look at it and had to yank Maverick away before he lifted his leg to pee on the stone column it stood on. Apparently, this priest was the man who first came up with the yellow arrow idea for marking The Way.

"Listen, Dude. You might have peed on every yellow arrow marker so far, but you can't pee on this guy's head.

That's not very nice," I scolded Maverick. He gave me a side
eye and then lifted his leg on a nearby stone wall.

As much as I would have loved to stay in O'Cebriero for
the entire day, we still had over twenty kilometers ahead of us
if we wanted to reach Triacastela by the end of the day. It was
time we kept moving. Not wanting to be stuck on a road all
day, I made sure to keep my eyes peeled on the way out of
the village for those famous yellow arrows. Apparently, most
pilgrims miss them and end up just following the road out of
O'Cebriero and down to Liñares. In fact, I almost fell into
this trap as well and we had to backtrack to find the Camino
past an albergue and into the forest.

There wasn't another pilgrim on this trail. It seemed the
guidebook was right for once; most did miss this trail. It
passed easily through tall pines and across what looked like
logging roads before spitting us back out on an asphalt road
that dropped down to the main road, where I could see the
little dots of fellow pilgrims below us walking on. We joined
up with them in time to pass through Liñares, which wasn't
much of a "hamlet" but rather a roadside pit stop. It was
definitely more run down, and perhaps there was more to the
town if we were to turn into it and explore, but all Maverick
and I saw was the gas station and auto shop where workers
watched pilgrims pass by.

I continued on with Maverick on the leash since we were
on the busy road now, crossing over it to look out over the
green valleys of Galicia laid out before us. On this side of the
mountain pass, it was clear these would be our last real
mountains of the trail. Below us, the land slowly flattened
out to rolling hills and patchwork farmland. The thick cloud
cover still hung low over us and kept the day raw and chilly,
but at least it didn't look like rain for the rest of our descent.

While the Camino remained on that side of the road
from Liñares to Hospital de la Condesa, I made sure no cars

were barreling down on us and dashed across the road one more time just after Liñares. Just beside the highway, an enormous statue of a medieval pilgrim appeared to be fighting against the mountain winds, looking down into Galicia. The bronze statue was immaculately carved, complete with a *concha* or pilgrim shell sewn onto his cape and the brim of his hat, as well as a pendant bearing the cross of Saint James around his neck. He stood at least ten feet tall and had one hand on top of his cap to keep it on in the eternal wind he seemed to be fighting and the other hand on a staff.

Despite the fact that I knew we probably looked really silly to any of the passing pilgrims, Mav and I set up my tripod and phone for a picture beside the pilgrim monument. Unfortunately, *bicigrinos* kept buzzing by us as I tried to snap the photo. One fellow walking pilgrim stopped across the road from us.

"Do you want me to take your picture?" she asked.

I had already snapped a few, so I trotted down from the statue to snatch up my camera and shook my head at her. "Oh, no," I said. "It's okay. We're used to this way of doing it by now. Thanks, though!"

She waited for me as I packed my mini-tripod back into the side pocket of my pack and tucked the remote into my hip pocket. It looked like we were going to have company for this next stretch.

"You've been walking the whole way with your dog?" she asked when we finally crossed back over the road and rejoined the dirt Camino trail.

"Yeah. We started in Saint Jean."

"That's amazing," she gushed. "How has it been? You said we, are you walking with other people, too?"

"Oh, no, sorry. We as in me and Maverick." I nodded down at him on the end of the leash. "That seems to confuse a lot of people. I guess I shouldn't say we but…" I shrugged. "He's just like any other person I'd travel with. *We* just makes sense."

"Wow. Just you and your dog. And how old are you?"

"Twenty."

"You're…twenty?" she gasped. "And you're all alone out here?"

"Well, I have my dog," I countered with a grin.

"Wow. I'm sorry, I keep saying that, but it's all I can think to say. I would never think of doing this alone. My friends are up ahead."

"It must be nice to do it with friends," I told her.

She nodded and began to tell me a bit about her experience and we continued together for a little while, but like so many walking companions on the Camino eventually you just end up drifting apart. She returned to her friends and then it was just me and Mav again, winding our way downhill. Sure, walking with friends must be nice, but I already had my best friend with me.

Just before Hospital de la Condesa, we passed by a field being worked by three men and a black, fluffy farm dog. It looked like a man was in the tractor, while his father and his son were on the ground, all working together to harvest the grain. The dog, however, didn't appear to be helping all that much. In fact, the men didn't even realize when he decided to leave them when he saw Maverick come into view.

"Oh, no," I muttered. "Maverick." I called him closer to me and made to pick up his leash from where it had been resting in the handle of his pack, but the dog didn't seem to be upset by our presence. Instead, he just seemed curious. He came across the field towards us, his fluffy black tail held high, and trotted all the way up to Maverick. I waited with bated breath, looking back to the field and hoping the men would call in their dog. Before that run in with the dog outside of Cacabelos, I wouldn't have thought twice about another dog approaching Maverick. We had passed by quite a few loose dogs on the trail so far, mostly in the small villages. Stray dogs were a known problem on the Camino. But aside from those dogs by the mobile café, we hadn't had any negative experiences.

For the most part, dogs just wanted to know what this new, foreign dog was doing in their territory. I'm sure Maverick smelled all sorts of strange to them. But I think when they realized he was just passing through, there was no real problem. Just as most dogs don't mind when others walk by their house but would get mad if a dog tried to come into their yard. I think the dogs along the Camino knew Mav was no threat because we were just walking through.

Maverick and this black, Spitz-like looking dog circled around each other as dogs do, attempting to sniff one another while also preventing each other from getting a good sniff. The men in the field still hadn't realized their dog had left them.

Maverick, never one to really interact with other dogs, had already determined he was over this new meeting and looked back up at me, ready to walk on. "Good boy," I praised him. But the other dog was being very good, too. He looked at me when I spoke and I saw his muzzle was all grey. I smiled. "Buen chico," I added and his tail, still raised high like a flag, gave a little wag.

"Okay, we're going now." I took a couple steps forward along the trail, away from the field behind us, and the dog trotted along ahead of me, just behind Maverick. "Oh, no." I looked between him and the field, getting further and further apart. "No, no. Uhm... ve a tu familia," I tried. The dog paid me no mind. Instead, he overtook Maverick and led the way down the trail.

"Perro," I tried again. "Vete." He should know that

command. Go away. Not that I necessarily wanted him to just *go away*, but the fewer words the better.

Maverick turned his head to look back at me like *what is this dog doing?* The farm dog turned to look at me as if he was saying *why does this dog have a backpack?* I looked between the two of them, my feet still planted back by the field. I glanced once more over my shoulder and then back ahead.

"Madre mía," I muttered. I guess we had a new companion for the walk into Hospital de la Condesa.

The dog seemed to know the way, not once straying from the dirt path that ran parallel to the road and then turned right into the little village of Hospital. "Vale," I told him as we turned onto the shaded streets. "¿Donde está tu casa?" I paused with my hands on my hips and surveyed the surrounding slate building and little patios. "Es tu pueblo, ¿no?" The dog stayed practically glued to Maverick's side as I unfurled his leash and took hold of one end. Mav looked up at me in confusion.

"Well, I figure he knows Spanish," I told Mavy. "He should know casa means house. Vete a tu casa." I tried to tell the farm dog sternly. He wandered over to a stone house and lifted a leg to pee. "Listen, boy. I can't just leave you out here now with no owner. Someone here must know you. Because you can't keep coming with us-"

A voice from a second-story window of a house to our right suddenly cut me off. "Rocky!"

I turned my head to spy a little old lady sticking her head out of the window. "¿Es su perro?" I asked her.

"Sí."

"Perfecto," I grinned. "See? This is your house. Go to your house." I waved him towards the little patio in front of the house, but the dog just continued down the road. I looked back up at the window, but the little old lady wasn't there anymore. *That's okay*, I thought to myself. *She must be on her way outside.* Only…she never appeared. I waited for another couple minutes. Still nothing.

"Alright, Maverick. Let's go. Clearly this is his town. I'm sure he's fine."

A woman was out hanging clothes on the line at one house as we passed by and I heard her call out to Rocky. "¿Conoce a este perro?" I asked her.

"Ah, sí, se llama Rocky."

"¿Es suyo?" I didn't think he was hers, since the old lady from before said he had been her dog, but this woman clearly knew him as well.

"No." She must have seen the confusion on my face because she smiled and continued. "Está bien. Él siempre pasea por el pueblo."

"Oh, vale. Fue en el campo con sus dueños, pero nos siguió," I explained.

She smiled again, not at all worried, then explained that he did that all the time. Apparently, he walked himself home whenever he got tired of being in the fields with his owners. After one final assurance that it was totally fine, she waved us off with a Buen Camino.

We continued down and off the main road to a little village that wasn't even marked as a town on our map, but it had a water fountain and what appeared to be a massive, stone water trough. The water was cold and crystal clear, so I allowed Maverick to jump up on the rock wall that was about waist-high and dip his head to drink. When he tried to put a foot down in it, I had to yank him back.

"Oh, no you don't," I scolded. "You'd never get yourself out of there and I am *not* planning on going for a swim to save you today. It's still way too cold for that." Reluctantly, he remained balanced on the edge of the pool of water until he had drunk his fill and hopped down again. Then he led me up the steep climb to the café at Alto do Poio where we stopped to rest and have lunch. Unfortunately, there were no empanadas to be had here and I had to settle for a measly *bocadillo*.

Fellow pilgrims stopping for lunch were interested in hearing all about Maverick, so I entertained them with stories of our Camino so far between bites of my sandwich and trying to figure out how many more kilometers we had to walk today. It was already one o'clock and we still had twelve kilometers and I was starting to drag. As much as I would have liked to stay somewhere in one of the little villages along the way between here and Triacastela, Maverick was out of food. Which meant we really needed to make it to a town that may actually have dog food. I couldn't be sure if Triacastela would, but the small villages on the way there definitely wouldn't. Plus, there was a place that allowed dogs in Triacastela. It looked a bit strange on Booking.com, but it was cheap and right in town so I couldn't complain. Despite my fatigue, we had to continue on. So what if we still had about twelve kilometers until we reached Triacastela? It was all downhill. It couldn't be that bad.

It could. It could definitely be that bad.

Between Alto do Poio and Fonfría, the low hanging clouds turned from benign to misting on us. One of my boots came untied, but I was too tired to bend down and tie it, so I just let it be. Except, every step I took somehow made it so the lace slapped against my opposite calf and bit into it. By the time we arrived in Fonfría, there was a trail of blood trickling down my calf to the edge of my sock. I took a seat on a rock wall and laughed. Maverick sniffed at my bloody leg tentatively.

"I mean, it is kind of funny, isn't it?" I said to him. He made to lick the blood and I bopped him on the head so he wouldn't. "What a stupid injury. Just because I was too lazy to tie my shoe." I bent over and laced up the boot, triple knotting it this time. This town was apparently famous for its frigid water fountain, although I couldn't find it anywhere. It wasn't much of a town, just one road through some barns, and it smelled like cows. The whole region smelled like cows. That smell didn't leave us for the rest of our descent. In fact, I would soon find out that it wouldn't leave us for most of our time in Galicia. It was everywhere, even when no cows were in sight, seeping into your hair, your clothes, your pores. It was inescapable.

From Fonfría down to Fillobal was a blur. Luckily, the rain stopped but the clouds were so low they obscured much of the view out along the valley ahead of us. Though it was promising to see we were getting closer and closer to being on the valley floor. The trail alternated from passing through walls of greenery and cutting through wide open fields. Thick mosses covered the rock walls beside the trail so it was hard to even tell there was a structure of rock beneath the plants, but sometimes Celtic symbols could be spotted carved into the stone.

Despite being tired and ready for a nap, it really wasn't *all* that bad. Until we rounded the corner into Fillobal, just three kilometers shy of Triacastela. Fillobal was an interesting little village, tucked just under a ledge and wrapped around the twists and turns of the road as it winds its way back to open farmland. It was just as we came around that first curve, with the ledge of the mountains on our right, that I heard a low growl. I hadn't been holding onto Maverick's leash, because the little villages had been pretty empty as we passed through, and I had been letting him trot ahead happily. I looked up ahead of him, to the right where a driveway cut back into the rock, and saw the source of the growl. A massive dog, definitely part Mastiff, stood from his spot by his owner's feet when Maverick and I came into view. In the blink of an eye, the dog was flying down the driveway towards us. I didn't even have time to think, let alone react. I just prayed it somehow would stop at the end of the driveway; that it would know not to come out into the road.

The owner called its name from behind him, but the beast didn't slow down at all. Instead, that seemed to make him run faster. Within seconds, he was on top of Maverick, biting down into the skin on his shoulders.

"Maverick!" I screamed, running forward, but what could I do? I had always been told never to get in the middle of a dog fight. My nana had her thumb ripped open and needed to get it stitched back together when she had tried to intervene on one. But I couldn't just let my baby get mauled right in front of me. "¡Señor!" I yelled, looking back at the owner. He had to do something. He had to call his dog back. But when I looked back, rather than seeing the owner running to get a handle on his dog, I saw two more Mastiff-mixes charging down the driveway. "Señor, por favor," I cried. The man just stood and watched, not even opening his mouth despite my distress. I turned away, running towards Maverick who was doing his best to get away from the dog that was already on top of him.

"Go, Maverick," I screamed. "Just go!" I did my best to get a hold on his pack and the two of us took off running, whipping around the next sharp corner in the road. It had been easier than I thought to get Maverick separated from that beast of a dog. Luckily, he hadn't latched on fully yet. We skidded to a stop at the patio of an albergue in town and I paused to catch my breath and start checking Maverick over for any injuries.

The woman who ran the place must have come outside to see what the commotion was, because she was already standing on the patio with a blank look on your face. "¿Es tuyo?" she asked. I was about in tears, every inch of my body shaking, and I was more concerned about making sure

Maverick was okay than I was in answering her stupid question. *Obviously* he was mine.

"¿Es tu perro?" another voice asked, this one deeper and gravelly. I turned my head and looked uphill to see the old man, the owner of the dogs. Beside him, his three animals were making their way down the street. He eyed me disdainfully. "Por favor-"

I had no idea what he was going to say, but I could already tell from his tone that it wasn't anything I wanted to hear. Somehow, he was going to blame this on me. I could hear the disapproval in the few words he had spoken so far. However, I had no time to worry about that. His beasts were on the move again. They had spotted Maverick and started to trot towards us, growls coming from each of them.

"¡Señor!" I gasped, but I knew it would be no use. He didn't give a shit if his dogs mauled Maverick right in front of his face, that much was apparent. So even though I had no idea if Maverick was hurt, we took off running again.

"Go, Maverick. Run!" My legs that had been completely exhausted just minutes ago were suddenly pushing me on, sprinting to keep up with Maverick as we tore out of the village. My pack was heavy against my back and I could feel tears falling down my cheeks, but I didn't care. I sprinted across the road, through a little garden, and then out onto a wide farm track straight ahead. My lungs were burning, but Maverick seemed fine to keep going. I looked behind and the three massive dogs were still following, but clearly at a slower pace. They had just made it to the edge of the village and slowed to a walk as they came on to the farm track. *Please*, I prayed. *Please let them stop.*

I allowed myself to slow down a little, knowing they had slowed, too. I checked over my shoulder again and they had stopped. Two had already turned and started to head back to the village. The last one was standing still, staring at us where we still jogged ahead of him. Finally, he turned his back and headed towards the village and trees. I heaved out a breath and collapsed with my hands on my knees. My tears were falling unchecked now and I was still shaking.

"Maverick," I croaked. "Mavy, are you okay?" I straightened up and made my way over to him. Once again, I started running my hands through his fur. I didn't see any blood. He hadn't been limping. But I had seen that first dog take two bites on his back, and who knew what I hadn't been able to see. "Are you okay, baby?" I asked him through my tears. He shook out of my grasp and tried to lick his own shoulder, but there were no puncture wounds. Somehow, he had come out of that without a wound on him.

Unfortunately, in our haste to get away, we had strayed off the Camino. So we had to retrace our steps back towards the village. I waited another few minutes to make sure the dogs returned to their house, and then we hesitantly made our way back onto the main road. There were still three kilometers until we got to Triacastela, so I spent the last stretch in a panic, just waiting for another dog to pop out and attack us.

When we finally arrived, I didn't even have the mental capacity to think too much of how strange the place we were staying was. It wasn't so much of a *casa rural* as simply a woman's *casa*. If I hadn't shown my reservation on Booking.com to the old lady hanging clothes outside, I doubt she would have believed I was actually supposed to be staying there. She tried to make a big deal about Maverick, claiming something about only small dogs being allowed inside, but after what we had just gone through together, I wasn't having it.

Whether it was due to my tone, or tear-streaked face, or just the sheer exhaustion I'm sure was visible in every line of my body, she somehow found it in herself to take pity on us and allow Maverick to stay in the little bedroom with me. As much as I would have loved to take a shower and then go to bed and try to forget everything about this afternoon, Maverick was out of food.

I pulled my quick-dry, backpacker's towel through my wet hair one last time, not that it did much, and sighed at where Maverick lay on the purple, furry rug. Like I said, this wasn't a hostel. I felt like I was intruding on some little girl's room. Would she come back from her summer camp while I was here and kick me out? Who knows.

"Come on, stinky. Let's try to find some dinner."

We slipped out of the room, which did actually have a key so I was able to lock it behind us, and down the stairs that led to the garden. Two little girls were pushing each other on a spindly swing set and eyed us warily as we came down the stairs. Maybe they were sharing a room tonight so that I could use the spare room. I shook the thought from my head. This was supposedly a certified place to stay, at least according to Booking. I'm sure that room was always for guests.

We made our way out of the little neighborhood and back to the main road, then turned back up towards where I had caught a glimpse a store when we came barreling into town. Despite the guidebook singing Triacastela's praises, I wasn't all that impressed with it. It seemed like a mix between a quiet Camino village and an industrial suburb, though it certainly wasn't near any large city. Unless you wanted to count Sarria, which was almost twenty kilometers away. Regardless, it did indeed have a little grocery store, though no vet or pet store to be found unfortunately.

"Looks like you're stuck with canned food for the night," I told Mav as we crossed the road to the side where the store was situated on the corner right beside an albergue that was overflowing with happy pilgrims. I could see some chatting at little coffee tables inside in what looked like a café area, while others were lounging on the sidewalk so they could smoke a cigarette and others spilled over to the laundromat next door. In a damp climate like Galicia was already proving to boast, a clothes dryer would be much needed for pilgrims. "I'm sure we'll be able to find a vet in Sarria tomorrow. So just tonight you'll be stuck with canned food. Not that you really minded it last time, but-"

"Colby! Maverick!" I turned at the sound of our names, trying to find the face behind the familiar call. She was leaning against the corner of the store, a stream of cigarette smoke wafting up behind her blonde hair. "How are you?"

"Rose," I smiled. She immediately enveloped me in a one-armed hug so that her cigarette didn't singe me, then bent to smother Maverick in affection.

"Oh boy," she laughed. "Somebody has acquired a new… smell." She straightened up and smiled at me.

"Yeah, he stinks like cows," I grumbled back, but I couldn't stop the grin from overtaking my face. Just seeing her made everything that happened today seem not so bad. "One day in Galicia, and he already smells like the cows here."

Rose burst into laughter, the sound like tinkling bells even in the gloomy atmosphere of this region. She could brighten any place she went. "You look tired. Long day today?"

As always, with Rose it was easy and soon I had told her all about our day without a detail missing. She gasped at all the right places, and was just as appalled by the dog owner's behavior as I had been, and diligently checked Maverick over for any injuries I might have missed.

"Are you okay?" she finally asked.

"Me?" I clarified. "Me? Yeah, I'm fine. They didn't do anything to me. Just Maverick and-"

"Yes, yes, the dogs did not get you. But are *you* okay?" she asked adamantly, giving me a hard look, like a mom who knew that when you said *fine* you really weren't fine.

"I'm, uh, yeah," I tipped my head from side to side. "I'm okay."

"You are sure?" she asked. I nodded. I was. Okay, that is. Shaken up, but okay. We were both here, not injured, almost on to the last hundred kilometers of our journey. That was reason enough to be thankful. "You know, most people would not keep going. All the things you two have gone through? Most people would have stopped." She took a drag from her cigarette and blew the smoke back over her shoulder then pointed to me. "But not you. You are special. You two are something special."

I tried to brush her off, because we were nothing special. If anything, we were pretty weak considering how easily I let things bother me. But she wouldn't have it.

"You are. But what can I do to help you? There must be some way I can help."

"Well...would you mind if I left Maverick with you while I go in the store? I need to get him some food for dinner."

"I would not mind at all." She smiled and held out her hand for his leash.

"Thanks," I told her, but I held her gaze for an extra beat. I was thankful to her for so much more than just this one little favor. "Thank you. For everything."

Live and Die

Day Thirty-Three: Triacastela to Barbadelo
28.3 km ~ 39,926 steps

July 22nd

I went to bed with Maverick cuddled up against me last night, yet again questioning if this was really the right thing to be doing with him. Over thirty days later, and I still had the same questions bouncing around in my head that I did when we had stopped to rest on that grassy knoll looking out over the Pyrenees. Like everyone had tried to tell me before we set out on this trek, this wasn't Maverick's choice. Did he really want to be doing this?

However, it was his cold, wet nose that was nudging me awake at the crack of dawn today, eager to keep walking. The air was cool as we made our way down the back stairs and slipped out of our odd abode without seeing anyone else. It seemed the family was still asleep. After consulting the guidebook again last night, I had decided to take the San Xil route towards Sarria rather than the Samos route I had originally planned on. Samos is home to one of the oldest and largest monasteries in Spain, which I think was why I had first planned to walk that way, but it also looked like it followed a highway through most of the path to Sarria. The San Xil route looked a bit more primitive, and the guidebook made sure to warn that there wouldn't be many amenities, which meant it was right up my alley.

Despite the warning, there were a few little villages between Triacastela and Sarria that were happy to welcome pilgrims. Although, there weren't many pilgrims on this route. It seemed most pilgrims took the Samos route today. We did end up walking with a trio of young people for a little while between Triacastela and Alto do Riocabo, but those were the only other pilgrims we saw for most of the day. I've become accustomed to being alone on the trail, so the long stretches without other pilgrims had actually become some of my favorite times. Plus, Galicia as a whole was quickly becoming a favorite of both Maverick and myself. There had been a couple times where we had felt like we were walking through tunnels of greenery yesterday, but today took that to a new level. In fact, much of the paths in Galicia are sunken into the ground, with walls of moss and plants that rise up on either side of us. I've since found out these sorts of trails are known as "holloways" in some places, coming from the Old English "hola weg" meaning sunken road. They had been formed through hundreds of years of foot traffic, horses, and carriages passing on the same trail over and over again and wore it down into the bedrock. Everything else continued to grow up around it, making a tunnel of vegetation to pass through. Sometimes, it cut into a rocky area, creating a miniature valley to walk through.

Between these sections of "holloways" and open stretches beside farmlands with a blue sky and rolling clouds overhead, today really was the perfect day. Which was just what we needed after yesterday's debacle. We got to do a bit of climbing up to the high point of the day, then wound our way back down through the tight, gravel roads at the edge of Montán with its old, empty stone buildings, and grabbed some breakfast in the last little village of Pintín before the trail rejoined with the Samos route on the way into Sarria.

The tunneled path seemed to get even deeper once the Samos route rejoined, as if the added pilgrim traffic had worn the bedrock down even more over the years. Despite both trails converging, we still didn't see any other pilgrims, which didn't really bother me. I would have liked to have seen Rose again, but seeing her last night in Triacastela was a gift in itself. That was the funny thing about the Camino. You got so close with people so quickly and then, just like that, you never saw them again. I'm sure there was a lesson in there that I hadn't quite grasped yet.

Soon enough, the trail gave way to roads again and the bigger buildings of the city came into view. Sarria was known far and wide as the starting point for many pilgrims. The fact was, in order to receive a Compostela upon completion of your pilgrimage, you had to show proof of walking at least one hundred kilometers of the route. Therefore, Sarria, situated a mere one hundred and eleven kilometers from Santiago de Compostela, was the ideal place for pilgrims to start who were eager for that special piece of paper to commemorate their trek. I had been told that in the years since *The Way* came out, the route from Sarria to Santiago could get so busy you couldn't find any solitude on the trail.

Hoping that wasn't the case, Mav and I paused just before the city to drink some water and take a rest. Whether this was our last part of the trail we had to ourselves or not, I always liked to take a break before we went into a city. I pulled out my phone and did a quick search for any pet stores or vets in the city. I hadn't had much luck last night in that tiny market in Triacastela. I ended up buying what was basically a log of wet food. From what I read of the ingredients, it was almost entirely crude protein. So despite not seeming all that appetizing, I knew it wasn't bad for Maverick at all. Either way, I had only bought two of the disgusting-looking logs of food last night so he was out of food yet again.

I really hadn't thought it would be a problem since Sarria was such a major hub of the pilgrimage and a normal city besides that. There were sure to be veterinarian offices or stores. Only, the vet's office that was right by where we had stopped to take our break was closed for the day. I walked closer to see the sign on the door and had the horrible realization that it was Sunday.

"It's Sunday," I moaned to Maverick as I came back and sat against the concrete wall next to him. He cocked his head at me. "I know. It's a great thing to have in this culture. Makes everyone slow down. Spend time with family. Really enjoy the day with everything closed on a Sunday. But that is *not* helping us today." Mav stood and snuffled at some grass nearby, then watched as a man in full mountain-biking attire rolled a massive bike up the street past us. I raised an eyebrow at him as he went.

Once he was out of hearing distance, I turned back to Maverick. "I don't know where that guy thinks he's gonna find a mountain around here. We're in the midst of a concrete jungle. Granted, it looks like this is a hilly city, but still. It's a city."

Just then, a second man came around the corner. Same get up, big helmet on his head as if he were about to compete in Motocross, wheeling his bike up the street. Maverick tugged on his end of the leash, wanting to follow after him. "Okay, now that's just weird. Seriously, I don't see this as any place to be racing dirt bikes. But yeah, we can go that way. The Camino goes that way anyway. Plus, we need to find some sort of store. I'm sure we can at least find a grocery store."

I gathered our stuff up, considerably lighter now that there wasn't a drop of dog food in either of our packs, and let him tug me up the sidewalk into the city. Within minutes, it was clear that an overabundance of pilgrims wouldn't be our issue today. Instead, it was the crowds of spectators that were clogging the streets. The yellow arrows were pointing us upward, and yet I couldn't even see through the wall of people in that direction.

"What in the…" My words were drowned out but the *clunking* of what sounded like wheels over wood, like a bike speeding over a wooden bridge, and then a *swish* as whatever it was took a quick corner, followed by even more *thunks*. Maverick whined in response to the crowd's *ooh*'s and *ahh*'s. "Alright," I grumbled under my breath. "Pilgrim coming through."

As gently as I could while still making progress, I began to squeeze my way through the crowd and up the street which was supposed to be the main road through Old Town here in Sarria. It was no easy feat seeing as I was laden with one giant bag on my pack with a bedroll, another bag across one arm, and a seventy-five-pound dog attached to me that could part the crowds far easier than I could.

"Perdón. Lo siento. Perdóname. Disculpa. Lo siento." I shuffled forward, following in Maverick's wake as the people around us grumbled at our passage. *Well excuse me,* I grumbled internally. *So rude of me, thinking this was the route for pilgrims.*

The crowd seemed to be thinning, and then we were shoved to the right and I stopped short. We were now against a metal barrier, like the ones that held back crowds at concerts, and I could see up the entire street to where it branched at the top of the hill by the two churches. Only, the road had been covered with different wooden structures. Somehow, it had been turned into some sort of downhill bike track. And was that...a car? They had set up wooden ramps, turns, and obstacles all along the street. At one point, it looked like the bikers would have to jump a car, pass over a truck with barrels in it, and bounce down the countless stone steps. "What the-"

Again, my musings were cut off as a bike appeared at the top of the hill and the spectators gushed in anticipation. Without missing a beat, he came barreling down the street at breakneck speed. The countless stone steps didn't even seem to faze him as the mountain bike bumped down them, then he banked a right turn up on the wooden bridge that had been constructed, down again to the main road, pedaled hard to hit the ramp over the car and went soaring, and then he was out of view with a left turn on the boards that took him down a side street. Within a couple seconds, he was back on the main road, bearing down on us fast. As he came closer, the crowd around us cheered and clapped, prompting Maverick to let out the shrill bark he always felt the need to contribute when he got excited.

"Alright, alright," I hushed. The biker banked off the wooden curve we happened to be right next to, the *thunks* of his wheels over the boards echoing off the tight street. Maverick redoubled his barking. "Shh! Come on." I tugged his leash, forcing our way through the crowd and up the street. Between the barriers and the buildings, there was barely four feet of space where spectators were crowded. I did my best to make our way steadily upwards, towards the churches, but it was slow going. Each time a new biker started down the course, the crowd would surge forward to get a better look and we were essentially stuck in place, forced to watch along with them. And each time they cheered, Mav would bark, and I would wince and apologize to whoever was around us at the time.

What should have been a quick walk up the main road was a whole ordeal until finally we emerged from the crowd at the open door of *Iglesia del Salvador*. I heaved a big breath of fresh air, happy to be out of the crowds, and promptly had my arm just about ripped out of its socket as Maverick yanked back towards the bike track and the next biker that was zipping past. "Maverick!" I snapped. In an instant, he was by my side, head lowered in apology. I sighed and took another deep breath. "Sorry," I muttered. I ran my free hand over my face, sweaty and grimy from the nineteen kilometers we had already walked today.

"Let's just find some food and get out of here." I paused, noting the open doors of the church here. As of Sarria, it was required that a pilgrim get at least two stamps in their credential per day. It was some way to ensure that they really did walk the last hundred kilometers. This was new for us, since I had grown accustomed to just having our credentials stamped at whatever place we stayed for the night. I needed to remember to get another stamp every day now. Well, I might as well start now.

Even though it was much quieter at the top of the street than it had been down the track, I still wasn't fully comfortable leaving Maverick outside the church while I went in. There was a woman just inside the door, though.

"Disculpe." She looked up at the sound of my voice just outside the threshold. "¿Es posible que mi perro entre conmigo?" I asked. She hesitated. "Solo necesito sellos."

She looked around the inside of the church. "Ah, sí, si lo hace rápido."

I stepped up and into the church with Maverick, which was open and made of wood. It was one of the only churches on the Camino thus far that had a wooden interior. I had gotten so used to the stone cathedrals that this clearly stood out.

"¿Solo necesita un sello?" the woman asked me.

"Sí," I confirmed, turning from my perusal of the room and back to her. "Pues, necesito dos. Mi perro tiene una credencial también."

She smiled, not at all fazed by this. I slipped my bag from my shoulders and dug out our credentials to hand her so she could stamp them. "Oh!" she gasped upon receiving them. She looked up at me. "¿Has estado caminando desde Saint Jean? ¿Con el perro?" she asked in amazement, her eyes flitting back down to inspect the multiple stamps we had acquired.

I tilted my head, not quite following how she was so confused. "Sí," I answered slowly. Then I realized why it was so astounding to her. She was used to pilgrims starting their Camino in Sarria. To see a pilgrim with a dog doing just the last hundred kilometers probably wasn't all that jaw dropping to her. After all, from Sarria to Santiago was less than a week's worth of walking. Any dog could do that. But to see a pilgrim who had already walked seven hundred kilometers with a dog? That was something new.

She ended up telling me about a specific credential that was available for dogs now and I had to refrain from scoffing. A credential for dogs? It seemed unlikely to me based on how unwelcoming so many of the albergues had been up to this point. Maybe things would change in the last hundred kilometers, but I wasn't holding my breath. Besides, I had given up on the idea that albergues would welcome us. Booking.com had become my best friend over the past few days.

Mav and I followed the Camino markers outside the church after that, which took us along the top of the town, looking down the slope towards the more industrial parts of

Sarria. At least we could breathe up here, not being shoved back and forth by the pressing crowds along the bike race route. It was actually a nice part of the city with greenery, some limited views, and a final pass by *Monasterio de la Magdalena* just before leaving town.

"Wait…" My feet stuttered to a stop and Maverick turned back to look at me. "Leaving town already? We haven't even gone *through* town. Where are the stores? Where is the dog food?" I asked him out loud. I groaned and looked towards the yellow arrows marking the way out of town, then down the steep hill that led back to the heart of the city. "Come, Nug. Back into the city we go."

Over a half hour later, and a trek through the grimier, industrial parts of Sarria that weren't all geared around the pilgrim lifestyle, I was tired and defeated. "This is ridiculous," I moaned to Maverick as he tried to yank me forward along the sidewalk while I held his leash. "Where are the grocery stores? There's always at least a grocery store that is open on Sunday. There's nothing here. Literally, not a single thing is open."

Aside from many of the storefronts being boarded up in this part of the city, the ones that were still functioning were closed due to the day of rest. We had walked all the way back to where the Camino came into the city in our search for dog food and hadn't come across a thing. I sighed. "Well," I started. "I guess you're eating human food wherever I eat tonight."

With that decision, we turned back and headed the way we had come. There was no way I was fighting through the bike race crowd again to get back onto the Camino. We'd pick it up at the other end of the city.

I had purposefully looked for a place to stay on Booking that was just beyond Sarria. I knew the bustle of the city in addition to all the new pilgrims that joined in Sarria wasn't our speed, so we were staying at an albergue in Barbadelo tonight. It was just under four miles to the little village from the outskirts of Sarria and the trail there was magical.

We passed over rivers on ancient stone bridges that were overgrown with vines, hopped along rocks where the path coincided with little brooks or pools of water, and weaved our way through old forest until it opened up in the little hamlet of Barbadelo. Being so close to Sarria, I hadn't expected it to be much more than a suburb, but it was reminiscent of the miniscule villages we had fallen in love with along the way. There were only two albergues in the town and just one little shop that sold souvenirs, other than that it was pretty empty.

We walked up to the albergue, which really just looked like a big, stone house on the main road through town with a well-kept front lawn. The hospitalero was thrilled to welcome us and had been ready to accept us since he had seen our reservation in Booking. After fawning over Maverick for a bit, he got down to business taking my passport to write down all my information and stamping our credentials with a flourish.

"Pues, tiene una cama en uno de los dormitorios, pero no tengo muchos peregrinos hoy. Aún tengo dos habitaciones privadas disponibles. ¿Quiero uno de esos?"

"Uhm…" For once I had the option to choose between a dormitory bed or a private room? I wasn't being forced into a private room by some unhappy pilgrim or rules? This was just a nice offer he was making? "No," I answered. "Está bien. Quiero la cama en el dormitorio."

"¿Sí?" he confirmed with an air of confusion. Naturally, he would be confused. I'm sure most pilgrims would jump at the chance for a private room just because there happened to be rooms open that night.

"Sí," I smiled. "Estamos bien en un dormitorio."

"Bueno. Ven conmigo." He smiled at me warmly and led the way upstairs where he directed us to the right on the landing and into a small dormitory that had about five or so beds. He said I was welcome to pick any bed I wanted since I was the only pilgrim in this dormitory as of right now, the others were in a separate dormitory room downstairs. Then he pointed out the communal bathroom just at the top of the stairs and left Mav and I to settle in.

It was only two or so, and I wasn't really all that tired from today's walk, so after claiming a bed and leaving our bags behind, we decided to explore more of the town that we might not have seen on our way into the albergue since it was just at the start of the village. The hospitalero smiled and waved as we made our way outside and back through the front gate of the garden, taking a right to head further into the village.

This village was more spread out than the few others we had passed through so far in Galicia. The buildings were free-standing for the most part, not built one on top of the other to make tight streets between the tightly packed stone walls of the houses. Instead, this was more of a farming village which became even more apparent the further we walked. Within just a couple minutes, we were through the part of town that had buildings and found ourselves back on a forest path. A little rest area with old stone benches and a water fountain was on the left of the path just at the end of town, but after that there wasn't another structure as far as I could see. Just the barbed wire fence held up by both wooden posts and large, slate stones where it lined the path and separated the rolling fields from the thoroughfare. About one or two kilometers from the village, we made it to a split in the road and a crumbling stone church.

A couple of vans full of young teenagers were unloading by the stone church, the kids piling onto the lush grass of the nearby field and joking and laughing as they lounged on their big backpacks and rolled up sleeping bags. Of course, there was no way to know for sure, but it seemed like they were having a field trip for a campout overnight here. A few tents had already been erected further off the trail up the hill. I could see some of the kids pointing Maverick out to each other, so before we distracted them too much from whatever it is they were supposed to be doing, I turned and urged Maverick back towards the village.

On our way back to Barbadelo, I stopped at the rest area on the edge of town and called my parents. I filled them in on how relaxing of a day it had been, told them all about the nice albergue we were staying in tonight, and shared my worries about Maverick's dinner.

"Well, it's not the first time he'll be eating human food on the trip," my dad said over speaker phone.

"I know. But honestly, I don't even know if there's a restaurant in this town. It's super cute, but there really isn't anything."

"There has to be *something*," my mom added. "Pilgrims go through there all the time. The place you're staying doesn't have a restaurant?"

"I don't think so?" I wondered aloud to them. "I didn't see anywhere that would have food, like a dining area or anything there."

"The man sounds really nice that you said runs it. I'm sure he knows."

"Yeah , that's true." We chatted for a while more, talking about how close we were to finishing, and how tomorrow we would cross over the 100 km marker, making us officially less than one hundred kilometers from Santiago. Eventually I hung up to go in search of food for Maverick and myself.

As much as I had come to love the solitary experience of my Camino and didn't feel like I was missing anything when it was just me and Maverick, it definitely would have been nice to have my parents here with me. I know how rare that is to think. That a young girl actually *wants* to spend lots of time with her parents, but mine are my best friends. This whole trip, I've found different things that made me think of them or wish they were with me. The different trees I'm sure my dad would be able to point out. Or the laughs my mom and I would have over dinners and Spanish wine I'm sure she would have loved. Or just the idea of having the comfort of having someone you know with you on a trip like this.

But this was no time to dwell. I really was doing fine; I wasn't in a funk. Despite Maverick being attacked just the other day and not being able to find food for him, I wasn't upset. For whatever the reason, my depression hadn't reared its ugly head in quite a while. Without it fogging everything else and making every little thing seem so hard, I was able to see things clearly and work through problems rather than crumble.

It turned out the one real restaurant in town was at the other albergue just down the road from where we were staying tonight. Although the waitress had been confused, she did bring out both my meal and a full steak that I had ordered for Maverick. I felt a little bad putting the nice plate down on the cement patio for him to eat off of once I had cut the steak into smaller pieces, but what else was I supposed to do? I wasn't going to make my baby just eat straight off the ground.

Unfortunately, this was definitely one of the fancier places I had eaten at along the Camino. Aside from even the tables outside being coated in heavy, white tablecloths, everyone seemed to be dressed immaculately. There were no raggedy pilgrims in sweat-stained clothes and torn shoes here.

"Maverick, are you seeing this right now?" I muttered to

him as yet another van pulled up on the road outside the albergue. The driver hopped down and started unloading full suitcases from the van, bringing them up to the albergue on their rolling wheels.

"Mom!" a teenage girl called as she came out to the front of the albergue, dripping with water from the pool out back. "Our bags are here!"

I watched as the family came around from the pool and rolled their luggage into the albergue. I had heard about bag transfer services before, but this seemed to bring it to a new level. Rolling suitcases? For a Camino? "And so it begins," I whispered to Maverick. He ignored me to focus on licking every inch of his plate of steak clean.

"You're right," I sighed, popping another fry in my mouth. "I shouldn't judge. Everyone has their own way of doing a Camino." I looked up and watched as the driver wheeled more suitcases from the van up to the albergue. "But wheely suitcases? *Really?*"

Only Human

Day Thirty-Four: Barbadelo to Portomarín

20.6 km ~ 29,113 steps

July 23rd

The next morning we woke up before the sun, just like we had on each day of the Meseta. It was the first time I had really tried to wake up early in a while, so it took a little extra effort on my part. Maverick was unfazed by the early start, boinging around our empty dormitory (no other pilgrims had ended up checking in last night, so we did indeed end up with a "private room") as I packed up our gear and double-checked that we had everything before setting off for the day.

"Sorry, Baby Dog. No breakfast today." I bit my lip as I looked down at his wagging tail. I really didn't have a plan on how to get him food any time soon. I had really been counting on Sarria to have some since it was the last major city until Santiago. I would just have to check every single town we went through. At the very least, I should be able to find those log-like things I had gotten him in Triacastela. Not at all appetizing, but at least it was nutritious.

I put my finger to my lips and waited until he had calmed down enough to crack open the door and make our way outside. Even in the still-dark morning, it was clear that mist hung heavy in the air. It was a good thing we had followed the Camino route on our walk yesterday afternoon. If I hadn't known where I should be going, I probably would have lost the trail due to the fog cloaking the whole town. The views we had been able to see yesterday across the open fields were nonexistent now. Maverick didn't mind the gloom at all. He had found a stick and was frolicking along like he wasn't at all bothered by his lack of breakfast this morning.

After the crumbling church, where I could barely even make out the school group's tents off to the right of the road, we left the open fields behind and followed the dirt trail through a forest of gnarled trees. Paired with the heavy fog, it made it feel like we were walking through some sort of enchanted forest. Although, not the nice kind of enchanted forest. More along the lines of one where something sinister could pop out at any moment from behind the thick foliage or creep through the mist towards us.

Despite the forest's ominous look, I didn't feel at all anxious. We had yet to pass another pilgrim, so we were most certainly alone, and still I felt at ease. There was something comforting about the way the trees curved and bent over the path, almost like they were there just to shelter a pilgrim on their way.

The trail weaved in and out of forest and through farm-land after that, yet we only came across one other pilgrim on our way. At times, the trees were so tightly packed they made walls on either side of the path. Other times, actual rock walls had been built beside the trail which had been slowly swallowed by the forest so they looked more like a thick hedge than rock. Sometimes, our views would open to fields of grass that were over Maverick's head and yet I could only see about fifty yards out into them. Even though it was almost nine, the fog had yet to lift.

We walked with an older couple from the Netherlands for a little while, but when they turned off for breakfast in one of the little villages, Mav and I continued on. I wanted to reach our big destination for the day with as little people around as I could. I knew it was a big photo op for so many pilgrims – just as big as the sign in Roncesvalles that stated there were 790 KM left to walk to Santiago.

Just before the little farming village of A Pena, we finally came up to it. Just another granite marker, no bigger or more exciting than any of the others we had passed on our way through Galicia so far. Same dark blue square with the tell-tale yellow lines of a pilgrim's shell and a yellow arrow just beneath that. What made it so different, so special, was that instead of "160.948" etched on a copper plaque beneath the yellow arrow, KM 100.000 was carved into the granite itself. We officially only had one hundred kilometers to go before we reached the cathedral.

Previous pilgrims had graffitied the stone marker so that around the yellow arrow there was a bubble of blue spray paint and the granite was more black than grey now from the amount of sharpie covering it in pilgrims' notes. I know some people are so disappointed to see that, but to me, it still looked perfect. It looked exactly as it should.

I stood back for a while, just taking it in. Sure, it was just a stone marker, one that I heard got replaced often due to the amount of graffiti that was put on it all the time. But it meant so much more than that. It was a physical manifestation of everything we had done so far. The seven hundred kilometers we had already walked to get here. As I stood staring at the marker, with the stone wall behind it and a green field beyond that, still cloaked in fog, I couldn't help but feel…sad.

I had so much excitement leading up to this and yet seeing it, truly realizing that we were almost done our journey was definitely a sad feeling. We had been struggling for so long, every day brought a new challenge, that I hadn't had any time to really see how far we had come. I couldn't believe we had already been out here for thirty-four days. Sometimes, it felt like entire weeks had passed in the course of three days. Sometimes, it felt like we had just barely arrived in Spain. I wasn't ready for this to be over. I felt like I was just starting to enjoy it.

We had been doing really long days since we got into Galicia, sometimes over thirty kilometers in a day, but from now on, I wanted to slow down and soak up as much as I could of the experience we had left. There was no reason for us to be walking such long days; it had just kind of happened. With the cooler weather and the fact that we were definitely in walking shape now, it was easy to just keep walking. From today on, I wanted to split our days up to shorter distances. I wanted to stop and take everything in.

Thanks to Maverick, I thought we had been doing a pretty good job of that so far. He had a way of making me slow down whether I had wanted to or not. Because of him, I had seen far more of the villages than most pilgrims did. We stopped to play in every river we passed. We hung out in whatever shady spot we could find. We explored different streets, different parts of towns, that were at times very far off the marked Camino trail. Whether that was because I needed to find him food, or a toy, or just to take him for walks in the evenings, it had been our time and our time only. I guess there had been a plus to all those times when it was just the two of us, not spending time in a big bunk room or cooking dinner with other pilgrims.

"Excuse me?" A girl's voice pulled me from my thoughts. "Would you mind taking a picture for us?"

"Oh, of course." I stood and brushed the dirt from my shorts and took her outstretched phone. She looked to be about my age and the gentleman with her had to have been older than my dad. They positioned themselves on either side of the hundred-kilometer marker and I snapped a few pictures, always wanting to give a person some options.

"I took a few for you." I smiled and handed the phone back to her. "Let me know if they're good."

She flipped through on her screen, showing her dad. "Thank you so much. Would you like us to take one of you? And…is that your dog?" she asked with what I thought was a Dutch accent.

"Oh, uhm," I hesitated, *no, that's fine* on the tip of my tongue. I could count on one hand the times someone else had taken a picture for us. I was more than happy to use my tripod. But for some reason, I found myself agreeing to her offer. "Sure." I handed over my phone and called Maverick to me, but he was more interested in the birds twittering in the branches above us than the phone to look for a picture.

"Is there a way you could make him look?" the girl asked.

"Actually, yeah. Sorry. Here, if you just take…this." I snatched up a branch that was broken off to the side of the trail and Maverick immediately sprung into action. I positioned him back in front of the stone marker with a sit command and then told him to wait. "Okay. Yeah, if you just hold this, he'll look right at you." I passed off the stick to her and then scrambled around to kneel next to Maverick.

"Wow," the dad murmured from behind his daughter. "That definitely works."

The girl finished up with the pictures with a smile. "So

what do I do with this now?" she asked. Only, she waved the
stick out as she asked the question and Maverick launched,
chomping down around the wood. "Oh!" she gasped. Her
shock quickly dissolved into laughter, though. "Oh, my."

I laughed with her. "I'm so sorry. Yeah, he really likes his
sticks."

He had run away with it initially but was already back,
dropping the stick at the father's feet and taking three tiny
steps backwards before looking up at him expectantly. "Oh,
boy," the dad said. "What am I supposed to do with that?"

I smiled and shook my head at Maverick, who darted his
gaze to me for half a second before staring down the father
again. "He wants you to throw it for him. Sorry about that."
I lifted my pack from the edge of the trail and slipped my
arms through. "Maverick, no," I added to him. "He doesn't
want to throw your stick."

Mav's gaze flicked to me, then back to his stick as if he
couldn't take his eyes off it for a second in case the man was
really doing to throw it. "Ah, you just want me to throw it? I
see. Hmm." The older man bent down and gently picked up
the stick. Maverick's paws danced in anticipation. Carefully,
he tossed it further down the trail and Maverick took off at a
sprint, catching the stick before it had even hit the ground.
"Goodness me! He is fast!"

"And now he will never leave you alone," I joked with
them. I buckled my pack across my chest and hips and
shrugged Maverick's saddlebags over one forearm. Without a
word, the three of us fell into step on our way into A Pena.
Maverick had already scampered ahead and placed his stick
in the trail directly in front of us, waiting for the old man to
reach it. Of course, just as he was going to get it, Maverick
snatched it up again and took off.

"He does not want me to have it anymore?" the man
asked, glancing at me.

"He does and he doesn't. It's a game he plays."

"How very strange."

"Why yes, yes he is," I countered. The daughter laughed.

"Have you been walking the whole way with him?" she asked.

"Since Saint Jean, yeah."

"And no one else?" her dad asked as we came into A Pena and found a little station set up at the end of a driveway for pilgrims. There was a little box for donations and a sign that said to take whatever you needed. Power bars, juice boxes, and plastic-wrapped croissants were scattered over the table.

"No, just me and Maverick," I answered as we paused by the rest area. I grabbed a juice box and a power bar. This would apparently count as breakfast today.

"But you are so young," he said as he tore open the wrapping on a danish of some sort.

I shrugged and then spoke around my bite of power bar. "I'll be twenty-one in a few days."

"Just twenty-one!" he gasped. "That is younger than my daughter."

The daughter in question smiled sheepishly. "I am twenty-four."

"And you guys are having a wonderful time walking this together I bet." They both agreed emphatically. "I'd love to walk this with my dad. And my mom. Either of them. But for now, yeah. It's just me and Mavy."

Who, of course, had dropped his stick by the man's feet again and had been staring up at him in anticipation this entire time. At that point, I had finished my juice and power bar and tossed my trash in the bucket that was left for pilgrims, but the older man and his daughter were still sitting on a bench to rest.

"Well, I think we'll be heading on. It was really wonderful to meet you." I smiled at them genuinely. You could just tell they were very close and were loving this journey together. Just in the brief time I had spent with them, that much was clear. It was an easy thing to see. "Enjoy the rest of your Camino together."

"You too!" the daughter replied. "It was so nice to meet you."

"Buen Camino," the man grinned.

"Buen Camino."

Mav and I lazily made our way along the next stretch of trail, through more holloways and past more farmland. The ever-present smell of cows clung to us with each step and I kept thinking the fog and mist was sure to burn off at any time, but it didn't at all. It stayed grey and gloomy until the afternoon.

About an hour after we had left behind the father-daughter team from Denmark, we came up to a little gift shop off to the left of the trail. It was one of the only buildings around, made from the same grey stone as everything else in this region – the rock walls, the houses, the shops. It would have blended right into the grey day and gloomy surroundings if it hadn't been for the display of colorful *conchas* that was leaning against the building just to the left of the open doors. Each pilgrim's shell was painted a different color, from maroon to periwinkle blue to lime green. And on each *concha* was a different message. I took a step closer to inspect the writing, only to find out that it looked like every shell was written in a different language. I recognized the English and Spanish sayings easily enough. Ones that read "lucky is the man who has time to wait" or "*la guerra es la soledad infinita*" meaning war is infinite loneliness. I could pick out German but had no idea what they were saying and I could see some were written in French, but there were other languages I didn't even recognize bearing phrases I would never know.

I brushed my fingers over the different colors, then dipped inside the store to see what else they had. By the time I came back out, a little crowd of pilgrims had gathered around Maverick where I had left him tethered to my pack by the stone wall. They were fresh and clean and full of energy, a sure sign they had just started in Sarria. I answered all the typical questions about Maverick and then waved them goodbye as we continued down the misty lane.

We weren't alone for long after that. The swell of new pilgrims had caught up to us as the afternoon approached so we were constantly being passed or passing by others. In typical Galician style, a group of us was halted at one road crossing as a little old man ambled behind his herd of cattle, lazily directing them down the country road. Luckily, Maverick kept his mouth shut at the sight of all these cows. Apparently he wasn't so tough when they were right in front of him, no fence to separate them.

We broke off from the group in order to grab an empanada at the last village before Portomarín and *finally* it looked like the sun was coming out to burn off the fog. Leaving that village, we got our first views down into the valley and the río Miño. Though I was hard-pressed to call this a river. With the dam built across the river, the Belesar reservoir was created, flooding the previous lowland and making this seem more like a massive lake than part of the river anymore.

Maverick and I angled left on the optional route just before Portomarín and were suddenly free of all the other pilgrims that had been coming in droves for the past hour. They continued right to stay on the road and what appeared to be the main route, but the old route was calling me. It left the asphalt of the road and picked its way between a low stone wall and an overgrown field covered in yellow dande-lions. Soon though, it became a narrow lane between two tall stone walls, only wide enough for two people to walk side by side and angled downward pretty steeply. Mav and I scampered along, loving the tight walls and towering trees above us as the path twisted and turned until it took a sharp left and the reservoir was revealed to be just ahead of us, peeking over the stone wall.

At the sharp turn, the dirt trail gave way to smooth stone beneath my boots, worn down by hundreds of feet that had passed this same way before me. Suddenly, the trail dropped down steeply just after the turn but in the stone, steps had been worn away. They hadn't been carved or manmade. No, they had simply been worn into the rock by thousands of pilgrims passing this very same way over the course of centuries.

My feet froze and I felt my breath catch in my throat. I knew going into this trek that it had been a part of history for decades. I knew the history behind it. I knew the first pilgrims started making journeys to the remains of Saint James back in 950. I was aware that tens of thousands of pilgrims had walked the route to Santiago in the Middle Ages, that whole Orders had evolved in an effort to keep pilgrims safe. I had read that pilgrim numbers had soared in recent decades. The movie *The Way* had apparently inspired many to take off and start walking just in recent years. I *knew* all this. Yet somehow, for the first time on this entire journey, it really hit me. For the first time, I could see physical evidence of all those people. All those souls who had chosen, for whatever reason, to pause their normal lives and walk hundreds of kilometers on their way to Santiago de Compostela.

I was standing on stone that had literally been carved away into the shapes of stairs simply from the vast numbers of pilgrims who had walked these very same steps.

It was a humbling experience that I wasn't sure I could

ever adequately put into words. Just like Cruz de Ferro, this was one experience that couldn't quite be explained. It had to be experienced. I placed my foot carefully down into the next step. And then the next. And I added my own weight to the path that had been worn before me.

The narrow passage between the stone wall and cliff face continued to angle down, dropping to the river and where we would cross into Portomarín. It had grown so tight that even Maverick and I couldn't walk side by side through the last bit of it until we were spit out onto the side of the busy highway that ran parallel to the river. We continued along the highway, hugging the cliffs we had just come from, while I kept checking for a break in the traffic. When it looked like we had a big enough window, I tugged Maverick's leash and we darted across the lanes and onto the sidewalk on the river side of the road.

Just ahead, the road turned to cross over a massive bridge into Portomarín at one of the widest parts of the reservoir. Luckily, the sidewalk was barricaded from the highway at that point so pilgrims had a safe zone to walk right next to the speeding cars. A little group of pilgrims looked to be stopped, taking a break just before the bridge. I was judging them a bit, wondering why they would choose there of all places to stop, when one of them called my name.

"Colby! Maverick!"

I squinted into the now-blinding sun and held tight to Maverick's leash as he pulled towards the voice. I lifted my free hand to shade my eyes. "Oh my gosh! Gio!"

I practically ran the rest of the way to him and his group and he enveloped me in a huge hug. I hadn't thought I'd ever see him again. I think the last time I saw him was back in Terradillos de los Templarios when I had dinner with him and his friends, who were standing beside us smiling now. "Hola. ¿Cómo estás? ¿Cómo te va?" I asked him, but also looked around at his friends, knowing he would speak for them all.

"Bien, bien. ¿Y tú? ¿Estás bien? ¿Maverick?" he fired back in his Italian/Spanish accent.

"Sí, sí. Estamos bien. Nos encanta Galicia," I smiled. In spite of mist, mean dogs, and the smell of cows, we really were loving Galicia. "¿A ti también?"

"Sí, es muy hermoso. Mejor de la Meseta, ¿no?" he laughed.

"¿Para Maverick y yo? Sí, claro," We fell into step next to each other with Maverick tugging us over the long bridge into Portomarín and the two Italian girls he had been with back in Terradillos fell in behind us. "¿Te quedas en Portomarín esta noche?"

He made a face and shook his head at me. "No, no sé dónde vamos a quedarnos. Quiero estar en Melide mañana."

I made a face back at him. If he wanted to be in Melide by tomorrow night, he had quite a bit of walking still ahead of him. Melide was the next big(ish) town after Portomarín and was close to forty kilometers from where we were now. I huffed. "Pues, vamos a quedarnos aquí esta noche." I nodded down at Maverick so he knew what "we" I was talking about when I said we were staying here tonight. "¿Estás seguro de que quieres andar más hoy?" I waggled my eyebrows at him in an attempt to entice him to stay in town with us tonight.

He laughed. "Sí, estoy seguro. Lo siento."

I decided to give him a pass because at least he sounded like he really meant it. So together we climbed the massive stone stairway up into the main part of Portomarín, but that was where we parted ways. Just minutes after meeting up with him again, I was already saying goodbye. We hugged once more, he bent down to squeeze Maverick and ruffle his fur, and then I waved goodbye to him and his fellow Italian friends before taking a seat on one of the little park benches at the top of the old staircase. I took out my phone and pulled up GoogleMaps in an attempt to find a pet store or vet where I could get Maverick food.

In the end, there was no vet in town. I was able to find a feed and grain store here in town, right on the main strip heading towards the church. The men there were extremely helpful but unfortunately the store didn't carry any smaller bags of dog food and none that were the Science Diet brand I had switched Maverick to. They did tell me there was a vet that should have it in Melide, so hopefully we could stock up on food then. In the meantime, I found more of the log-like wet food and grabbed four of them to last us through until we reached Melide.

I popped back outside, where Maverick had become the center of attention for some locals who were dining on the patio outside of the café next door. I unhooked his leash from around the big column I had tied him to and shoved the food logs into his pack. "Come on, Reek Freak. Let's go hope this albergue really does let us in and is as nice as they sounded on the phone this morning."

Little Boy

Day Thirty-Five: Portomarín to Palas de Reí

29.0 km ~ 40,907 steps

July 24th

"Ah, look. Rain again. Are we surprised?" I glanced back at Maverick who was chowing down on his log of wet food. My nose wrinkled in disgust, but he just glanced up briefly before tucking back into his meal. At least he seemed to enjoy it even if I found it gross. I shook my head and stepped out into the mist on our balcony to pull in my clothes that I had been attempting to dry. Clearly, they did not dry overnight. I gave my toe sock a sad poke and it squished a bit. It may be clean, well, as clean as could be expected from washing in sinks this whole journey, but it still smelled like wet dog.

The private room we had in this albergue was so cozy and the staff was so welcoming I almost didn't want to leave. The weather sure wasn't helping matters. The drizzle didn't let up at all as I packed our gear up and rinsed out Mav's bowl once he was done. No way was I packing that into his bag still stinky from the food log. I sighed and took one last look around the sunny, yellow-painted room that didn't match the outside weather at all. "Shall we?" I asked Maverick. He spun in a circle by the door, waiting for me to take the end of his leash.

I thanked the girls at the front desk profusely on our way out, telling them again just how nice it was to have a welcoming place to stay, and then we were back on the damp sidewalk of Portomarín, heading back down towards the main plaza. Yesterday afternoon had stayed pretty nice out, so we were able to walk around town a bit and take in the sights. I didn't get a chance to go in the big stone church in the center of town because there was no good place I felt safe leaving Maverick tied out to. I had made sure to check out the exterior of it, trying to find any of the numbers that were marked onto the heavy stones. Every block in this church had been numbered so that the church could be completely dismantled and then rebuilt in its current location. Each individual stone had been painstakingly moved uphill to this site before the dam was built that had flooded the valley, creating the Belesar reservoir. I wondered just how much was underwater now. All the buildings that hadn't been important enough to save; to pick up and move uphill. They say during times of drought you can still see the Roman bridge that used to cross the river and the remains of the town that had been left.

Of course, this church had definitely been worth saving. As we walked past it this morning, I was reminded again that it was not just a church. It was also a fortress. From afar, the single nave looked like one massive, grey, rectangular block. Up close, you could see more details in it. The thin slots for archers' arrows, the battlements, the dark stained glass in the rose window just above the carved arch leading into the main doors. I took in the structure one last time, and then we headed back downhill, following the blue ceramic blocks inlaid in the sidewalk with a bright yellow arrow. They stood out even in the gloom of the early morning rain.

We plodded along up the wide, dirt track through the forest amidst hoards of other pilgrims. I hadn't expected it to be so busy being so damp and early in the day, but I had been wrong. I'm not sure if there will be a time that isn't busy between here and Santiago. About five kilometers into the trek, I swung my pack off to see if the toe socks and bra I had rigged onto it to dry were still hanging on. I gasped in a breath of damp, woodsy air.

"Mavy." He looked up from sniffing at the edge of the trail at my voice. "My sock. Where's my other sock?"

He trotted over to me and began sniffing my pack earnestly. I looked back down the trail where a steady stream of pilgrims were coming, then back to my pack where my sports bra and one sock remained. I unfastened them and shoved them, still wet, into the main compartment of my pack. It was early. Maybe eight in the morning. We really hadn't gone all that far in the day. I suppose I *could* retrace my steps and try to find my missing sock.

"Are you okay?" an older woman asked as she huffed her way up to us on the slight incline.

"Hm?" I asked distractedly. Maverick sniffed around her wooden walking stick and I snapped my fingers absentmind-edly so he would return to my side. I knew he was eyeing that stick. "Yeah, I'm good. Why?"

She paused in front of me and pulled out a big bottle of water from her little daypack. "You look upset. Did something happen?"

"Oh, I lost one of my socks," I said sadly.

She laughed in response, but then realized I wasn't

kidding. "A sock? Just one sock?"

"Yes…"

"It's just a sock." She must have seen me looking back down the way we had just come longingly. "You're not actually thinking of walking back to try to find it, are you?" she asked seriously.

"No," I hedged. But I was. I really was.

"It's just a sock. I'm sure you have others. If not, you could probably buy more at a store."

I pulled my eyes away from the trail we had come up and focused back on the woman, tucking her water back into her bright, clean, daypack. She didn't get it. She was clearly new to the trail. She hadn't been walking for the past thirty-five days with only two sets of clothes and whatever she carried on her back. When you have so little, you realize the value of what you did have. And sure, it was just a sock. But it was a good sock. I hadn't had a single blister this entire trek and I was going to attribute that partially to my toe socks for making it so the skin on my toes didn't rub against each other in my boots. Now I was down one toe sock and that was sad. It wasn't worth trying to explain it, though.

"You're right," I said instead. I took one last, half-hearted look around us, hoping the sock would magically appear, then slipped my pack back over my shoulders.

Maverick and I walked with the woman for a little bit longer, but soon found we easily outpaced her. As was the case with many of the pilgrims we passed by this morning. Somewhere over the past month we had found our walking groove and we seemed to be speeding by all these new pilgrims who weren't yet in Camino shape. Regardless, as the trail left the forest behind to come next to the main road into Gonzar, there were so many pilgrims it was shoulder to shoulder.

Maverick must have realized this wasn't a time to run

ahead, because in the pack of pilgrims he stayed close to my left side while cars zipped by just to my right on the busy highway.

"Aren't you worried he'll dart out into the road?" a man asked as he sidled up beside us in the throng of pilgrims. His clothes looked crisp and clean as well, a sure sign of a new addition to the trail.

I glanced down at Maverick, his leash lazily circling his neck that I hadn't even thought of picking up until that moment. But the man was right. The cars passing on the road were going at breakneck speed. It wouldn't end well if Mav decided to sprint into the road. And yet, I wasn't at all worried.

The past few days I had been increasingly annoyed because I felt like I was yelling at Maverick all the time. With so many people on the trail now, I was constantly trying to keep him close to me instead of herding any pilgrims or trying to get them to throw a stick for him. I felt bad because it seemed like I was calling his name every other minute. But when we came to the road today, I hadn't even thought of grabbing his leash. I had just said "sidewalk" as I said any time we had been along a road so far on this journey, and he stayed off to the side of the road in the dirt. I hadn't realized it as I was doing it, but I had a feeling he had already learned "sidewalk" as a new command.

I smiled unconsciously. My little boy was growing up. I turned my eyes from Maverick to the man who had asked the question. "Actually, no. I don't."

He let out a low whistle. "You must really trust him then."

My smile grew. "Yeah, I really do."

All of the tables at the café in Gonzar were overflowing with pilgrims when we finally arrived and I normally would have just kept walking, but I really was hungry. We had already walked almost eight kilometers and I had yet to eat breakfast. I plopped down our packs at the base of a tree and hooked Maverick to them to stand guard before squeezing my way through the crowds to get into the café and order some food. Only, there were no empanadas. No croissants. Not even any tortillas españolas. What the heck was I supposed to eat? Those were my go-to foods for the past month. I had thought if I never saw another tortilla Española it would be too soon, but I took that back. I would have loved to see one now.

Through the din of so many other people packed into one small space, I finally was able to order a sandwich from the rude man at the counter and escape out of there back to open air with Maverick. He had already become like an animal at a zoo while I was gone, other pilgrims coming over to see him while others stayed at their tables but their eyes followed our every move. I answered the questions many fired my way once I came out about where we started, how our trip had been so far, if it was hard. All the typical ones. As soon as I was done with my food and Maverick had finished his water, we were out of there.

Of course, just because we escaped the multitudes of pilgrims stopped for breakfast didn't mean there weren't plenty more on the trail. At times, looking up ahead at the trail along the road, it looked like a line of ants. Or a first-grade class lined up to go to recess. That is, if a class had upwards of fifty people in it. The line stretched for what seemed like forever. So much for solitude on the trail. I had to laugh, really. I had been so upset at the beginning of this journey that we didn't walk with other people. That we didn't have a typical Camino Family. I remembered texting my dad one of those first mornings to lament about it. And here I was now *wishing* Maverick and I were on our own.

Luckily, just after Castromaior we were able to dip off the

main trail and curve to the left, away from the road as well. No other pilgrims turned off with us from the main route, so Mav and I had a delightful solitary stroll through a little scrubby area before coming upon a little information plaque. *Castromaior*, it said. *One of the most important archeological sites of the peninsular Northwest. It was habited from IV Century B.C. to I Century A.D.*

The attempted translation from Spanish to English may have a few grammatical mistakes, but the message was clear. Just ahead was a piece of history I didn't want to miss out on. We were still alone as we followed what appeared to be a tractor path through an outer mound of dirt, almost like a ringed barrier into a little flat area that had been hayed recently. The tractor path dwindled down to just a footpath through the cut hay as we approached another ring of raised dirt. Only this time, as we passed through the gap between two hillocks, stones raised up on either side of us. Almost as if they were walls of buildings and we were walking through a street rather than through a gap between two hills.

And then before me was a whole maze of low stone walls. We really were walking through a village. A village from the fourth century B.C. I paused and looked around, but there was not another soul in sight. It truly was just us in this world from so many years ago. I reached out tentatively and touched the tight-packed stones. They looked no different than any of the stone buildings of the villages we had passed through so far in Galicia, except the walls only came up to my waist, like these were merely the remnants of foundations.

My hand trailed along the cool, damp rock as I ventured further into the complex. At first, it had appeared over-whelming, but now I could tell I was on a main road. A larger opening branched off between two walls of stone to my left and I turned with it, up what was once another ancient street. There was a gap in the wall of the next rectangular foundation, stone steps leading into it. The remains of a doorway. I stepped up onto it and looked around myself once more, imagining what this must have been like when people lived here.

People had raised their families here. Kids had played in these streets. I wondered if they had balls back then. I could imagine a few boys chasing after one down the street. A woman hanging wash out to dry. A dog barking from another house. Whole lives had been lived between these stone walls. A time so different from now it was hard to even fathom. I sank down to sit on one of the rock walls while Maverick sniffed along, his tail peeking up over the stone from a few foundations over.

I couldn't believe I was sitting here. All alone. After all those pilgrims on the trail today and not a single one had come to see this? How could they not? It was less than half a kilometer off the main trail. How was no one else as in awe of this as I was? I was once again reminded of my thoughts from a few weeks ago about how people are so focused on the end goal that they don't enjoy the small moments along the journey. They were truly missing out.

A moment later, Maverick launched himself onto the rock beside me with a piece of hay in his mouth. I smiled at him and reached out to stroke his fur. He understood. He knew to seek out the joy in the little moments. He taught me that lesson every single day.

"No, I'm not throwing a blade of grass for you," I chuckled. My fingers kept stroking his neck as I surveyed the little settlement. "Do you know?" I asked him. "Do you realize what this place is?"

He whined impatiently, dropping his piece of hay onto my leg. I rolled my eyes. "Nah, you don't, do you? You have no idea."

I must have spent close to an hour just soaking up the history of Castromaior. Only one other pair of pilgrims came in all that time. They walked through the settlement with barely a pause before continuing to the other side and back towards the main trail.

When I finally did go to leave, I turned and climbed up the hillock that surrounded the main settlement on the way out. Maverick scampered up the bank after me and skidded to a halt at the edge of the sharp drop down to the main road of the ancient village we had just been walking on. From this vantage point, it was all laid out clearly. Which parts were narrow alleyways between houses, what were once streets. Where two buildings backed up against each other and where doors used to be. And just like that, it faded into grass, eaten up by the earth where more had yet to be excavated. From here, it looked like someone had peeled off the top crust of a pie to reveal the filling inside. Just one little corner of earth had been peeled up to reveal this gem.

"Incredible," I whispered to Maverick.

The rest of the day passed by at a seemingly excruciatingly slow pace. Perhaps that was due to the clogged trail thanks to so many new pilgrims. Dipping into roadside chapels just to get a stamp was new to me. So was having to get a stamp at any bar you stopped at along the way. I was still used to only getting one at whichever place we stayed for night. I certainly wasn't accustomed to waiting in line for one. Maverick was a fan of the influx of people, though. He had discovered that it was far easier to con a stranger into throwing a stick for him than it was to get his own mother to throw it.

"Really," I sighed to the group of mid-twenties Australians I found us walking with at the moment through a little farming village. "You do not need to throw it for him. If you just ignore him, he'll stop trying to get you to throw it," I told them for what had to be the seventh time in the past five minutes.

One of the guys grinned at me and bent down to pick up the stick yet again. "We don't mind. This is great." He flung the piece of wood ahead of us on the desolate road and Maverick went tearing after it. I rolled my eyes when the guy turned back around to watch Mav skid to a stop, his nails clattering across the asphalt, and snatched up the stick again. It could be worse, I suppose. They could hate dogs. Luckily, other than the mom and her son we met really early on, most pilgrims weren't too afraid of Maverick.

For most of the day, I continued to try my hardest to breathe in deeply and then exhale any negativity I was feeling. It wasn't fair of me to be annoyed at the multitudes of pilgrims on the trail now. They were all here for their own reasons, just as I was. Unfortunately, my little exercise wasn't yielding promising results. My frustration was still bubbling under the surface. So I had taken to making up stories for the new pilgrims in my head as we passed by them on the trail. Different reasons for what might have brought them here.

"What do you think, Baby Dog?" I had asked him as we were approaching a pair of women who looked to be in their late forties. They were each wearing pristine, white tennis skirts and visors, though there was no sun to need shading from today. Neither had a big backpack, just fancy trekking poles and fanny packs. "I think these two are new divorcees. Mary just recently caught her big-wig husband cheating with the secretary. So cliché," I whispered to Mav. "And Sue has been divorced for a while now, so she suggested they do this together to shake off their past."

Maverick spared me half a glance before putting his nose back to the brush at the side of the road and snuffling around for more sticks. I cut off as we came closer to the ladies and plastered a big smile on my face. "Buen Camino," I greeted nonchalantly, as if I hadn't just made up their lives in my head.

They looked up as Maverick scooted by and one pulled out an earbud. "Buen Camino!" she replied shrilly. I tossed a wave over my shoulder and we moved on past them. Of course, Maverick never contributed to my little game of make-believe, so it got old pretty fast. Luckily, it seems that the pilgrims who have been walking for a long time have a way of gravitating towards each other unknowingly. We ended up walking with a man from London for a little while, weaving in and out of pilgrims as we passed through more tiny hamlets of stone buildings interspersed with pastures of cows before making it into the park just before the city of Palas de Rei.

We passed by a clump of teenagers, another organized tour group or field trip by the looks of it, with their music blasting, and the man turned to me. "It just has a different feel now, doesn't it?" he asked me.

I took a sip from my waterspout and nodded. "It does," I agreed once I had swallowed.

"I'm trying not to be judgmental, but there's a different energy on the trail now."

"Right. Less about the pilgrimage and more..." I struggled to find the right word.

"Commercialized?" he offered.

"Definitely. Like it's a tourist attraction rather than a spiritual pilgrimage."

"I agree. I do my best to keep to myself now."

I made a face. "Which isn't exactly what the trek is supposed to be about."

"Well, no. Then again, you must have a different experience. The dog must make things different," he added.

"It does. We've basically kept to ourselves most of the trip. But that doesn't mean that most pilgrims do."

"You're not most pilgrims," he grinned.

I smiled back. "No, I suppose not."

Once we got into the main part of the city, which was really more industrial than I had expected, we broke off with a "Buen Camino" to our new friend. I had called an albergue last night and they had said there was no problem with a dog staying there. Since we had such a great experience at the last albergue, I had high hopes for tonight as well. It seemed Galicia was much more dog friendly. Only, I couldn't find this albergue for the life of me. Mav and I went up and down the streets, going to what was almost the edge of town, and yet I couldn't find it. Finally, I decided to just go to a hostel I had seen on Booking that allowed dogs. Only, when we got there, the man had just booked his last room.

"¿Sabes ningunos albergues que permite perros?" I asked him. If I couldn't find the albergue I had called ahead to, maybe he would know of other places that would allow us in.

He shook his head sadly. "Lo siento, señorita. No conozco."

I nodded with a sigh. "Vale. Gracias, señor." I heaved my pack back onto my shoulders and trotted back down the stairs into the narrow side street that the hostel had been on. "Alright, kid. We have no other option. We've got to find this albergue."

Retracing our steps through town, which seemed like quite a ghost town considering it was the end of a stage, we made our way down the main road in the direction I had thought the albergue was. According to GoogleMaps, it should have been right on the main road, but that clearly wasn't the case. Finally, I managed to find it down one of the last roads on the way out of town. It was in a neighborhood of rather nice houses, blending in like it was just another big house. I sighed in relief and made my way inside with Maverick.

Everything was shiny and clean. Fresh paint in pastels coated the walls and an artful welcome sign featuring countless languages was behind the reception desk. I eyed the place carefully, feeling extremely out of place with my smelly bag and clothes. "Uhm, hola." I stepped up to the desk and the young girl working there with a neat polo shirt. I fought down the urge to raise my eyebrows at their neat uniforms. "¿Tiene una cama o un cuarto libre esta noche?"

"Sí, claro." She punched in a few things in her computer, barely looking up at me. "¿Pasaporte?"

"Pues, sí," I reached in to get my credential and passport out, aware that she still hadn't looked up to realize I had a dog. "Pero, tengo un perro. Llamé ayer y me dijo que permite perros." That got the girl's attention. She looked up, first at me, then glanced to her matching-polo wearing counterpart at the desk before standing up to look over the desk at Maverick. He had plopped himself down by my feet, soaking up the cool concrete floor. The girl's eyes widened at the sight of him and frantically turned to the guy next to her.

She gave him a nudge with her elbow. "¿Permitimos perros?" she hissed to him.

The man finally pulled his eyes from his own computer screen and looked over the desk. "Hmm?"

"Llamé ayer," I reiterated. "El hombre en el teléfono dijo que ustedes permiten perros."

The man stood and evaluated Maverick. "Sí," he said slowly. "Puede tener una cama en el dormitorio, pero el perro necesita dormir en un cuarto con las bicicletas."

I blinked rapidly. "¿Perdón?" I asked again.

"Tenemos un cuarto abajo donde se guardan las bicis."

I bit my lip to keep from saying something rash. He

expected me to leave Maverick in a room…in the basement…where they kept the bicycles? Was he insane? I took a
deep breath in to gather myself. "¿Puedo tener una
habitación privada?"

"Sí, pero el perro no puede dormir allí. Solo en el cuarto
abajo."

I sucked in another deep breath. "Bueno," I bit out. Well,
if Maverick couldn't stay in a room or a dormitory, then I
would just stay with him. They couldn't say no to that.
"Puedo dormir en el cuarto con él?"

The man burst into laughter. At least the girl I originally
talked to had enough sense to realize I wasn't joking. Her
eyes pinged between me and her boss. When he realized I
was still standing stoically before him, his laughter died
down. "¿En serio?" he asked. I folded my arms across my
chest. "No. No puede."

"¿Por qué no?" I demanded to know.

He launched into a lengthy explanation of how that
would look bad. What if other pilgrims saw me sleeping
down there? What if they started to take pictures of me? That
would be a very bad image for the albergue. They couldn't
have pilgrims thinking they had put me there. That would
hurt tourism. At his idea of tourism, I couldn't help it
anymore. I burst into humorless laughter.

"Esa es la única cosa ahora, ¿no? El turismo. Solo se
preocupa por el turismo. Nadie se preocupa por la peregri-
nación o los peregrinos. Solo por turismo." I shook my head
in disgust. The guy from London we walked with early was
right. The trail had lost the energy it once had. I had been
turned away before, but never for the sake of having a bad
image for tourism.

"Señorita," he started, but I shook my head and held up a
hand.

"No se preocupes. No quiero la reservación." I snatched

back my passport that was still lying on the desk between us and picked Maverick's pack back up off the floor beside him. He stood, ready to head to our place for the night. Only, that clearly wasn't happening. I had put on a brave face, but tears were pricking my eyes.

"Señorita, lo siento pero es una mala imagen si-"

I didn't care to hear what else the man had to say, I turned and pushed my way through the doors. The busy place that this "albergue" was, there were pilgrims in line behind me waiting to check in and more by the door. I kept my head down so they couldn't see how upset I was and uttered my apologies as I made my way out.

Once I was free of that suffocating place, I realized I had nowhere else to go. I made it about five feet down the sidewalk and then collapsed, my back against the sunny yellow exterior paint of the albergue. I wiped a fist under my nose, trying my best to brush away the tears. This was stupid. I shouldn't be crying. But it really got to me. It was almost worse to be turned away like this than it had been back on those times along the Meseta. At least they didn't give out bullshit reasons like it would hurt their image or their tourism. That wasn't what this walk was about.

I pulled out my phone and dialed my dad's number. I knew in the States my parents would still be at work, but at least he was able to answer a call while he was working. I just really didn't want to feel so alone right now.

He answered on the third ring. "Hey, Colb. What's up?" To anyone else, he would have sounded perfectly normal, calm. But I could catch the hint of concern laced in there. I shouldn't have been calling at this time. I also had a tendency to call my parents when things went bad.

"Hi," I mumbled, trying to hide my hiccups.

"What's wrong? What happened?"

So much for hiding it. "Nothing. I mean, not really. We

just got denied again. It shouldn't matter."

"Oh, Colb," he cooed. "Is there somewhere else you can go?"

"No," I sniffled. I swatted a stray tear from dripping down my cheek. "I already tried the one other place that's supposed to allow dogs and they're full."

"What happened at this place? I thought you called them yesterday?"

"I did. Except, when I got here they said Maverick had to stay in the basement with the bikes," I rushed out. "And when I said I didn't want to do that, they didn't care. I asked if I could just sleep down there with him, not that I want to sleep in a smelly, gross, bike room, but I would. And they said that I couldn't do that. Because it would hurt their image! They didn't want to hurt their tourism!" I hiccuped, my tears coming faster as my words jumbled together. Maverick nosed his way into my lap on the sidewalk and I knotted the fingers of my free hand through the thick fur on the nape of his neck.

"Their tourism? Really?" I sniffled some more and nodded, not that he could see me. "Is there anywhere you could pitch your tent around there? Or a town close by you could try?"

"¿Perdón? ¿Señorita?" I looked up to see the girl from behind the desk hovering over my shoulder. She was probably here to tell me I couldn't stay sitting here, crying on their sidewalk. That would definitely hurt their image, too. I had already garnered quite a few side eyes from passing pilgrims heading out to explore the town or on their way in to check in.

"I gotta go," I said hastily to my dad. "One of the ladies just came out."

"Call me back," he urged. I hit end and looked back up at the girl. If she thought I was going to stand up and try to look dignified, she was sorely mistaken. I was happy to keep sitting here.

"Señorita, no puede quedarte aquí."

"Yo sé," I spat. I was well aware they would not let me stay here. Could they just give me a couple minutes to collect myself before shooing me down the road?

"No, quise decir en la calle. Vamos a hacer una excepción. ¿Sí?"

I shot her a doubtful look. "¿Una excepción?" I repeated.

"Sí. Ven. Tenemos una habitación privada."

Though I was still leery, I pushed myself to a stand and gathered up my things. She offered to take Maverick's pack from me, but I hugged it to my chest as if it was some kind of shield. She led me back inside and checked me in at the desk, which the older man was mysteriously absent from, then led me to a private room just inside the main entryway. It was extremely modern, with all sleek appliances, and resembled more of a concrete cell than a welcoming room, but it was a room with bed. One we more than likely didn't deserve.

I was well aware that the only reason they had made this "exception" was because too many other pilgrims had probably witnessed them turning me away. It was already a bad look for them. If they made it up to me by giving us a place to stay, it might save their image. Whatever the reason, I wasn't about to question it.

"¿Necesito algo más?" the girl asked, her hand back on the doorknob to leave after she had laid down the ground rules.

"No." I shook my head, still clutching my belongings like they would protect me. Finally, I looked up to meet her eye. "Gracias."

She made a face and nodded once, then closed the door behind her.

Come Down

Day Thirty-Six: Palas de Reí to Melide

19.1 km ~ 26,989 steps

July 25th

I hid in my room for the majority of last night. Well, we went out and wandered around the city some and found a place to get dinner, but other than that I stayed hidden in my room. Even when I went to shower, I tried to do so as quickly and quietly as possible. I certainly didn't feel welcome in that albergue, even though we had been given a room. I suppose in any other situation, it would have been a really nice place. I saw plenty of pilgrims gathered in the common areas, some playing music, some cooking dinner together when I did scuttle out of my room to the bathroom. But my dog and I were certainly not welcome.

On the plus side, the waiter where we had eaten dinner had been so kind to us last night. Not only did he hang out while I ate outside and tell me stories of his own dog, he also came out at the end of the meal with a massive T-bone for Maverick to chew on. There was still plenty of meat hanging off the bone, too. It was basically a whole meal for him. Which, not that he knew it, was so incredibly meaningful for us. With Maverick still living off of those logs of wet dog food, this was the equivalent of a Thanksgiving feast for him. I couldn't thank the man enough. Even the cook came out to say hi to Mav and give him some love. So even in the midst of a rough day, with people who showed us the uncaring side of humanity, we were still shown the amazing parts of it, too.

In an attempt to avoid the crowds on this part of the trail, I decided to try different times to start walking in the morning. Today's attempt was a late start and I wasn't complaining. It was nice to be able to have that opportunity now. For so long, a late start would have meant blistering heat, but in Galicia it was a nonissue. Plus, since I had decided to slow down and really take in these last hundred kilometers, it wasn't like we needed to get a certain distance each day. Our grueling days on trail were starting to look like nice, relaxing strolls. Or so I hoped.

Oddly enough, my late start idea paid off. It looked like most of these new peregrinos were early risers so we actually got some of that old Camino vibe back on our walk today. We even had quite a bit of the trail all to ourselves without another soul in sight. When we did catch up to other pilgrims, we had a nice time talking with them. We didn't come across any other pilgrims who had started back in Saint Jean or even before Sarria, but the few we did chat with were definitely here for the real Camino experience. It was nice to be back around people who really understood the magic of the Camino.

It really did have a magic to it. Especially here in Galicia. The tunnels of greenery between each tiny village continued along the trail today as the stone markers ticked us down, closer and closer to Santiago. Sixty-five, sixty-four, sixty-three… Holloways grew deep again, the walls of earth rising up above my head on either side and the trees curving in like a canopy. Little stone bridges from centuries past rose up and over what could have once been rivers but were now merely trickles of water. Light blue hydrangeas bloomed along mossy fence posts and pink rose petals sprung up beneath stone windowsills in the quiet villages we passed through.

When we did come across the stray pilgrim here and there, I answered their many questions about Maverick and how our trip had been thus far. I spared them the nitty-gritty details but didn't shy away from admitting how hard this had been. Regardless, each time we passed another stone marker, I felt a little bit sadder. I still wasn't ready for our journey to be over. So we stopped for a break in every hamlet. We splashed in each little stream. I paused to take pictures of things most people probably missed.

We reached Ponte Velha, the medieval bridge that crosses río Furelos just before Melide, just after noon. Since the gloomy morning clouds had finally burned off, the sun was warm on our backs and Mav was itching for a good swim. I meandered my way across the long bridge which angled up to the center over the biggest arch and then dropped back down to the town of Furelos while Maverick scampered ahead. The village looked like an eclectic mix of modern suburbs of Melide encroaching on the ancient stone buildings with their thatched roofs. The shiny, new-model cars parked on the grass alleyways just seemed so out of place that I couldn't help but smile.

"Alright, Freak Reek. Let's get you to play in some water." Mav smiled up at me in the wolfish way he had. Unfortunately, the Camino tried its best to funnel pilgrims up the main road, giving no access to the river. But we had all the time in the world. I took a left down a side road through some of the older buildings in town in hopes of finding access to the river. Just a few feet down that street, there was a little stake shoved into the ground by a low rock wall that was covered in moss. A small wooden arrow had "RIO" painted in faded blue letters. I grinned at Maverick.

"You know what that means?" I asked. I tipped my head to the left, down the hay-covered alley where the sign pointed. Though there were power lines above us, everything else about this part of Furelos looked like it could have still been in the Middle Ages. The houses were made of big, round rock put together and covered with hay and wooden beams for a roof. The "windows" were merely holes in the rock walls covered with two planks of wood nailed together haphazardly, hanging awkwardly off their hinges as a crude form of shutters. Many of the buildings looked to be growing whole forests inside of them, proving it had been quite some time since anyone had stayed in them.

Before long, the alley continued straight forward into the shallow waters of the river. Maverick splashed in without hesitation, immediately lying down and looking back over his shoulder at me as if to say thanks. I smiled back at him and shrugged my pack off my shoulders, placing it on a rock that would be out of reach if Mav decided to come back up the bank and shake water everywhere. I dropped his bag beside it and began to slip off my shoes.

The river was so overgrown here. Big bushes seemed to grow straight out of the water in places. It looked like a river through a tropical rainforest, not part of Spain. But it was also incredibly clean and little waterfalls bubbled from just a bit upstream, beneath the medieval bridge we had crossed into town. Downstream, under the shade of a lush tree, a little rowboat with a blue stripe painted on it bobbed from its spot tethered to a rock.

Maverick had taken to chasing a pair of dragonflies as they flitted from bush to bush. Each leap after them sent a plume of water into the air so any time he got close to the rock I was perched on, I ended up soaked again, but I didn't mind. The sun was warm enough and there was no rush for us to walk on to Melide. As long as he was having fun splashing around, so was I. We must have stayed down by that river for close to an hour, him romping through the water, me just lounging.

It was funny, not another soul came down to the water during that whole time and yet I could easily imagine this as a busy part of town in centuries past. Maybe I was just in the mindset of thinking about what these places must have been like so long ago because of the Roman ruins from the other day, but I could clearly picture this being the gathering place for women of the town. The way the little alley had emptied directly onto this flat bank of the river made it seem like this had been somewhere villagers may have come to do laundry together, or wade in the cool waters when it got too hot. Maybe I was completely off-base, but it was fun to imagine a life back then. How simple things must have been. And even then, the pilgrims that must have passed through town and stopped for a rest here. There was so much history along this trail, most of it we would never even know.

I smiled to myself as I waded back to shore and gathered up our things. Maverick was still digging for something in the river, probably a rock he would want me to throw, and I looked at him with an insane sense of gratitude. Without him, I never would have stopped here. I never would have pictured how the villagers in Furelos lived. I wouldn't have wandered down the side streets or found this back alley with the crumbling houses that had mini jungles growing in them now. I would have walked on by, just like any other pilgrim, and missed all of this.

"C'mon, Mavy," I called, finally summoning him from his play in the river. He stopped digging for a moment and I looked at him, his soaked head cocked to one side and dripping. I laughed. "Let's go, kiddo."

He gave himself one last shake and bounded towards me, all hyped up from the cool water. I bent down, sacrificing my dry clothes, and wrapped my arms around his neck in a hug. "Thank you," I whispered.

The Camino followed a paved road up and out of Furelos once we rejoined it, meaning I had to keep Maverick on the leash as we made our way into Melide. Since he was so excited from his play in the river, I let him have his little pink ball. Except, he kept dropping it to sniff something along the way, and since we were on an uphill climb, it would roll down the road each time. After the fifth time he yanked my arm halfway out of its socket in his attempt to rush after the ball rolling downhill, I finally gave up and clipped his leash back in a loop around his neck.

"You are not worried he will run away?" a pilgrim asked who happened to be walking just behind us when I clipped Maverick's leash around his neck. Mav went tearing by him and dipped under the guardrail just in time to clamp his jaws around the rubber ball before it went down the steep embankment.

I took my eyes off him once I knew he was safe to face the pilgrim talking to me. He came to my side and matched his steps with mine. "No," I responded easily. "I know he'll be fine. I'll grab him if there's a car coming, but he just wants his ball." Maverick went trotting by us then, tail held high like a flag, tongue hanging out the side of his mouth behind the ball.

"He's all wet," the man commented.

"We just went for a little swim in the river."

"Oh. I did not know there was a way to the river."

I smiled to myself. I wouldn't have either if it hadn't been for Maverick. "Yeah, it was nice."

"You say 'we.' Are you with the others up there?" He nodded his head to a couple pilgrims rounding the curve ahead of us.

"Oh, no, sorry. I meant just me and Maverick." At his confused expression, I clarified. "My dog."

"It is just you and your dog?" I nodded. "But you said *we*."

I shrugged. I'd been saying *we* this whole journey. "Maverick makes it a we," I rationalized.

The man made a face like he wasn't convinced, but didn't push it. Of course we were a *we*. We were always a *we*. There had never been a time during this journey where it hadn't been the two of us against whatever was going on. He was my constant companion, for better or worse. Whatever I did, he did. There was nothing more *we* than that in my mind. His ball came bumping down the road towards me and I absentmindedly kicked my foot out to stop it like a soccer ball just as Mav came barreling down the hill. He snatched it up from the inside of my foot and then glanced up at me as if to say 'thanks, Mum" before running up ahead.

"You have been walking for a long time?" the man asked after a little while of walking in silence.

"Yeah, a little over a month now. We started in Saint Jean." I noticed him raise his eyebrows and I realized I had unconsciously used *we* again. *Oops*, I thought with a grin. "Did you just start?"

"In Sarria, yes."

"And you like it so far?" I asked politely.

"Very much. It is a beautiful trail. Very serene." Now it

was my turn to raise my eyebrows. While I was loving Galicia, I wouldn't exactly call much of the trail serene with the influx of pilgrims. Then again, I had managed to find some quiet times, especially today, so maybe he had as well.

We had reached the industrial suburbs of Melide and traffic was picking up, so I grabbed hold of Maverick's leash again and popped his ball back into his bag. The man made to take a right hand turn, following the Camino's yellow arrow spray painted on a street sign, then paused when I didn't join him. He glanced between me and the arrow. "Are you not coming?" he asked.

"I have to find some dog food for him." I nodded down at Maverick, not that it needed clarification. "There's supposed to be a vet this way, I think." From what I remembered when I had been looking it up while I was resting by the river, we needed to continue straight at this split for a more direct route to the vet.

The man looked at the road ahead in question. I agreed with his less-than-impressed look. It wasn't exactly the nicest looking street I had ever seen. It looked like it passed by quite a few abandoned buildings and half-built lots. And they weren't the kind of nostalgic, old abandoned stone houses like we passed in the villages. No, these were those kinds of empty concrete, city buildings with the shattered windows that seemed to be everywhere in the bad parts of town. I shoved down any trepidation and smiled at our fellow pilgrim.

"It was nice to meet you," I told him. "Buen Camino."

He glanced one last time between me and the road ahead. "Good luck," he offered. "And Buen Camino."

Mav and I continued on as I pulled my phone out to look up the vet on GoogleMaps to ensure we were heading the right way. There was no one else on this road, no cars going by, so it was a bit eerie to dip off the Camino and head this way, but it was nothing if not a new adventure. Maverick may have allowed me to find cute, hidden river hangouts, but he also took me way off the beaten path in search of food and supplies.

About a kilometer and a half later, we finally emerged back onto a busy road lined with shops on either side that resembled more of a downtown than the seedy suburbs we had been trudging through. I scanned the storefronts and found the vet almost directly across from us. "Perfect. C'mon, Mav. Let's get you some dinner."

A large black sign with block letters greeted us at the door. *CERRADO.* "Is this a joke?" I said aloud to no one in particular. I glanced at the printout of hours in the window beside the door. Siesta was from one-thirty to three-thirty and it was only one-nineteen now. There was no way they should be closed, but the sign was clear. CLOSED.

My teeth ground together as I pressed my face up against the glass with my hands cupped over my eyes to see in better. The place was dark, not a soul in sight. I scanned the waiting area for what I could see. There was dog food in there alright, but it wasn't Science Diet. I guess I could take a little comfort in that. They didn't even have the brand I needed. So even if they had been open, this would have been a wasted trip.

My hands dropped from shading my eyes and I took a step back from the windows, Maverick trailing along beside me. My shoulders drooped in a massive sigh and I suddenly wanted to sit down right on that grimy sidewalk. I was exhausted. I shouldn't have been. We had been doing short days recently. The weather was nice. Yet suddenly it hit me how exhausted I was mentally.

Have we ever had a day when everything went right? I couldn't remember. And sure, just earlier today I had been tearing up over the dwindling numbers on each of the markers, counting down our kilometers until Santiago but now I was cursing those very same markers. I was ready to be done. I was tired of wandering all over to find dog food, only to not find what I was looking for. I was tired of having to call ahead to multiple places and get denied for having a dog, or worse, be accepted then turned away later. My *feet* were tired. Every time I rested for just a little bit now, it took a solid five minutes of walking again before my feet stopped aching. The list could go on and on. Apparently, I was becoming bipolar on this journey. Add that to the depression and anxiety. One minute was happy and relaxing, the next I wanted to cry.

Maverick whined from beside me and I realized I had been standing, staring at this empty shop, for a good five minutes. Cars continued to whiz by us on the freeway at our backs. Shoppers were weaving around us on the sidewalk, casting a backward glance at my attire once they were past. We were a few kilometers off the Camino at this point, they probably all thought we were lost. If they even put together the fact that we were pilgrims. Mav whined again.

"I know," I sighed. "There's no food here. I'm sorry." He cocked his head to one side to listen, then tugged on the leash to keep moving. Because that's what we did. Kept moving, no matter what.

In the end, I found him some more of the wet food logs for another day and prayed we would be able to find some real food in Arzúa, where I was planning to stay tomorrow night. We had a nice hostel for the night in Melide, though it was a full three kilometers up the freeway from the vet and then back down a main road almost to where we had first parted ways with the pilgrim on our way into town so by the time we checked in I was dead on my feet. Even though we weren't walking full days, we somehow still managed to put in the mileage. I was too beat to wander far from the hostel for dinner, so I opted to just use their restaurant and sit out on the sidewalk with Mav.

Plus, I had noticed on our walk down the main boulevard, there weren't many typical restaurants in town. Every other café seemed to be advertising as *pulperias*. Octopus stores. Apparently, Melide is very famous for their traditional Galician Octopus dish. I would kill for an empanada, but apparently that wasn't an option tonight.

My eyes skimmed over the menu for the hostel's restaurant as I sat outside with Maverick late that night. It was past nine but the sun was still high in the sky. Almost every dish on the menu was fish, or shellfish, or the beloved *pulpo*. I suppose that should have made me feel good, knowing we were getting closer and closer to the coast and Santiago, but I hated seafood. As someone who had grown up so close to the Atlantic, I could say that confidently. It wasn't that I had never had good seafood, I just was not a fan of the slimy stuff – delicacy or not. But it looked like I didn't have much choice tonight.

A few minutes later, a round platter almost overflowing with little white and red pieces was placed before me. The whole meal was sitting in a pool of melted butter with paprika flecked all over it. "Huh," I said aloud. Maverick lifted his head to sniff at the table, then thought better of it and laid back down. I glared at him. Then I tentatively picked up my fork and poked at one of the pieces. It sprang back like an elastic.

The melted butter pooled in the holes of the octupus' suction cups in a somewhat satisfying way as I poked at those with my fork, too. "Well, here goes nothing," I muttered to Maverick and shoved a piece of *pulpo* into my mouth.

Sleep on the Floor

Day Thirty-Seven: Melide to Arzúa

19.2 km ~ 27,145 steps

July 26th

Okay, so it turns out, octopus wasn't *that* bad. Did I finish the entire plate for dinner last night? Of course not. Did I spend the majority of my time at dinner playing with the little suction cups and filling them up with melted butter by dipping my fork into them? Maybe. But overall, it really wasn't terrible. I dare say I would try it again. Not that I would be out looking for a *pulperia* any time soon, but I could eat it again.

For better or worse, Maverick was not trying any new food last night or this morning. He was still on the same, unappetizing logs, but he seemed to be enjoying them well enough. I just wasn't sure they were giving him the nutrients he needed for all of this exercise. He had definitely lost weight along this trip. Not so much that I was overly concerned, but his ribs were becoming somewhat visible when he breathed heavily and I really would have liked to get him some real food if that was ever possible.

We exited our hostel to another grey morning. I was really enjoying these late mornings. If it meant we didn't have to deal with so many crowds, all the better. I kept a hold of Mav's leash as we made our way out of town, past all the *pulperias* that were closed up for the morning. After a while, we finally broke free of the concrete sidewalks and grimy streets in favor of wooded pathways.

Today's stage passed over a couple of rivers, which Maverick was more than happy to dive into even though it wasn't hot or sunny yet. We alternated between sparse forests and open farmland. And although we didn't see many other pilgrims due to our later start, we did run into a boy we had last seen in Sahagún while we hid from the rain at that café. I had assumed he would be long gone by now, already in Santiago for Saint James' Day like so many other pilgrims we started with had been aiming for. It was nice to walk with an old, familiar face even if it was just for a little while.

We waved goodbye and Buen Camino to him as we turned into a little café that appeared to be in the middle of nowhere. Just one building amidst open farmland with at least fifteen picnic tables scattered around. Since no other pilgrims were here, I picked one at random and threw our bags down on a bench before tying Mav's leash to it. The sight of whole plates of empanada greeted me inside the café. After last night's dinner of octopus, this was like food for the gods. I had been craving an empanada for *days* now. If the little old lady behind the counter thought my excitement over food was at all strange, she didn't comment. She just smiled and handed over my *empanada de atún* with a warm smile.

"Look, Mav," I sang as I made my way back out to our table. "Empanada."

He sniffed at the corner of my plate, much more interested in this than he had been in my dinner last night. As excited as I was to scoff this down myself, I cut off a little corner for him and plopped it onto the dirt in front of his nose.

I was facing away from the café, staring blankly at the open farmland, lost in my enjoyment of the empanada, when the little old lady appeared by my side. "Perdón," she said quietly. I startled and turned to see her holding a metal bowl in her hands. "Tengo comida para el perro." She tipped the metal bowl to show dog food covering the bottom of it. "¿Puedo dárselo?"

My eyes widened. "Oh, sí," I said emphatically. If I had stopped to think more, I probably shouldn't have let him eat some random dog food. But at the time, I was too grateful for this woman's act of kindness to be thinking of anything else.

Even though she had asked if she could give Maverick the food, she seemed to hesitate, not knowing if she could put the bowl down or not. "Está bien," I tried to tell her. "Él es muy simpático." As if to prove this, Maverick sat like a good dog and patiently looked up at her with the bowl.

She glanced between his waiting face and me before thrusting the metal bowl towards me with a smile. "Pues, tú puedes dárselo," she laughed.

I took the bowl from her with a laugh. "Muchas gracias," I told her seriously after I had put the bowl down in front of Maverick. "De verdad," I added and caught her eye. "Esto significa mucho para nosotros."

"Ah, no te preocupes." With one last smile, she turned and headed back into the café. I looked down at Maverick, devouring the bowl of food she had given to him, and I felt tears sting my eyes.

She had no idea how much this meant to us. She had no idea we had been unable to find dog food for days now. She didn't know Maverick's sole source of food had been weird logs of wet food and scraps from my plate or the bone from the waiter the other night. She didn't know the frustration I had felt yesterday at yet another town not having anywhere to get actual dog food. She didn't know how I had been cursing this whole Camino with a dog on our walk back from the vet in Melide to our hostel last night. To her, she was just giving food to a dog because she liked dogs and it was a nice thing to do. For us, it meant the world.

I pulled out my journal, intending to write a note that I could leave behind for her to let her know just how much this meant to me when she reappeared. This time, there was a plate in her hands. I smiled up at her. "Hola."

"¿Cree que él le gusta empanada?" she asked tentatively, showing me a massive slice of empanada on the plate she was holding.

I couldn't help it, I laughed. "Sí, le gusta empanada." For a dog who didn't like carbs, I had found he was very fond of a good empanada.

"¿Está bien?" she double-checked, making sure it was okay to give him human food. I smiled and nodded, taking the plate she extended to me because she was still too nervous to bend down and give it to Maverick herself. He stretched his neck to sniff at the plate and she laughed quickly, then cut herself off as if she wasn't sure that she was supposed to find him funny.

"Muchas, *muchas,* gracias, señora." I said as seriously as I could. I would finish my letter to her, telling her more eloquently how much this meant, but I still wanted her to know just how grateful I was in this moment.

She waved her hand, brushing off my thanks, and then gave one more small smile before turning to hurry back to the café. Maverick squirmed beside me, waiting for his empanada to be put down. I looked between him and the café. "This is a *huge* piece of empanada. You definitely want to share, right?" His nose peeked over the edge of the plate. "Okay, okay. Hold on." I quickly cut off a little bit of his empanada and transferred it to my own plate, then plopped his down on the dirt in front of him.

He gave me one last disdainful look, as if he knew I had just stolen his food. "Oh, get over yourself. I offered you my octopus last night. You can't say I don't share with you." With that, he dove into his own plate. "That's what I thought."

The rest of the day passed by pretty peacefully through a mixture of eucalyptus forests and cornfields, which I was quickly coming to realize were very popular in Galicia. With the abundance of cornfields came even more *horreos*, odd little structures that the region was well known for. They're long, skinny things that are raised off the ground by granite in order to keep rodents out and come in both entire granite rectangular buildings or wood and are often topped with a cross. Their main purpose was to store feed for the farm animals or any produce that needed to be ripened further. We had passed quite a few of them since we entered Galicia, but I had yet to determine if I thought they were used as much as they had been in past decades or if they were more of a vestige of a past time. They could range anywhere from a meter long up to almost thirty-five meters in length – over one hundred feet long!

We hadn't seen any insanely long *horreos* yet, but we had seen plenty of little ones scattered about. One on the way into Arzúa was even decked out with a cute, copper-painted roof and sandy slats that made it seem more like a terracotta house than a grain storage. Signs as we entered the village outskirts of Arzúa welcomed us to the "land of cheese, honey, and philosophy." I paused to study these vibrant, laminated signs strapped to one of the trees in a park. "Huh," I muttered down to Maverick, who was sniffing around for the best tree to lift his leg on. "Quite the eclectic collection of things to be known for if you ask me." He caught my eye mid-stream, leg lifted on the very tree the signs were posted to. "Right. You don't care. But really," I added as we wound our way out of the park and along tiny roads through cute, Galician neighborhoods. "Cheese, honey, and philosophy? The cheese I get. You've seen all the cows around."

Maverick scampered ahead, so I took that as a yes. "And sure, honey can make sense, too. But why throw in philosophy when you're boasting about the good food you make? You know any famous Arzúian philosophers?" He trotted back to me, this time with a twig dangling from his mouth.

I huffed. "Me neither."

The sound of bagpipes interrupted my ramblings. I looked up to Maverick, who was unfazed by the random notes being pumped through the seemingly empty forest. He was picking his way ahead over the fallen eucalyptus leaves without a care in the world. I clicked my tongue a couple times to call him back to me and spotted the bagpiper as we crested a rise in the trail. There was no one else around, just him, posted up on the side of the Camino trail, piping away. As if the lush greenery of this region and the tunnels of wet moss and rock hadn't been enough to convince me of its Celtic heritage, the added bagpipe music certainly added to the allure.

I smiled at the man as we passed by, but his playing never wavered. He had no collection jar, no desire to be tipped for his music. He simply wanted to play for passing pilgrims. There was certainly nothing else out here to play for, save the trees. It was the kind of selfless Camino magic that made this trail so special, and so difficult to describe to others what this pilgrimage really was.

The trail dipped down again after that, heading down to the river Iso and the medieval bridge over it to the village of Ribadiso. It was as if all the pilgrims we had avoided today by starting so late had congregated on the riverbanks here to soak their feet and wade in the shallow waters after a day of walking. "Maverick," I warned in a low voice as I saw his pace unconsciously pick up speed ahead of me.

His paws stuttered to a halt as he looked back at me, then quickly ahead to the river. Most of the pilgrims had grouped together on the opposite bank, on the village side, so we had an entirely clear path down to the river on this side. I sighed. "Fine." I glanced ahead of us once more, ensuring he couldn't accidentally take someone out in his haste to get to water as soon as I gave him the go ahead. "Yes," I said in the way he knew to be his release word. In the blink of an eye, he was off, careening into the river at top speed.

My eyes rolled as I shook my head. His obsession with water was truly special. A moment later, I caught up to him and put our bags down on a dry spot of the bank. He was lying in the water just in front of the bank. It wasn't that he needed to sprint to water to romp around in it. No, he just wanted to lie down as soon as he made it to water. He grinned his wolfy grin at me as I bent over to unlace my boots and peel off my socks.

"Oh! He's yours," a voice carried over to me from the opposite bank. I straightened up and smiled across the river, wading in beside Maverick, who hopped up and went in search of something I could throw for him.

"Oh yes," I smiled. I wasn't exactly sure where the voice had come from, since there were close to fifteen pilgrims milling about on that side of the river. "He's mine." Mav had returned, a pebble he must have found on the bank in his mouth. He dropped it by my feet, where it sank under the surface.

"We thought he might just be one of the village dogs," another voice added.

I bent down absentmindedly and plucked the rock he had given me from the bottom of the river. "Nope, he's with me." I tossed the rock out into the river, downstream towards the bridge so that he wouldn't go crashing towards any of the other pilgrims and splash them. It disappeared as soon as it hit the water, but Maverick was already off, water flying in every direction as he bounded towards the ripples where the rock had sunk.

The water was up to his chest, but not deep enough that he had to be fully swimming. Only, it wasn't shallow enough for him to actually find the rock I had thrown. He snuffled around the surface of the water for a while, circling and sniffing as if he'd actually find it.

"You're walking with your dog?" one of the women on the bank asked. Maverick sloshed his way back towards me and I already had another pebble ready. When he got closer, I tossed it back towards the center of the river and he spun on his heel and took off after that one.

"Yeah. We started in Saint Jean," I replied as I kept my eyes on Maverick. A couple of the younger girls across the river were giggling at his antics, having already caught on to the fact that I was throwing rocks that he most assuredly could not actually fetch.

"My goodness! That's a long way to go with a dog!" an older woman exclaimed.

Maverick gave up on that rock and started fording the river back to me, his eyes alight, knowing I would be ready for him yet again. I had a new rock dripping in my fingers. This one I sent sailing a bit more upstream, into a shallower area of the river. He flew by me in a wave of water. A few other pilgrims, realizing the futile game we were playing, joined in with the laughter from the younger girls.

"It's been quite the trip," I told the person who had last commented as Maverick alternated between dunking his head into the water in an attempt to grab the pebble that had sunk and dug at the river bottom with his paws, stirring up dirt in the water. The laughter of the pilgrims across the way grew louder. A moment later, Maverick's head popped up, water dripping from his jaws and he bounded back towards me. He deposited the pebble I had just dropped in front of my feet.

"No way," one of the younger girls across the river commented. I looked up at her with a grin. She caught my eye, realizing I had heard her, and clarified. "He did not just really find the same rock you threw."

I nodded and plucked the very same pebble from the water where he had dropped it. His feet danced back and forth in anticipation of where I may throw it next, his whole head dripping from the dunking he had done to retrieve this one. I tossed it back upstream and it landed a bit closer to the opposite bank this time. Now the whole cluster of pilgrims on that side of the river was watching this game of his, laughing at his ridiculous antics as he bobbed and dug to get the rock again.

Yet again, he came up victorious. Only this time, instead of bounding back towards me, he realized he was closer to the opposite bank. "Maverick..." I warned. He paid no mind. Instead, he scampered off to the opposite bank and found one pilgrim wading in the water that he deemed acceptable. With a splash, he dropped the rock right in front of the girl's feet, then looked up at her expectantly.

"I'm sorry," I called to her. "Maverick," I commanded, but he didn't move. He just waited for his next victim to pick up the rock for him. "You really don't have to throw it for him. I've got another one."

The girl was laughing. "This is great!" she called back, hesitating for just a moment before bending to retrieve the rock. She tossed it ungracefully downstream and Maverick was off, a plume of water thrown up in his wake, soaking the poor pilgrims who happened to be standing too close.

I covered my face with my hands and groaned. "I am so sorry. He didn't get you too wet, did he?" I asked, but it didn't seem to matter. Instead, almost all of the pilgrims around were laughing together. Many of them were gathering up a rock of their own, ready to throw if Maverick couldn't find this one again. I bit my lip and shook my head. It was clear I was not the focus anymore, if I ever had been. Maverick had stolen the show, just as he always did. And instead of causing any issues, he brought joy.

I eased down onto a big rock sticking out of the river, my feet kicking lazily back and forth in the water as Maverick waded back towards the group of pilgrims, no rock this time. Another one took up the duty of tossing a new rock for him. He took off again with water flying, and their smiles beamed. I smiled, too. And once again this journey, Maverick told me to just sit back and watch. Let it happen and just *be here now*. His head broke the surface again, his jaws clamped around the rock the pilgrim had just thrown, and he turned until his eyes caught mine. I smiled at him and he didn't say a word, didn't come towards me, but for some reason we just connected. Like he just had to check in. *You still good, Mum?*

My smile grew even more. "I'm still good, bud," I whispered back. He turned and bounded back to the group of pilgrims waiting for him, tail dripping but wagging nonetheless. I wondered just how many people saw him as their Camino Angel.

Lost!

Day Thirty-Eight: Arzúa to A Rúa

23.5 km ~ 33,235 steps

July 27th

We ended up in the busier town of Arzúa last night, despite it not being the typical end of stage according to Brierley's guidebook. It was a good mix of village and city, a regular sort of town, not too big or too small. There were even more pilgrims joining the trail here. The Del Norte route connected up to the Camino Francés at this point, and even last night I noticed a bit of an influx in pilgrims around the town square while Mav and I split a roast veal dinner. Still no dog food available in this town, despite there being a vet here. Luckily, the nasty logs of food seem readily available in any grocery store, so Maverick isn't going hungry. Though he sure did enjoy the roast veal off my fork last night.

Though yesterday had been pretty bright and somewhat sunny all day, it was back into the gloom today. Grey clouds hung low over the lush fields as we made our way out of town onto dirt farming roads. With the increased number of pilgrims coming from Del Norte onto Francés route today the trail was extra busy leaving town, even with our late start. Maverick was enjoying all the new people, though.

Over the course of this pilgrimage, he had definitely come to realize I was the last person he should ask to throw his stick while we were walking. I was of the mind that he should not be sprinting back and forth endlessly throughout the entire day when we were already walking over twenty kilometers. He didn't need to unnecessarily tire himself out even more. However, he had learned that other pilgrims did not share this viewpoint.

This morning he bounced from new pilgrim to new pilgrim on the wide farm tracks we were walking. I silently judged from a distance, making sure he wasn't actually annoying anyone with his behavior. For the most part, he delighted the pilgrims we were walking with, though. They thought he was "so cute" and "has so much energy!" and was "too funny." Personally, I think if he keeps hearing stuff like this, he's going to get a big head.

He seemed to settle on one group of four pilgrims just outside of town, so I ended up falling into step with them as they tossed his stick every time he brought it back. "Does he do this all of the time?" one of the men asked me in a German accent.

"Unfortunately, yes."

The group chuckled as the girl bent down to pick up Mav's stick yet again. "You guys have been walking for a while?" she asked. Her accent was Irish and her question was more of a statement.

"Since Saint Jean. You guys seem like you have, too?" There was just a vibe of pilgrims who had been on trail longer than ones who had recently joined.

"Yeah, but this is our first day on the Francés route. There are a lot more people here. It's a bit crowded, yeah?"

"Yeah," I sighed. "It definitely is. It wasn't always this way. Before Sarria was way different than it is now. You've been on Del Norte then?"

"Yes, just joined in last night," one of the guys added.

"How was that? I hear it's beautiful."

"Definitely. Absolutely gorgeous," another German man agreed.

"But exhausting," the Irish girl added with a grin.

"So many hills," one of the men said. "You get used to them I suppose. But it is hills every day."

"Yeah, I can see that. We took a little side trip up to Bakio, just past Bilbao, and walked along the coast one day and it was so hilly. I couldn't imagine doing that every day. Plus, the humidity."

"It was awful!" the girl laughed.

"I'm not sure what would have been worse, though. The humidity on Del Norte or the dry, baking sun where we were," I grinned.

"After Del Norte, I would welcome some baking sun."

"You say that now," I joked while one of the guys attempted to wrestle the stick out of Maverick's mouth. If he wasn't dropping it for them right away, it normally meant he was getting tired and needed a little breather from sprinting after the stick nonstop. "I'm just going to stop for a bit to give him some water. You guys can walk on if you want."

I peeled off the trail and took out one of his water bladders from his pack across my forearm, but the group of four also slid to a stop. "We can wait," the girl said with a smile.

They watched as I detached Mav's water dish from his pack and popped it open, careful not to expand it too aggressively because the rubber bowl part was beginning to separate from the hard plastic ring that was the top edge of the bowl.

"That bowl is not in very good shape," one of the guys commented.

I shrugged and filled it up with water that Maverick quickly came over to lap up. "It's been almost forty days of constant use. I'm just hoping it holds together to get us through to the end."

"Hey, I have a plastic bowl actually! Yeah, I packed it thinking I might need it if I camped out or anything but, yeah. We never had to camp out at all. So I've never even used it. You totally need to take it."

I laughed at her enthusiasm. "Well, I won't say no if you're offering it."

"When we stop, I'll have to get it out of my bag because it is buried deep in there."

The group of us walked on after that, trading stories from different aspects of our Camino routes. Eventually, when they turned off to stop for a morning coffee, Maverick and I chose to walk on a little further. It totally slipped my mind to ask about the plastic bowl again, and so on we went, with hopes his water dish would make it the next few days. A few hours later, as I was sitting on the patio of an outside café eating an empanada for lunch, the Irish girl came running up to me again.

"I totally forgot to give you this! When we stopped for coffee earlier, I dug it out of my bag. I'm so glad we caught up to you again."

I put down the forkful of empanada I had been just about to shovel into my mouth and laughed as she thrust a red, plastic, collapsible bowl toward me. "Oh my gosh, you really didn't have to give me this. But thank you."

"I wanted to! When I saw you sitting here, I had to run over." She nodded her head back towards the trail where the three German boys she had been walking with were waiting on the other side of the stone wall, one of them leaning lazily against a big tree. The trio lifted their hands to wave a greeting when they saw us looking at them.

I laughed and nodded back before turning back to look at the girl. "Seriously, thank you so much."

"No problem! I'm glad it'll finally get some use this trip. It was so nice to meet you!" She reached down and scratched Maverick between the ears with a smile. "Buen Camino!" And then she was off, bouncing away, a little bundle of energy back to regroup with her Camino family. I watched them leave together with a sad, little smile. I loved walking with them. I loved running into nice pilgrims like that. Loved getting to see how close pilgrims grew to one another on this trip. But sometimes I still missed having a tight-knit Camino family of my own.

I reached down and stroked Maverick's soft fur on top of his head, running my fingers over his ears. "You're the only Camino family I really need, though. Right, Baby Dog?"

Today's route continued in and out of small villages and through lush forest and open farms, with the occasional traffic stops for passing cattle. Just before the village we were staying in tonight, as we were stopped to let a farmer and his herd of massive cows lumber by on the narrow road, two young women caught up to me. Both were toting clean packs, not beat up or dust-coated at all, and had the happy grins of new walkers.

"Hello," one finally said just as the cows cleared the road and we took the turn where they had just come from, towards A Rúa.

"Hi." I briefly smiled back at her and reached down to loop Maverick's leash back around his neck. He hurried ahead once he was clear to roam, sniffing at any cow drop-pings along the way. I wrinkled my nose at him in disgust.

"May we ask you a question?" the other girl asked. Both of them were clearly Irish.

I chuckled a bit. No one out here ever asked if they could ask questions when it came to me and Maverick. They normally just launched into it. I had a strong guess what they wanted to know, but I humored them. "Of course."

"How long have you been walking?"

Ding, ding, ding, I thought. One of the most popular questions we got. "Today is Day Thirty-Eight for us."

Her reaction, however, was *not* what I had been expect-ing. "Okay, you win," she said to her friend. That caught my attention. My eyebrows rose in surprise, but I didn't say anything. Her friend must have seen my expression, though, because she was quick to jump in.

"I'm sorry, it's just, we saw you at the café buying water earlier. When the waiter came out to give your dog some scraps. And then a bit later. We'd been hoping to catch up to you again," she said sheepishly.

My curiosity was piqued. "We've been trying to guess how long you guys had been out here," the other girl added.

I laughed out loud. "And what did you come up with?"

"Well, she had thought more," she said, tipping her head to indicate her friend who had "won" their little game. "But I said there was no way. You couldn't go that long with a dog. I figured you just started in Sarria, like us. But…you didn't. You've really been out here for that long with a dog?" she asked excitedly.

"Yep. Since Saint Jean." And so it went. My quiet walk into town for the night was now consumed with questions to recount our entire journey. I guess now with so many new pilgrims joining in, we were somewhat of a novelty again. Just like the first few days on the trail when everyone was shocked to see Maverick, all the new faces were excited to hear his story.

When we reached A Rúa, I gently disengaged from conversation with the two girls. I thanked them for their company, and wished them a Buen Camino, and then dipped into what looked to be one of the few albergues in town. I had found it on Booking.com as the only place near O Pedrouzo that would allow dogs. However, when I had booked and told them in advance that I had a dog with me, I don't think they had been expecting Maverick. The hospitalera looked a little uneasy with just how big he was, but she didn't say anything against him.

She showed me around the cute, little albergue in a big, stone house that from the outside had looked a bit decrepit but from the inside was absolutely incredible. Huge, modern windows looked out from our private room over an empty lot next door and the quiet village street. The exposed rock of the wall had been artfully enhanced with white plaster to fill the cracks and give the room a rustic, quaint feel. The lobby was decked out with couches made from wooden pallets and colorful cushions so that pilgrims could lounge together and pilgrim silhouettes and inspirational quotes pasted on the walls. I'm sure if it had been a busier town, one that was an end of stage in the guidebook, pilgrims would be clambering for a spot to stay here. I certainly was enjoying it.

The only downfall was that A Rúa didn't boast many amenities. In fact, there was only one restaurant in town. As such, they had complete control to set prices exorbitantly high. I glanced up from the menu that was posted near the road towards the restaurant that was set back a bit, then down at Maverick on his leash beside me.

"This is *not* a pilgrim menu, I'll tell you that much, Mav." He looked back up at me and cocked his head to one side. "No, I know. It is ridiculous. I'm just trying to get a little steak and some fries. Some bread to go with my *menu del día*, you know what I'm sayin'?"

His tongue lolled out from his mouth and I smiled at him. I looked away from the restaurant, back up the main road through town that we had walked down to find this place. It wasn't all that late yet. We could probably walk into O Pedrouzo to find some food. Plus, he needed more of his logs for dinner and breakfast tomorrow and it was clear nowhere in A Rúa would have any dog food. "What do you say? Want to go for a walk to get dinner?" I asked him.

He bounded forward, tugging my arm where I hung onto his leash. "Okay, okay," I laughed. "We'll go."

It turned out, the walk from A Rúa to O Pedrouzo wasn't just a quick jaunt into town. It was actually quite a long distance. But the weather had cleared up since earlier in the day, and it wasn't like I had my pack over my shoulders or Maverick's in my arms, so it was actually really nice. We passed a few other people, who looked to be A Rúa locals out for an evening walk of their own, and exchanged a few words with them. It was kind of cool to feel like just another villager taking her dog for a walk and going to get food from town.

As we turned off of the quiet road from A Rúa and onto the sidewalk beside the rushing highway into O Pedrouzo, I was insanely grateful we weren't able to find a place to stay in this town. In our little village, it felt just like the old Camino towns we had loved in the past. This bustling, dirty suburb had a completely different feel to it. But it did have bars and stores galore in comparison to A Rúa, so for that I was grateful.

"Maverick? Colby? Sì! Che bello!"

I turned my head as we passed by the first bar in town and was shocked. I knew that voice, but I wasn't ready to believe it was really him. "Dario?" I called, trying to pick him out from the crowded patio of pilgrims.

Lo and behold, there he was. He squeezed his way out from between a few tables to meet us on the sidewalk. "Che bello! Che bello!" he cooed, his favorite words since we had met him on the bus to Saint Jean. Only now, his clothes had become more brown than any other color, his face was covered in a beard I hadn't known before, and he looked like he had lost quite a few pounds.

"Dario! How are you? What are you doing here? I didn't think I'd see you again!"

He embraced me and kissed both my cheeks before crouching down so that Maverick could attack him with kisses. "I am good! I am good! How are you? How is Maverick? He is thin, no? Che bello!" he repeated again, wrapping his arms around Mav's neck in a hug.

"We've been good. Almost there." I couldn't hide my grin, I was sure it was taking over my entire face. There was something about meeting up with someone you had started this whole journey with that was special. It felt like just the other day he was walking up to us while we rested by that food truck in the Pyrenees. We hadn't even crossed into Spain yet.

"Tomorrow, yes?" he asked, his smile matching mine as he pushed his way back to his feet. I was reminded of the leg cramp he got that night in Zubiri. He may not have gotten a cramp just now, but he was definitely moving a lot slower. The Camino had worn him down this time around, you could tell.

"Not for us," I shook my head slowly. "I'm planning to stop for the night just before Santiago."

"But why? It is only twenty kilometers from here. Easy day after this trip."

"I know. But I want to get there on the twenty-ninth."

He eyed me and then nodded with a smile. "Very well. Then this is where we say goodbye. For real this time, no? And Buen Camino."

"Buen Camino, Dario."

He hugged me once more, two more kisses on my cheeks, and roughed up Maverick's fur around his collar. "Che bello!" he cooed one last time, then shot me a wink, before disappearing back into the busy bar.

I'm Gonna Be (500 Miles)

Day Thirty-Nine: A Rúa to San Lázaro

22.7 km ~ 32,080 steps

July 28th

I stayed up way too late last night. Maybe it was because we were so close to Santiago. Maybe it was because my time to think seemed to be late at night now, when everything was quiet and it was just me and Maverick again. Or maybe it was just because I ate a sleeve of chocolate chip cookies I had bought at the store and had too much sugar late at night.

Whatever the reason, I came to the conclusion that as crazy as it may sound, I think I've taken this trip for granted. As much as I tried not to by taking pictures, and journaling, and taking time to reflect, I think it's in human nature to normalize things. You get wrapped up in the here and now – in what you're doing at the moment. You forget that what you're doing is actually a big deal - something life-changing. I've allowed myself to be overwhelmed at times, to be sad, or frustrated, and I focused on that. I've also laughed while talking to others and walked past things too quickly, not stopping to really appreciate things I passed. But the thing is…that's living.

I can't beat myself up over talking to a new friend and missing something along the way. If I had stopped and let the person walk on, I would have missed out on a new friend. I would have missed out on that conversation. Every little decision we make in life is part of a bigger picture. It's part of this whole thing called living, which I hadn't been doing very well up until now. So when I take a step back, and really take in these last thirty-eight days, I'm reminded of just how incredible this trip has been. And now it was almost over.

When we woke up this morning, our last late wakeup before Santiago, the fog was so thick I could barely see fifty yards ahead of me and mist soaked Maverick's fur. I suppose I couldn't complain all that much since it was clear heavy rains had already passed through last night or early this morning and the road into O Pedrouzo was still wet. Maverick splashed in and out of the puddles on our way past O Pedrouzo and into the forest, his red pack bumping along the trail ahead of me.

I had decided he could wear his pack on this second to last day of walking. It wasn't like it was weighed down with dog food since we had yet to find any. Plus, he had all sorts of energy pent up now that we had been walking shorter days. Of course, this resulted in a new stick being dropped by my feet on every other step I took.

With our late start, the trail towards Santiago was mostly empty. I was sure most pilgrims intended to reach the cathedral today so they must have left early. We ended up walking with two guys from Denmark for a bit this morning, through the thick tunnels of greenery and eucalyptus forest. The fancy

Camino markers that had been common all through Galicia gave way to an older style of stone, with carved Camino shells and thin red numbers counting down the kilometers until the cathedral. As we looped our way around the airport outside the city, an intricately carved marker welcomed us into the city limits. The shell was joined by a staff and gourd that ancient pilgrims carried water in, as well as a scroll bearing the city name. **SANTIAGO**. We had arrived.

The mist was still heavy as we waved goodbye to our Danish friends who wanted to stop for coffee in the hamlet of San Paio and bumped into our Del Norte friends who were just coming out of the little stone church here.

"It's Colby and Maverick!" the girl cried excitedly. She bounded out of the church to give me a big hug with one of the Germans bent down to give Maverick a scratch. "How's that bowl working for you guys?"

"It's been great," I smiled. "Seriously, thank you for that. I'm not sure his dish would have held on much longer. How have you guys been?"

"We have been great. On to Santiago today. Will we see you there?" one of the guys asked.

"No, I'm going to stop just short of the cathedral tonight. But I'll be there tomorrow for Mass."

"Ah, yes, us as well. We are hoping to see the *botafumeiro*."

My eyes lit up. "Of course," I chimed in. "Do you think it will swing?"

"Oh, I hope so."

"It will be a Sunday. We can hope," another man added. I tipped my head in acknowledgement of that. He was right, tomorrow would be a Sunday and if there was a chance of seeing the legendary *botafumeiro* swing, it would be on a Sunday. But it had also just been Saint James Day this past week, so I'm sure the massive incense burner would have swung to celebrate that day. I was worried they wouldn't go through the effort to swing it again in the same week, but I still had hope. Just like this group of Del Norte pilgrims, and probably any other pilgrim on the trail, I had hope. I think we all would want to be at a mass where the *botafumeiro* would swing.

"It was great to see you guys again," I added as they began to pull on their packs and buckle into them again, double checking their rain covers to keep all of their gear dry. Maverick shook himself of the mist that was soaking him and tried to drop another stick at their feet. Of course, one of the group bent down to grab it and tossed it into the churchyard for him to go tearing after. "Hopefully I'll see you guys tomorrow, then."

"Buen Camino," they called with smiles and waves as they disappeared further down the trail.

After dipping into the miniscule stone church, Mav and I continued down the trail behind the Del Norte group. From that point on, we remained on roads through the outer villages of Santiago. First was Lavacolla, which got its name from the fact that this was the place pilgrims would stop to wash themselves before entering the holy city of Santiago. *Lavar* is the Spanish word for wash. After weeks of grueling travel, pilgrims of centuries past would stop here at this stream to cleanse themselves. This would often be the first time they washed throughout their journey. It was a sign of respect that even the most tired of pilgrims were clean upon entering the cathedral.

It was really just a tiny stream now, though perhaps it was a bigger river decades ago. Either way, Maverick was happy to rush into the water and "cleanse" himself. He plodded around in a circle, lapping at the water, until he laid down and looked up at me with that wolfy grin.

I raised my eyebrows as I watched him from higher on

the bank. "Is this your way of washing off your sins before the church?"

He let out a whine and started to dig at the clear water for a rock beneath the surface. I rolled my eyes. "I don't think you're fully comprehending the significance of this place, sir." His muzzle dipped under the stream like he was bobbing for apples and he came back up a moment later with a pebble in his jaws. "You're supposed to be washing the grueling journey from you before entering the city."

He leaped out of the stream and up the bank towards me, immediately getting muddy from the dirt embankment and his dripping coat. So much for "cleansing." I laughed down at him. "No, I'm not throwing that. Let's go, kiddo."

The Camino remained along the road as it wound upwards to Monte de Gozo. There was still no break in the clouds, though it wasn't misting quite so heavily anymore. As we were passing through Vilamaior, a *bicigrino* slowed to ride beside us for a bit, laughing at Maverick's attempts to keep pace with his bike. Even though there weren't all that many other pilgrims around, there was an excitement hanging in the air that was almost palpable. Santiago was a stone's throw away. The wet, asphalt trail wasn't bringing down anyone's spirits today. Even though my feet were sore and I was soaked to the bone, I was still smiling.

We reached the top of the hill at Monte de Gozo, complete with its more modern statue of...I wasn't exactly sure what. Whatever it was, plenty of pilgrims were stopped taking pictures of the massive structure and posing at its base. Though I had been looking forward to a pilgrim monument in this place, this wasn't the one I had in mind.

A table was set up just beyond the crest of the hill in front of a small chapel, welcoming pilgrims and giving information on navigating the city and checking into Santiago. Mav and I queued up in line to get our credentials stamped and take their handouts, though I didn't intend on walking all the way to the cathedral today. I had already booked a place in San Lázaro, less than three kilometers from here. So while the man handing out information was all excited to tell me there was only five kilometers left until the cathedral, I wasn't too interested in it. I was more interested in finding those massive pilgrim statues I knew had to be somewhere around here.

I glanced around at the open hilltop one last time, then at the trail of pilgrims headed down hill, dropping down to the city without a care in the world. Didn't they want to find the two, giant, pointing pilgrims? Didn't they want to see the spires of the cathedral for the first time? Did nobody care about this landmark but me?

"Huh," I huffed aloud. "Well, Maverick. Maybe they're further downhill?"

Mav peeked up at me from his end of the leash, then tugged forward where other pilgrims were passing by, headed down *Rua do Peregrino,* the name of the road leading towards the cathedral. Following Maverick's lead, and all the other pilgrims, I started down the steep sidewalk. Only...we never found the pilgrim statue. We had almost reached the base of the hill, clearly no longer in Monte de Gozo and on the edge of the industrial part of Santiago, and I had yet to find the statue. I mean, really? How hard could it be to find two enormous, green, medieval pilgrims? Shouldn't they stick out?

I looked to my left, back towards the city park that Monte de Gozo had become and the compound of housing that looked like barracks more than anything. No pilgrim statues there. Then I looked back up the steep sidewalk we had just descended. I didn't exactly *want* to hike back up that. My feet were killing me. Over the last thirty-nine days, my feet had slowly come to hate me for walking so much every day. Camino Fact not many people share: after so many days of walking, your feet will hurt. So much so that every time you stop and rest, you'll look like a ninety-year-old grampa when you try to get up again. It will take a solid five minutes of hobbling before you can walk normally again after that. So yeah, my feet hurt. I was soaked. The clouds were still so thick I doubted I would even be able to see the spires if I did find this lookout with the statues. I could just keep walking, get to my hostel for the night. It would be fine. But something pulled me back up that hill.

"Come on. We're finding these pilgrims."

We turned into the park, weaving our way up the cement trails that crisscrossed the area. Finally, I was able to find an information board with a map of the park and sure enough, the pilgrim monument was marked on it. We set off in the direction it noted with a pep in our step. I would see them. And then, around a bend in a dirt path on the outskirts of the park, they appeared. Two medieval pilgrims, complete with staffs that were topped with crosses and *conchas* and gourds for drinking water. *Conchas* inlaid into the edges of their carved capes draped over their shoulders. The cross of Saint James carved as necklaces around their necks. Rope belts meticulously etched into the metal dangling by their legs. Straps of flat sandals carved over their feet and detailed, bare toes. They were everything I had imagined and more.

Above all, both stood with their right arms extended towards the city below them, their eyes forward on what had to be the location of the cathedral. I had dreams of arriving to this spot and the clouds clearing. The rain would stop and suddenly the sun would come out and there would be the spires of the Cathedral of Saint James, nestled into the bustling city of Santiago below us. As if some miracle would allow the clouds that had prevailed all day to suddenly break. Life wasn't a movie. It had been silly of me to think that would happen. But as I leaned against the staff of one of the pilgrims, who each towered above me at over ten feet tall, I could imagine the cathedral out there. I could imagine the joy medieval pilgrims must have felt upon reaching this overlook. To have been walking for so long and finally have a first look at their destination, the cathedral where the remains of Saint James were laid to rest? It would have been incredible for them. It was incredible for me.

So amongst the dreary mist and thick clouds, I took out my trusty tripod for my phone and Maverick and I had our own little photo shoot with our new giant, green friends. Not another pilgrim came to visit this amazing spot the whole time we were there. We goofed, and played with sticks, and posed in fun ways, and in the midst of it all, I looked up and saw that the clouds were breaking. The raindrops had stopped and I hadn't even realized it. And there, in front of me in the valley surrounded by the red roofs of the city buildings, were the three tall spires of the Cathedral of Santiago.

"Oh," I breathed, my arm still outstretched in a silly pose to match with the statues. It fell to my side with a hollow *flop*. "It's beautiful."

With rays of sunshine and peeks of blue skies, Mav and I finally descended from Monte de Gozo and followed the Camino arrows into the bustling metropolis of Santiago de Compostela. We stopped for pictures with road signs bearing the city's name and murals of street art. We passed by various restaurants catering to incoming pilgrims and endless shops. Even walking beside the busy highway and through roundabouts couldn't wipe the smile from my face. We had made it. The sun was shining. All was well.

Of course, something always has to go wrong to spice things up a bit. The place I had found in San Lázaro that was supposed to allow dogs…apparently didn't allow dogs. Luckily for us, the hospitalero was reasonable. When I showed him the information on Booking.com that clearly stated their establishment allowed pets, he couldn't argue with that. Although he couldn't justify letting us stay in one of the dormitories with other travelers in case they were afraid of dogs.

"Tengo este cuarto," he told me sheepishly as he led me past the doors of dormitories and into what looked like a storage room slash office of some sort. I glanced around the space, which had a long coffee table, a leather couch against one wall, and a glass door back to the hall we had just come from.

"¿Puedo dormir en el sofá?" I asked him. Honestly, I was totally okay with that. Sleeping on a couch was like sleeping on a feather bed compared to some of the places we had stayed so far.

"Sí." I could tell he was a bit ashamed to be offering me this space, clearly not meant for travelers, but he didn't have any other single rooms where Maverick and I would be alone.

"Perfecto," I smiled. "Está perfecto, señor."

"¿De verdad?" he asked doubtfully.

"Oh, sí, claro. Muchas gracias, señor."

"Vale. Pues, dime si necesitas cualquier otra cosa." I knew he thought I was strange, but who hadn't on this journey so far? He had given me far more than most had by allowing me a room of our own and a couch to stay on. I couldn't imagine needing anything else from him.

After shucking out of my damp clothes and taking a hot shower in the communal bathroom here, I decided to retrace our steps back a few blocks to the laundromat we had passed on our way in and finally give my clothes a real washing. It may not be Lavacolla, but I should arrive at the cathedral tomorrow cleansed.

Just behind the laundromat happened to be a mall. At

this point, with Maverick's ribs becoming more and more visible as the days passed, I knew he couldn't keep living off these logs of wet food. I changed over my wet, clean clothes to the dryer in the laundromat, started the machine up, and then headed back outside to grab Maverick's leash from where I had tied him out to a lamppost just outside. "Alright, kiddo. Let's get you some real food."

We snuck down the alley beside the laundromat which backed up to an extremely steep hill. Sure, this wasn't the conventional route to get to the mall, but with my tired feet I wasn't about to make a giant loop around on the roads when I could just scramble up this hill and be in the parking lot. Luckily, it looked like some locals had the same idea and some switchbacks had been carved into the loose dirt. With minor slipping and sliding, we clawed our way over the guardrail at the top of the hill and into the sprawling parking lot of the modern-day shopping center.

"Right then," I huffed out, brushing off my hands on my shorts since I had pulled myself hand over foot to get up that. "It says there's a pet store in here. We've done this before. No big deal. You wait outside the mall, I run through the shiny shopping center like a madman, and I make it back with a bag of food. Piece of cake, right?"

Unlike at the mall in León, I felt more comfortable leaving Maverick outside the doors here. For one, it seemed to be in a more rural area than León had been and there were definitely less people around. Plus, we had grown even more in the time since León that allowed me to have full trust that he would be perfectly fine waiting for me while I ran in for food. As it happened, the pet store was the very first store to the left of the doors when I walked into this mall. I quickly dipped inside, found a bag of Eukanuba which he had been on when we first came to Spain, and snatched it up. I didn't even care that it was one of the large, thirty-pound bags. I was taking it. I would figure out how to deal with all that weight later. Now, I just needed to get my dog some real food.

I hurried back outside to where Maverick was lounging in the shade. No one was around him and he looked as if he had no cares in the world. His head popped up at the sound of my footsteps coming closer and I hiked the bag up in my arms.

"See, baby? Real food. Things are looking up. You have food, I have clean clothes, and tomorrow? Tomorrow, we have Santiago."

Like Gold

Day Forty: San Lázaro to Santiago de Compostela

July 29th

    The muffled sounds of me packing away all of our gear one last time was the only noise in the entire hostel this morning at five a.m. The *click* of the buckles on Maverick's pack seemed to echo in the silent office we had called home for the night as I strapped him in. On tiptoes, we snuck out from the room and through the narrow hall until we exited onto the stairwell and made our way down to the street level. For once, it was a dry morning and I could see the full moon peeking out from some clouds as they skirted by. The bustling city street from yesterday was no more. Not a single car was on the roads this early, no Spaniards out and about or pilgrims hurrying past in excitement. All was still. All was silent.

    I didn't bother to click on my flashlight. The light of the

moon with the streetlights was enough to guide us down the empty sidewalks. Maverick scampered ahead, his pack bumping along on his sides while I carried the giant bag of dog food like a baby in front of me. I hadn't quite figured out the best way to carry this yet, but that was okay. We were only going a few kilometers today. Our final steps through the city. The dank, grimier parts of the outer city began to give way to buildings that were centuries old. The heart of the city grew closer.

A burst of laughter and staggering footsteps cut through the otherwise silent morning. A group of young adults were leaning on each other, laughing and talking raucously as they stumbled through an alleyway to our left. Maverick cocked his head at them, as if he couldn't understand what was wrong with them, but I just smiled as we passed by without their notice. Some people were just ending their Saturday night festivities and for us, our day was just beginning.

The noise from a few other drunken parties carried through the narrow alleyways as we twisted and turned closer to the cathedral and then, without warning, we had arrived.

My feet stuttered to a halt as the alley opened up to *Praza Obradoio*, the immense plaza that was empty before the front façade of the cathedral. There were just three other people in the entire space, camped out with a Chinese flag sitting directly in front of the massive structure. Though the sky was still pitch black, the face of the cathedral was lit by flood lights, illuminating the thousands of intricate details that had just been painstakingly restored this past year. The final scaffolding that had been covering this impressive façade since 2013 finally came down this month. And boy, was it an incredible sight to see.

My footsteps echoed across the paving stones of the empty plaza as I slowly made my way closer. With the bright lighting on the building, and the pure black night sky behind it, the carved statue of Saint James stood out from an arch at the top of the centermost peak of the cathedral. Two of his disciples, also carved in traditional pilgrim garb, stood just below him. In between, the urn representing the body of Saint James that is laid to rest here was shown with a carving of a star above it. It had to be the star that was believed to have guided the Hermit Pelagius to this very spot. Columns that stretched up from the doors, raised above the plaza, looked to be covered in the most minute carvings. Vines and *conchas* and delicate designs. The cross of Saint James and more stars and shells all brought the focus to the tomb of the great apostle buried here.

Slowly, my feet carried me to the center of the plaza, Maverick trailing by my heels. Somehow he could sense the importance of this place, too. So at five thirty in the morning, the morning of my twenty-first birthday, I slowly lowered myself down to the ancient bricks of the plaza and leaned back against my pack, looking up at El Catedral de Santiago. Forty days since we had set out. Forty days of walking, and crying, and laughing, and singing. Forty days of pain and happiness and loneliness and companionship. Forty days, but truly many years, had finally brought us to this place.

Without a noise, Maverick curled himself up on the cool cobblestones and pressed himself into my side. I smiled and reached an arm out to rest it across his back, scratching under his collar, then swallowed hard. "We made it, Mav," I whispered as the sky slowly began to lighten. The pitch black morphed into indigo, which lightened even more to cobalt, which finally revealed the cloud cover that had been blocking out any stars before. And yet, as we laid there on the cold, hard ground with my pack as a pillow, the rising sun started to play on the clouds, lighting the bottoms of them golden, giving the cathedral a dusty rose color.

"Buen Camino, Colby. Maverick."

I finally startled out of my reverie and looked up to see our Del Norte friends standing over us. They were all in new clothes, no longer looking ragged and dirty. Each of them wore a smile that took up their entire face. Mav jumped to his feet and bounded over to them, dropping a miniscule stick he had managed to find somewhere in the plaza by their feet.

I quickly rose to greet them, my joints popping and groaning in protest. *Just how long had I been laying on those bricks?* I thought vaguely as I returned the hugs of my friends. "Buen Camino," I whispered back.

Even though the plaza was beginning to grow busier now that the sun had risen, it still had a holy hush to it. "I see you've had a wardrobe change," I chuckled.

One of the young guys struck a pose, another pulled out his sweater he had on this morning to examine it further. "Pretty nice, right? It is amazing to wear fresh clothes. Will you be shopping today?" he asked.

"Oh, no," I laughed. "No, we still have a few days to go. I'm afraid I'll be spending my birthday in the same smelly clothes today." I pulled on the sleeve of my long-sleeve shirt as proof of this.

"Today is your birthday?!" the Irish girl exclaimed.

"Yeah, twenty-one."

"That is a big deal in your country, yes?" one of the guys asked. I nodded. "You must get a drink today!"

"We'll see," I grinned. "I'm just happy to be here." At that, all of us turned to look back at the façade of the cathedral. It somehow had the power to glue your eyes to it at all times.

"Will you come to *Portico de la Gloria* with us? We came early so we could get a good spot in line," the little Irish girl said now.

I followed her gaze to see that metal fencing had already been set up, stretching from the stairs leading up to the main doors of the cathedral down the right side of the structure. About a dozen people were already waiting in line within the barriers. "That's what these people are lining up for?" I asked. "To see *Portico de la Gloria?*"

"Yep," she sighed. "We wanted to go yesterday, but the line was through this entire plaza. So we figured we'd wake up early to get in this morning."

"That's insane," I muttered. There was something wrong about having to wait in line and pay to see a part of a church that was the end of a pilgrimage. Not that I had any solutions on how to manage the immense crowds that I'm sure flocked to see this, but still.

"Well, it has been closed for nearly a decade."

"Really? That long?" I asked.

"Yes, the restoration on *Portico de la Gloria* started in 2008. It has just finished this summer. We are some of the first to be able to see it. Will you join us?"

"Uhm," I debated for a minute, looking between the growing line and then feeling my stomach growl. It was almost eight. I had been up for close to four hours and still hadn't eaten anything. Plus, I heard the Pilgrim's Office was known to get really crowded, too. "Thanks, but I think I'm going to get our *Compostelas* first and find some breakfast. But I appreciate the invite."

"Well, it was great to see you one last time. And happy birthday!"

After one last round of goodbyes, Maverick and I finally gathered up our gear and made our way out of *Praza Obradoiro.* Since it wasn't quite time for the office to be open yet, I figured it couldn't hurt to scope out the place I had reserved for us to stay tonight and ask if we could leave our bags there ahead of time. That way I could go into the cathedral without having to use a storage locker for it.

Just behind the plaza, I found our place which was also a café and was staffed by the kindest people. They were more than happy to hold our bags for me until we checked in later in the afternoon and even let Maverick sit at a table inside the café with me while I ate some breakfast. By the time we made our way back towards the cathedral after breakfast and up *rua Carretas* towards the modern-day office, pilgrims were already beginning to flood in for their *Compostelas*.

"Señorita. Él no permite." I stopped just inside the doors to the office and found a massive guard staring down at me hard.

I looked between him and where he was glaring at Maverick at the end of the leash. "Oh, sí, pues él caminó todo el Camino también. Tiene una credencial." I held up Maverick's credential as proof of his walking the whole way. The man's face didn't change at all.

"No permite aquí."

"Pues…necesita su Compostela." I really hadn't been expecting an issue here. I mean, ever since Sarria there had been so many places advertising for *perro-grino* credentials. We had just walked past an office for the protection of animals along the Camino featuring a sign with a dog in booties on it yesterday as we entered the city. If anything, I had been expecting the office to welcome a pilgrim dog with open arms. This harsh rebuttal hadn't been at all what I was anticipating.

The guard's face was impassive at best. I moved to walk further into the office. "No. Puede esperar en el jardín."

"Uhm…vale. Supongo," I huffed. I *guess* he could wait in the garden. But that seemed wrong. After all this? All we had faced and accomplished together? He couldn't even walk up to the desk and get a *Compostela* with me?

I followed glumly after the security guard into a "garden" of sorts off the main hall. It was just a small, square space filled with pebbles and potted plants. "¿Dejálo aquí?"

"Sí," he grunted.

I raised my eyebrow at him in disdain, but bent down to Maverick's level nevertheless. "I have to leave you here, buddy. I know, it's stupid. I promise I won't be long. I'm going to get our Compostelas, okay?"

Maverick gave a little whine, then went to snuffle around the base of a plant for a stick. I looped his leash around a bench leg and clipped him back in, then looked over my shoulder to where the security guard was still watching me. I straightened up to full height and grabbed up my credentials from the pebbles beside Mav. "¿Cómo?" I asked rather rudely. He didn't need to keep staring, I had done what he asked. "¿Está bien?"

"Vale," he grunted. I think all he knew how to do was grunt. I rolled my eyes when he finally turned away and then slipped back into the hall and into line. It was only a moment before I was being called forward to one of the many clerks along the endless desk. There had to be at least twenty stations here to accept pilgrims at the same time.

I stepped forward with a smile, trying to put the security guard out of my mind. We had done it. We were getting our *Compostelas*! I could squeal with excitement. "¡Hola!" I chirped as I skipped up to the open place of the desk. "¿Cómo está?"

"Credential, por favor," the man droned.

I blinked in surprise. *Alright, then*, I thought. *Not a morning person. Noted.* I slid my credential across the desk and his hand reached up to snatch it.

"No tienes fechas en todos los días," he snapped.

"Uhm…" I stood on my tiptoes in an attempt to see over

the desk and to my credential he was scrutinizing. "Pues, hay muchas fechas, no?"

So what if not every single stamp had a date on the bottom of it? I'm pretty sure ninety-eight percent of them did. The man paused in scouring my credential and looked back up at me, as if assessing if I had just made up these stamps all on my own to fake my way through this. Once he deemed me worthy enough, he went about giving me my final stamp and asking all the necessary questions. When we started. Where. If we had walked the entire time. Then finally, he was filling out my information on a piece of parchment paper and handing it over. He filled out a certificate of completion and passed that along the desk, too before rushing to call the next pilgrim forward.

"¡Espere!" I cried. "Tengo una otra credencial."

"¿Otra?" he asked doubtfully.

"Sí, para mi perro."

The man laughed humorlessly.

"No, es verdad. Él caminó todo el Camino de Saint Jean conmigo. Tienes todos los sellos, también."

"No tenemos Compostelas para perros," he sneered.

"Pues…¿puede darle su último sello?" That was the least he could do. At least authorize Maverick's credential. He had gone this whole way, gotten almost all the same stamps I had. And he wasn't going to be allowed to get a *Compostela*? The least the man could do was stamp his credential here for the official final stamp. He continued to stare at me blankly, like he couldn't believe I was stupid enough to ask for such a thing. But this meant a lot to me. To Maverick. "Por favor, señor. Por favor," I pleaded.

He sighed as if I had just asked him to do the most tedious thing in the world rather than push a rubber pad into some blue ink and then onto a piece of paper. "Vale. Dámelo."

"Oh, gracias, señor. Muchas gracias." I quickly thrust Mav's credential over the wooden surface, scared that if I was any slower he would change his mind. His eyes scanned over the front and back, taking in all the stamps from Saint Jean, to Agés, to Carrión de los Condes and Sahagún, all the way to San Lázaro. "Bien. Aquí tiene."

He slammed down the stamp with a bit more force than necessary, then put Maveick's credential back onto the desk for me. "Muchas gracias, señor."

"Sí." He raised his arm, yet again ready to wave the next pilgrim forward.

"¿Es posible tener un certificado para Maverick?"

His eyes raised one last time to meet mine and I saw just how done he was with me in that moment. *Well you know what, sir? I was pretty all set with your attitude myself,* I wanted to yell. I gritted my teeth and forced my lips into a calm smile to placate him, though I'm not sure how much it was working.

"No," he bit out.

"Pero-" I started.

"No," he repeated harshly, this time brooking no arguments. I raised my hands in surrender but my teeth were grinding together.

"Muy bien." I swallowed hard and took a deep breath through my nose. "Gracias."

Finally, I stepped back from the desk and he was able to call forward his next pilgrim. "Buena suerte," I muttered as I passed by the poor man who had to deal with him next. He could use all the help he could get with that curmudgeon.

I skirted back out to the mini garden and found Maverick just where I had left him. The surly security guard was still eying him from the corner as if he was about to jump up and start vandalizing the place. I bent down and unclipped him from his post. "Come on, Nug. Let's go."

He sniffed at the red tube decorated with tiny golden shells which held my new *Compostela* and certificate of completion, but only mine. Not his. I swallowed down my disappointment and tried to smile for him. "You want to carry it?" I asked, extending the tube to him. Tentatively, he closed his mouth over it. "Now don't break it. Just hold it."

With a lurch, he started to pull us back outside. "Okay, okay," I laughed. "We're going."

As we made our way back up *rua Carretas* towards *Praza Obradoiro,* multitudes of pilgrims were already streaming towards the office to get their *Compostelas*. Each one stopped to stare at Maverick, trotting along with the tell-tale red tube in his mouth, prancing up the street like he was on a special mission. I shook my head in amusement, listening to others gushing over him and pointing him out to friends. He truly was the star of this entire trip. He didn't need his own certificate to tell him that.

The plaza was already getting crowded with tourists and pilgrims alike. Stalls were being set up around the edges where vendors could hawk their trinkets and trades. A troop of pilgrims on horseback were clip-clopping their way to the center of the square to take their pictures in front of the cathedral. It looked like they had some sort of guide with them. I'm sure they hadn't been riding very far. Various school groups and tour groups were making their way into the open space, all in t-shirts with matching obnoxious colors like neon green and pink. Some group was blasting music from a boombox. Everything was moving and shifting and alive under the cloudy sky now. The hushed, holy vibe we found here this morning was a thing of the past.

Already, the line to enter *Portico de la Gloria* was almost to the end of the metal barriers along the edge of the cathedral. The Del Norte group hadn't been kidding about it getting busy. Maybe they were right to jump in line when they did. I looked down at Maverick, then back up to the line ahead. I didn't even know if I *could* go into the cathedral. What was I supposed to do with Maverick? I should have arranged something with the Del Norte group earlier so they could have watched Maverick like Trish had done for me in Burgos. Even though I had become more and more comfortable with leaving him out when I went into places, this plaza was way too busy to do that. Unless…

Unless he waited just at the bottom of the stairs, inside the metal gates while I went into the cathedral. Only other pilgrims or visitors to *Portico de la Gloria* would be there. I'm sure it would be fine. They sent people in in small groups for a max of fifteen minutes. That would be no problem. And really, I couldn't *not* see this. Not see the column where thousands of pilgrims had placed their hands over the centuries, wearing away a handprint in the stone. Not see the intricate details painstakingly carved by Master Mateo. I had to.

"Alright, Mavy. This is what we're gonna do."

About an hour later, we finally reached the corner of the stairs that led up to the main doors of the cathedral. So far, we had made friends with the older couple just ahead of us in line who had walked the last stretch of the Camino with their granddaughter. And we had listened to the man behind us tell all his tales about his time on the *Camino Primitivo*. Now, I know it's supposed to be the "primitive" route, but I still had my doubts that he had really encountered a wolf out there. It was still a Camino route after all. I rolled my eyes with a grin as I heard him launch into another tale of just how quickly he had completed the trail to the poor tourist behind him. By now, the line to get into *Portico de la Gloria* had extended out across *Praza Obradoiro* and was almost to the government building on the other side of the square. The tourist train that ran through here was currently waiting to part the queue to continue on its tour.

"What's your plan with the dog now?" the grandfather in front of me asked just as the people in line ahead of us were counted out and allowed to ascend the stairs to the front doors.

"Well…" We were close enough to the front of the line, just one other group ahead of these three, that I was able to lean forward and catch the guard's attention. "¿Perdón, es posible dejar al perro aquí mientras yo visito?"

He looked between me and Maverick, then at the fence I was indicating I would tie him to. "Bueno. Sí, está bien."

I smiled brightly. "Muchas gracias, señor." I turned back to the grandparents and their granddaughter. "See? All is well. The guard said it would be fine to tie Maverick to this fence while I go in."

"Oh, how wonderful!" the grandmother clapped excitedly.

"Okay, Mav. Why don't you just wait on the other side of the fence so you're not in anyone's way. Go ahead, crawl under." I urged him to dip under the bar of the fence to the other side and he was just about to when the old woman who was selling cheesy trinkets just beyond the barrier started squawking.

"¡No! ¡No, no no! Aquí no. ¡El perro no permite aquí!"

"Lo siento, señora, pero el guardia me dijo que-"

"¡No! Estoy vendiendo aquí y no me gustan perros," she hissed, swatting at Maverick with a beaded scarf of some sort.

"¡Tranquila!" I tried. No need to hit my dog, jeez. I ushered Maverick closer to me just as the guard opened up the barrier to let in our group to be next. Only, I had nowhere to leave Maverick now if this woman wouldn't let me tie him here. The grandparents and their granddaughter hesitated, not wanting to go up the stairs without me.

"It's fine," I tried to tell them, but my own heart was

sinking. "No big deal," I laughed without humor. "Let me know how it is after!"

I turned before they could see how truly disappointed I was and started to make my way backwards, squeezing between the metal barrier and the other people in line to see *Portico de la Gloria*. Since I couldn't break from the barrier, I would have to fight against the crowd all the way to the edge of the cathedral. "Excuse me," I muttered while I kept my head down and Maverick tight to my side. "Perdón. Sorry. Lo siento. Perdón."

When we turned the corner of the stairs following the barriers back towards the main wall of the cathedral, an older woman stopped me. "Where are you going?" she asked.

I swallowed hard so I wouldn't sound upset and looked up at her with a wan smile. "I couldn't tie him outside. The vendor there wouldn't let me. So I can't go in." I shrugged weakly and made to move on, but her hand shot out to grab my arm. "What if we held him?" I stopped and turned to face her again, but didn't say anything. I wasn't sure what to say. She turned to her husband. "Right, honey? He can hang out here with us. Who's to say he isn't part of our family? We're all family on the Camino, right?"

"You're serious?" I asked.

"Of course! What are you waiting for! Go get in that next group!" She reached out for Maverick's leash, easily taking it from my lax grip. She shooed me away with her free hand and a smile.

"Okay. Mav, you're going to stay here, okay? I promise I'll be right back. These people are going to watch you. Okay?"

He gave out a little bark, as if saying to hurry up, and I quickly thanked the couple one more time before turning and hustling my way back up the line. The guard was just counting off the last of the group when I made it back to him. A younger man right in front of the guard cried out in protest when he smiled and waved me forward to let me in.

"She waited in line the whole time, sonny!" I glanced up to see the grandfather I had been standing with before leaning over the edge of the stairs above me. "You know she did! Don't act like you didn't just see her and her dog walk by you!"

The younger man just ahead of me clamped his mouth shut with an audible grinding noise and turned away from the guard to glare at me. Even his anger wasn't enough to wipe the smile off of my face from my recent turn of events. "Sorry," I muttered, though I didn't feel the least bit remorseful.

"¿Dónde está su perro?" the guard asked with a smile as he clicked the gate shut once I was inside.

"Con unos amigos," I grinned back. He waved me up the staircase on the right side and up to the expansive patio before the front doors. With a few minutes to spare before the previous group came back outside, I got to take in the carvings on the façade of the cathedral up close. There were simply no words for something as incredible as this. And to think, some of this limestone had been carried by pilgrims past from Triacastela to be fired in the kilns of Castañeda before being brought here to build this cathedral. Here, where the intricate details of shells and stars and statues were all carved into the stone. I wanted to reach out and touch it, but I was too scared. Even my hands, which were clean, seemed too dirty to touch something this awe-inspiring.

Soon enough, another guard emerged from inside the cathedral to tell us the strict rules in place for viewing *Portico de la Gloria* now. No photos of any kind. No electronic devices out. Stay quiet. It was all very strict, but no one needed to be told twice. There was a hush over the whole group upon entering those doors and seeing the *Door of*

Glory up close, unveiled for the first time in a decade. As one, the whole group seemed to gasp upon seeing the entrance.

Before us, one massive archway in the center, with a center column splitting the main opening where pilgrims had worn away a handprint in the stonework. A massive statue of Saint James commands everyone's attention first where he stands on the central column. With the new restoration, his robes look tan, his beard brown, and his cheeks have a rosy hue to them. All around me, in all these incredible details, I started to notice the color that has been revealed. For so many years, this portal had been merely grey and black and dirty. Centuries of grime had hidden what Master Mateo had once breathed life into. But now? Now it was incredible.

Jesus. Apostles and prophets with their robes of deep burgundy and blue and gold hues. Demons under the feet of the columns representing glory crushing sin. It's all almost too much to take in. All so astounding. And this is merely the entrance to the cathedral. Beyond the Portico, which was once the main entrance to the whole sanctuary, I could see people milling about the cathedral itself, let in from other entrances but not allowed to view this face of *Portico de la Gloria*.

We may no longer be able to enter through this door, or press our palms against the cool stone on that sunken imprint anymore, but this was still incredible. The feeling of standing here, looking at this masterpiece, knowing I had walked all the way to get to this point? That was a feeling beyond any words. The only thing more incredible than this would be to experience the Pilgrims' Mass here.

Mav and I left *Praza do Obradoiro* and started to make our way around the cathedral, intending to take it in from all sides. Only, upon reaching the southern façade, we came to a standstill. This side entrance to the cathedral looked like the general admission floor of a concert venue. Pilgrims were packing into *Praza das Praterías*, swarming the steps that led to the doors that would allow them in for Mass at noon.

I hadn't realized we should have been queuing up early to get into Mass as well. With wide eyes, Mav and I skirted our way around the crowd, almost bumping into the fountain in the center of the square because it hadn't been visible through the throng of people. We popped out on the far side, to the right of the cathedral doors, where we could get some air. Just beneath the steps up to the cathedral, there was a little alcove that had a place for people to store their bikes. Tucked into the corner of the stairs, it made a quiet hideaway just opposite the door to a tiny gift shop.

I looked up at the doors that were starting to open and let in the swarm of pilgrims, then down at Maverick by my side. Okay, so I really hadn't planned this out. I definitely should have thought this through more, but I thought I had more time. It wasn't even noon yet! I had thought maybe I would be able to get into our room early, leave Maverick in the room, and come back to go to Mass. Clearly, that wasn't going to happen. If people were already going in now? No way.

I looked down at my watch. It wasn't quite eleven-thirty yet. Pilgrims were shuffling forward endlessly, though. I bit my lip, then dropped to one knee next to Maverick. "Okay, here's the deal. This isn't ideal. However, I think you'll be fine. No, you will be fine. I promise. It's all pilgrims around. It's the holiest church in the land. No one will come into this little corner. Okay?"

I sucked in a breath as Maverick ignored everything I was saying to sniff at one of the bikes hooked up here. I wasn't convincing him, anyway. I was convincing myself. I looped his leash around one of the metal rungs meant to hold bikes and clipped him back into place. "There. You're in the shade. No one's going to bother you. I'll be right inside. Right there, see?" I pointed over my shoulder where pilgrims were showing their credentials and getting into the cathedral. The crowd still stretched past the fountain in the center of the square. "Okay? I'll be right back. I promise. I love you."

I took a step back, out of the alcove and into the throng of pilgrims. "I love you." Maverick watched me as I slipped into the crowds. I caught his eye once more from above as I peeked over the massive stone banister of the stairs. "I'll be right back. I love you."

Surprisingly enough, I found myself in front of one of the cathedral security guards almost immediately. He checked my credential and ushered me in for the Pilgrims' Mass without a word and I was left looking over my shoulder at the teeming crowd still waiting to get in like I had done something wrong to slip in that quickly and easily. "Oops," I muttered under my breath, but I quickly forgot about it as my eyes acclimated to the change from the bright light outside to the dim, candlelit interior.

"Oh. My…" I didn't finish that thought. Not in this holiest of places. This. *This* was a cathedral. Sure, the ones we had passed through on our way to this point were all massive. All beautiful. All with their own distinct touches and unique qualities. From Burgos to León to Astorga and all the little chapels in between, the whole Way had been marked by holy places. But *this* was the first place you could truly *feel* it. This was the first house of worship where it still felt as authentic as I imagined it must have felt for those pilgrims in the Middle Ages.

The interior of *El Catedral de Santiago* wasn't flashy. It wasn't brimming with sunlight or a kaleidoscope of stained glass. This transept where I entered was as wide as a nave in any other church. Grey, block columns lined the aisles of both the transepts and the nave to the crossing and gold winked at me from the altar to the right. Already, all the seats were occupied in the transept and pilgrims were crowding around columns and shuffling to get as close as possible to the altar.

After sneaking forward to get a view down the nave and to see the altar more clearly, I slipped my way back through the crowds and took up a post against one of the cool columns. I wasn't expecting to see anyone I knew aside from maybe the Del Norte group. For one thing, there were simply hundreds of people here. The odds of finding them in the crowd were slim. For another, most of our close Camino friends had probably finished their Camino around the twenty-fifth, Saint James Day. They would be long gone by now.

Of course, I should have known by now that the Camino never does what you expect it to.

As I leaned against that column before the Mass officially started, countless fellow pilgrims came up to me. They came to share hugs, and smiles, and Buen Caminos. Each asked where Maverick was and how he was doing. In the midst of it all, I realized we touched a lot of people's lives. I didn't even recognize half the pilgrims who came up to me before the Priest began the Mass. Yet somehow, Mav and I had influenced them. I had no idea all these people had worried about us, thought of us long after we had walked with them just for a few steps, even prayed for us. The outpouring of love was almost overwhelming. How I was just coming to realize it now was beyond me, but I was so grateful for it.

The Mass proceeded solemnly, with the whole congregation gathered falling to a hushed reverence as the Archbishop continued from reading the names of pilgrims who had arrived in the last twenty-four hours through his blessing. The entire ceremony was in Spanish so I had a feeling many, if not most, of the people in here had no clue what was being said. As unfortunate as it was, so many pilgrims I met along the way knew only the basics of the Spanish language. I suppose you didn't need to understand every word that was being said in this ceremony, though. There was an energy in the air in that massive cathedral; a holy presence that completely surrounded every single person crowded in the aisles and transepts and nave.

As moving as the ceremony was, it was also far longer than I had anticipated, and it didn't look to be wrapping up any time soon. When I couldn't hold in my anxiety anymore, I slid from my post against one of the massive columns and dipped through the crowds as quietly as I could to the back doors where I had come in. A security guard was standing post there.

"¿Perdón?" I whispered as I came up next to him. He barely glanced down at me. "¿Es posible ir afuera y volver? Mi perro está allí y yo quiero verlo."

I wasn't entirely sure if I had said that right, but I'm sure he could understand that my dog was outside and I wanted to check on him and be able to come back in. In the same hushed tone so as not to disrupt the ceremony, he spoke out of the corner of his mouth. "Si sales, no puedes regresar."

"Sí, pero quiero ver el *botafumeiro* si usan hoy pero necesito ver si mi perro está bien afuera. Solo necesito un minuto para verlo," I told him. If I could know if the *botafumeiro* was even swinging at all today, I could know if I even needed to come back inside or not. But since I couldn't be sure, I didn't want to miss it. The guard looked down at me fully, as if debating if I was being sincere. "Por favor. Puedo correr," I grinned. Between the offer to run, and my clearly dirty and ratty pilgrim attire, he must have decided to take pity on me.

With a barely there grin, he glanced around to make sure no one else was listening and then spoke in a whisper.

"Bueno. Pase por la tienda de regalos. Cuando regreses, pasaré por allí de nuevo y te dejaré entrar aquí."

"Oh, gracias, señor. Gracias, gracias, gracias," I whispered excitedly.

"Ven," he chuckled under his breath and waved me with him towards the right side of the transept where there was a separate door to a gift shop. With a mock little salute, I ducked into the shop. The woman behind the register looked up as I came in and I waved at her but true to my word, I practically ran through the shop and out the glass doors to the raised part of the street above where I had left Maverick tied. I quickly took in my new surroundings and then darted around this corner of a cathedral tower and to the edge of the raised street to the stone wall and peeked over. There was Maverick, laying exactly where I had left him, only now he had a big bowl of water next to him. I smiled and debated running down to see him, but figured it would be best if he didn't get excited.

I just grinned from above him, glad to see no one was bothering him and that he was indeed still there, and then sprinted back to the doors of the gift shop. The woman glanced up again as I came flying in. I waved again and called a quick "hola" before slipping over to the entrance to the cathedral. The heavy doors were closed now and I debated what to do. With a look around the empty alcove where these doors entered, I gently knocked.

Within a second, one door cracked open inwards and I stepped to the side to avoid being hit. The guard's kind eyes winked at me from the gloom of the cathedral and upon seeing it was me, he cracked the door just a bit more so that I was able to slip through. "¿Está bien?" he whispered as I passed by him. I nodded with a massive grin. "Perfecto. Mire. El *botafumeiro*."

My eyes widened at his words and my head whipped

towards the altar where sure enough, a group of men in rich, crimson robes were now at the crossing. There, lowered to ground level, hanging from the center of the crossing on a rope as thick as my forearm, was the *botafumeiro*. The silver shone from the light of the altar as two *tiraboleiros*, the men in crimson robes, held open the giant incense burner as the Archbishop loaded in the last of the incense and said a blessing. Already, it was smoking. Upon the blessing, the *tiraboleiros* closed the metal cover and one waited as the almost six-foot-tall metal canister was raised above his head from the pulley with a flourish. The man reached up, gripped the base of the silver burner that was coughing out incense and smoke, and with a mighty shove, threw it forward towards the south transept.

The *botafumeiro*, which could weigh up to three hundred and fifty pounds when full of charcoal and incense, swung forward on the rope and then back across the crossing slowly. And then the group of all eight *tiraboleiros*, each holding their own rope where it split at the other end of the pulley, in unison, pulled their ropes straight to the floor, so low so that each man was practically sitting on the floor of the crossing. The massive *botafumeiro* rocketed upward as it swung. Each time it made its way back to the center of the crossing, the group of men yanked again. Soon, the metal was spewing incense and smoke throughout the whole cathedral as it picked up speed, swinging up to the rafters in each transept.

I stood in awe of it. At the speed, the beauty, the history behind this tradition, and the fact that I was standing here able to witness this. In that moment, I felt truly complete.

I dipped out through the gift shop before Mass was officially over with one last secret nod to my friend, the security guard. I wanted to get out to Maverick before the crowds started pouring out. Sure, I would have liked to wander the cathedral some more, take it all in. But just like everything on this pilgrimage, it wasn't only about me. And that was okay. In fact, I preferred it like that. This was Maverick's trek, too, not just mine. So I skipped down the steps of *Praza das Praterías* to find him surrounded by fellow pilgrims.

"Colby! I'm sorry, we had to come take a picture of Maverick. Is that okay?" one woman asked as soon as she saw me approaching.

"We figured you must be in the Mass when we saw him laying out here by himself," another smiled at me.

"We recognized him right away," someone else added.

"Oh, by all means, you're welcome to take his picture. He loves it," I said to the first woman as I bent down to unhook him from the bike rack. I didn't remember any of their names, in fact I barely recognized them, but again, they clearly knew us. "Yeah, I was at Mass. Luckily, a security guard let me check on him partway through and still come back in to see the *botafumeiro*, so that was great."

"Did it swing?" one of the women asked excitedly. I nodded happily.

"You're so lucky to see that! And to have such a good dog. I can't believe he just sits and patiently waits here."

"I'm so glad we were able to run into you guys one last time. It was so, so nice meeting you along the trail."

With a flurry of goodbyes, and a thank you to the shop owner in this alcove who had been the one to put out the bowl of water for Maverick, we headed down the winding street, the *Catedral de Santiago* at our back. For the first time all trip, I acted a bit like a tourist. I bought myself a bracelet from one little vending cart with a silver shell on it, and a t-shirt from a gift shop, and even a sweatshirt from another shop. I popped into a chocolatier shop and bought myself a chocolate pop that had Buen Camino written in white chocolate script across it. The woman asked if I was buying it for a friend who had just finished the Camino and when I told her it was for myself, as a birthday gift because I had finished today on my twenty-first birthday, she was at a loss for words before sputtering out happy birthdays and congratulations.

Mav and I wandered the old parts of the city, took in the sights, got settled into our nice little hotel room right by the cathedral with a view of the spires from the balcony. I had splurged on a nicer place tonight to celebrate myself, which also happened to be right next to the post office. Since I had some time, I decided to pop in and check out what was up with this *Camino Correos* thing and sending bags ahead. By the time I came back out to meet Maverick, I had organized for his pack (and all the excess food we had now) to be sent ahead to the place we were staying tomorrow. For the first time in our trek, I was sending a bag ahead. And it felt *awesome*. To top off what had to be the perfect day, even though the restaurant I found for dinner said *paella* was for two or more people only, they made an exception for me when they found out it was my birthday. So I was able to have a whole pan of *paella mixta* to myself as the waiters fawned over Maverick. They even sent me home with a piece of chocolate cake to have later.

I sat on the bed in the hostel, Maverick by my feet, and popped open the plastic container of cake. I smiled at him weakly, but he was sleeping, not paying me any attention. It had been a perfect day. It really was. I don't think I'd ever be able to top this birthday. But in this moment, I still wished I wasn't alone. I stabbed at the chocolate frosting with my plastic fork.

"Happy Birthday to me," I sang softly. "Happy Birthday to me. Happy birthday dear me. Happy birthday to me."

Pon de Replay

Day Forty-One: Santiago de Compostela to Logrosa
27.0 km ~38,018 steps

July 30th

I swore this region had only one weather setting with various degrees of intensity: mist. This mist could range from barely there, to soaking, to full out raining but it was always present. I was grateful to have the sweatshirt I bought yesterday because there was a chill to the air this morning, as most mornings in Galicia had. I slipped it over my head and double checked my bag. It was lighter now, I had transferred some things I knew I wouldn't need throughout the day to Maverick's pack that would be getting shipped ahead. I had tried to fit as much of his food into his two food sacks as possible last night, but that still left almost half the bag for me to carry today. I couldn't ship that ahead. Instead, I would still be carrying it like a baby.

We skipped down the stairs of our hostel to the café on the first floor to check out with the owner and to make sure I left his pack in the right place to get picked up by *Correos*. Then we were off yet again, just as we had for the last forty days. We left the cathedral behind and wound our way through back streets of Santiago, on our way to the coast. Of course, since we were still in a city still, there weren't many green spaces. So when Maverick decided it was time for his morning poop, it happened right in the center of a sidewalk on the very outskirts of Santiago. No big deal, I opened up a hip pocket to take out a poop bag and realized I was all out. Which was fine, I had brought plenty of back up rolls of bags in…his pack.

"Oh, no," I said aloud. Maverick, now unburdened, was scampering ahead. I patted my pockets, but I knew I didn't have an extra roll in this backpack. I had shipped them all ahead. I glanced around, but obviously no solution appeared on the dreary, grimy side street. I took a step to be upwind of it and a shrill voice echoed down the street.

"¡Caca! ¡Caca del perro!" I startled at the voice of an old lady and looked around for the speaker. I finally found her, her head of grey hair sticking out from a second story window about three blocks down.

"Sí," I called back mildly. "No tengo una bolsa," I explained my predicament. Why I was explaining this to some old, Spanish woman hanging out a window was beyond me, but here we were.

"¡Caca!" she cawed again. I swear, if she said *poop* one more time… "¡Recógelo!" she demanded. Of course I meant to pick it up but…

"No tengo una bolsa," I reasoned again.

"¡No me importa! ¡Recógelo! ¡Encuentra una bolsa!"

I blinked slowly. One: I was in a shouting conversation with a senile Spanish woman who had to be at least ninety.

Two: she was yelling at me about dog shit. Three: the longer I was standing here, the more soaked I was getting. And four: she expected me to just find a bag somewhere. Where? Where did she think I could find one? I took another step forward, intending to see if there was anywhere open up ahead where I could get a bag because there had been nothing where we came from. The woman squawked again, this time more aggressively, that I needed to pick up the poop. I pinched the bridge of my nose. "Maverick," I gritted out under my breath. "Come."

I turned my back on the woman and headed back the way we came. I knew there was nothing in this direction. And the fact that I was retracing my steps, knowing we had a long day ahead of us, was not making my morning mood very happy. About five minutes later, we came to the first open business. It was a little, rundown hotel. But it was the only thing we had seen so far and I was sick of walking backwards, so I tied Maverick to a planter out front and headed into the lobby.

After a lengthy conversation with the receptionist where he was very confused as to why I needed a plastic bag and I attempted to do my best to get across what I needed, I finally emerged with a plastic shopping bag. Mav and I started back down the street. Only for me to realize about three blocks later that I had left his giant bag of food next to the planter I had tied him to and we needed to turn back to get it.

By the time we made it back to the pile of poop on the sidewalk, I think I had called the little, old lady every name in the book in my head. I scowled up at her, still sticking her head out the window once we arrived to make sure I did indeed pick up the poop. I glared at her, though I'm not sure if she could tell my expression from this far away, as I bent and picked it up. As soon as I had it secured in the bag, her head disappeared and I heard the window slam shut distantly. I muttered under my breath as I stood and finally continued forward on the trail, tossing the bag of poop in the nearest trash can.

On the plus side, that was our only negative experience of the day. Despite the extremely dreary weather and the trails being soaked everywhere from what must have been heavy rain last night, today was a joy. The trail after the city felt like a rainforest, lush and green, with everything dripping. After the influx of pilgrims from the last week, it was really nice to enjoy an empty trail for a while. Even with the crappy weather, on the last outlook back towards the city, I was still able to get in one last look at the spires of the cathedral.

"Goodbye, Santiago," I whispered before turning to follow Maverick's fluffy tail up the trail.

At the first village we came to, there were no cafes or bars. No stores or anything open for pilgrims, but there was a vending machine. So we paused for a healthy breakfast of Twix and Nestea before continuing on, up and down, for the next ten kilometers. When we finally did find a café, we met up with a couple from Philly who were walking on to Finisterre and chatted with them briefly. We had bumped into two or three other pilgrims so far, but it seemed like this part of the trail had a solitary vibe to it. There was no longer the oversharing that had been so normal on the Camino Frances. Instead, it's just a quiet Buen Camino and a nod, nothing more. It's almost fitting, though. Like the warm sun and long days of the Meseta or La Rioja brought out the warm, bubbly pilgrims and the quiet, mist of Galicia sets them to introspection.

Whatever it was, Mav and I kept our own banter going throughout the day as we marched on through little villages from Portela de Villestro to Ventosa to Castelo and on. I'd noticed that if it's just the two of us and I didn't talk out loud to him, his mood seemed to go down. I always had to keep up the chatter or tug on the sticks he brought me.

"What do you think, Reek? Think I could hack it back in the days when women carried everything on their heads?" I asked him as I attempted to balance his giant food bag on top of my head as we passed through another quiet hamlet.

He looked up at me, a stick dangling out from the side of his mouth, and cocked his head to one side. I tried to take a step forward, my arms outstretched and ready to catch the bag if it slipped, and immediately it fell from my hair. Mav scampered away.

"No, no, no," I muttered, repositioning the bag and trying again. Maverick weaved around my legs, making it next to impossible to walk and balance the bag. "You could carry it, you know. Just drape it over your back?" He ran ahead at that, not wanting to stick around. "That's what I thought."

Our lonely trail continued on, through little villages that definitely had a different feel than those found along Francés. Things were quieter now; life didn't revolve around pilgrim traffic in this part of the country. The roads we traveled were wide and devoid of any other pilgrims for hours at a time. Maverick continued bringing me damp sticks he found, so I tugged them to the beat of whatever song happened to be stuck in my head, causing his little head to bob to the beat.

"Hey, Mister DJ, song pon de replay," I sang to him, pulling the stick back and forth. "Come, Mister DJ, won't you turn the music up."

I let the stick go and shimmied along with him as we walked through puddles on the empty tar road. "All the gal pon the dance floor wantin' some more. Come, Mr. DJ, won't you turn the music up?" I grabbed onto the stick when Maverick trotted it back once more, happy as a clam with my horrible singing. "It goes one by one, even two by two, everybody in the club gon' be rockin' when I'm through." I tip-tapped my boots along with the steps, then bent down to bounce with Maverick.

"Come run, run, run, run, everybody move, run." I let go of the stick and ran beside Maverick now and laughed at how ridiculous we were. "Lemme see you move and rock it 'til the groove done. Shake it 'til the moon becomes the sun." At this, I grabbed hold of his stick and shook his head from side to side until he let out a play bark.

"Wow, you guys certainly know how to make your own fun," I suddenly heard from behind us.

My eyes bugged out of my head as I looked at Maverick. Then I slowly released his stick and straighten up from the squat I had been in, shaking my hips (horribly) to the beat of my awful singing. I turned around to see a pair of pilgrims a few yards behind us on the road.

"Hah," I said drily. "Well. This isn't embarrassing at all."

The couple laughed and shook their heads. "No, I love it," the woman said.

They were decked out with rain covers for their packs and each had rain jackets. Meanwhile, I had been caught shaking my ass, singing to a dog, and probably looked like a drowned rat because I had never bothered to put on any rain gear since it was just a mist all day.

Even though I was mortified, I quickly shrugged off the embarrassment and walked the rest of the way to the río Tambre with them. At that point, they continued on without the crazy lady and her dog while Maverick and I stopped for a bite to each where the Roman bridge, Ponte Maceira, crossed the river.

According to legend, Saint James and his followers were fleeing from Roman soldiers here and when they crossed over the bridge to the other side of the river, the bridge was suddenly destroyed. The Roman soldiers had been stranded on the other side of the river, unable to reach the Saint and his crew. Since then, the coat of arms for the council in Maceira is an image of a broken bridge.

Mav and I enjoyed a peaceful lunch to the sounds of the river, then headed off to explore the bridge and the other medieval structures around. Everything in this town was covered in green, so much so it felt like things were ready to burst. Vines crawled up the walls lining the streets, entire archways had been coated in ivy, and the leaves of bushes trailed into the rushing river. I thought we had known green before, when we first got into Galicia, but this was even better.

Just as we were leaving town, we happened to bump into a fellow pilgrim who was walking with her dog, Rango. She was from the area and they were just doing the Camino Fisterra, but it was nice to walk with a fellow perrogrino for the first time. Rango even looked a bit like Mav. His owner told me he was half shepherd and half mastiff, but he had the traditional black and tan coat of a German Shepherd. Luckily, Maverick took to him immediately. I was a bit worried he might be timid around other dogs after the attack near Triacastela, but it seemed like he was completely unfazed.

Rango and his owner waved goodbye to us as they continued on the main trail to Negreira and Mav and I bore left towards the hamlet of Logrosa. A little under a kilometer off the main trail, I had been able to find an albergue that had no problem accepting Maverick. The town was nothing more than a few houses and a tiny church amongst all the farmland, and the albergue in question ended up being a big, stone house.

When we walked in the door, Maverick's bright red pack was waiting for us at the foot of the front desk. He trotted over immediately and began to sniff it. "Yes, that's yours," I chuckled.

A man appeared from a back room at my voice and smiled brightly. "¡Bienvenidos!" he called out. "¿Son Colby y Maverick, no?"

"Ah, sí," I replied, a bit surprised he already knew who we were. I guess that's what happened when your bag got shipped ahead. Well, that and the fact that we were only one of four total pilgrims who ended up staying in this house for the night. The other three were ladies in their late seventies who showed up just after I had taken a shower. They reminded me of my nana and her two sisters and they were an absolute delight to share the albergue with.

Even though the dinner was terrible, and there was nothing else to explore in this little town, they made Logrosa one of the best places I stayed along the Camino. The four of us shared one room. They fawned over Maverick and asked all sorts of questions about our whole Camino and I loved hearing the many stories they had to tell as well. It was almost like being in a college dorm room with them, giggling late into the night. It was the magic of the Camino; that ability to bring together people of any age, any background, and suddenly forge a friendship between them.

Sink

Day Forty-Two: Logrosa to Olveiroa

39.3 km ~ 55,430 steps

July 31st

The next morning, we left our elderly comrades sleeping soundly and slipped out of the albergue. Once again, I left Maverick's pack (minus a new roll of poop bags) by the front desk with the tag for *Correos*. We had a long day ahead of us. That was the downfall of booking in advance and sending your bag ahead…you had no choice but to arrive at that place by the end of the day. In this case, it meant we had almost thirty-five kilometers ahead of us on the trail to Olveiroa.

We quickly passed through Negreira, where fellow pilgrims were waking up and getting their start from the bustling town. It was pretty, and it had plenty of stores and bars that would have probably served better food than the dinner we had last night in the stone house, but I was happy we stayed in Logrosa instead. I wouldn't have met those three old ladies if we hadn't, and that more than made up for any subpar dinner. Plus, I would always prefer the feeling of being welcomed into a true, Spanish home rather than a hostel or hotel.

The trail today alternated between paved roads through the small, scattered villages, farm paths, and holloways through the gnarled forests of Galicia that we were becoming accustomed to. Horreos dotted the trail in various lengths. Some were short and stubby, others were long, stretching alongside the road with their moss-covered stone and thatch roofs. The chill of the morning quickly burnt off as the sun actually made an appearance today and dried up all the puddles on the roads and trails. Even with the sun though, it wasn't as hot here as it had been along the Meseta. Plus, there were plenty of streams and shade trees for Maverick throughout the day, so we took our time at each river access for him to chase sticks and enjoy himself. Which was good because I was starting to wonder if I was pushing him too hard again. I hadn't thought that way in a while, not really since we had entered into Galicia. But a thirty-five-kilometer day was long even for me, and I wasn't the one running back and forth the whole time.

If it hadn't already been apparent from yesterday's walk, this part of the Camino was definitely not as equipped with pilgrim rest stops, so the options for food or a break were few and far between. Luckily at one bar we came to, the owner took one look at the pitiful plastic bag I was using to carry Maverick's food and emerged with a new bag for me, this one with handles still intact. I hadn't realized how much of a help that was until we set off again. I no longer had to cradle the food like a baby; I could actually sling it across my forearm by the handle again.

We skirted the edge of massive corn fields that stretched

as far as I could see, then climbed up steeply through the
farmland to have an even more impressive view of it all. A
little bench and viewing platform were at the very top of the
hill, so I threw down the food bag and unbuckled my pack. I
was tired of walking, honestly. We still had way too many
kilometers left to walk at that point and I was already
wanting to take a nap. Instead, I chose to take a seat on the
edge of the wooden platform and stretched my legs out,
leaning back on my palms. Maverick trotted over with a twig
in his mouth. I absentmindedly scratched at the fur around
his collar while he placed the twig daintily beside me.

"Who do you think we should get in contact with about
making corn mazes a thing over here?" I asked him. He
backed up two steps and then did a little bounce on his front
paws, hoping that would get me to throw his twig. I ignored
it and pulled my legs up, resting my arms on my knees. "I
mean, look at this place. This is prime corn maze country." I
waved an arm over the beautiful expanse of land stretched
out in front of us. The sea of bright green corn stalks waved
lazily in what little breeze there was.

"Just imagine how much money that would make. Think
of how massive that maze could be. It would be like the
freakin' Triwizard Tournament maze. Look at all this corn!" I
pointed more aggressively, then turned to Maverick to see if
he was seeing what I was seeing. His eyes were glued to the
stick he had placed closer to my hip. His gaze darted up to
meet my eyes, then zipped back to the stick as if it may take
off on him if he didn't focus. I ignored it yet again.

"Seriously, though. They're really missing out here. I bet
they could make all sorts of cool patterns in fields of corn
this big. Get some haunted corn mazes up in here in the fall.
Make them spooky. It's a brilliant idea, I'm telling you."

I stood and brushed off my butt while Maverick dove to
grab his stick and follow my every move. I heaved my pack

over my shoulders once more, feeling like it had gained ten pounds since this morning, and snapped the clips back in place before grabbing his bag of food. "We could be onto something here. An untapped business venture. Say we move to Spain, to Galicia, land of cows, corn, and rain and start up a corn maze business. We could strike it rich, don't you think?"

Maverick whined impatiently at the fact that I had yet to throw his stupid little twig. I finally tore my eyes from the view and focused on him. "I know. You're not a fan of all the cats here. But what do you think?" He apparently got bored of my ramblings, because with one last whine of disapproval, he turned and trotted along the dirt trail ahead of us. The good thing was it continued to be a mostly downhill trek after that grueling climb to the viewing platform. Plus, we got to stop at a nice little albergue/restaurant that had ice cream. I had originally only gotten an ice cream for myself, but after Maverick had stared longingly at the chocolate once I sat down outside, it was only a matter of time before I went back in to get his own cup of vanilla.

If I hadn't already booked a place in Olveiroa for the night, I would have stayed the night at that albergue with the delicious ice cream. The food coming out for other patrons of the restaurant looked incredible, too. And the owner loved Maverick. I knew we would have been welcome to stay. But alas, we still had about two more hours of walking after that pitstop before we would reach the outskirts of Olveiroa.

It was the biggest town we had come to since walking through Negreira this morning, but that wasn't saying much. From the start of the village to the edge of town where our albergue was located, it couldn't have taken more than five minutes to walk. It seemed like there were actually quite a few other pilgrims in town, though. Most of them were staying in the municipal albergue in town from the looks of the many people we saw hanging around on the rock walls that lined the main road outside the albergue. We stopped and exchanged pleasantries with a few pilgrims, but my feet were aching beyond belief, and I wanted nothing more than to take a shower and lie down at that point, so we didn't chat for long.

The place we were staying tonight felt more like a woman's home than a place for weary pilgrims. There was a main building that housed a little restaurant and individual rooms, but upon checking in and getting our credentials stamped, the woman who owned the place led us out the back of the house and through an enclosed courtyard where numerous kids were screeching and running around. They ranged in age from one who was no more than a toddler, to a group of teenage boys watching the younger girls run around with a hint of annoyance. I had to say, I was on the side of the teenage boys. I could have done without the screeching and immense energy those girls had after the long day of walking we had just done.

The woman showed me into a back guesthouse across the patio where there were only two doors and opened up the one on the left with a key she handed to me. The room was massive and beautiful with its own bathroom and a shower that could have fit four people inside of it. This was easily one the nicest places we had stayed so far. My previous annoyance at the plethora of kids the hospitalera had running around the property flew out the window as I quickly thanked her for everything and promised I would be back to the main house for dinner once I showered and laid down for a bit.

She left with a motherly smile and a wave and I watched from the window as she paused in the courtyard, a hand on her lower back in the way that all pregnant women seemed to do, and spoke with a few of the kids. I couldn't tell what she was saying, but I could tell just from where I was standing that the kids loved her. They couldn't all be her own children, but it seemed like she was the designated "cool mom" of the neighborhood and this was clearly a spot where all the children wanted to hang out. I watched as she gave a tired smile before waddling back into the main albergue, presumably into the kitchen where she had emerged from when I had arrived.

I turned away from the window, wishing to shower and then take a nap. The good thing about Spaniards and their super late dinner times was that I could squeeze in a nap in the late afternoon and still have plenty of time to get food without being worried anywhere would be closed. Maverick was already passed out on the tile floor, so I ducked into the bathroom to wash my clothes and myself. I was just getting ready to lay down on the bed when someone knocked on the door of my room.

I debated not even answering it, but who ever knocked on a door of a guest's room unless it was important? So with a longing look at the bed, I turned and unlatched the heavy wooden door. On the other side was one of the younger girls from the patio. Upon closer inspection, she couldn't have been older than seven. She was standing at the door with a mix of uncertainty and determination, the combination of two such different things causing an involuntary smile to twitch on my lips as she glanced behind her and looked to the group of kids watching our interaction from near the main house.

"Ehm…" she started hesitantly. I raised my eyebrows in amusement. "Pues…" She paused again, still not quite meeting my eyes. Then, in a rush, she spit out what she wanted. "¿Puedo el perro jugar con nosotros afuera?"

I laughed at her request since it was not at all what I was expecting. Not that I had been expecting anything, but it was cute that what she wanted more than anything was to see if Maverick could come out and play with them. I looked back at Maverick, who despite being exhausted from today, had perked up at someone knocking on our door and was currently trying to see around my leg to who was outside. "Pues, el perro es muy cansado hoy. Tuvimos un día muy larga," I told her with a grimace. It was true. Our day had been grueling. And he had walked even more than I had. He needed his rest, not to go chase a ball around a courtyard with kids.

Immediately, her face dropped. In fact, her entire little body deflated. Her eyes briefly lifted from the ground back to meet mine. "Ah, sí, está bien. Entiendo. Gracias, señora."

She turned and made to leave the entryway, but already I felt like a jerk. "Espera." She turned back to face me with hope all over her expression. I sighed and opened my door a little wider. "El puede jugar con vosotros. Su nombre es Maverick," I told her, pronouncing the 'v' like a 'b' and stressing the 'rick' to sound more like 'reek' just like I always did when introducing him in Spanish. He slipped out from behind my legs to investigate the kids, all of whom were now crowding into the entryway and cooing over him.

"Hola Mabereeek," the little girl tried. I smiled and gave her a half nod when she glanced up to see if that was right. One of the little boys kicked a dusty soccer ball across the patio and Mav immediately took off after it, the group of children running and screeching to catch up with him.

I leaned against the doorjamb of my room, my head tilted against the wood, and I felt my smile stretch wider. Another boy kicked the ball, trying and failing to get it past Maverick where he stood between them, and they shouted in glee at his quick reflexes. He chased after them as they dribbled it around the courtyard, dropping down to a play bow and bounding after the ball when they kicked it too far.

A flash of movement took my attention from the scene for a moment and brought it to a window of the main house across from me. The woman who owned the place, the mom of at least a few of these children, had pulled aside a curtain in the kitchen window to look out at what was causing all the commotion. When she saw Maverick at the center of it all, her eyes lifted and found me in the doorway across the patio. Before her expression could switch into one of apology, because I was suddenly sure I knew what she had been saying to the kids on her way back into the main house earlier and it was something along the lines of "do not bother the lady with the dog," I shook my head at her and smiled. I could see her let out a sigh, hand on her lower back again, and return my grin with a wan smile of her own. There was nothing for her to apologize for. This was fine. This was more than fine.

Wherever You Will Go

Day Forty-Three: Olveiroa to Muxía

39.3 km ~ 55,390 steps

August 1ˢᵗ

I stared at the ceiling through the gloom of morning. The room was chilly, outside the window the sky was still dark, and I wanted to cry. The idea of another thirty-plus kilometer day sounded like torture. Why did I think this was a good idea? Why did I think we could make it from Santiago to Muxía and then on to Finisterre in four days? Was I a masochist?

My alarm went off again until finally I rolled out of bed with a groan. Maverick lifted his head slightly at the sound of my feet hitting the floor. Just touching the soles down to the worn wood was painful; that's how sore my feet were. I flipped on one of the lights and squinted against the sudden brightness, then hobbled my way to the bathroom. I didn't bother closing the door since it was just Maverick in the room with me, which meant I had a perfect view when he wandered over to where I had left my empanada from last night.

"Don't you do it," I scolded. Of course, I was unable to jump up and shoo him away from the napkin-wrapped delicacy. I had ordered it last night at dinner and wrapped it up to bring with me today. I had wonderful visions of munching on it while we walked the first kilometers of the day. That dream was quickly going down the drain as Maverick nudged the empanada onto the floor with his nose.

"Maverick, no!" But it was too late. He had already gotten the napkin open and was licking along the flaky shell of the tuna empanada. "Mavy," I groaned. He paid me no mind. As soon as I could, I made my way back into the main room to assess the damage. As much as I loved him, I wasn't about to eat the empanada now that he had licked the entire crust. He looked up at me from beside the fallen pastry and gave a wolfy grin, his tail wagging slowly. I glared back down at him.

"Well, you might as well finish it. Don't just lick the edges." I bent and picked up the slice of tuna pie and held it out to him. He sniffed it tentatively, almost like he was worried this was a trap, before taking a miniscule bite off the end. I rolled my eyes. "Oh, don't be coy now. We both know you love these things." The next second, he took the whole piece from my hand and scoffed it down in record time.

"So much for my breakfast," I grumbled. I dished him out some actual dog food, as much as I could to lighten the load, and gathered up the few things I had left out overnight. Within a few minutes, we were once again on the road.

Every joint in my body was aching after yesterday's long day. I hobbled more than anything as we made our way down narrow roads that overlooked rolling hills and rivers.

Once again, I was grateful for my purchase of the sweatshirt in Santiago, because the wind was whipping today and the chill in the air could be felt even through the thick fabric. We plodded along for the first six kilometers, bumping into five or so fellow pilgrims out and about this morning, until we came to the massive roundabout where the trail split.

On the edge of the roundabout were two markers, their blazing yellow arrows pointing in two opposite directions. The group of four guys we had been trailing behind since Logoso were just finishing up taking pictures with the stone markers as we approached. They gave a wave and headed left. 29,693 A Fisterra was etched into the plaque beneath the left pointing arrow. Beside it, 26,589 A Muxía was pointed to the right.

"Two roads diverged," I muttered as Maverick circled the markers, sniffing around them like he was about to pee. "Don't even think about it."

He stopped and cocked his head to one side, then shuffled towards the right. I smiled because he was right, we were headed towards Muxía first. "And I took the one less traveled by," I muttered under my breath.

Grabbing Maverick's leash, since we were now walking along a busy motorway for a bit, we headed towards the right path. From that time on, we only saw two other pilgrims. The guidebook noted that this route was less traveled, but I hadn't realized it would be so completely empty of pilgrims. Apparently almost everyone headed straight to Finisterre, the "end of the world."

While, yes, the scenery was beautiful as it always was in Galicia, I couldn't find it in me to fully appreciate it. If it hadn't been for Maverick, I know I would have simply trudged through the grueling day just to make it to the final destination. But since it wasn't only about me, I did my best to keep things interesting for Mav by singing or talking to him or playing with whatever stick he brought me. Despite how exhausted I was, he still managed to bring a smile to my face with his goofy ways.

We wound up and down, through a couple little villages, but none with any great options for food so we never stopped for long. The trail alternated between road walking and wide dirt paths through eucalyptus forests. It brought us past a massive hórreo that stood atop twenty-two stone supports and by an old stone church with a small but impressive stained-glass rendition of Jesus Christ. After what seemed like forever, we finally caught our first glimpse of the sea. The breeze wafted the smell of salt up to us in the hills as the deep blue stretched out in front of us, so close it felt like I could reach out and touch it.

Of course, looks are deceiving. Because just as soon as we could see the ocean, it disappeared again. With still ten kilometers to go before we truly reached Muxía, the expanse of blue waves dipped in and out of view. The Camino slowly worked its way down from the hills of Galicia, in between scattered houses and over streams which Maverick made sure we stopped to wade in. He was plodding in one little brook when I felt my phone vibrating in the hip pocket of my bag. I pulled it out without really looking at it and slid to answer the call.

"Hola," I spoke into the phone, then realized I had no idea why I had just answered in Spanish. Apparently, I was so used to talking to people in the villages or on the trail that it had become a habit to speak in Spanish unless I was talking to my mom or dad.

"Colby Millsaps?"

I cleared my throat at the clearly English voice. "Uhm, yes, this is her."

It was a reporter from a local newspaper back home who wanted to interview me about our journey on the Camino. I pulled the phone away from my ear to look at the caller ID again, just to make sure this wasn't some prank, then returned it to my ear to hear him ask his first questions. I guess I had never stopped to think of my journey as anything that should be in a newspaper. I hadn't set out to do this for people to learn our story, or to be inspired somehow, but the way he talked made it seem like this was a special story to tell. That I was something special.

He asked about arriving in Santiago and I did my best to describe that feeling of arrival that I don't think anyone but a pilgrim who's experienced it can truly know. He asked about the hardest parts of our trek and I tried not to choke up as I described crying on sidewalks, in wheat fields, and over the phone to my mom. He asked about what had gone wrong, what parts had felt so incredibly right, and why we had ever come out here in the first place. He asked me what it was like doing this all alone, but I just smiled and shook my head even though I knew he couldn't see me. I had never been all alone. I watched as Maverick dipped into a trail ahead of me between two dunes covered in beach grass.

"I was never alone," I told him. "I had Maverick."

I ended the call just as I crested the hill between those short dunes. White sand and worn wooden boards were beneath my hiking sandals. In front of me, the sea kissed the creamy sands in soft waves and Maverick laid at the very edge of the water, his eyes and ears pricked in my direction. Despite being exhausted, absolutely bone-tired, a smile spread across my face. We had made it. From the mountains of France all the way to white sands and the Atlantic Ocean. My heavy pack slid off my shoulders and plopped into the sand by my feet as I slipped off my shoes and dug in my toes. Half a world away, it felt as if I had just come home.

The beach this trail had emptied onto was small, set in a little cove, and I could see the town of Muxía stretching up the shore to our left. The sand was covered in seaweed and plenty of driftwood logs that Maverick was already gathering up and dropping by my feet so I would throw them for him. The smell of salt and fish hung in the humid air. It was clear this was no sunbathing town. This was a fisherman's village, and it had a wild feel to it. Our walk through town a little while later on the way to the hostel only confirmed that even more. Though Muxía was a seaside paradise, the streets weren't crowded with tourists. Instead, we saw only locals and parents going for a stroll with their children.

Our hostel was located in the very center of town, which was clustered on a tiny peninsula that jutted into the sea. It turned out to be the most modern place we had stayed during our entire journey. Everything was black and white; sharp lines and fancy appliances. I had to double-check just to make sure it was the right place because I was sure this place had to cost more than the few euros I was spending on it. However, Maverick's smelly, dirt-coated, red pack was waiting for us at the foot of the front desk. As it turned out, the hospitaleros who ran this fancy place were some of the kindest people I had encountered. They weren't at all fazed by Maverick and were more than happy to show us to our private room and point out all of the amenities I was welcome to use. After a quick shower, they pointed us in the direction of the Virxe da Barca sanctuary.

On the very tip of the peninsula of Muxía, where the waves crash angrily against the stones, stands a stone church. Legend claims that in this spot, the Virgin Mary appeared to Saint James in a stone boat to tell the saint that his mission in Spain was complete. In September, people flock from all over for a ceremony to honor the legend. The sanctuary was built as a reminder of the tale. The rocks are a holy place, but above all, they are a beautiful place. The wildness I had felt on the beach when we first arrived and later through the tight streets of town came to a head here. The waves broke on the smooth stone on three sides, sending off spray that caught the evening sun and glistened. Even if I had wanted to talk to Maverick beside me, I would have to shout to be heard over the roar of the sea.

After a while, we scooted away from the sanctuary, up the rise and away from the many people who were milling about the sacred area, and I took a seat to watch the sun dip lower. The stifling humidity from midday was gone now, replaced with the whipping wind. My eyes scanned over the top of the large stone sanctuary, to the little pillar that read 0,000 km. In a way, we had reached our finish line twice now. Many stopped in Santiago once they reached the cathedral. Others stopped once they made it here, to the coast. Yet, we still weren't done. We had one more day. I just wasn't sure if my body could take it. So for now, I just wanted to enjoy this view.

Jack from Ireland's words came into my head from the movie The Way. He had stood near this same spot; watched these same wild waves. "Writers," he had said. "They always want the last word. But this…?"

***

The peace from watching the waves at the sanctuary was short-lived. Upon arriving back at the hostel and checking with Correos, I found it was too late to arrange for baggage transfer onto Finisterre tomorrow for Maverick's pack. Between the still-too-full bag of food we had picked up in Santiago, my own pack, and his pack, there was no way my exhausted body would be able to carry everything on my own.

"I can't do it," I cried into the phone in our dark room late that night. My voice shook and I hated it. I hated that I was crying to my mom yet again from an ocean away. I thought I had gotten past this. I thought I had become stronger. I thought I had left all my troubles behind with my stone at Cruz de Ferro. I thought I had conquered all my weaknesses when we arrived in Praza Obradoio and looked up at the stonework of the cathedral.

"You don't have to," my mom answered over the phone, her voice on the speaker mingling with the waves I could still hear crashing through my open window. "You've already done more than anyone could have ever anticipated. No one said you could do it all with a dog, and you did. You could have quit a hundred times already, but you didn't. You made it to Santiago. The two of you made it. You have nothing else to prove. You don't have to go on to Finisterre tomorrow. You can be done now."

"But I can't," I wailed again, only this time for a different reason. I said I couldn't keep going. But I also knew I couldn't just give up.

It was stupid. What she was saying was right. There was absolutely nothing that was forcing me to go on. By all accounts, I definitely could stop here. I had made the trek from Saint Jean to Santiago. I had gotten my Compostela. I was a "true pilgrim." Maverick and I really had done it. No one would judge me if I stopped here. We made it to Muxía after all. Many people stopped here, just as I had been thinking about earlier this afternoon. But that wasn't what I had set out to do. I said we would finish in Finisterre and I intended to finish in Finisterre.

"Colby…you can do anything you want. This is your trip. This is your Camino. If you don't want to do this last stage, you don't have to."

"I do," I sniffled. "I do want to do this last stage. I have to. But I can't."

"Yes, you can. You are one of the strongest people I

know. You are my inspiration. And you can do anything you say you want to do. So if you want to do this, I know you can. You'll find a way. You always do."

"You think so?" I whispered.

"I know so."

We're Going Home

Day Forty-Four: Muxía to Finisterre

27.2 km ~ 38,339 steps

August 2nd

I woke up to the sound of my phone ringing. I hadn't gone to bed in the best of moods and I wasn't exactly looking forward to being woken up at some ridiculous time since I still had no plan on what we were going to do today, but I rolled over and felt around for the vibrating phone. A Spanish number was lit up. I slid to answer and put the phone to my ear.

"¿Hola?" I said groggily into the line. A chipper voice answered me right away, telling me they were from *Correos* and was wondering if I still needed a bag transferred this morning. I scrambled to sit up in bed.

"Oh, uhm, sí, por favor," I stammered. Within minutes, it was squared away and I had a half hour to get my crap together and leave Maverick's pack at the front desk for *Correos* to pick up and transfer.

I hung up and blinked, still in a state of shock, then looked over the side of the bed to see Maverick watching me with his head on his paws. "Well, I guess we're walking, Reek. We're really gonna finish this thing." His tail made a swishing sound against the wood floor. One last day of walking. We could do this.

We could do this, sure, but I had to accept the fact that my body could not take another thirty-kilometer day. Somewhere in the midst of my breakdown last night, I had realized that we could make it happen today, but I may need to make some accommodations. So I didn't feel guilty when I went to the front desk on our way out today and asked if they knew of a taxi that would allow a dog in it. With the help of the amazing hospitalero, I called a cab and arranged for them to take us to Lires, almost exactly halfway between Muxía and Finisterre. I left Mav's pack at the front desk, and we hopped into the waiting cab just as *Correos* pulled up to collect the bags for the day.

The almost fifteen-kilometer drive between Lires and Muxía flew by in just minutes. It was kind of weird to think that if I had attempted to walk that exact same route, it would have taken me hours. Not that I was salty at all. Mav and I were deposited with a friendly wave goodbye just at the foot of what looked like a Spanish bed and breakfast. Pilgrims were hanging out on the porch enjoying morning coffee and *tortillas* so it felt a little odd rolling up in a taxi, but I quickly forced that out of my head. If I had learned anything over these past forty days, it was that everyone had a story you couldn't see and there was no need to judge. From all this time being completely alone, with just a dog as a companion, I wasn't all that concerned with the opinion of others anymore. It was a very liberating feeling.

After pausing for a quick breakfast on the wide, old porch, Mav and I set off along the coastal route towards Finisterre. Regardless of the time, the weather was already shaping up to be a brutal day. The humidity was oppressive being so close to the ocean and I was already starting to sweat. However, the views more than made up for it. Empty white sand beaches stretched beside us as we curved along the coastline. The beach grasses waved lazily in what little breeze there was. The ocean looked lighter here than it did back home. It was more of a teal than the deep blue I was used to in New England, which gave it almost a tropical vibe.

I felt my phone vibrate in my hip pocket and pulled it free. *My way to kick depression.* The title of a newspaper article stared back at me yet again, a little picture of Maverick and I smiling in front of the cathedral right below it. I had already received about ten texts just this afternoon alerting me that from an ocean away, Mav and I had made the front page of the paper. *Chester woman finds renewal on Spain's Camino* was printed next to another picture of us I snapped just by the city limits walking into Santiago. I clicked the lock button on my phone and the screen went black, then shoved the device back into the hip pocket of my pack and started hiking on without bothering to read the article. I could read it later.

But even though I hadn't stopped to read it, I couldn't keep my mind from wandering back to that article as I followed Maverick through the oppressive midday heat. *My way to kick depression.* I snorted a laugh, though no one was around to hear me. We were a scant ten kilometers from our finish line, had traveled over five-hundred miles on foot, and I wasn't sure if I had really accomplished that goal. Had I truly kicked depression? I didn't think so. I had had plenty of depressive episodes along the trail. I thought back to the side-walk bar in Sahagún after we had been denied on the train. I thought back to the dirt lot in Hornillos. I thought back to just last night. Could I honestly say I thought I beat depression along this trail? Of course not. But maybe, just maybe, I had discovered how to live with it. Maybe my depression would never be fully gone. Maybe it would always be a part of my life, but it didn't have to *control* my life anymore.

As we walked up the last hills of our journey that overlooked the ocean and through the last stretch of open forests, I thought back on how I had been living my life for the past few years, since depression had taken control. Recently, I had started thinking about what I wanted from life when I got back home. The goals I had for my career. Where I wanted to live and work and how I wanted to spend my life. I thought back on the past years and the relationships I had formed, or rather the ones I had *not* formed, and realized that depression had been in control of every aspect of my life. I had been so deep into that dark hole that I hadn't seen any point in getting close to other people. How could I, in good conscience, allow someone to get close to me when I knew I was suicidal? That I might take my own life and leave them nothing but sadness? I hadn't set a solid plan for my career or where I wanted to live because I wasn't able to see a future. Depression had blocked all of that.

So in the end, maybe this journey hadn't been my way to kick depression, despite what that article claimed. The Camino wasn't about getting what you want. I had learned that more than anything over the past forty-three days. Instead, the Camino gave you what you needed. My Camino had reminded me what it felt like to live again. It taught me how to take back control of my life from the invisible force that had tainted it for years. That darkness may never be gone, but I had hope for a future now. I felt the lightest I had in years. Well, at least I did metaphorically.

Physically, my entire body felt heavy today. Even

Maverick was struggling as we made our descent into Finisterre. The temperature had risen to a sweltering ninety-eight degrees and the humidity hadn't waned at all. Once we left the shade of the forested hillside to dip down to the sea, the Camino followed along paved roads that I was sure were burning Maverick's paw pads. Luckily, he was able to find a little drainage canal that ran beside the road and plodded along through that as I slogged through the heat. In short, our final walk into a Spanish town on this journey was brutal. I suppose it was fitting to end such a long, hard journey.

Even though I was exhausted and just wanted to collapse into a bed and take a shower to wash off all the sweat pouring from my skin, I couldn't pass up the opportunity to let Maverick go for a swim in the ocean once I spied a beautiful, secluded beach. The only problem with my plan was that I had no clue how to actually *get* to said beach. The sidewalk we were on through Finisterre wound along a cliffside overlooking a calm, turquoise bay with water so clear I could clearly see the reefs and rocks beneath the surface. At the end of the cove was what appeared to be a popular white-sand beach, but just beneath the cliffs we walked along was a more secluded area with barely any people. I craned my neck, trying to see a way down to the sand, and finally spotted an old, stone stairway leading down.

"Come on, Mav." I gave his leash a little tug to prompt him up from his shady spot beneath a bench. "Wanna go for a swim?" He perked up at that thought and trotted ahead again, tugging me along even though he had no idea where we were going. Not that I really did, either. All I knew was that somewhere up ahead there was an old stone staircase. I just had to find it.

After exploring various grimy alleyways that emerged onto sharp cliffs, not stone stairs, I was ready to call it quits on our endeavor. I pulled Maverick away from yet another dead-end to trudge back up the damp alley. We pressed against the wet, stone wall of one building to let a worker pass on his way to a boat, then emerged back into the sunshine. "I don't know, dude. I can't find our way down. Maybe we won't get to swim today. Maybe we should just go to the albergue."

I unclipped his leash as we entered a quiet pull-off on the end of a street that opened into a sitting area overlooking the bay and plopped down on one of the granite benches. Maverick sniffed his way along the scrubby grass, then disappeared from view over a ledge.

"Hey!" I called, groaning as I pulled myself up to stand again. "I said you can't go over the cliff. I don't think we're going to find a way down to-" My voice cut off as I saw where Maverick had disappeared to. In the very corner of this sitting area was an opening to stone steps. The very same steps I had seen from above that led down to the water. Maverick was already at the bottom step, launching into the sand below and scampering into the water. I felt my lips lift in a smile and suddenly my pack didn't feel so heavy. Suddenly my feet weren't quite so sore.

I hurried down the steps after him, passing two local girls on their way up who smiled at me, and finally made it down to the sand to see Maverick already laying in the water. There was a small group of people nearby, a pair of younger ladies chatting with an old couple. I smiled at them and called out a "lo siento" for Maverick's behavior. After a double-take, I realized the older woman was indeed very much topless. I quickly averted my eyes and headed straight to Maverick rather than stopping to make conversation. I knew that nudist and topless beaches were a thing in Europe, but that didn't mean I was prepared to see it. I blinked a few times and focused forward on Maverick. *This is fine. All is well. We're just gonna scoot, scoot over that way and…*

"Is your dog?" one of the younger ladies called to me. I squeezed my eyes shut. So much for the escape plan.

With a smile plastered on, I turned back to face them. "Yes, he's mine." I reluctantly made my way towards them across the sand as Maverick ran over with a piece of seaweed dangling from his jaws. Luckily for me, the two younger women were clothed, so I kept my focus solely on them.

"He is very handsome. What is his name?"

"Maverick." I enunciated slowly, drawing out the 'v' like a 'b' as I did when speaking to any Spaniard. Despite them speaking to me in English, it was obvious they were locals.

"You are walking The Way?" the older man asked with a nod to the shell on my pack, which was still sitting heavy on my shoulders. I joined their little group but purposefully kept my eyes averted from his wife. No offense to her and this common European practice of topless bathing, but I had already gotten an eyeful of old lady boobs with that first glance and I wasn't keen for a second look.

"Just finished, yes."

"With the dog?" I turned my gaze from his face straight to his wife's once she spoke. *Do not look down. Do not look down.*

"Yes. We started in Saint Jean in June. Took us forty days, but we finally made it here."

"Wow." The woman didn't say anymore, possibly because she didn't know much English, possibly because she didn't want to, but either way it gave me an excuse to focus on the other fully clothed members of the group.

"Your English is very good," one of the other women said happily.

I laughed and a genuine smile broke across my face. "Well, thank you. But that's because I'm American."

"Oh!" she gasped and slapped a hand over her mouth. Her friend tittered and the old man's deep laugh joined theirs.

"But thank you. I do believe that's the first time I've ever been complimented on my English. Feels kind of nice," I joked.

"I feel silly," the girl laughed.

"Oh, no. Don't at all. I should tell *you* that your English is very good. Because it really is."

She blushed and I could tell she didn't believe my compliment so I added one more *really* for good measure. "I should get going, though. I know the boy wants to swim and I could use a swim, too. Have to rinse off all this sweat." I waved a hand over myself with a little laugh. "It was nice to meet you guys. Enjoy the rest of your afternoon."

I waved to all of them, then internally cursed myself because my eyes had drifted too far. *Damn these topless beaches. Damn my prudish American mentality.* I scurried away down the beach after that, happy to put some distance between us. The water here was even warmer than it had been in Muxía and much calmer, so I ended up stripping down just to my underwear and joining Maverick for a swim. Any time I dunked under, he came paddling over to make sure I was still okay. I tossed different rocks for him to dive after, and we watched some boys on a float out in the middle of the bay as if this was a small lake, not the Atlantic Ocean, until eventually it was time to dry off and head in search of our final albergue of the Camino.

We climbed back up the steps to the streets of Finisterre and found the albergue I had booked ahead of time not far from our hidden little locals-only beach. As soon as we stepped over the threshold, I could tell this was not going to go well. The hospitalera at the front desk immediately stiffened and gave us a disdainful look.

"Hola," I called as I made my way to the desk and took out our credentials and my passport to check in. "Tengo una reserva."

"No."

"Uhm… ¿perdón?" I asked in confusion. She didn't even know my name yet, how could she know if I had a reservation or not?

"No tienes una reserva aquí con *ese* perro." Her chin jerked up at that statement so she could look down at Maverick in disgust. *That* dog, she had said. I couldn't *possibly* have a reservation with *this* dog.

"Sí…usé Booking y le dije que tengo un perro. Este albergue admite mascotas, ¿no?" Their establishment had said pets were allowed. I had left a message saying I would be here with my dog. I had done everything right.

"No. Sólo admitimos mascotas de menos de seis kilos."

"¿En serio?" I gasped. A stipulation of dogs under six kilograms? Was this a joke?

"Sí," she sniffed.

"No dijo eso en línea. Sólo dijo que permitía perros." The hospitalera didn't even dignify me with a response to that. She clearly didn't care what their albergue said on Booking.-com. I sighed deeply. This *would* be happening to us. It was our last night. No way this could have gone smoothly. That wouldn't have been right for us.

"Señora," I tried one last time. "Es nuestro último día del Camino. Por favor, ¿podemos quedar aquí? Sólo es una noche."

"No. Lo siento."

I turned away just so I could roll my eyes without her seeing it and bent to grab Maverick's pack which was waiting beside the front desk. I was too tired to fight any harder at this point. Maybe if it had been earlier in our trek, I would have had more false hope or perseverance to press the issue, but now? Now I was just tired. "Come on, Baby Dog. We can't stay here."

I turned and made my way out through the hanging beads that formed a door to this albergue and back onto the narrow, seaside streets of old Finisterre. I wish I could say this was a new feeling of disappointment but we had made this walk of shame too many times by now. A pair of American pilgrims followed us out, the beads tinkling against each other as they pushed their way into the street beside us.

"They won't let you stay here?" one of the men asked once his eyes had readjusted to the bright sun and he had found me leaning against the outside wall of the albergue.

"Nope." The 'p' popped as I let out the word with a sigh and tipped my head to look in their direction. Not only was I exhausted at this point, but I was also still slightly damp from my swim and I'm pretty sure just the walk here had caused me to chafe. I wasn't looking forward to searching out another place to stay.

"Does this happen to you often?" the other man asked.

I gave him a wan grin. "You'd think I would be used to it after over forty days, wouldn't you?" They each made a sympathetic face back at me. I pushed off the wall and straightened up, hiking my pack up on my shoulders and bending to grab Maverick's pack from the ground beside me. "It's okay. One last adventure."

"I'm not sure if this is helpful at all, but there's another albergue just up the street. I think they had some private rooms left when we passed by just now. If you'd want to do that?"

It was my best option, so I followed their directions and found the albergue in question. The hospitalera there was a bit hesitant, but in the end she agreed to let us into a private room just as the men had said. In truth, this albergue looked even nicer than the one I had originally booked. It was a little more expensive, especially for a private room, but I had long ago passed the point of caring about that. While Maverick slept, I washed my clothes in a sink one last time and hung them out the window to dry, then took a shower to wash off all the dried sweat and salt from my skin.

A little before sunset, we set out on foot one final time for the last three kilometers to the lighthouse at the very "end of the world." The Romans were the first to name this cape. *Finis terrae* in Latin directly translates to "end of the earth" which the current name of Finisterre has emerged from. To them, and many generations since, looking out at the expanse of ocean from the precipice of this cape felt like they were looking out to the very edge of the earth itself.

The narrow, gravel path that clung to the cliffs along the one lane road to the end of the cape was crowded this evening. Some were pilgrims, still with their packs on their shoulders. Others were families with small children giggling and playing while their parents tried to keep them simultaneously off the road and away from the cliff edge. Foot traffic was going both ways, but more seemed to be heading towards town than towards the tip of the cape like we were. I couldn't imagine why. It seemed wrong not to watch the sun set off the edge of the world, but I wasn't about to complain. If that meant the end of the cape was less crowded once we got there, I was okay with that.

Despite not carrying our packs, Maverick and I were both dragging. The three kilometers felt more like ten and when we were less than halfway to the lighthouse, Maverick started to limp on the gravel of the path. I cursed myself for not bringing his booties with us for this little walk, but I hadn't even thought about needing them for it. I debated turning back. We didn't *really* need to do this. We had made it to the town of Finisterre after all. We had gotten our Compostela in Santiago. But of course, my stubborn pride pushed us on. After a short rest at the pilgrim statue along the way, we trekked on the final kilometer and a half to the lighthouse and the very last Camino marker. This time, when we saw the blue and yellow *concho* and its bronze *KM 0,000* marker it really felt true. We had made it. We had truly made it to the end of the earth.

Though this was no church, no hushed temple, no ornately carved chapel, the whole space felt sacred. Maverick and I weaved around the many pilgrims, tourists, and locals until we found a spot on the bluffs to watch the setting sun dip towards the Atlantic. The sea breeze was strong, carrying excited voices to where we sat tucked into the rocks and rustling the long grasses around us. The humidity of the day still hung in the air, even the wind couldn't brush it away, and a haze shrouded the sun so you could look at it fully without your eyes burning. For a long time, Mav and I just sat and watched the world. We watched the shadows grow. Watched our final moments as pilgrims on El Camino de Santiago drift away.

I had come here with a purpose. I had decided this journey would heal me. I had so many ideas in my head of what this walk would be when I set out. It was supposed to teach me so much about myself. And maybe it has. Maybe it will continue to teach me for many months after we've stopped walking. But maybe, instead of teaching me new things, this journey has shown me what it means to truly be myself. Because I don't exactly feel like *I've* changed, but somehow in two months, *everything* has changed.

The sun approached the ocean, one edge dipping below the waves and disappearing over the edge of the earth, and I stood from my spot on the bluff. I stepped up to the edge of a rock outcropping and I felt Maverick step up beside me. Without looking, I reached my hand down and sank my fingers into his thick fur. We stood like that, just the two of us, what felt like the last two souls on the edge of the world, until the last of the sun sank beneath the horizon.

Everything may have changed. But one thing was certain. I would have never been able to complete this journey without Maverick. My fingers tightened in his fur.

"Thank you," I whispered into the wind.

Afterword

When I stood at the end of the earth with Maverick in 2018 at the end of our journey, I wasn't magically healed or "fixed" as I had hoped to be. I wish I could tell you that in the four years since completing our Camino, I have somehow managed to completely beat depression. But if you've learned anything from reading this tale, it's that I don't hide the truth. And the truth is, depression will always be a part of who I am. I want you to know that that's okay, though. I learned on that sweaty walk between Muxía and Finisterre, I don't have to let depression control me. In the last four years, I've learned to live with depression. I haven't ended up back in a ward like I was in 2017. I've had suicidal thoughts, but I haven't acted on them. Instead, I take Maverick for a walk. Even if it's just a walk around our neighborhood. Or I throw myself into planning our next trip.

The thing is, there is always something new around the corner. A new adventure. A new friend to meet. A kind woman to take you in. A nice man to sit with you while you cry. The Camino taught me that there is good in this world full of color. You don't need to live in black and white. You can learn to live through the good and the bad. Thank you for taking a journey through our goods and bads with us.

A Note About Chapter Titles

As a huge music lover, I am never without a song in my head. When Maverick and I find ourselves completely alone on a trail, I'm known to break out in whatever song happens to be in my head at the time. While I know all the words to far too many songs, more often than not this singing will devolve into simply a song about Maverick to the same tune of the original song.

While on the Camino, I got into a habit of noting my "Song of the Day" for each day we walked. This was the song that I was normally singing out loud to Maverick any time we found ourselves alone. It was the song that was on loop in my brain as I pushed myself forward. So if you'd like a listen in to what our trek sounded like, head to this link to check out the Spotify playlist I created of the songs during our time along El Camino de Santiago. Bonus points if you can find out ways to weave "Maverick, Mavy Nugget, Freak Reek, and Baby Dog" into the lyrics. Happy listening!

Con el Perro

> *Put One Foot in Front of the Other – Ether Park*
> *Follow the Yellow Brick Road – Judy Garland*
> *Calling All Angels – Train*
> *Foreplay / Long Time – Boston*
> *Castle on the Hill – Ed Sheeran*
> *All My Friends – Dermot Kennedy*
> *Take Your Time – Vance Joy*
> *Whenever God Shines His Light – Van Morrison*
> *Don't Stop Believin' – Journey*

Colors of the Wind – Judy Kuhn
Featherstone – The Paper Kites
Realize – Colbie Caillat
God Undefeatable – Austin Stone Worship
New Slang – The Shins
Alone with Me – Vance Joy
Better – Declan J Donovan
Until The Sunrise – Timeflies
Don't – Ed Sheeran
Only Love – Ben Howard
Halfway Gone – Lifehouse
Waves – Dean Lewis
Poetry - Wrabel
The Reason - Hoobastank
Boulevard of Broken Dreams – Green Day
Rivers and Roads – The Head and the Heart
All In - Lifehouse
Drops of Jupiter – Train
Take Me to Church – Hozier
Mykonos – Fleet Foxes
Wild Things – Alessia Cara
Live and Die – The Avett Brothers
Only a Human – George Ezra
Little Boy – Vance Joy
Come Down – Noah Kahan
Sleep on the Floor – The Lumineers
Lost! - Coldplay
I'm Gonna Be (500 Miles) – The Proclaimers
Like Gold – Vance Joy
Pon de Replay – Rihanna
Sink – Noah Kahan
Wherever You Will Go – The Calling
We're Going Home – Vance Joy

Acknowledgments

I have so many acknowledgments to make for this project. Because it really was a project. It's been so much more than just a book.

More than anything, I have to say thank you to my parents. They have supported me every single step of the way, literally and figuratively. I have put them through what I'm sure no parent ever wants to experience. They have seen me at my absolutely lowest and I've terrified them. But they've also seen my accomplish things most people only ever dream of. So thank you. Thank you for believing in all my wild dreams. For knowing, sometimes more than I do, that I can do it. I can do anything. Thank you for being my cheerleaders, my sounding board, my publicists, my editors, my everything. I could never ask for better parents.

Thank you to my extended family as well. To my Nana and Grampa, who had their own copy of the guidebook back home to follow along where I was day by day. Thank you again to my Nana, for being one of my first editors. For always being in my corner. For sharing a love of writing with me.

Speaking of guidebooks, I can't forget to thank (and curse) John Brierley for his truly wonderful guidebook. *A Pilgrim's Guide to the Camino de Santiago (Camino Francés): St. Jean, Roncesvalles, Santiago* in a wealth of knowledge and there wasn't a single day on the trek where I wasn't pouring over it. I may have cursed it at times, but it is a beautiful guide. I believe it has been updated in recent years to be even more accurate. If you're looking to walk the Camino, this is your guide.

To Chelsea, I can never thank you enough for all you have done for me in the almost five years I was lucky enough to be your patient. You changed my life in ways I will never be able to fully thank you for. You taught me it was okay to be who I was and to accept every part of myself, good or bad. You were there for the worst moments and you celebrated my best moments. There isn't a week that goes by where I don't curse you for closing your practice (kidding…but not really. I miss the shit out of you). I hope you are proud of the work you do, because you truly save lives.

I also want to take the time to thank my high school Spanish teachers and current friends. Jenny Barriere and Señor Hastings, I have a million thanks I could say to each of you. For one, it is you, Jenny, who first introduced me to the Camino my freshman year of high school. Thanks for telling me about a tiny, indie theater in Concord that was playing a cool movie that summer. And Señor, I could take pages for all the ways I want to thank you. Thank you for being such an amazing person. A wonderful mentor. An endless fountain of knowledge on any and all things. A man I'm happy to consider just as close as family at this point. Thank you for all your time and care and café dates to share travel stories and compare Camino memories. I hope for many more in the future.

To the Camino Facebook groups, you hardened me to criticism before I set out and you built me up like no other throughout our journey. I posted daily blogs into one group as we walked and I received the most beautiful outpouring of support every single day. Urging us on. Laughing at our stories. Commiserating when we were down. Offering their support in any way they could. To this day, I have gained many friends from these forums who I know I could call up and find a couch to crash on, with Maverick, in countries all over the world. Sometimes the internet is cool that way. If you're thinking of planning your own Camino, join some Facebook groups. They are a wonderful community to gain information from.

To Jen. Thank you. Thank you for breeding this incredible dog. For giving me my very best friend. He wouldn't be here without the care and love and time you put into your German Shepherd Dogs. And thank Ollie Bug for me. She's one hell of a mama. But thank you to who you are as a person, too. Thank you for being my friend far beyond just dogs. Thank you for cheering us on, for celebrating our victories, for always being in my corner no matter how far we drift.

To all the people I bugged throughout the writing process and all the needs you fulfilled for me, thank you. To the wonderful team at Bespoke Book Covers, Peter and wife, Caroline. Thank you for creating three beautiful covers for me now. Thank you for making this book the best it could be. I am so happy to have found you and get to work with you.

And last but perhaps most important of all, thank you to my fellow pilgrims and the Camino Angels who helped us along the way. Some I can mention by name because I'm lucky enough to still have them as friends and contacts. Some I have changed names in the book to maintain their anonymity. Some I was silly enough to never get their names but am forever in their debt. Thank you, if you happen to be reading this wherever you are, thank you. Trish. Joanne. Tobiah. Txema. Amy and Beth. Thank you. Thank you, thank you, thank you. You truly made our Camino what it was.

About the Author

Colby Millsaps is the author of two previous novels, *Crossing Lines* and *Doors*. After leaving Ohio State and finishing her Camino, she went on to finish a degree in English Language and Literature and Creative Writing. She now teaches high school English in her home state of New Hampshire. In the summers, she and Maverick continue to travel. They have since walked another pilgrimage, this one through Switzerland and Italy, before their travels were put on hold. They plan to walk the Camino Portugués from Porto to Santiago next.

In the meantime, be sure to check out her website www.colbymillsaps.com or follow her writing page on both Instagram and Facebook @cmillsapswrites. Her website contains a blog where she posted far more pictures from their Camino Francés as well.

Also by Colby Millsaps

Made in United States
North Haven, CT
16 September 2023

41631072R00339